# WRITINGS FROM THE *PHILOKALIA*
# ON PRAYER OF THE HEART

# WRITINGS FROM THE
# *PHILOKALIA*
## ON PRAYER OF THE HEART

Translated from the Russian Text

'DOBROTOLUBIYE'

by

**E. KADLOUBOVSKY**

and

**G. E. H. PALMER**

*faber and faber*

LONDON · BOSTON

First published in 1951
by Faber and Faber Limited
3 Queen Square London WC1N 3AU
Tenth impression 1979
This paperback edition first published in 1992

Printed and bound in Great Britain by Mackays of Chatham PLC.

ISBN 0-571-16393-9

4 6 8 10 9 7 5

✠

# FOREWORD

In the Name of the Father and of the Son and of the Holy Spirit.

The 'Philokalia' is a collection of writings of the Fathers from the earliest times after the Declaration of Constantine the Great. It shows the way to awaken attention and consciousness, and to develop them; it provides the means of acquiring the quickest and most effective conditions for training in what the Fathers, who reached the highest levels, called the art of arts and the science of sciences, leading a man towards the highest perfection open to him. The present selection is extracted from the 'Philokalia' in order to make the task easier for the mind which undertakes this training. The selection represents the essential lines of that training, and the practice of centuries has given it a definite value.

The most effective form of that art of arts and science of sciences is manifested as the practice of the Prayer of Jesus, to use its traditional name.

The primordial condition and absolute necessity is to know oneself. To gain this knowledge the beginner must learn to be alive to the many-sided possibilities of the ego; and he must eliminate all obstacles, personal as well as external, to acquire the best conditions for success. Silence and quiet are indispensable for concentration.

Practice of the Jesus Prayer is the traditional fulfilment of the injunction of the Apostle Paul to 'pray always'; it has nothing to do with the mysticism which is the heritage of pagan ancestry. This latter appeared in the first two centuries in the Gnostic movement, but was readily rejected by the clear insight of the Fathers, and had no further significant development in Eastern Christianity.

The attacks made against Gregory Palamas by Barlaam of

Calabria and others, and the resulting distortions that have gained currency in the West, have created a false picture of the meaning of the practice of the Prayer of Jesus.

It has not, in consequence, been realised in the West that this practice dates from the start of the Christian era and has been kept unchanged through the centuries in the East. It gives access even to the highest attainment, as will be seen from the writings in this selection.

The practice of the Jesus Prayer offers the most efficacious help and support for development of consciousness to those who think it wise to undertake such training. The 'Philokalia' is the thread leading the way through the hardships, vicissitudes and spiritual penury of modern life; it is the most active power showing a man the road and leading him to success in that doing.

The Orthodox foundations are: the Scriptures and the traditions, some oral, and some recorded in the writings of the Fathers, who belonged to the period of the most perfect attainments of Christian consciousness, and the centuries which followed it.

The Greek 'Philokalia' was compiled in the eighteenth century by Macarius of Corinth (1731–1805) and Nicodemus of the Holy Mountain (1748?–1809) and first published in Venice in 1782. It is a selection of the writings of holy men who attained the summit of the spiritual heights. It was translated into Slavonic under the name of 'Dobrotolubiye' by Paissy Velichkovsky (d. 1794), a monk who visited Mount Athos and worked afterwards in Moldavia. This translation had a fundamental importance for the rebirth of monasticism and the practice of the Jesus Prayer in Russia from the beginning of the nineteenth century. Later, the 'Philokalia' was translated into Russian by Bishop Theophan the Recluse (d. 1894), from whose text this English translation has been made.

Although the original 'Philokalia' consists of Greek texts, the Russian text has a value of its own, justifying translation into English, owing to the spiritual understanding of Theophan and of the period in which he lived.

Like all attempts to reach a certain spiritual level the practices described require a man's care, attention and constant watchful-

ness, to evade the very real and unsuspected dangers of trying anything *in his own way*; the lack of spiritual leaders in our days neces-
sitates the constant study of these sacred writings in order to follow
without harm this wonderful way of the art of arts and science
of sciences; the essential conditions which allow hope for success
are genuine humility, sincerity, endurance, purity . . .

Inaccessible to human conception is the inexpressible glorious
Majesty of the most holy, sublime Sacraments and Revelations
on earth of the Divine Incarnation and supreme Holocaust of
Love of our celestial Saviour and God Jesus Christ. They open
for us the way to possibilities that are not of this earth, forming,
purifying and developing the unseen part of our being, helping
us towards Salvation.

Whenever human consciousness begins to be alive to the
questions Who am I? Whence do I come? Whither do I go? then
there arises the possibility of taking and following the narrow,
long, blessed path to wisdom.

By and by circumstances show that our individual capacities
are quite insufficient, and Supreme Help is vitally needed. The
obstacles that arise are numberless and multiform, such as will
lead us, if possible, in a false direction and make us lose sight
even of the ultimate goal.

These writings of the Fathers, who were inspired, define
most of the difficulties and tell us how to vanquish and master
them. To facilitate the training in preparation, the Fathers gave
guiding instructions and helpful advice.

The two principal Commandments include the absolute
necessity, the duty, of Love, which for those practising the
Prayer is more than essential. If the Path is taken and followed
in the spirit of genuine Love, irrevocable self-denial and humility,
there is a great chance of successful attainments in this life
leading imperceptibly to the farthest future.

These holy Fathers were of the Christian Church of the first
millennium and their teachings, instructions and help are
accessible only in the light of genuine, primordial Christianity,
devoid of any human considerations, additions and alterations,
in its integrity and purity of the times of the holy Apostles. ✠

MOUNT ATHOS, *May* 1951.                          ✠    ✠

7

Facsimile, in reduced size, of the 'Philokalia' title-page:

# ΦΙΛΟΚΑΛΙΑ

## ΤΩΝ ΙΕΡΩΝ

# ΝΗΠΤΙΚΩΝ·

### ΣΥΝΕΡΑΝΙΣΘΕΙΣΑ

### ΠΑΡΑ ΤΩΝ ΑΓΙΩΝ ΚΑΙ ΘΕΟΦΟΡΩΝ

# ΠΑΤΕΡΩΝ ΗΜΩΝ

### ΕΝ Ἧ,

Διὰ τῆς ᾧ τὴν Πρᾶξιν κ᾽ Θεωρίαν Ἠθικῆς Φιλο-
σοφίας ὁ νῦς καθαίρεται, Φωτίζεται, κ᾽ τελειῦται·

ΕΠΙΜΕΛΕΙᾼ, ΜΕΝ ΟΤΙ ΠΛΕΙΣΤΗ, ΔΙΟΡΘΩΘΕΙΣΑ·

### ΝΥΝ ΔΕ ΠΡΩΤΟΝ ΤΥΠΟΙΣ ΕΚΔΟΘΕΙΣΑ

### ΔΙΑ ΔΑΠΑΝΗΣ

ΤΟΥ ΤΙΜΙΩΤΑΤΟΥ, ΚΑΙ ΘΕΟΣΕΒΕΣΤΑΤΟΥ ΚΥΡΙΟΥ

# ΙΩΑΝΝΟΥ ΜΑΥΡΟΓΟΡΔΑΤΟΥ

### ΕΙΣ ΚΟΙΝΗΝ ΤΩΝ ΟΡΘΟΔΟΞΩΝ ΩΦΕΛΕΙΑΝ.

αψπβ. ΕΝΕΤΙΗΣΙΝ, 1782.
ΠΑΡΑ ΑΝΤΩΝΙῼ, Τῼ ΒΟΡΤΟΛΙ.
CON LICENZA DE' SUPERIORI, E PRIVILEGIO.

Facsimile, in reduced size, of the 'Dobrotolubiye' title-page (the date is that of the fourth edition):

# ДОБРОТОЛЮБІЕ

## ВЪ РУССКОМЪ ПЕРЕВОДѢ,

## ДОПОЛНЕННОЕ.

## ТОМЪ ПЕРВЫЙ.

### ИЗДАНІЕ ЧЕТВЕРТОЕ.

Иждивеніемъ Русскаго на Аѳонѣ Пантелеимонова монастыря.

МОСКВА.
Типо-Литографія И. Ефимова. Большая Якиманка, собственный домъ.
1905.

# CONTENTS

* The Volume numbers refer to the edition of 'Dobrotolubiye' published in Moscow 1896–1901.

# TRANSLATORS' NOTE

The text of each author in this selection has been translated in full as it appears in the 'Dobrotolubiye'.

The Biographical Notes relating to the authors are all taken from the 'Dobrotolubiye'.

No parenthetical clauses have been inserted by the translators; all those occurring in the English text are translated from the Russian.

All Biblical quotations are taken from the Authorized Version. Footnotes have been inserted to indicate where serious differences of meaning occur as between the A.V. rendering of the Old Testament and the Slavonic, which is translated from the Septuagint.

E. Kadloubovsky
G. E. H. Palmer

# DOBROTOLUBIYE
# (PHILOKALIA ; or the Love of Good)
## INTRODUCTION[1]

In offering to lovers of spiritual reading a Russian translation of
the well-known 'Philokalia', with certain additions, we deem it
necessary to say a few words about what the 'Philokalia'
represents.

The word 'Dobrotolubiye' is the translation of the Greek
title of the book, 'Philokalia', which means love of the beautiful,
the exalted, the good. More precisely it contains an interpretation of the secret life in our Lord Jesus Christ. Secret life in our
Lord Jesus Christ, which is the truly Christian life, begins,
develops and rises to perfection (for each in his own measure),
through the good will of God the Father, by the action of the
grace of the Holy Spirit present in all Christians, and under the
guidance of the Lord Jesus Christ Himself, Who promised to
abide with us for all time.

God's grace calls all men to such a life; and for all men it is
not only possible but obligatory, for it is the essence of
Christianity. Not all who are called participate therein, and not
all who actually participate, do so in equal measure. The chosen
enter deeply into it and gradually climb high by its steps.

The manifestations of this life, as well as the richness of the
realm where it is revealed, are no less abundant and varied than
the manifestations of ordinary life. And, if it were possible
clearly to understand and to depict all that takes place there:
hostile attacks and temptations, struggles and victories, falls and
recoveries, the birth and strengthening of various manifestations
of spiritual life, degrees of general progress and the state of mind

[1] This is the Introduction to the Russian translation from the Greek.
(Translators' note.)

13

and heart corresponding to each of those degrees, the interaction in everything of grace and freedom, the sensations of God being near or far, the perception of the power of God's Providence over all and one's own final and irrevocable surrender into God's hand, the renunciation of all one's own methods of activity, together with a constant and intense activity—if all this, we repeat, and many other things, representing an integral part of true life in the Lord, could be clearly and plainly described, it would give a picture as attractive as it is instructive, a picture like a journey round the world.

Travellers write accounts of all they see worth noting on their journey. So did the chosen of God, who had explored, in various directions, all the paths of spiritual life, write notes of all they met with and experienced in their arduous journeying. But the purpose and meaning of these notes is different.

Those who have no possibility of travelling may form, without moving from where they are, a fairly accurate idea of foreign lands, through reading the travel notes of other wayfarers, because the mode of life of all creatures is more or less similar in all countries. It is quite different in spiritual life. Only those can understand such notes as are following the path of that kind of life. For those who have not entered this path, it is quite an unknown science. But even those who have entered upon it, cannot understand everything in those notes at once. Their ideas and conceptions become more and more clear as they advance further and penetrate deeper into the country of the spirit. As personal experiences of spiritual life accumulate, indications derived from experience, which had been noted down by the holy fathers, gradually become more clear and intelligible to them.

At the same time, however, descriptions of various manifestations of spiritual life, contained in the writings of the holy fathers, may be a gift useful even to all Christians in general. They give everyone to understand, that if he has not yet had experiences contained in such descriptions, it means that his established mode of life (though capable of being reconciled with Christian conscience) is not the final perfection, above which there is nothing to wish for and beyond which there is nowhere to go. To understand this, cannot but excite zeal for achievement; it must beckon a man to move on, pointing to something better than he has.

For those who have already entered the path leading to the best and the most perfect, such reading provides the necessary guidance in doubtful and puzzling circumstances, both when the guidance of direct experience is lacking, and when this latter (guidance) encounters problems which it cannot solve, and which do not permit of final decisions that would banish all vacillation from the traveller. It is often very important, in some particular case, to know how and where to put one's foot, so as to avoid a mistake. And here one or another saying of the fathers disperses the darkness, shining like a streak of lightning in the night.

Generally speaking, these writings are a spiritual forcing house, into which the faithful enter with their consciousness and their heart, by reading instructions concerning phenomena of spiritual life. A man is there subjected to the palpable influences of the contemplations so evoked. Thus stimulated, he feels that at those moments he floats in another atmosphere, life-giving and light-giving. Those are moments of joy, and it is at such moments that fresh shoots are born and strengthened on the tree of spiritual life. Therefore it is not to be wondered at that he, who has had this experience, hastens to read descriptions of spiritual life from the experience of others as soon as he finds a free moment, just as a man who likes making profit hastens to places which promise him profit, and as a man bent on pleasure is drawn to places of amusement. Such a man often longs to breathe the inspiring and revitalising spiritual air. And yet it is not idle curiosity. No, it is a matter of essential necessity for the progress and welfare of our spirit.

This is why among true Christians there always has been and still is a need to have the writings of the holy fathers on spiritual life within their reach. But just as this craving is praiseworthy, so also its satisfaction is obligatory, for those who have such duty and the means to satisfy it. This craving has been satisfied in the past both by editions of those writings in full, as for example, of St. Macarius, Isaac and Ephraim the Syrians, John of the Ladder and many others, and, no less, by collections of extracts from those writers. The well-known 'Philokalia' represents one such collection and is the best of them.

Now it is clear what 'Philokalia' is. It gives us the teachings and the salient points of sacred sobriety, that is, both complete discourses and short sayings, concerning the inner spiritual life, with all the manifestations and activities accompanying it. This book has been composed to satisfy the spiritual need of men striving towards spiritual achievement. Those who read it know what treasures of spiritual wisdom are contained in the 'Philokalia'—they read and they rejoice. But rejoicing and receiving instruction from this reading, they cannot, all the same, hide their regret that many things in the book remain incomprehensible, not owing to the high level and depth of the contents, but simply owing to obsolete translation. This fact makes the need for a new translation self-evident.

This need was realised long ago, and was partially met by translations published in the 'Christian Reading'[2] from the very first years of its publication, and by the publication of separate papers from the 'Philokalia', as for instance, St. Maximus (on love—which forms part of the Greek 'Philokalia'), Hesychius of Jerusalem and Peter of Damascus, etc. The compiler[3] of the present collection had originally in view merely a revision of what had already been translated, the translation of what had not been translated, and the publication of the 'Philokalia' in Russian in the same form as in Greek. But later, he came to the conclusion that it was necessary to amplify the 'Philokalia' as compared with the Greek edition, because, although the Greek 'Philokalia' was fuller than the existing Slavonic translation,[4] it did not contain all the guidance left to us by the holy fathers concerning spiritual life. Therefore it seemed desirable to afford help and comfort to those who valued such reading. The result is the present collection, which is the 'Philokalia' itself, only augmented.

[2] A religious periodical published in Russia in the nineteenth century. (Translators' note.)

[3] The compiler is Bishop Theophan the Recluse (d. 1894). (Translators' note.)

[4] i.e. the translation made by the Moldavian Staretz Paissy Velichkovsky (d. 1794). (Translators' note.)

# INTRODUCTION

Our new collection follows in the steps of the old 'Philokalia'. But, noticing that some particular father, whose sayings are included in the old version, has yet other sayings, the compiler turns to them and, if he finds them relevant, includes them too in the collection. Also, noticing that besides the number of fathers, whose sayings are quoted, there were others who had left descriptions of spiritual life and who were omitted, the new 'Dobrotolubiye' is enriched with the latter. For example, the old 'Philokalia' included only 170 texts of St. Antony, whereas the new version includes his other writings as well. St. Macarius is missing in the old version (except 150 texts paraphrased by Simeon Metaphrastes) whereas here we include his precepts arranged in a certain systematic order in his own words. Of Isaiah the Hermit there were only 27 texts of short sayings; here we have all his well-known 29 chapters in a new translation from the Greek. The same was done with Abba Evagrius and St. Mark the Wrestler. This system will be followed also in the next volume of collected writings.

This then is the method adopted in compiling the new 'Dobrotolubiye'. It will conform to the old one, with additions. We have only one end in view: not to deprive the reader of anything we find which may be of value in guiding his life in God.

As regards the actual texts, we deem it necessary to say that not all writings will be included in full. Many things are best presented in excerpts. This will be done at times with some systematic order, at other times without, in the form of separate sayings. But the precepts themselves will always be quoted in the author's own words.

We accompany our collection of writings with a sincere wish that lovers of spiritual reading should find in it what their compiler desired to include for their sake.

*PART ONE*

# NICEPHORUS THE SOLITARY
## Short Biographical Note

Our holy father Nicephorus lived a life of spiritual endeavour[5] on the holy Mount Athos and died a little before the year A.D. 1340. He was teacher and guide to Gregory of Salonika (Palamas) in the study of the way of training in the higher love of wisdom, as his pupil himself testifies. In silence, undisturbed by worldly cares, he kept attention within himself alone and, reaching indescribable inner union with God Eternal, he received in his heart the blessed illumination of Divine grace. Himself enriched by this Divine gift, he is like a father guiding us by his writings towards the same goal. He collected from the books and lives of the holy fathers passages on sobriety, attention and prayer, and finally added advice derived from his own experience. Therein he invites all to ascend to the most perfect communion with the Lord through prayer of mind and heart.[6]

[5] The meaning of the Russian word подвигъ includes: task, as well as struggle, effort or endeavour, and feat. It occurs frequently throughout the texts, and has been variously translated according to the emphasis which seems most dominant in each case.

The related term подвижникъ renders the Greek ἀσκητής. It does not seem right to translate this as 'ascetic', since in modern popular English usage this latter word has acquired too exclusively a distorted meaning, implying a morbid element of self-maceration. The original meaning implied primarily a man who *trained* for something, whether in the field of a trade or an art, of athletics or of spiritual endeavour. The Russian word has the same implication but is limited to the field of spiritual endeavour. The translators have therefore used such terms as 'spiritual worker'. (Translators' note.)

[6] Literally 'mind-heart' prayer. There is no equivalent composite epithet in English. As will be seen from the texts, the joining of mind and heart represents a definite stage of attainment; that attainment is wisdom. (Translators' note.)

# NICEPHORUS THE SOLITARY

## A Most Profitable Discourse on Sobriety and the Guarding of the Heart

You, who desire to capture the wondrous Divine illumination of our Saviour Jesus Christ—who seek to feel the Divine fire in your heart—who strive to sense the experience and feeling of reconciliation with God—who, in order to unearth the treasure buried in the field of your hearts and to gain possession of it, have renounced everything worldly—who desire the candles of your soul to burn brightly even now, and who, for this purpose, have renounced all this world7—who wish by conscious experience to know and to receive the kingdom of heaven existing within you—come and I will impart to you the science of eternal heavenly life or, rather, the method leading him who practises it, without labour or sweat, into the harbour of passionlessness, freeing him from the fear of prelest8 or of defeat by the wiles of the devil. Such fear is proper only when through our transgression the circle of our life revolves far outside the life of which I intend to teach you. For then it happens to us as to Adam;

---

7 Настоящій, here translated 'the world', means literally 'actual'; in this context it means the apparent reality of the world of the senses, the passions and the discursive reason. The Greek is τὰ πάροντα. (Translators' note.)

8 Прелесть. The nearest English equivalent seems to be 'beguilement' (cf. 'The serpent beguiled me, and I did eat' [Gen. iii. 13]). But the meaning of prelest is both wider and more technical. It has seemed best therefore to leave the word untranslated throughout the texts, in which will be found many passages on the subject.

Прелесть in general translates the Greek word πλάνη; the latter literally means 'wandering' or 'going astray' (cf. πλάνος, deceiver, impostor). Prelest is the resulting state in the soul which wanders away from Truth.

If we may paraphrase Bishop Ignatiy Brianchaninov (d. 1867), we could define prelest as the corruption of human nature through the acceptance by man of mirages mistaken for truth; we are all in prelest. (Translators' note.)

associating with the serpent, he disregarded God's commandment; trusting the serpent's counsel, he tasted of the forbidden fruit and was utterly filled with prelest. Thus to our sorrow he plunged himself and all after him into the depths of death, darkness and corruption.

So let us return to ourselves, brothers, and be filled with disgust and hatred for the counsel of the serpent and of all that crawls on the ground; for it is impossible for us to become reconciled and united with God, if we do not first return to ourselves, as far as it lies in our power, or if we do not enter within ourselves, tearing ourselves—what a wonder it is!—from the whirl of the world with its multitudinous vain cares and striving constantly to keep attention on the kingdom of heaven which is within us.

Monastic life is called the art of arts and the science of sciences; for it does not bring perishable blessings akin to the things of this world, which drive the mind from what is best and engulf it; but monkhood promises us wonderful and unspeakable treasures which the 'Eye hath not seen, nor ear heard, neither have entered into the heart of man' (1 Cor. ii. 9). Hence, 'we wrestle not against flesh and blood, but against principalities, against powers, against the rulers of the darkness of this world' (Ephes. vi. 12).

If therefore present existence is but darkness, let us flee from it, let us flee by retuning our mind and our heart. Let us have nothing in common with the enemy of God, for 'whosoever . . . will be a friend of the world is the enemy of God' (James iv. 4). And who can help the enemy of God? Therefore let us imitate our fathers and, like them, let us seek the treasure existing within our hearts and, having found it, let us hold fast to it in doing 9 and guarding—for which task we were destined from the beginning. But if some other Nicodemus appears and begins to argue, saying: 'How can anyone enter his own heart and do and dwell therein?'—as that one said to the Lord: 'How can a man enter the second time into his mother's womb, and be born?', let such an one also hear: 'The wind bloweth where it listeth' (John iii. 4, 8). But if, even amidst the events of active life, we display such doubts through lack of faith, how can we enter into the

9 'Doing' here, as in many passages throughout, refers to inner activity and work. (Translators' note.)

mysteries of contemplative life? For ascent to contemplation is active life.

But it is impossible for such unbelievers to be convinced without written proofs; so, for the service of many, let us include in this discourse features of the lives of the saints and some of the ideas they have recorded to bear out this truth, so that all may be convinced, and cast away their last doubts.

Let us begin with our first father, Antony the Great, and then, taking those who followed him in order, let us collect, as best we may, their deeds and words and offer them as evidence to unbelievers.

## From the life of our holy father Antony

Once two brothers were on their way to St. Antony, and when all their water was gone, one died and the other was near to dying. Having no strength to go on, he lay on the ground and awaited death. Meanwhile St. Antony, seated on a mountain, called the monks who happened to be with him and told them: 'Take a jar of water and run along the road towards Egypt. There there are two men who were coming here; one of them is already dead, and the other too will die unless you hurry. This I saw when I was at prayer.' Coming to the spot, the monks indeed found one man dead and they buried him; the other they revived with the water and brought him to the staretz.[10] The distance was a day's walk.—If anyone were to ask why St. Antony did not send them earlier, before the first one died, it would be an ill-judged question. Allowing the first brother to die was the business not of Antony but of God, Who gave this decision for the first and sent a revelation to Antony about the second. To St. Antony belongs only the miraculous deed that, seated on a mountain, he was sufficiently sober in heart to be found worthy for the Lord to reveal to him that which was a great distance from him. You see that, through sobriety of the heart, St. Antony was given divine vision and clairvoyance. For, according to the words of John of the Ladder, God appears to the mind in the heart, at first as a

[10] 'Staretz' is literally 'elder'; in these texts it sometimes means head of a monastic community, sometimes 'spiritual teacher'. (Translators' note.)

flame purifying its lover, and then as a light which illumines the mind and renders it God-like.

## From the life of Theodosius the Cenobiarch

St. Theodosius was so deeply wounded by the sweet arrow of love and held so fast in love's fetters that he practised in actual deed the highest of God's commandments: 'Thou shalt love the Lord thy God with all thy heart, and with all thy soul, and with all thy strength, and with all thy mind' (Luke x. 27). And this can be achieved by no other means than concentrating all the natural powers of the soul in single desire for the Creator alone. Such also was the work of his mind, that when offering consolation he inspired awe, and when reprimanding someone, he was always kind and sweet. Who else, like him, could converse with many and appear quite at their service, yet at the same time could collect his senses and marshal them back within him? Who, like him, could enjoy, in the midst of tumult, the same inner peace as others who live in the desert? And who else has remained the same in a crowd as in solitude? Thus the great Theodosius, through collecting the senses and turning them within, became pierced by love for the Creator.

## From the life of Arsenius the Great

The divine Arsenius strictly preserved the rule—never to write to anyone and never to receive letters, and in general to say practically nothing—not because he could not (how could this be thought of someone who could speak eloquently with the same ease as others speak simply?) but through the habit of much silence and in order to avoid vanity, that is, display. And in church gatherings, for the same reason, he made every effort to stand where he could not see others nor be seen by anyone; he never mixed with the crowd of brethren but hid away somewhere. Such was the care he took to keep attention within himself and to hold his mind collected inwardly in order to raise himself with less hindrance to God. Such is the example left to us by that divine man and earthly angel.

## From the life of Paul of Latros

This divine Paul spent almost all his time in mountains and deserts, having none but wild beasts to share his solitude and his food. Only seldom did he come down to the Lavra, to visit the brethren, whom he was wont to teach not to be faint-hearted and not to give up the most difficult and painful practices of virtue, but to persevere with all their attention and all their power of reasoning in leading a life according to the Gospels and in fighting the spirits of evil with all their heart. Moreover he revealed to them a method through which they could gain strength, free themselves from their former passionate dispositions and avoid new seeds of passions. You see how this father teaches his pupils, who do not know him, a method through which they could turn aside the impinging of passions. And this method is none other but the guarding of the mind, for the repelling of suggestions is the business of the mind and of nothing else.

## From the life of St. Sabbas

Whenever St. Sabbas noticed that a monk, who had renounced the world, had thoroughly mastered the rules of monastic conduct, had become strong enough to watch over his mind and struggle with thoughts from the enemy, and had completely banished from his thoughts all memory of earthly things and deeds, then, if his body was weak and sickly, he gave him a cell in the Lavra, but if he was healthy and physically strong, allowed him to build a private cell for himself. You see how St. Sabbas demanded from his pupils above all things that they should guard their mind and did not allow them to live in a separate cell unless they had acquired habitual skill in this practice. What are we to do, who sit idly in our cells and do not even know what is this guarding of the mind?

## From the life of Abba Agathon

A brother asked Abba Agathon: 'Tell me, Abba, which is greater, physical labour or the guarding of the heart?' The Abba replied: 'Man is like a tree; physical work is the leaves, and the guarding of the heart is the fruit. Since, according to the Scriptures, "every tree which bringeth not forth good fruit is hewn down, and cast into the fire" (Matt. iii. 10), it is evident that all our care must be for the fruit, that is, for guarding the mind. Yet the covering and adornment of leaves, that is, physical work, is also necessary for us.'—In this marvellous way this saint has condemned all those who do not guard their mind but boast only of their practice of virtues, in saying: 'Every tree which bringeth not forth good fruit, that is, has no guarding of the mind, and possesses nothing but leaves, that is, externally correct behaviour, is cut down and cast into the fire.' Terrifying is your definition, Father!

### From Abba Mark's epistle to Nicholas

'If you wish, my son, to acquire within you your own lamp shedding the mental light of spiritual knowledge, so that you can walk without stumbling in the deep night of this age, and to have thy "steps . . . ordered by the Lord" (Ps. xxxvii. 23), because you delight greatly in the way shown by the Gospels, in other words, if you wish to practise Christ's commandments strictly and with the warmest faith and prayer, I will show you a marvellous spiritual method or means to achieve this, a method not requiring physical labour or exertion, but demanding spiritual work—attention of mind and thought, assisted by the fear and love of God. By the use of this method you will always be able easily to defeat the enemy host. So, then, if you wish to gain victory over passions, abide within yourself by prayer and with God's help, and descending into the very depths of your heart discover there these three strong giants: forgetfulness, laziness and ignorance. These act as supports to intruders in the mind, who bring back other evil passions to act, live and grow strong in the souls of lovers of lust. But you, having found all these unknown evil giants, by strict attention and exertion of the mind, together with help from above, will find it easy later to get rid of them, again through prayer and attention. Then your zeal for true knowledge, for remembering the word of God and for

27

harmonising your will and your life therewith, together with your attention constantly standing on guard in the heart, carefully protected by the active power of grace, will destroy and wipe out the last traces of forgetfulness, ignorance and laziness.'

## From St. John of the Ladder

'A hesychast [11] is he who being without body strives to retain his soul within the bounds of its bodily home. A rare and wonderful feat!' (Ch. 27, 6). 'A hesychast is he who says: "I sleep but my heart waketh" (Song of Songs v. 2).' 'Close the door of your cell to the body, the door of your lips to conversation, and the inner door of the soul to evil spirits' (Ch. 27, 17–18). 'Sitting on high, observe, if only you know the art, and you will see how and when and whence, how many and what kind of robbers are trying to enter to steal the grapes. When the sentinel gets tired, he gets up and prays, and then sits down once more and again resumes his work with new courage' (Ch. 27, 22–3). 'The guarding of thoughts is one thing, but safe-keeping of the mind is another; and "as far as the east is from the west" (Ps. ciii. 12), so far is the latter higher than the former, but it is incomparably more difficult' (Ch. 26, 78). 'Just as thieves, when they see the king's weapons lying ready somewhere, do not attack that place carelessly, so he who has joined prayer to the heart is not easily despoiled by mental robbers.'

Do you see these words which reveal the wonderful inner doing of this great father? But we, walking in darkness, give no attention to these soul-saving sayings of the spirit and, like those who are wilfully deaf, we do not hear them.

[11] Безмолвникъ is the Russian equivalent of the Greek 'Ησυχαστής, that is one who practises hesychasm. The latter word means silence or stillness, rest after warfare; in these texts its principal significance is of an inner kind. The translators recognise that there is some risk in using the word 'hesychast', owing to the misunderstanding attached to the word in certain quarters and books of reference, more especially since the Palamite controversy of the fourteenth century. At the same time it is the correct description of the traditional spiritual method described in these texts, and has, for this reason, been used from time to time. (Translators' note.)

# PROFITABLE DISCOURSE ON SOBRIETY

## From Abba Isaiah

'When a man withdraws from what is on the left side, he will know clearly all his sins which he has committed before God. For he does not see his sins unless he separates himself from them by bitter separation (with much suffering of the heart). Those who have attained to this degree have obtained tears and prayer, and the power to be ashamed before God when they remember their friendship with passions' (Ch. 17, 21). 'Let us strive then, brothers, according to our powers, and God will help us in His infinite mercy. If we have not preserved our hearts secure, as did our fathers, let us do all we can to keep at least our bodies pure of sin, as God demands. And we believe that, in times of famine, if such a time comes, He will vouchsafe us His grace as He did with all His saints' (Ch. 21, 20).

Here the great father consoles the very weak, saying: 'If we have not preserved our hearts secure as did our fathers, at least let us preserve our bodies free from sin, as God demands—and He will be merciful to us.' Great is the compassion and the indulgence of this father!

## From St. Macarius the Great

'The most important work in spiritual struggle is to enter the heart and there to wage war with Satan; to hate Satan, and to fight him by opposing his thoughts. If a man keeps his body outwardly free from lust and corruption, and yet inwardly commits adultery before God, by fornication in his thoughts, then is there no profit whatever in keeping his body pure. For it is written that "whosoever looketh on a woman to lust after her hath committed adultery with her already in his heart" (Matt. v. 28). There is adultery committed by the body, and there is adultery of the soul, communing with Satan.'

This great father seems to contradict the words of Abba Isaiah quoted above. But this is not so, since the other also advises us to care for our bodies and keep them such as God demands. But God demands not only bodily but also spiritual purity as is shown in the Gospel commandments.

## From Bishop Diadochus

'He who always remains in his heart is remote from the attractions of this world and, walking in the spirit, can no longer experience carnal lusts. Such a man proceeds on his way protected by virtues, posting these virtues as door-keepers, as it were, to his city of purity. Then all the wiles of the devils, directed against him, fail' (Ch. 57).

Truly did the holy father speak when he said that the wiles of the enemy fail as long as we abide in a certain place in the depths of our hearts, and the more so the more firmly we hold there.

## From St. Isaac of Syria

'Try to enter your inner treasure-house and you will see the treasure-house of heaven. For both the one and the other are the same, and one and the same entrance reveals them both. The ladder leading to the kingdom is concealed within you, that is, in your soul. Wash yourself from sin and you will see the rungs of the ladder by which you can ascend thither.'

## From St. John of Karpathos

'Much labour and effort is needed in prayer in order to attain to an untroubled state of thoughts—that other heaven of the heart where, according to the Apostle, Christ dwells: "Know ye not your own selves, how that Jesus Christ is in you, except ye be reprobates?" (2 Cor. xiii. 5).'

## From St. Simeon the New Theologian

'When the devil with his demons had succeeded in having man banished from the garden of Eden through transgression, and in separating him from God, he acquired access to the reasoning power of every man, so that he can agitate a man's mind by day or by night; sometimes much, sometimes a little, and sometimes exceedingly. And there is no protection against this except through constant remembrance of God; in other words, if the memory of God, engraved in the heart by the power of the cross, strengthens the mind in its steadfastness. To this end lead all the efforts of mental struggle, which it is the duty of every Christian to practise in the field of faith. That man will struggle in vain for whom this is not so. It is to achieve this that all the various spiritual exercises are undertaken by anyone who seeks God through voluntary privations, and to attract the compassion of the all-merciful God; so that he may be once more granted his first status, and so also that he may have the imprint of Christ on his mind, as the Apostle says: "My little children, of whom I travail in birth again until Christ be formed in you" (Gal. iv. 19).'

Have you understood, brethren, that there exists a certain spiritual method swiftly leading whoever follows it to passionlessness and the vision of God? Are you convinced that the whole of active life is regarded by God as nothing but leaves on a tree which bears no fruit and that every soul which has no guarding of the mind will labour therein in vain? Let us then take care lest we die having borne no fruit and suffer vain regrets for all eternity.

## By Nicephorus himself

*Question* (to Nicephorus). We have learned from the foregoing evidence of the doing practised by the fathers who were pleasing to God, and that there exists a certain doing which speedily frees the soul from passions and by love unites it to God; which doing is necessary for everyone warring for Christ. All our doubts are now dispelled, and we are firmly convinced of this. But we beg you to teach us what is attention of the mind and how to become worthy to acquire it. For this work is quite unknown to us.

*Answer* (by Nicephorus). In the name of our Lord Jesus Christ Who said: 'Without me ye can do nothing' (John xv. 5). Having called Him to help and assist me, I shall try as far as is in my power to show you what attention is and how, God willing, one can succeed in acquiring it.

Some of the saints have called attention the safe-keeping of the mind, others—the guarding of the heart, yet others—sobriety, yet others—mental silence, and others again by other names.

But all these names mean the same thing. Just as of bread one can say: a round, a slice, a piece, so also understand about this. As to what attention is and what are its characteristic features, you shall learn forthwith.

Attention is a sign of sincere repentance. Attention is the appeal of the soul to itself, hatred of the world and ascent towards God. Attention is renunciation of sin and acquisition of virtue. Attention is an undoubting certainty of the remission of sins. Attention is the beginning of contemplation, or rather its necessary condition: for, through attention, God comes close and reveals Himself to the mind. Attention is serenity of the mind, or rather its standing firmly planted and not wandering, through the gift of God's mercy. Attention means cutting off thoughts, it is the abode of remembrance of God and the treasure-house of the power to endure all that may come. Therefore attention is the origin of faith, hope and love; since he who has no faith cannot bear all the afflictions coming from without, and he who does not suffer them willingly cannot say: 'He is my refuge and my fortress' (Ps. xci. 2); and he who has not the Almighty as his refuge cannot be truly sincere in his love for Him.

This greatest of all great doings can be gained by many, or even by all, mostly by being taught. A few men receive this gift from God without being taught, working from inner compulsion and the warmth of their faith. But what is rare is not the law. Therefore it is necessary to seek a teacher who is not himself in error, to follow his instructions, and so learn to distinguish, in the matter of attention, defects and excesses of right and of left, encountered through diabolical suggestion. From his own sufferings from temptation he will explain to us what is needful and will show us correctly that mental path which we can then follow with less hindrance. If there is no such teacher in view, one must search for one, sparing no efforts. But if, even after such a search, he is not to be found, then, with a contrite spirit, calling to God with tears and praying to Him assiduously and with humility, do what I shall tell you.[12]

---

[12] What follows is an abbreviated paraphrase because the original instruction applies to a method of breathing which is now expounded differently. (Footnote in 'Dobrotolubiye'.)

You know that our breathing is the inhaling and exhaling of air. The organ which serves for this is the lungs which lie round the heart, so that the air passing through them thereby envelops the heart. Thus breathing is a natural way to the heart. And so, having collected your mind within you, lead it into the channel of breathing through which air reaches the heart and, together with this inhaled air, force your mind to descend into the heart and to remain there. Accustom it, brother, not to come out of the heart too soon, for at first it feels very lonely in that inner seclusion and imprisonment. But when it gets accustomed to it, it begins on the contrary to dislike its aimless circling outside, for it is no longer unpleasant and wearisome for it to be within. Just as a man who has been away from home, when he returns is beside himself with joy at seeing again his children and wife, embraces them and cannot talk to them enough, so the mind, when it unites with the heart, is filled with unspeakable joy and delight. Then a man sees that the kingdom of heaven is truly within us; and seeing it now in himself, he strives with pure prayer to keep it and strengthen it there, and regards everything external as not worthy of attention and wholly unattractive.

When you thus enter into the place of the heart, as I have shown you, give thanks to God and, praising His mercy, keep always to this doing, and it will teach you things which in no other way will you ever learn. Moreover you should know that when your mind becomes firmly established in the heart, it must not remain there silent and idle, but it should constantly repeat the prayer: 'Lord, Jesus Christ, Son of God, have mercy upon me!' and never cease. For this practice, keeping the mind from dreams, renders it elusive and impenetrable to enemy suggestions and every day leads it more and more to love and longing for God.

If, however, in spite of all your efforts, you do not succeed in entering into the realm of the heart, as I have described, do what I shall now tell you and, with God's help, you will find what you seek. You know that in every man inner talking is in the breast. For, when our lips are silent, it is in the breast that we talk and discourse with ourselves, pray and sing psalms, and do other things. Thus, having banished every thought from this inner talking (for you can do this if you want to), give it the following short prayer: 'Lord, Jesus Christ, Son of God, have mercy upon me!'—and force it, instead of all other thought, to have only this one constant cry within. If you continue to do this constantly, with your whole attention, then in time this will open for you the way to the heart which I have described. There can be no doubt about this, for we have proved it ourselves by experience.

If you do this with strong desire and attention, full of sweetness, a whole host of virtues will come to you: love, joy, peace and others, through which, later, every petition of yours will be answered in the name of Jesus Christ, our Lord, to Whom, with the Father and the Holy Ghost, is glory, and power, honour and worship, now and always, and for ever and ever. Amen.

# ST. GREGORY OF SINAI
## Short Biographical Note

Our holy father Gregory, who took his monastic vows on Mount Sinai and is therefore called 'of Sinai', lived in the reign of Andronicus Palaeologus in the middle of the fourteenth century. Coming to Mount Athos, he visited all the monasteries and hermitages existing there and found many fathers who possessed knowledge and led a pure life. But all their endeavours were concerned with active life; and of guarding the mind, of true silence and contemplation they knew so little that they did not even understand these words themselves.

He met only three monks in the Magul Skete, opposite the Philotheus Monastery (Isaiah, Cornelius and Macarius were their names) who practised contemplation to a small degree. Seeing this, he was filled with zeal and began to teach sobriety, guarding the mind and mental prayer not only to those who practised silence, living in solitude, but also to all cenobites. In addition to organising three large lavras in Macedonia, he visited many other places and dioceses, giving everyone in general his blessed instruction in the practice of ceaseless mental prayer. Thus he converted many sinners and, making worthy men of the unworthy, was the means of their attaining salvation. His life has been described in detail by Callistus, the holy Patriarch of Constantinople, who was his pupil.

As during his life he was generally recognised as the teacher of holy sobriety, so after his death he guides us in that direction by these writings, in which he clearly and fully expounds for our instruction the active method of the prayer of mind-in-heart; he teaches us how to lead a good life and to fight passions, and shows us clearly the characteristics of prelest, and of grace. Therefore these writings, above all others, are useful to beginners, to those who are already on the way, and to the perfect. All who read them, except from mere curiosity, will discover the nature and greatness of the spiritual treasures hidden in his words and in obtaining this treasure will rejoice exceedingly. He died in the year 1360.

# ST. GREGORY OF SINAI

## Texts[13] on commandments and dogmas, warnings and promises; also on thoughts, passions and virtues; as well as on silence and prayer

1. True reason, such as man had in the beginning, cannot be had or acquired by any man, who has not first been purified and become passionless. Of purity we are deprived by unreasoning tendencies of the senses, and of passionlessness—by the corrupted state of the flesh.

2. True reason belongs only to those who have become saints through acquiring purity. None who are wise in words have ever had pure reason, because, from birth, they let their reasoning powers be corrupted by unseemly thoughts. The sensory and prolix spirit of the wisdom of this age, so rich in words, which create the illusion of great knowledge but actually fill one with the wildest thoughts, has its stronghold in this prolixity, which deprives man of essential wisdom, true contemplation and the knowledge of the one and indivisible.

3. By knowledge of truth,[14] understand the direct apprehension of truth through grace. All other thoughts should be

[13] In the Greek original, these texts are arranged acrostically, the initial letters serving as acrostics. (Footnote in 'Dobrotolubiye'.)

[14] There are two words in Russian each of which may be translated 'truth': истина and правда. The former, which is used in this passage, means absolute Truth beyond relativity; e.g. it is used in John xiv. 6: 'I am the way, the truth, and the life.' правда means truth in the sense of what is correct or right, but it is contingent or relative truth. It can be said that истина is правда always, but not every правда is истина. The translators have found no complete remedy for the lack of two equivalent words in English; but правда has often been translated 'righteousness'. (Translators' note.)

called manifestations of the significances of truth and demonstrations of its applications.

4. Those who lose grace, suffer this loss through lack of faith and neglect; and those who acquire it again, do so through faith and zeal. These latter move forward step by step, but the former turn right back.

5. To fall into stonelike insensibility is the same as to die; so also to be blind in mind [15] is the same as to lose the sight of one's bodily eyes. For he who has fallen into insensibility is deprived of the life-giving force; and he whose mind is blind is deprived of Divine light by which a man can see and can be seen.

6. Only a few receive power and wisdom from God. For wisdom is to share in Divine blessings, and power is to show them. But this sharing and passing to others is a truly Divine activity, beyond the powers of man.

7. A true sanctuary, even before the future life, is a heart free from thoughts, made active by the Spirit. For there all is said and done spiritually. He who has not attained to such a state, although for the sake of some virtues he may be a stone suitable for use in building a temple to God, is not himself a temple nor a celebrant of the Spirit.

8. Man is created incorruptible—and as such he will be raised from the dead; but neither unchanging nor yet changing, but possessing the power, according to the inclination of his desire, to change or not to change. Desire has no power to give to nature the character of complete unchangeability; this latter is the mark of the future unchanging deification.

9. Corruption is born of the flesh. To feed, to excrete superfluous matters, and to hold one's head proudly even when lying down to sleep are the natural characteristics of animals and wild

---

[15] The Greek original has νοῦς for the word here translated 'mind'. It is essential to realise that 'mind' in this context is not limited to the thinking power or reason. The νοῦς includes in its qualities the faculty of direct knowledge or intuition of Truth (истина). The word 'mental' in paragraphs 111 and 116 is to be understood on the same level. See, too, paragraphs 23, 31, 45, 79, 112, 123 and 130 below, as well as many passages throughout these texts. Owing to the lack of precise English equivalents the translators must in general leave the reader to interpret the words 'mind' and 'mental' on the correct level according to the context. (Translators' note.)

beasts in which we share; for, through trespasses, we have become akin to beasts and have lost the natural blessings given us by God, becoming as beasts instead of reasoning beings, and animal instead of divine.

10. Paradise is of two kinds—of the senses and of the mind; that is, the garden of Eden and the paradise of grace. The garden of Eden is the place where all kinds of sweet-scented plants have been planted by God. It is neither entirely incorruptible nor entirely corruptible. Placed between corruption and non-corruption, it is for ever rich in fruit and flowers, both ripe and unripe. The trees and ripe fruit, when they fall, become transformed into sweet-scented earth, free from the smell of corruption belonging to trees of this world. This is due to the abundance of sanctifying grace for ever flooding the garden of Eden.

11. The creature as he is to-day was not originally created corruptible, but has fallen into corruption because it 'was made subject to vanity, not willingly' but unwillingly, 'by reason of him who hath subjected the same in hope' of the renewal of Adam, who became subject to corruption (Rom. viii. 20). He who has renewed Adam and sanctified him has renewed also the creature, but he has not yet freed them from corruption. This freedom from corruption is understood by some as a transition to a better state, and by others as a total abandonment of everything sensory.

12. Those who receive grace are people who have conceived and are active with the Spirit. But it happens that they cast away the Divine seed either through downfalls or through being widowed of God by communion with the enemy concealed within them. The forsaking of grace is brought about by the action of the passions (if one takes pleasure in the impulse of passions), and grace is utterly lost through the committing of sins. For a passion-loving and sin-loving soul is deprived of grace, sweeps it away and becomes widowed; hence, it becomes the abode of passions—if not of demons—both in this world and in the next.

13. Anger is tamed and becomes transformed into benevolence only through courage and mercy; for these destroy the enemies that besiege the city of the soul—the first, the enemies outside and the second, those within.

14. Many people, though they act in accordance with the commandments, are like wayfarers who seem to follow the way, yet remain outside a city instead of reaching it. For they travel without sense or method, take wrong turnings at cross-roads and thus deviate from the king's straight highway. In other words, they mistake vices which are near to virtues for the actual royal road. For the true fulfilment of the commandments does not require merely forbearance from excesses or defects, it also demands an aim acceptable to God, that is the fulfilment in everything of God's will alone. If we do not work thus, then all labour is in vain; for without this it is impossible to follow the 'right ways of the Lord': in all he does it is demanded of a man constantly to keep this aim before him while he acts.

15. On your path of obedience to the commandments seek the Lord in your heart. When you listen to John, crying in the wilderness, 'Prepare ye the way of the Lord, make his paths straight' (Mark i. 3), understand by these words commandments for the heart as well as for actions; for it is impossible rightly to follow the commandments and to do rightly unless the heart too is right.

16. When you hear the prophetic words in the Bible: 'thy rod and thy staff they comfort me' (Ps. xxiii. 4), understand by these words judgment and Providence, and, in a moral sense, psalmody and prayer. For when 'we are chastened of the Lord' with the rod of chastisement (of teaching) (1 Cor. xi. 32), we are learning to be converted. And when we chastise our foes with the rod of courageous psalmody, we become strengthened in prayer. Thus, with mind active and holding the rod and the staff in its hand, let us not cease chastising and being chastised, until we are entirely under Providence (until we surrender to it) so that we may escape judgment both now and hereafter.

17. It is ordained that man must put before all things the universal commandment—to remember God—of which it is said: 'thou shalt remember the Lord thy God' (Deut. viii. 18). For, by the reverse of that which destroys us, we may be secure. What destroys us is forgetfulness of God, which shrouds the commandments in darkness and despoils us of all good.

18. Those who struggle, regain their original state by keeping two commandments—obedience and fasting; for all evil entered

into the generation of mortals through practices opposed to them. Moreover, those who keep the commandments through obedience ascend to God more quickly, and those who keep them through fasting—more slowly. Besides, obedience is more suitable for beginners, and fasting for those on the way, who possess courage and vision of mind. But in fulfilling the commandments it is given to very few always to obey God undeceived, and even for the most valiant this achievement is very difficult.

19. 'The law of the Spirit of life' of which the Apostle speaks (Rom. viii. 2) is such as acts and speaks in the heart; just as the written law (according to the letter) acts in the flesh (or is fulfilled by the flesh). The first frees the mind from the law of sin and death; but the second allows one to play the pharisee in secret, the body being seen obeying the law and fulfilling the commandments for display.

20. They say that the whole body of the commandments as practised in deed, 'fitly joined together and compacted' in the spirit (Eph. iv. 16), shows a man as he is—whether perfect or not yet perfect, according to his achievements. Moreover, actions in accordance with the commandments are the body; virtues, that is, established inner tendencies, are the bones; and grace is the living soul, inciting to actions in accordance with commandments and assisting their performance. The degree of zeal in acquiring stature in Christ shows whether a man is an infant or a perfected man in the present world and the world to come.

21. He who wishes to make the body of the commandments grow (by actions in accordance with the commandments, virtue, righteousness) should seek the true word of the milk of grace, for it feeds all who desire and strive to increase in stature in Jesus Christ. As breasts give forth milk to infants, its wisdom yields warmth for growth, and, like nourishing honey, provides the perfect with the joy of purification. 'Honey and milk are under thy tongue' sings the Song of Songs (iv. 11); wherein by milk Solomon meant the nourishing and growth-giving force of the Spirit, and by honey, Its purifying power. The great Apostle, pointing to the differing actions of the Spirit, says: 'Even as unto babes . . . I have fed you with milk, and not with meat' (1 Cor. iii. 1, 2).

22. He who seeks to understand commandments without fulfilling commandments, and to acquire such understanding through learning and reading, is like a man who takes a shadow for truth. For the understanding of truth is given to those who have become participants in truth (who have tasted it through living). Those who are not participants in truth and are not initiated therein, when they seek this understanding, draw it from a distorted wisdom. Of such men the Apostle says: ' the natural (16) man receiveth not the things of the Spirit' (1 Cor. ii. 14) even though they boast of their knowledge of truth.

23. As the physical eye looks at written letters and receives knowledge from them through the senses; so the mind, when it becomes purified and returns to its original state, looks up to God and receives Divine knowledge from Him. Instead of a book it has the Spirit, instead of a pen, thought and tongue ('my tongue is the pen' says the Ps. [xlv. 1]); instead of ink—light. Plunging thought into light, so that thought itself becomes light, the mind, guided by the Spirit, traces words in the pure hearts of those who listen. Then it understands the words: 'And they shall be all taught of God' (John vi. 45), and 'he that teacheth man knowledge' (Ps. xciv. 10).

24. Understand that the law of the commandments means direct faith acting in the heart. For faith gives birth to every commandment and brings illumination to souls, which thereon produce these fruits of true and active faith: abstinence, love, as the end of perfection, and humility as a special gift of God, holding them firmly together.

25. Real Orthodoxy is true knowledge of things visible and invisible: visible—that is, sensory; invisible—that is, of thought, intellect, spirit and God.

---

16 'Natural'; see paragraphs 46, 127 and 128 below. The Russian word here translated 'natural' is душевный which is the word used in the Russian version of 1 Cor. ii. 14. It is an adjective meaning 'of the soul', for which there is no English equivalent, the term 'spiritual' being inadmissible as a substitute in these texts, where it has a wholly different meaning. The translators have therefore used the word 'natural' where it seemed appropriate, but more often have employed 'of the soul'. Cf. also: 'It is sown a natural body: it is raised a spiritual body. There is a natural body, and there is a spiritual body' (1 Cor. xv. 44). (Translators' note.)

26. The final end of Orthodoxy is pure knowledge of the two dogmas of faith—the Trinity and the Duality; to contemplate and know the Trinity as indivisible and yet not merged together; to know the Duality as the two natures of Christ joined in one person—that is, to know and to profess one's faith in the Son of God both before incarnation, and after incarnation, to praise Him in His two natures and wills unmerged, the one Divine and the other human.

27. The three unchanging and immutable properties of the three Persons of the Holy Trinity should be rightly professed: non-begottenness, begottenness and procession: the Father, non-begotten and without beginning, the Son, begotten and also without beginning, and the Holy Spirit, eternally co-existing, who proceedeth from the Father and is given by the Son, as says St. Damascenus.

28. Faith, full of grace, supported by the keeping of commandments would by itself lead to salvation, if we kept it in full force and did not prefer dead and inactive faith to living and active faith in Christ. It behoves a believer to establish the image of faith in his heart and to organise his life according to active faith in Christ. But nowadays ignorance teaches the pious a faith manifested in words, dead and unfeeling, instead of the faith of grace.

29. Trinity is simple unity; it is not merged together—it is three in one. The One three-hypostatical God has the three hypostases perfectly distinct in Himself.

30. God is known and understood in everything in three hypostases. He holds all things and provides for all things through His Son in the Holy Spirit; and no one of Them, wherever He is invoked, is named or thought of as existing apart or separately from the two others.

31. Just in the same way, man has mind, word and spirit; and the mind cannot be without the word, nor the word without the spirit, but the three are always in one another, yet exist in themselves. The mind speaks by means of words, and the word is manifested through the spirit. This example shows that man bears in himself a feeble image of the ineffable prototype, the Trinity, thus demonstrating that he has been made in God's image.

32. Mind is the Father, word is the Son, spirit is the Holy Spirit, as the divine fathers teach in this example, expounding the dogmatic teaching of the consubstantial and pre-existing Trinity, of one God in three Persons, thus transmitting to us the true faith as an anchor of hope. According to the Scriptures, to know the One God is the root of immortality, and to know the dominion of the three-in-one is the whole and entire truth. The word of the Gospel on this subject can be understood thus: 'This is life eternal, that they might know thee, the only true God' in three hypostases, 'and Jesus Christ, whom thou hast sent' in two natures and two wills (John xvii. 3).

33. Torments differ, as do the rewards of the righteous. All torments are in hell, according to the word of the Scriptures, 'a land of darkness, as darkness itself; and of the shadow of death, without any order, and where the light is as darkness' (Job x. 22), where sinners dwell before judgment and whither they return after the pronouncement of God's final decision. For what else can the words of the Scriptures mean—'The wicked shall be turned into hell' (Ps. ix. 17) and 'death shall feed on them' (Ps. xlix. 14)—than the final verdict and eternal condemnation?

34. Fire, darkness, worm, hell correspond to passions—lusts of all kinds, the all-embracing darkness of ignorance, the unquenchable thirst for sensual pleasures, the stench of evil-smelling sin, which, like precursors and foretastes of the torment of hell, even now begin to torture sinners in whose souls they take root through long-established habit.

35. Passionate habits are the precursors of the torment of hell, just as active virtues are the forerunners of the kingdom of heaven. By good deeds one should understand actions in accordance with the commandments, and by virtues good tendencies rooted in habit. In the same way also do sinful deeds and tendencies differ from one another.

36. Future rewards and punishments are equally eternal, although some people view this differently. To some, Divine justice gives eternal life, to others, eternal torment. Whether they have spent their present life in good or in evil, all alike will receive their reward according to their merits. The amount and

49. In the future life (or in heaven) the saints hold inner converse with one another, the Holy Spirit speaking in them.

50. If we do not learn what we were created by God, we shall not know what we have become through sin.

51. They are equal in spiritual stature who have in this world acquired the fullness of perfection in Christ.

52. To whom the labour, to him the reward. But the amount and nature of rewards, that is, their measure, degree and state, will there appear in actual deed.

53. Minds equal unto the angels, in freedom from corruption and in deification, will be those saints who are the children of the resurrection (Luke xx. 36).

54. It is said that in the life to come the angels and saints shall never cease to progress in increasing their gifts, striving for greater and ever greater blessings. No slackening or change from virtue to sin is admitted in that life.

55. In this life, regard that man as perfect who has received the likeness of the stature of Christ as a pledge, so to speak; but in the life to come, perfection will be shown by the degree of deification.

56. In the future, a man shall have the degree of deification corresponding to his present perfection in spiritual stature.

57. It is said that true glory is knowledge, or spiritual contemplation, or the exact understanding of the dogmas and knowledge of true faith.

58. Wonder is a total transport of the powers of the soul towards what is discerned of the wondrous glory of the Deity. Or again, wonder is a pure and entire stretching of the mind outwards towards the limitless power of the light. Ecstasy is not only the ravishing of the powers of the soul to heaven, it means, also, transcending the limits of the senses themselves.

59. There are two forms of ecstasy in the spirit: one, of the heart (going deep into the heart, in forgetfulness of all things), the other, enravishment (being carried beyond the limits of all that is). The first belongs to those who are still learning, the second to those who have attained to perfection in love. Both alike place the mind in which they act outside the senses (or the consciousness of outer relationships); for Divine love is an intoxicating

forcing of thoughts by the spirit towards the most excellent, which deprives a man of the sense (or the consciousness) of outer relationships.

60. The origin and cause of thoughts lies in the splitting up, by man's transgression, of his single and simple memory, which has thus lost the memory of God and, becoming multiple instead of simple, and varied instead of single, has fallen a prey to its own forces.

61. To cure this original memory of the deceitful and harmful memory of thoughts means to bring it back to its ancient simplicity. The weapon of evil—transgression—has not only disordered the simple memory of good in the soul, but has corrupted all its powers, darkening its natural desire for virtue. Memory can be cured by a constant remembrance of God, consolidated by the action of prayer; for it is thus imbued with the spirit, and is carried from the natural to a supernatural state.

62. The causes of passions are sinful deeds; of thoughts—passions; of imagination—thoughts; the cause of opinions is memory (become multiform); of memory—forgetfulness (of what is true and needful); the mother of forgetfulness is ignorance; of ignorance—laziness; laziness is born of lustful desire; desire is born of movement in a false direction; movement in a false direction comes from committing an action; such action is the fruit of a foolish tendency to evil and of adherence to the senses and sensory things.

63. In the thinking power of the soul thoughts are born and act; in the excitable part—passions of wild beasts; in the desiring part—animal lusts; in the mind—images and fantasies; in the reason—opinions.

64. The influx of evil thoughts is like a flowing river. They contain the suggestion with which later there occurs a sinful identification, which covers (floods) the heart like a deluge of water.

65. Regard the sweetness of the bodily humours as a deep moat filled with mire; likewise the rot of adultery and all pother over material possessions, thoughts of which burden the passionate mind and cast it down into the depths of despair.

66. Passionate thoughts present images of passionate things. The action of thoughts is not material, but they remind and attract one towards material things, and so cause carnal sins.

67. Thoughts are the words of the demons and the fore-runners of passions; for it is impossible for anything good or bad to be done, without its first suggesting and exciting thought about itself. A thought is the movement of a formless suggestion of one thing or another.

68. Things in themselves give birth to simple thoughts, but suggestions of the devil engender evil thoughts. Natural thoughts are distinguished from the unnatural and the supernatural by comparison.

69. Thoughts change instantly from one to another: the natural into the unnatural, and again those on the level of nature into thoughts above nature. But the devil's suggestions can stick to anything, even to Divine thoughts.

70. Take note that before thoughts stand their causes; before imagination—thoughts; before passions—imagination; before the demons—passions, forming a kind of graded chain of de-graded spirits holding on to one another. But nothing here comes to pass without the demons: neither does imagination paint images, nor does passion act without their hidden power. All the same, what gives them power over us is mostly our own carelessness.

71. The demons fill our mind with images, or rather clothe themselves in images for our benefit and impinge on us (introduce a suggestion) according to the ruling passion habitually acting in the soul. For generally they make use of passionate habits to multiply in us passionate fantasies and even in sleep they fill our dreams with varied imaginings. Moreover, the demons of lust sometimes turn into pigs, sometimes into donkeys, or into frenzied and fiery stallions, sometimes into the most intemperate Jews. The demons of anger turn sometimes into pagans, some-times into lions; the demons of cowardice into Ishmaelites; the demons of inconstancy into Idumaeans; the demons of drunken-ness and gluttony into Saracens; the demons of greed sometimes into wolves, sometimes into tigers; the demons of deceit some-times into snakes, or into vipers, or into foxes; the demons of

shamelessness into dogs; the demons of laziness into cats. It happens that the demons of lust sometimes take the shape of snakes, and sometimes that of crows or rooks; the shape of birds is usually taken by the demons of high places. Our fantasy changes the images of demons in a threefold manner corresponding to the tripartite nature of the soul, presenting them in the form of birds, wild beasts and domestic animals, in accordance with the three powers of the soul: the desiring, the excitable and the thinking. For the three princes of the passions rise up against these three powers, and assuming the image akin to whatever passion qualifies the soul, assault it in this disguise.

72. The demons of sinful lust often attack like fire or like burning coals. These voluptuous demons set fire to the excitable force of the soul, but, at the same time throwing the reasoning part of the soul into confusion, they plunge the soul into darkness. The chief cause of lustful burnings, confusion of thoughts and the darkening of the soul lies in voluptuous passion.

73. The night of passions is the darkness of ignorance. Or again: night is the realm where passions are born, where the prince of darkness holds sway and where wild beasts, birds of the air and reptiles of the earth, figuratively understood, like spirits of evil, snarl, seeking to devour us.

74. When the passions are in action, some thoughts take the lead, others follow after. Those that take the lead are dreaming thoughts (succession of images), and those that follow are passionate thoughts (incited by those images). Passions precede the demons, and the demons follow after passions.

75. The origin and cause of passions is misuse; of misuse— inclination; of inclination—the movement of habitual desire. To experience a desire is suggestion, and suggestion comes from the demons whom Providence allows to show up what our self-will is like.

76. The poisonous sting of sin unto death is passionate habit of the soul; for it is hard to change or eradicate the character of a man who has willingly surrendered himself to passions.

77. Passions have different names; but they are divided into those of the body and those of the soul. Bodily passions are sub-divided into sorrowful and sinful; the sorrowful are again

subdivided into those of suffering and those of punishment. Passions of the soul are divided into excitable, slothful and mental. The mental are subdivided into those of imagination and those of reason. All of them are either voluntary, through misuse, or involuntary, through necessity. The latter are so-called non-shameful passions, which the holy fathers described as due to surroundings and natural characteristics (dispositions).

78. Some passions are of the body, others are passions of the soul; some are passions of lust, others passions of the excitable part, yet others are passions of thought. Of the latter some are passions of the mind and others of reasoning. All of them combine with one another in various ways and affect one another—and thus change.

79. Passions of the excitable part are: anger, bitterness, quarrelsomeness, hot temper, insolence, haughtiness, boastfulness and the like. Passions of desire are: graspingness, debauchery, intemperance, insatiability, voluptuousness, love of money, self-love—the most evil passion of all. The bodily passions are: fornication, adultery, impurity, unseemliness, gluttony, laziness, absentmindedness, attachment to the world, attachment to life and the like. Passions of speech and tongue are: unbelief, blasphemy, deceit, craftiness, curiosity, duplicity, slander, calumny, blame, disparagement, talkativeness, pretence, lying, ribaldry, invective, flattery, mockery, pushing oneself forward, servility, being puffed up, perjury, idle talk, etc. Passions of the mind are: conceit, self-exaltation, self-praise, argumentativeness, rashness, self-satisfaction, contrariness, disobedience, dreaminess, fabrications, love of showing off, love of fame, pride—the first and last of all evils. Passions of thought are: wandering, heedlessness, captivity and slavery, darkening of thoughts, blindness, evasions (of work), suggestions, identifications, inclinations, distortions, rejections and the like. In a word, all evil thoughts, feelings and dispositions, contrary to our nature, are divided according to the three powers of the soul, just as all the good ones, consistent with our nature, are similarly divided.

80. David cries out in wonder to God: 'Such knowledge is too wonderful for me; it is high, I cannot attain unto it' (Ps. cxxxix. 6). It is inaccessible for my weak mind and powers.

81. It is worth investigating why the holy fathers call lust and anger sometimes forces of the body and sometimes forces of the soul. We mention this, because the words of the saints never disagree if they are carefully examined; all alike speak the truth, wisely changing their judgments on these subjects when necessary. The soul possesses in itself the power to wish and a courageous energy for action, which belongs to the excitable power. But since it was created both intelligent and spiritual, neither lust nor anger were included in its being; just as the flesh, having been originally created free from corruption, did not possess the humours which later gave rise to lust and animal rage. Already after transgression, when man fell into corruption and coarseness of flesh, this fact of necessity produced in him lust and rage. Therefore, when flesh holds sway in him, lust and anger resist the desires of his soul. But when these forces of death are made subject to reason, they assist the soul in doing right.

82. When God's breath created the soul possessing mind and reason, He did not, at the same time, create rage and animal lust; He endowed the soul only with the desiring power and with courage in fulfilling desires. In the same way, when He created the body, He did not first include therein anger and unreasoning lust. It was only later, through transgression, that death, corruption and bestiality were added. Theologians say that the body was created incorruptible and that such it will be resurrected, just as the soul was created passionless. But just as the soul was free to sin, so also the body had the possibility of becoming subject to corruption. Thus both of them, that is, body and soul, became corrupted and compounded together, in accordance with the natural law of combining and interacting with one another. Moreover the soul acquired the qualities of passions, or rather demons, and the body became akin to beasts devoid of reason and was plunged into corruption. Thus joined together, the forces of the two formed one animal being, unreasoning and senseless, subject to anger and lust. This is how, according to the Scriptures, man has become 'like the beasts that perish' (Ps. xlix. 12).

83. The origin and the source of virtues is will or desire directed towards that which is good, just as God is the cause and the source of all good. And the origin of good is faith, or rather

Christ, the foundation stone of faith, Whom we have as the origin and the basis of all virtues, in Whom we stand and by Whom we perform every good action. He is the corner stone which joins us together, and the precious pearl, seeking which a monk, entering into the depth of silence, sells all his desires in exchange for obedience to commandments, that he may possess it.

84. Virtues are equal in the sense that they all reduce themselves to one, all leading to the same end and, in their totality, forming one complete image of virtue. But some virtues are greater than others, embracing and comprising in themselves a great many, or possibly even all, other virtues. Such as—Divine love, humility and Divine patience. Of the latter the Lord says: 'In your patience possess ye your souls' (Luke xxi. 19). He did not say: in your fast or in your vigil. By patience I mean that patience which is of God and is the queen of virtues and the basis of manly valour. It is in itself—peace amid strife, stillness in the midst of storm and an impregnable position for those who have acquired it. He who has attained it in Christ cannot be harmed by any weapons, or javelins, or attacking armies, or even the hosts of demons or the legions of hostile powers.

85. Virtues, though born of one another, have their origin in the three powers of the soul—all but those that are Divine. For the origin and cause of the four Divine parent virtues which contain and constitute all others, namely, wisdom, courage, chastity and truth, is the Divine wisdom made active by the Spirit which has a fourfold movement in the mind. However, it does not yield them all at the same time (or does not set them all in motion), but each one separately, in its own time, as the Divine wisdom wills: the first as light, the second as life-giving force and impelling inspiration; the third as sanctifying and purifying force; the fourth as the dew of purity, giving joy and cooling the arid heat of passions. Each upon each man, it bestows according to his achievements; and on the perfect, it bestows perfection of action.

86. The practice of virtues, even though performed with care and effort, does not afford complete security to the soul unless grace transforms them into an essential disposition of the heart. Each of the virtues has its own special capacity and its own particular action, and once it has been bestowed it remains

unchanged and unfailing. For those who have earned this gift possess in their members, like a living soul, the grace for practising them. But without grace the whole bevy of virtues is usually dead, and in those who appear to possess them and practise them this appearance is but a shadow, a phantom of virtues and not the real thing.

87. Thus there are four original virtues: courage, good sense, chastity, righteousness. And there are eight other moral qualities, originating either from an excess or a defect of these and following them closely on either side; these we consider and call vices, but the world calls them virtues. On either side of courage, go audacity and timidity; on either side of good sense—artfulness and senselessness (tactlessness); on either side of chastity go intemperance and lack of sensibility; on either side of righteousness being over-exacting and unrighteousness. Along the middle way, between them, proceed not only the original virtues which are beyond all excess or defect, but also individual good deeds. Those in the centre are moved by the will for good within a righteous heart; the others (those on the sides) by depravity and conceit. The fact that right virtues move along the middle way is testified by the proverb: 'Then shalt thou understand . . . every good path' (Prov. ii. 9). They are all contained in the three powers of the soul where they are born and grow, rooted in the four parent virtues, or rather in Christ. Moreover the natural virtues are purified by the active ones (the good inherent dispositions and features of temperament—by good deeds in accordance with the commandments), whereas the Divine and supernatural virtues are bestowed by the grace of the Holy Spirit.

88. Among the virtues some result from action, others are natural, the third category are Divine (the last come from the Holy Spirit). The virtues resulting from action are the outcome of a will for good, the natural come from a man's constitution, and the Divine—from grace.

89 Just as the virtues are born in the soul, so are the passions. But the first are born in the soul in accordance with its nature, and the latter contrary to its nature. The starting point in the birth of good or evil in the soul is the inclination of its desire:

whatever the desire is inclined towards, that the soul takes for its stimulus, and acts.

90. The Scriptures call virtues virgins (Song of Songs i. 3) owing to their marriage with the soul, through which they are regarded as one in body and spirit. The face of the virgins is the symbol of love, and the testimony of the purity and saintliness of those holy virgins is their garments and adornments.

91. There are eight ruling passions; three principal: gluttony, cupidity and vanity, and five subordinate to them: lust, anger, melancholy, laziness and pride. In the same way among the virtues opposed to these there are three principal ones: self-mastery, non-acquisitiveness and humility, and five others, derived from them: purity, meekness, joy, courage and self-belittlement—and then the whole series of virtues. To study and know the power, action and quality of each virtue and each passion is not given to every-one who desires it, but only to him who has experienced every-thing in practice and has received from the Holy Spirit the gift of discernment and discrimination between them.

92. Virtues either act or are practised. They act in us coming at their own chosen time, whenever they will, as much as they will and how they will. But we practise them according to our will, moral disposition and habit. In themselves they have their own independent essence, and we approach them only approxi-mately by morally conforming to them. Very few can absorb the spiritual in its essence before they have the unchanging taste of it, which is to come. Most of us possess only certain similitudes of virtues, instead of their real essence.

93. That man ministers the Gospels who, having participated in them himself, can also actively pass on to others the light of Christ. Like some Divine seed he sows the word on the fields of his listeners' souls, according to the indications of the Apostle: 'Let your speech be always with grace, seasoned with salt' of Divine benefaction (Col. iv. 6); 'that it may minister grace unto the hearers' with faith (Eph. iv. 29). In another place the Apostle, calling the teachers, tillers, and the pupils, the field they till, clearly describes the former as the labourers and sowers of the Word of God, and the latter as the fertile soil of virtues, bearing rich fruits.

94. The oral word, spoken for the instruction of others, differs according to the different ways in which it is gathered. For one word comes from teaching, another from reading, yet another from practice, and another from grace. But just as water, essentially the same everywhere, changes and acquires a peculiar quality according to the composition of the soil under it, so that it tastes either bitter, or sweet, or salt, or acid; so a word differently spoken is different according to the level of each speaker and therefore produces a different effect and its usefulness is not always the same.

95. Speech is given to all sentient beings for use and, just as the value derived from different kinds of food varies, so does the profit of speech to the soul and the satisfaction derived therefrom. The word of teaching acts like a teacher who moulds the disposition of the soul; the word derived from reading is like 'still waters' which feed it; the word which comes from practice is like 'green pastures', rendering it more fertile; the word of grace is like a 'cup' which 'runneth over' (Ps. xxiii. 2, 5) quenching its thirst and making it glad; and the unspeakable joy of grace is like 'oil to make his face to shine' (Ps. civ. 15) which gladdens the heart and fills it with light.

96. In truth, not only does the soul contain this in itself as very life, but when it hears such teaching from others it straightway feels it, so long as both are guided by love and faith—when one listens with faith and the other teaches with love, speaking of virtues without arrogance or vanity. Then the soul accepts the word of teaching as a teacher; the word of reading as a nourisher; the word derived from practice (the most inner word) as the loveliest bridal adornment; the illumining word of the Spirit as the word of the bridegroom, joining her with himself and rendering her glad. Every word, proceeding from God's lips, is either a word from the mouth of the saints made active by the Spirit, or the most delectable inspiration from the Spirit which not all, but only a few, are given to enjoy. For, although all intelligent beings enjoy words, there are very few in this world who rejoice in the words of the Spirit. The greater part know only by memory the various forms of spiritual words; they can only participate in them in this way, since they cannot as yet directly apprehend the

Word of God, that true bread of the world to come. For there this bread alone is offered in abundance to those who are worthy of every kind of enjoyment, for it is never consumed, used up nor stolen.

97. If a man has no spiritual sensibility, his senses cannot savour the sweetness of Divine things. For, just as a man whose senses are dulled cannot perceive sensory things, does not see, does not hear, does not smell, being quite feeble or rather half-dead, so a man, who through passions has deadened the natural powers of his soul, renders them insensible to the action of, and communion with, the mysteries of the Spirit. For he who is spiritually blind, deaf and insensible is dead in spirit, since Christ does not dwell in him and he himself does not act and move in Christ.

98. Equally with the powers of the soul, the senses have a similar, if not the same, action, especially when they are healthy. Then the senses see sensory things clearly, while the powers of the soul discern mental things, especially when they are free from the onslaughts of Satan, who wages war against mental and spiritual law. But when they are joined into one by the Spirit, and have but one outlook, then they know directly and essentially what is Divine and what is human, clearly discerning their nature and their meaning, and see, as clearly as is possible, the one cause of all—the Trinity.

99. He who practises hesychasm must first of all possess the following five virtues, as a foundation upon which to build his actions: silence, abstinence, watchfulness, humility and patience. There are three practices pleasing to God: psalmody,[20] prayer and reading—and work with the hands for those weak in body. The virtues enumerated not only embrace all the others but enter as component parts into one another. From early morning, freeing oneself from everything, it is necessary to keep remembrance of God, by prayer and silence of the heart, and for the first hour to

[20] The meaning of the word 'psalmody' is explained by Bishop Ignatiy Brianchaninov as follows: 'By the word "psalmody" . . . should be understood a very slow, long-drawn intoning of psalms and other prayers. . . . It was done from memory. The monks of those times had to learn the psalms by heart.' (Writings. Vol. II. 'On prayer with voice and lips'.) (Translators' note.)

pray patiently; for the second hour to read; for the third hour to psalmodise; for the fourth—to pray; for the fifth—to read; for the sixth—to psalmodise; for the seventh—to pray; for the eighth—to read; for the ninth—to psalmodise; for the tenth—to eat; for the eleventh—to rest, if need be; for the twelfth—to recite the vespers. Thus spending the day in a goodly manner, man pleases God.

100. Like a bee, one should extract from each of the virtues what is most profitable. Thus, taking a little from all of them, one builds up a great store of the practice of virtues, to form that honey of wisdom which makes the heart glad.

101. Now hear, if you will, how it is best to spend the night. Night vigil can be of three kinds; for beginners, for those who are already on the path and for the perfect. The first is as follows: sleep half the night and stay awake the other half, either from evening till midnight or from midnight till morning. The second kind is to be awake for one or two hours in the evening, then to sleep for about four hours and to get up for matins; to psalmodise and pray for about six hours till morning; then to psalmodise for the first hour, and then to sit practising silence as described above—after which, either to follow the order of definite practices given for every hour, or to keep ceaseless prayer without interruption. The third kind consists of standing all night and keeping vigil.

102. Now let us speak about food. A litra (about a pound) of bread is sufficient for everyone practising silence; for drink—two cups of undiluted wine and three cups of water; as to other victuals, one should eat not as much as lustful nature craves, but use what the Lord provides sparingly. The best and shortest guiding rule for those who wish to live as they should is to keep to the three all-embracing practices of virtue: fasting, watchfulness and prayer, which give the necessary stability to all virtues.

103. The first requirements of silence are to have faith and patience, and, with one's whole heart, strength and power—to love and to hope. Even if through lack of zeal, or for some other reason, a believer fails to attain here what he seeks, on leaving this world it is impossible that he should not receive confirma-

tion of the fruits of faith and struggle, and should not gain liberation through Jesus Christ, Who is the salvation and redemption of our souls, the incarnate God—the Word. But an unbeliever, on leaving this world, will be eternally damned. Indeed he is damned already, as the Lord says (Mark xvi. 16). For he who is a slave of lusts, and seeks honour among men, instead of from God, is not one who is faithful (John v. 44). Though by his words he may appear to be faithful, he merely deceives himself without realising it. For he will have to hear: 'As you did not receive Me in your heart but did cast Me out behind your back, so shall I cast you out.' But he who is faithful should be filled with hope, and believe in God's truth as testified by all the Scriptures, confessing his weakness, in order to avoid a worse damnation, from which there is no pardon.

104. Nothing is better for rendering the heart penitent and the soul humble than wise solitude and complete silence. Nothing has a greater power of disturbing the state of silence, and of depriving it of God's help, than the following principal passions: presumptuousness, gluttony, talkativeness and vain cares, arrogance and the mistress of all passions—self-regard. Whoever readily permits himself to acquire the habit of these passions will become, in the course of time, more and more shrouded in darkness, until finally he is completely deadened. If, however, he comes to himself and begins to practise the necessary observances with faith and zeal, he will once more obtain what he seeks, especially if he seeks it with humility. But if, through negligence, even one of the passions mentioned begins to rule in him, then the whole host of evils, with pernicious unbelief at its head, attacks and overpowers him and completely devastates his soul. The soul is then filled with diabolical confusion and turmoil and becomes another Babel, so that 'the last state of that man is worse than the first' (Matt. xii. 45). Then the man turns into a violent enemy and defamer of those who practise silence, always sharpening his tongue against them, like a razor or a double-edged sword.

105. The waters of passions, having troubled and muddied the sea of silence, flood the soul, and can be crossed only in the light and empty boat of complete self-mastery and unpossessiveness. For intemperance and attachment to things cause torrents of passions

to flood the soil of the heart and deposit there all the mud and filth of thoughts, thus confusing the mind, darkening the heart and weighing down the body. In the heart and the soul they produce negligence, darkness and death and deprive them of the feeling and disposition natural to them.

106. Nothing renders the soul even of zealous strugglers weaker, more negligent and senseless than self-love, that nourisher of passions. Teaching men to prefer bodily ease to labours for the sake of virtue, and to esteem it provident good sense not to burden oneself with work voluntarily, self-love is wont to deprive the soul of willingness and zeal in its progress on the path of silence, by urging it to undertake only the lightest and easiest work in keeping commandments, and thus produces in it a strong and overpowering laziness for action.

107. For those who have become lazy in fulfilling the commandments and desire to banish murky obscurity, there is no better or more efficient physic than complete obedience in everything, with faith and without argument. Such obedience is the medicine compounded of virtues, giving life to those who drink it, and the knife which, with one cut, cleans festering wounds. A man who, in faith and simplicity, has chosen to wield this knife, at once cuts off all passions, more completely than anyone, and not only enters into silence but, through obedience, fully masters it, having found Christ and become His imitator and His slave (as he is also called).

108. Without the practice of constant weeping, it is impossible to bear the boiling cauldron of silence. He who weeps and thinks of the horrors which both precede and follow death, before they actually come to pass, cannot help but have patience and humility—the two foundation stones of silence. Without them a man who has entered the path of silence will always have conceit and negligence as his companions; and these will more than ever multiply the captivities and wanderings of thought, resulting in weakness. From this follows the daughter of negligence—intemperance, which renders our body listless and weak and the mind darkened and hard. Then Jesus is hidden from the crowd of thoughts and dreams which throng the market place of the mind.

109. It is not the fate of everyone to taste pangs of conscience either here or in the future, but only of those who sin against faith and love. Grasping the unsheathed sword of fervour and denunciation, conscience pitilessly tortures the guilty. He who resists sin and the flesh is comforted thereby; but he who submits to them is persecuted and tormented until he repents. If he does not repent, the torment passes with him into the other life and will there last for ever.

110. Of all passions two are especially cruel and grievous: lust and despondency, that is, laziness, when they take possession of the soul and weaken it. The two are closely connected and blended together; this is why it is so difficult to struggle with them and overcome them; a complete victory over them is even impossible for us. The first flourishes in the desiring power of the soul but embraces both parts of our composite nature—soul and body—spreading its voluptuousness through all our members. The second, gripping the mind—our ruler—spreads like ivy over the whole soul and body and makes our whole being lazy and enfeebled, as though stricken with paralysis. Although lust and despondency cannot be finally conquered before acquiring the blessed passionlessness, they can nevertheless be driven away when the soul, through prayer, receives force from the Holy Spirit, which gives it comfort, strength and profound peace, and gladdens it with respite from their tyranny in the heart. That passion (of lust) is the origin, the mistress and the queen of all voluptuousness; this most voluptuous voluptuousness of all, and its companion laziness, bring in the tristate of pharaoh, and are an unconquerable chariot. Wretched as we are, all other passions afflict us through these.

111. The beginning of mental prayer is the purifying action or the power of the Holy Spirit, together with the mysterious officiating of the mind, just as the beginning of silence is withdrawal from all things or freedom from all cares; the middle stage is the illuminating power (of the Spirit) and contemplation, and the end—ecstasy or the soaring of the mind towards God.

112. Before attaining the future delights beyond the mind— the Sanctuary of the spirit is the mysterious mental performing of mind on the altar of the soul, both officiating and partaking of the

Lamb, in betrothal with God. To eat of the Lamb on the mental altar of the soul means not only to know It, or to partake of It, but in the future to be like as the Lamb, fashioned in Its own image. Here we have only the words, but there we hope to receive the very substance of the mysteries.

113. For beginners prayer is like a joyous flame bursting out of the heart; and for the perfect it is like a sweet-scented light acting within it. Or again, prayer is the Gospel of the Apostles, an action of faith, or rather it is direct faith, it is the foundation of hope, love brought to life, angel-like movement, power of the bodiless spirits, their work and their joy, the Gospel of God, informing of the heart, hope of salvation, sign of purification, symbol of sanctity, knowledge of God, manifesting of baptism, or purification in the bath of eternal life, betrothal with the Holy Spirit, the rejoicing of Jesus, gladness of the soul, mercy of God, sign of reconciliation, the seal of Christ, a ray of the mental sun, the dawn of hearts, the affirmation of Christianity, token of reconciliation with God, grace of God, wisdom of God, or rather the beginning of self-wisdom, a manifestation of God, the doing of monks, the way of life of the silent, the cause of silence, the sign of angelic life. But why say so much? Prayer is God, making active all in all, for single is the action of the Father, the Son and the Holy Spirit, all-doing through Jesus Christ.

114. If Moses had not received from God the rod of power, he would not have become god to pharaoh and would not have punished both him and Egypt. In the same way the mind, if it does not wield in its hand the power of prayer, will be unable to conquer sin and the powers of the enemy.

115. Those who say or do something without humility are like a man who builds a house in winter or without cement. It is given to very few minds to acquire humility and to know it through experience. Those who speak of it in words are like people measuring a bottomless pit. We others, who are blind and guess but little the meaning of this great light, say: true humility does not say humble words, nor does it assume humble looks, it does not force one either to think humbly of oneself, or to abuse oneself in self-belittlement. Although all such things are the beginning, the manifestations and the various aspects of humility,

humility itself is grace, given from above. There are two kinds of humility, as the holy fathers teach: to deem oneself the lowest of all beings and to ascribe to God all one's good actions. The first is the beginning, the second the end. Those who seek humility are advised to keep in their minds the following three thoughts: that they are the most sinful of all men, that they are the most despicable of all creatures since their state is an unnatural one, and that they are more damned than the demons, since they are slaves of demons. He who seeks humility should reason thus: are there in the world sinners whose sins are equal to mine, let alone exceeding mine? No, my soul, you and I are worse than all men, we are dust and ashes under their feet.—How can I help considering myself the most despicable of all creatures, when they behave according to the order of their nature whereas I, owing to my innumerable sins, have sunk below my nature? Truly animals and beasts are purer than I, sinner that I am, for I am the lowest of all, since I have brought myself down into hell and am lying there even before death.—Who does not know or feel that a sinner is worse even than the demons, since he is their subject and their slave, even here sharing their prison in the outer darkness? A man possessed by demons is truly worse than the demons. Therefore with them I inherit the abyss, cursed as I am. You who dwell in the abyss of hell even before death, how dare you delude yourself and call yourself righteous when through evil deeds you have made of yourself a despicable sinner and a demon? Woe to your delusion and your error, you offspring of the devil, you unclean dog, condemned for this to fire and darkness!

116. Wisdom moved by the Spirit is, according to theologians, the power of mental, pure, angelic prayer; a sign of this is that during prayer the mind is free from forms, with no image either of itself or of anything else appearing even for an instant, since it is drawn away from the senses by the light acting within. For then the mind is removed from everything material and is like light, being ineffably merged with God into one spirit.

117. There are seven different actions and dispositions leading and guiding towards this God-given humility, which are born of one another and enter one another as components. These are: silence, humble thoughts about oneself, humble speech, humble

apparel, self-belittlement, contrition and considering oneself last in everything. Silence accompanied by reason gives birth to humble thoughts about oneself. Humble thoughts about oneself give birth to three kinds of humility: humble speech, wearing poor and humble clothes and self-belittlement. These three give birth to contrition, which comes from temptations attacking one by God's leave, and is called being taught by Providence and humbled by demons. Contrition soon constrains the soul to feel that it is the lowest of the low and that all others are above it. These two lead to the perfect and God-granted humility which is called the force and perfection of all virtues. It is this humility which ascribes good deeds to God. Thus, the first practice leading to humility is silence of the lips from which come humble thoughts about oneself. And this leads to three kinds of humility. These three give birth to one—contrition; and contrition gives birth to the seventh kind of humility—considering oneself to be lowest of all, which is called providential humility. Providential humility brings God-granted, perfect, unassumed, true humility. The former of these (the providential) comes thus: when a man, left to himself, becomes overpowered and enslaved by every passion and every thought, then, becoming a prey to the hostile spirit and finding no help either in works, or in God, or in anything whatever, and ready to fall into despair, he is humbled in everything, is filled with contrition and regards himself as the lowest and last of all, a slave of all, worse even than the demons themselves, since he is subject to their tyranny and constantly vanquished by them. This is providential humility which leads God to grant the second, higher humility, which is a Divine force, all-doing and all-creating. Through this force a man sees himself as an organ of Divine powers and by its action performs inscrutable works of God.

118. It is impossible in our generation to achieve essential spiritual contemplation of the light, to acquire a mind free from wanderings or dreams, the true action of prayer, surging continuously like a fountain from the depths of the heart, the resurrection and ascension of the soul on high, Divine awe, complete ecstasy in spirit, and an angelic rousing of the soul moved by God, since, through many temptations, we are governed nowadays by

the tyranny of passions. Our mind is wont to dream of all these things prematurely, for this is an easy occupation; but because of such dreams it often loses even the little good order given it by God. Therefore it is wrong to seek prematurely, with much speculation, that which comes in its own time and, thereby rejecting what is in hand, to dream of something else. It is natural for the mind to build easy fantasies and imaginings about the aforesaid achievements before it has attained them. Therefore a man is in considerable danger of losing what he has and, by falling into prelest, of being deprived of good sense, thus becoming a dreamer instead of a hesychast.

119. Grace is not merely faith, but also active prayer. For the latter shows in practice true faith, made living by Jesus, for it comes from the Spirit through love. And so faith is dead and lifeless in a man who does not see it active in himself. More than that —a man has no right to be called faithful, if his faith is a bare word and if he has not in him a faith made active by love or the Spirit. Thus faith must be made evident by progress in works, or it must act in the light and shine in works, as the divine Apostle says: 'Shew me thy faith without thy works, and I will shew thee my faith by my works' (James ii. 18), thus showing that the faith of grace is made evident by works performed in accordance with the commandments, just as the commandments are fulfilled in deed and are made bright through the faith which is in grace. Faith is the root of the commandments, or rather the spring, whose water feeds their growth. It has two aspects: profession and grace, remaining at the same time essentially one and indivisible.

120. The large and the small (the long and the short) ladders of monkhood alike have five rungs, leading to perfection. The first is renunciation (of the world), the second—submission (entering a monastery with a vow to keep monastic statutes), the third—obedience (submission in deed, in living), the fourth—humility, the fifth—love, which is God. Renunciation of hell raises him who is prone and frees the captive from matter. Submission gains Christ and serves Him, according to His word: 'If any man serve Me, let him follow Me; and where I am there shall also My servant be' (John xii. 26). And where is Christ? In heaven, sitting

on the right hand of the Father. And where the Master is, there should also the servant be. Let this be remembered by him who places his foot on the first rung to ascend the ladder. Obedience, practised entirely in accordance with the commandments, builds a ladder out of the various virtues and disposes them in the soul as rungs of ascent. The lofty power of humility receives the obedient one from this ladder, takes him on high to heaven and hands him to the queen of virtues, love, and leading him up to Christ, presents him. Thus the obedient one ascends unhindered to heaven by the short ladder.

121. There is no shorter ascent to the royal and Divine mansions by means of the short ladder of virtues than through subduing the five passions hostile to obedience, namely: disobedience, argumentativeness, self-gratification, self-justification and pernicious high opinion of oneself. These are the limbs and organs of the recalcitrant demon who devours false monks and casts them down into the abyss of the serpent. Disobedience is the mouth of hell; argumentativeness is its tongue, whetted like a sword; self-gratification is its sharp teeth; self-justification its throat; high opinion of oneself, which casts one into hell, is the belching of its all-devouring belly. But he who, through obedience, conquers the first, by one stroke cuts off all the rest and with one stride reaches heaven. Such is the truly ineffable and inconceivable miracle performed for us by our merciful Lord, Who gave us the possibility of straightway reaching heaven by means of a single virtue or rather of a single commandment, just as through a single transgression we have descended and are descending into hell.

122. The second, the new man, is and is called a new world, according to the divine Apostle who said: 'Therefore if any man be in Christ, he is a new creature' (2 Cor. v. 17). Moreover, since the Apostle says: 'We wrestle not against flesh and blood, but against principalities, against powers, against the rulers of the darkness of this world, against spiritual wickedness in high places' (Eph. vi. 16) so, in accordance with this, we must suppose that those who secretly wrestle with us abide in another great world which, in its nature, is akin to the natural powers of our soul. For the three princes of evil, in their fight with spiritual

strugglers, attack the three powers of our soul, and if a man has
failed in something or does not strive at something, they overcome him in this very thing. Thus, the dragon—the prince of the
abyss—rises in arms against those who keep attention on their
heart, as one whose 'strength is in his loins, and his force is in the
navel of his belly' (Job xl. 16). He sends the lust-loving giant of
forgetfulness against them with his clouds of fiery arrows, stirs up
lust in them like some turbulent sea, makes it foam and burn in
them and causes their confusion by flooding them with torrents of
insatiable passions. The prince of this world, who is in charge of
warfare against the excitable part, attacks those who follow the
path of active virtue. Using the giant of laziness, he encompasses
them with all kinds of witchery of the passions and wrestles with
those who always put up a courageous resistance. Thus he either
vanquishes or is himself vanquished and so he gains them either
crowns or shame before the faces of the angels. The prince of
high places attacks those who exercise themselves in mental contemplation, by offering them fantasies; for, in company with the
spiritual wickedness in high places, his task is to affect the thinking and speaking part. Using the giant of ignorance, he brings confusion into the thought striving to rise on high, darkens and
frightens it, introducing into it vague fantastic images of spirits
and their metamorphoses and producing phantoms of lightning
and thunder, tempests and earthquakes. Thus each of the three
princes, impinging upon the corresponding powers of the soul,
wages war against it, conducting his attacks against the particular
part allotted to him.

123. At one time they too were minds; but having fallen
away from immateriality and refinement, each one of them
acquired a certain material coarseness, gaining flesh according to
the level and nature of the deeds whose practice qualified him.
For since, just like man, they have lost the delights of angels (the
angelic taste or the angelic heaven of delight) and have been
deprived of Divine bliss, so too, like ourselves, they began to
find pleasures on earth, when they became material and acquired
the habit of material passions. Nor should we wonder at this,
since our own soul, created wise and thoughtful in the image of
God, having refused to know God, has become bestial, senseless

and almost insane through delighting in material things. For habit is wont to alter nature and change its action in accordance with the direction of the will.

124. The rising of passions and warfare of the flesh against the soul can be of five kinds in us. At times the flesh misuses what it has, at other times it seeks to do what is unnatural as if it were natural; sometimes it forms a close friendship with the demons who arm it against the soul; sometimes it happens that the soul acts lawlessly of itself, when pervaded by some passion; and, finally, the demons may sometimes be allowed to wage war against us to make us more humble, if they have not succeeded in tempting us by any of these means.

125. All people and things cause this warfare in us for three chief reasons; namely, through habit, through misuse of natural things and, by God's leave, through the envy and onslaught of the demons. The arising and lusting of the flesh against the soul, and of the soul against the flesh, is the same in habit and action as the arising of passions of the flesh against the soul and the valiant struggle of the soul against the flesh. And our foe himself, being shameless, at times daringly attacks us, without cause or warning. So, my friend, do not let the blood-lusting leech suck the blood from your arteries, for it is insatiable; nor let the serpent and the dragon have their fill of the flesh; and you will easily subdue the arrogance of the lion and the serpent. So sigh, until you are delivered from the valley and endowed with higher life and become transformed in the likeness of the image of Jesus Christ, your Creator.

126. Indeed, those who are nothing but flesh and are addicted to self-love always serve sensuality and vanity; envy too is rooted in them. Consumed by malice and saddened by the success of their neighbour, they calumniate good as bad, as a creation of prelest; they do not accept it as coming from the Spirit, or simply do not believe in it. Neither can such men know and understand God in their blindness and lack of faith. So, there, they will justly hear: 'I know you not' (Matt. xxv. 12).

127. A true lover of wisdom is he who, through natural[21] things, has learnt to know their Creator, and from the Creator has

[21] See Note 16 to paragraph 22 above. (Translators' note.)

understood natural things and things Divine; and such as knows not from teaching only but from experience. Or: a perfect lover of wisdom is he who has perfected himself in the moral, natural and Divine love of wisdom, or rather in love of God.

128. Those who write and speak without the Spirit, and wish to instruct the Church, are natural, 'having not the Spirit' (Jude 19). They come under the curse, which says: 'Woe unto them that are wise in their own eyes, and prudent in their own sight' (Is. v. 21). For they speak from themselves, instead of from 'the Spirit of their Father which speaketh in them' (Matt. x. 20), as the Lord has defined. Those who speak from their own thoughts, before having acquired purity, are seduced by the spirit of self-esteem. Of these the proverb says: 'Seest thou a man wise in his own conceit? there is more hope of a fool than of him' (Prov. xxvi. 12). And again wisdom teaches us: 'Be not wise in your own conceits' (Rom. xii. 16). And the divine Apostle, filled with the Spirit, himself testifies, saying: 'Not that we are sufficient of ourselves to think any thing as of ourselves; but our sufficiency is of God' (2 Cor. iii. 5) and 'We speak before God in Christ' (2 Cor. xii. 19). The words of such men neither delight nor instruct, for they come not from the living spring of the Spirit but from their own heart which is like some slimy mire, harbouring the leeches, snakes and toads of lusts, conceit and intemperance, and the water of their knowledge is evil-smelling, muddy and tepid, revolting to those who drink it and producing giddiness, disgust and vomiting.

129. The divine Apostle says: 'Now ye are the body of Christ, and members in particular' (1 Cor. xii. 27) and again: 'There is one body, and one Spirit' (Eph. iv. 4). Just as the body without spirit is dead and senseless, so a man, who is deadened by passions through neglect of commandments, remains inactive after baptism, since he is not enlightened by the Holy Spirit and by the grace of Christ. For, although he possesses the Spirit through faith and regeneration, the Spirit remains inactive in him and does not move since his soul is deadened. Though we have a single soul, while our body has many members, our soul holds them all; but animates and moves only those which are capable of receiving life. Those that have withered to death and immobility

through some accidental disease, though they may be held by the soul, are lifeless and without sensation. It is the same with the Spirit of Christ: it abides wholly in all the members of Christ's body, and moves and gives life to those who can take part in life. But those also whose weakness prevents them, it still mercifully keeps as its own. Thus each believer, though sharing through faith in spiritual sonship, may remain passive and unenlightened through lack of faith and zeal, deprived of the light and life of Jesus. So, although every believer, as a member of Christ, possesses the Spirit of Christ in him, he may remain passive and unmoving, as one incapable of sharing in grace.

130. We affirm that there are eight main objects of contemplation: the first is God, invisible and formless, uncreated and without beginning, the cause of all that exists, one transubstantial Deity in three Persons; the second is the hierarchy and order of immaterial powers; the third—the composition of visible things; the fourth—dispensation[22] through the advent of the Word; the fifth—general resurrection; the sixth—the terrible second coming of Christ; the seventh—eternal torment; the eighth—the kingdom of heaven. The first four are passed and accomplished; the latter four are yet to come and still unmanifest, but are clearly contemplated and recognised by those who have attained to complete purity of mind through grace. Let him who approaches this without the light of grace know that he only builds fantasies, and does not contemplate; since, ensnared by the spirit of dreams and fantasies, he is but a dreamer.

131. It is imperative to say as much as possible about prelest, since for many it is difficult to recognise and almost incomprehensible owing to the multitude and variety of its snares and pitfalls. It is said that prelest appears or rather comes upon us in two forms—in the form of fantasies and in the form of outer influences, although its sole cause and origin is always pride. The first is the

---

[22] Домостроительство. The original Greek word is οἰκονομία. The literal meaning includes both the construction of a house and the proper setting up and running of a household. The word 'economy' is widely used in theological works, but its popular modern use fails to convey the idea of Divine bounty and provision for the ordering of every detail of the processes of the created Universe. The word 'dispensation' has therefore been used, though not wholly satisfactory. (Translators' note.)

origin of the second, and the second is sometimes the origin of yet a third—frenzy. The origin of the illusory contemplation of fantasies is opinion (pretending to know all), which produces a false representation of the Deity in one fantastic form or another; this is followed by prelest, leading one into error through dreams and engendering blasphemy, which further plants fears in the soul both in sleeping and waking. For puffing oneself up is followed by prelest (from fantasies), after prelest comes blasphemy, after blasphemy fear, after fear trembling, and after trembling frenzy (being out of one's mind). Such is the first form of prelest, that which comes from fantasies. The second kind of prelest, in the form of outer influences, is as follows: it has its origin in lust born of natural desire. This lust gives birth to irrepressibility of unspeakable impurities. Firing all one's being and darkening the mind by identification with imagined idols, its burning intoxication drives the mind to frenzy and madness. In this state the seduced man takes it on himself to prophesy, gives false prognostications, asserts that he sees certain saints and repeats words supposedly said to him, for, intoxicated by the frenzy of passion, his nature is changed and he appears like one possessed. Laymen, misled by the spirit of prelest, call such men 'psycharii'; they are to be found sitting by the shrines of saints, and are supposed to be inspired, influenced and tortured by them, and announce revelations received from them. But such men should simply be called possessed, seduced and fallen into error, rather than prophets of the present and the future. The demon of obscenity, having confused their mind with the fire of lust, drives them insane, presenting to them dream images of certain saints, making them hear their words and see their faces. But it happens also that the demons themselves appear and trouble them with fears. Subjecting them to the yoke of Belial, the demons drive them like faithful slaves to act sinfully, against their will, meaning later to lead them to hell.

132. It should be known that the onset of prelest has three main causes: pride, the envy of demons and permission for punishment. Of these, the cause of pride is vain heedlessness (or vanity); of envy—desire of success; of permission for punishment—sinful life. Prelest coming from envy and proud conceit is

quickly cured, especially if one humbles oneself. But the prelest due to punishment—deliverance to Satan through sin—God often permits, by forsaking a man, to last until death. It happens sometimes that even the innocent are delivered to the torment of demons for the sake of their salvation. It should be known that the spirit of proud conceit himself at times prophesies in those who do not keep careful attention on the heart.

133. All devout kings and priests are truly anointed in the new grace, just as those of old were anointed symbolically. For they were symbols of our truth, not in part, but wholly presaging us all. The meaning of it is that he who is anointed, being pure and free from passions, is wholly consecrated to God, now and for ever.

134. He whose 'mouth shall speak of wisdom; and the meditation of' whose 'heart shall be of understanding' (Ps. xlix. 3) is the man who, from the natural works of God, will show clearly the Word, the hypostatical wisdom of God and Father.

135. Prelest is to-day's great enemy of truth, leading men to perdition; through prelest the darkness of ignorance, alienating men from God, has established its rule in the souls of the heedless. Three passions are its main offspring: unbelief, wickedness and laziness, which engender and support one another. Unbelief is the teacher of wickedness, and wickedness is the companion of laziness which leads to total sloth. Or conversely, laziness gives birth to wickedness, as the Lord said: 'Thou wicked and slothful servant' (Matt. xxv. 26), and wickedness is the mother of unbelief, for every wicked man is unfaithful, and the unfaithful has no fear of God. Absence of the fear of God gives birth to laziness—the mother of negligence, which makes men neglect every good and commit every bad deed.

136. True knowledge of God and a right understanding of things constitute the perfect, orthodox, dogmatic teaching. Therefore we must glorify God thus: Glory be to Thee, Christ our God, glory to Thee Who has deigned to become man for our sake; Thou transubstantial God, great is the mystery of Thy dispensation. Our Saviour, glory be to Thee!

137. According to Maximus the Great, there are three different purposes for which gifted men write without fault or constraint:

the first, as memoranda for themselves; the second, for the benefit of others; the third, for obedience. With this last purpose many writings have been composed for those who humbly seek the word of truth. But he who writes to please men, for fame or for display, loses his reward and will receive no profit from this either here or in the life to come; more, he will be condemned as a sycophant and a wicked poacher of the Word of God.

# ST. GREGORY OF SINAI
## Instructions to Hesychasts

1. *How to sit in the cell*

Sitting in your cell, remain patiently in prayer, according to the precept of the Apostle Paul (Rom. xii. 12; Col. iv. 2). Collect your mind into your heart and send out thence your mental cry to our Lord Jesus, calling for His help and saying: 'Lord Jesus Christ, have mercy upon me.' Do not give in to faint-heartedness and laziness, but labour in your heart and drive your body, seeking the Lord in your heart. Compel yourself by every means to do this work, for 'The kingdom of heaven suffereth violence, and the violent take it by force'[23] (Matt. xi. 12), as the Lord said showing that this attainment demands severe labour and spiritual struggle.

2. *How to say the prayer*

Some of the fathers taught that the prayer should be said in full: 'Lord, Jesus Christ, Son of God, have mercy upon me.' Others advised saying half, thus: 'Jesus, Son of God, have mercy upon me', or 'Lord Jesus Christ, have mercy upon me', or to alternate, sometimes saying it in full and sometimes in a shorter form. Yet it is not advisable to pander to laziness by changing the words of the prayer too often, but to persist a certain time as a test of patience. Again, some teach the saying of the prayer with the lips, others with and in the mind. In my opinion both are advisable. For at times the mind, left to itself, becomes wearied and too exhausted to say the prayer mentally; at other times the lips get tired of this work. Therefore both methods of prayer should be used—with the lips and with the mind. But one should

[23] A literal translation of the Slavonic version would be: 'The kingdom of heaven is taken by forcing oneself, and is ravished by those who make effort.' (Translators' note.)

appeal to the Lord quietly and without agitation, so that the voice does not disturb the attention of the mind and does not thus break off the prayer, until the mind is accustomed to this doing and, receiving force from the Spirit, firmly prays within on its own. Then there will be no need to say the prayer with the lips; indeed, it will be impossible, for he who reaches this stage is fully content with mental doing of the prayer and has no wish to leave it.

### 3. *How to hold the mind*

You should know that no one can hold the mind by himself, if it be not held by the Spirit. For it cannot be held, not because of its mobile nature but because, through neglect, it has acquired the habit of turning and wandering hither and thither. When through transgressing the commandments of Him who has re-generated us (in baptism) we became separated from God, we lost our union with Him and destroyed in our feeling a mental feeling of Him. A mind thus inclined and withdrawn from God is led captive everywhere. And there is no way of regaining its stability except by repenting to God and uniting with Him, by frequent and patient prayers, and by mentally confessing our sins to Him each day. God immediately forgives those who ask forgiveness in humility and contrition and who ceaselessly invoke His holy name. When through this working at prayer the action of the prayer becomes established in the heart, then prayer begins to keep the mind near by, fills it with joy and does not let it be made captive. However, wanderings of thoughts occur even after this, for thoughts submit fully only to those who are perfect in the Holy Spirit and who, through Jesus Christ, have attained a state free from wanderings.

### 4. *How to drive away thoughts*

No beginner can ever drive away a thought if God does not drive it away. Only the strong are capable of struggling with them and banishing them. But even they do not achieve this by themselves, but with God's help rise up to wrestle with them, armed with His weapons. So, when thoughts come, call to our Lord Jesus, often and patiently, and they will retreat; for they cannot bear the warmth of the heart produced by prayer, and flee as if scorched by fire. John of the Ladder tells us to flog our foes with the name of Jesus; for our God is fire, devouring evil. The Lord is quick to help, and will speedily revenge those who wholeheartedly call to Him day and night.—But he who does not possess the action of prayer can conquer thoughts in another manner, by imitating Moses. For if he rises up and lifts his eyes and hands to heaven (Exod. xvii. 11) God drives thoughts away. After this he should again sit down and patiently resume his prayer.—This method is for a man who has not yet attained the action of prayer. But even a man who already possesses the action of prayer, when bodily passions, such as laziness and lust, grievous and violent passions, stir in him, often gets up and raises his hands to seek help against them. Still, to avoid prelest he does not do this for long, but after a while sits down again, to prevent the enemy from seducing his mind by showing him some phantom. For only the pure and perfect can have a mind safe from harm, even though the mind be safe from downfall no matter where it is, whether high or low, in the heart or elsewhere.

## 5. How to psalmodise

Some say one should psalmodise often, others—not often, again others—not at all. But I advise you neither to psalmodise so frequently as to cause unrest, nor to leave it off altogether, lest you fall into weakness and negligence, but to follow the example of those who psalmodise infrequently. For, in the words of simple wisdom, moderation is best in all things. To psalmodise much is good for those who follow active life, since they are ignorant of mental occupations and lead a life of labour. But it is not good for those who practise silence, for whom it is more fitting to abide in God alone, praying in their heart and refraining from thought. For, according to John of the Ladder, silence means setting aside thoughts about things, whether of the senses or the mind. Moreover, if it uses up all its energy in too much psalmody, the mind will not have force enough steadily and patiently to remain in prayer. John of the Ladder further advises that at night it is better to give more time to prayer and less to psalmody.—So also must you do. When, sitting in your cell, you see that prayer is acting and does not cease its movement in your heart, never abandon it to get up for psalmody, until it leaves you of its own accord. For otherwise, leaving God within, you will address yourself to Him from without, thus passing from the higher to the lower. Moreover, in this way you will disturb the mind, and remove it from its peaceful calm. Silence, in accordance with its name, has in itself such actions as work in peace and quiet. For our God is peace, being above all speech and tumult.

In accordance with our mode of life, our psalmody too should be angelic and not carnal. Oral psalmody is a sign of the mental cry within and is given us lest we become lazy and coarse, to bring us to the state in which in truth we should be. Those who are ignorant of prayer (have not experienced its power and action) —this prayer which, according to St. John of the Ladder, is the source of virtues watering, like plants, the powers of our soul— such people should psalmodise much, psalmodise without measure, be always occupied with various works and never know rest from them, until, through much intensive laborious work, they enter into the state of contemplation, having acquired the action of mental prayer within them.—The work of silence is one thing and that of a cenobite another; but each, abiding in that to which he has been called, shall be saved. Therefore I hesitate to write to you, because of the weak ones, for I know that you move among them. He who works at the prayer from hearsay or reading and has no instructor, works in vain. According to the words of the fathers, he who has tasted grace must psalmodise sparingly, and must concentrate on the practice of prayer. However, if he is attacked by laziness, let him psalmodise or read the writings of the fathers. A ship has no need of oars when the wind swells the sails, for then the wind gives it sufficient power easily to navigate the salt sea of passions. But when the wind dies and the ship stops, it has to be set in motion by oars or by a tugboat.

As an argument against this, some people point to holy fathers who performed all-night watches, spending all their time in psalmody. Our reply to this is, that not all travelled by the same road, or followed the same rule to the end. Many passed from active life to contemplation and, having ended their works, kept

Sabbath according to spiritual law and rejoiced in God alone; and they were fed by the Divine sweetness of grace which would not allow them to psalmodise or think of anything else. They remained always in a state beyond mind, having attained the end of desires, even if only in part. Others kept to a life of action to the end and attained salvation, dying in the hope of receiving their reward in the future. Some have at death received a testimony of their salvation, or exuded a sweet aroma after death, in token thereof. These latter are those who have preserved the grace of baptism but who, owing to the captivity or ignorance of the mind, failed to taste while alive the palpable, though mysterious communion with that grace. Yet others successfully practise the one and the other, that is psalmody and prayer, and spend their life in this way, richly endowed with grace, which moves all things to activity and makes them overcome all obstacles. Others again, although they were simple people, kept silence to the end, and being one became one with the One God, finding contentment in the one prayer. To the perfect all is possible through Jesus Christ Who is their strength—to Whom be glory for ever and ever. Amen.

## 6. *How to partake of food*

What shall we say of the belly, the queen of passions? If you can slay it or half kill it, keep a tight hold. It has mastered me, beloved, and I serve it as a slave and a vassal. It is the colleague of the demons and the home of passions. Through it we fall, and through it we rise again, when it behaves itself. Through it we have lost the first Divine rank and the second. For after the old corruption we have been renewed in Christ; but now we have once more fallen away from God, through neglect of commandments (whose observance would preserve and restore grace to us); and without knowing it, we puff ourselves up, imagining that we are with God.

According to the fathers, physical nourishment may differ greatly: one man needs little, another much to sustain his natural strength, and each reaches satisfaction as regards food in accordance with his strength and habit. But the practiser of silence should always be starved, never allowing himself to eat his fill.

For when the stomach is heavy and, through this, the mind is clouded, a man cannot practise prayer with purity and firmness. Under the influence of the vapours produced by much food he becomes drowsy and longs to lie down and sleep—and this leads to innumerable dreams filling his mind in sleep.

Thus a man who strives after salvation and forces himself, for the sake of the Lord, to lead a life of silence, should be satisfied, in my opinion, with one litra (three-quarters of a pound) of bread; three or four cups of water or wine a day, and a little of any other victuals which may be to hand. He must not let himself eat to satiety; so that, through such wise use of food, that is through eating all kinds of food, on the one hand he may avoid boastfulness and on the other may not show disdain of God's creations, which are most excellent; and he thanks God for everything. Such is the reasoning of the wise! To those whose faith is weak, abstinence in food is most salutary and the Apostle orders such men to eat herbs (Rom. xiv. 2), for they do not believe that God will preserve them.

What shall I say to you? You have asked for a ruling, and a ruling is usually hard, especially for you in your old age. The young cannot always keep to a definite weight and measure, so how will you keep to it? You should be free in partaking of food. When you happen to be overcome, repent, blaming yourself—and make new efforts. And never cease behaving in this way, falling and rising again, and with this blaming yourself alone and no one else—and you will find peace, wisely attaining victory through downfalls. Yet do not exceed the limit which we have established above.—This you should do, for no other victuals strengthen the body as much as do bread and water. Therefore the Prophet, counting all the rest as nothing, merely said: Son of man! Thou shalt eat bread by weight and shalt drink water by measure (Ezek. iv. 9, etc.).

The partaking of food has three degrees: abstinence, adequacy and satiety. To abstain, means to remain a little hungry after eating; to eat adequately, means neither to be hungry, nor weighed down; to be satiated, means to be slightly weighed down. But eating beyond satiety is the door to belly-madness, through which lust comes in. But you, firm in this knowledge, choose what is best for you, according to your powers, without over-stepping the limits: for the perfect, according to the Apostle, ought 'both to be full and to be hungry . . . and do all things through Christ which strengtheneth' (Phil. iv. 12, 13).

## 7. Of prelest and other subjects

See, I want to impart to you true knowledge of prelest, so that you should guard against it, and not cause great harm to yourself and ruin your soul through ignorance. For human self-will is easily inclined to the enemies' side, especially in the case of the inexperienced, since these are more assiduously pursued by them. All around, near to beginners and the self-willed, the demons are wont to spread the nets of thoughts and pernicious fantasies and prepare moats for their downfall, since their city is still in the hands of the barbarians. It is not to be wondered at, if any one of them goes astray or loses his reason, or accepts or has accepted prelest, or sees something foreign to truth, or says something unseemly, through lack of experience and ignorance. Often a man, while discoursing about truth in his ignorance, says one thing instead of another, not knowing how to express the true state of affairs correctly, and by this unwise action horrifies his listeners and brings abuse and ridicule on the heads of hesychasts. There is nothing strange in the fact that beginners make mistakes even after much labour: this has happened to many who sought God, both now and in the past.

Remembrance of God or mental prayer is higher than all other works; as the love of God, it stands at the head of all virtues. But a man who is arrogant and shameless in his efforts to enter into God and worship Him with purity, and who attempts to acquire God in himself, is easily destroyed by the demons if this be allowed them. For, daringly and presumptuously seeking that which does not correspond to his state, he strives in his pride to attain it before its time. The merciful Lord, seeing how hasty we are as regards things which are above us, often prevents us from falling into temptation, in order that each of us, realising his arrogance, should by himself turn to right action before making himself an object of abuse and ridicule for the demons, and of lamentation for men. Especially is this so, if a man seeks this marvellous doing with patience and humility, with obedience and asking the guidance of the experienced, so as to avoid reaping tares instead of wheat, gall instead of sweetness, and finding ruin instead of salvation. For the strong and the perfect should always wrestle alone with the demons, ceaselessly wielding against them the sword of the Spirit, 'which is the word of God' (Eph. vi. 17). But the weak and the beginners use flight as their stronghold, with reverence and fear, refusing to join combat and not daring to be involved in it before their time—and in this way they escape death.

But you, if you are truly practising silence hoping to be with God, and you see something either sensory or spiritual, within or without, be it even the image of Christ or of an angel or some saint, or if an imaginary light pervades your mind, in no way accept it. The mind has in itself a natural power of dreaming and can easily build fantastic images of what it desires in those who do not apprehensively pay attention, and so cause themselves harm. Memories, too, of good and bad things will often suddenly imprint their images in the mind, and thus entice it to dreaming. Then the man to whom this happens becomes a dreamer instead of a hesychast. Therefore beware, and avoid being enticed into believing something, however good it may be, without questioning the experienced and making thorough investigation, and then you will suffer no harm. Always be displeased with such images and keep your mind colourless, formless and imageless. It has often happened that even things sent by God, as a test before victory, have turned into harm for many. Our Lord wishes to test our self-will, to see whither it inclines. But a man who has seen something, whether with mind or senses, even if this thing be from God, and who accepts it without questioning the experienced, easily falls or will fall into temptation, since he is quick to accept thoughts. Therefore a beginner should pay attention to the action of the heart, which is not led astray, and refuse to accept anything else until his passions are pacified. God is not angry with him who keeps careful attention on himself if, through fear of temptation, he refuses to accept what comes from Him, without questioning and due investigation. On the contrary, He praises his wisdom, although He has been wroth with some.

One should not, however, question everyone, but only him

who has been entrusted with the guidance of others, whose life shines, and who is himself 'poor, yet making many rich', according to the Gospels (2 Cor. vi. 10). Many inexperienced men have done harm to many unwise people, for which they will be judged after death. For not everyone has the right to guide others, but only those who have been endowed with Divine discernment, according to the Apostle (1 Cor. xii. 10), namely that discerning of spirits which separates good from evil by the sword of the word. Each man has his own reason and his natural discernment, either practical or scientific, but not all have discerning of spirits. Therefore the wise Sirach says: 'Be in peace with many: nevertheless have but one counsellor of a thousand' (Ecclus. vi. 6). It is hard to find a guide unerring either in deeds, words or understanding. That a man is unerring can be recognised if he has testimony from the Scriptures both for practice and for understanding, and is humbly wise in the realms of wisdom. For it is no small labour to know truth clearly and to keep clean from what is opposed to grace. For the devil is wont to present his prelest in the guise of truth, especially to beginners, transforming his deceit into something spiritual.

Therefore, a man striving to attain pure prayer in silence must proceed towards it with great trepidation, lamenting and begging the guidance of the experienced, constantly shedding tears for his sins, in sorrowful contrition and with a fearful apprehension of being cast into hell or of falling away from God and being separated from Him now or in time to come. For the devil, seeing a man leading a life of lamentation, hastens to him, fearing the advent of humility born of weeping. But if someone dreams of reaching on high with conceit, moved, not by true desire, but by the suggestion of Satan, the latter easily enslaves him in his nets. Therefore the safest armour is to remain in prayer and lamentation so as not to fall from the joy of prayer into self-conceit, but to keep oneself unharmed by choosing the joy of sorrow. For prayer free of prelest is warmth, when joined with prayer to Jesus, Who brings fire to the soil of our heart; this warmth scorches passions like tares, and brings joy and quiet to the heart, coming neither from the right nor the left, nor from above, but issuing forth in the heart itself like a spring of water from the life-giving Spirit. It is this prayer alone that you should wish to find and attain in the heart, keeping your mind free from dreams and stripped of all thoughts and reasonings. And be not afraid, for He Who said: 'Be of good cheer; it is I; be not afraid;' (Matt. xiv. 27) is Himself with us, He Whom we seek and Who always protects us. So in calling to God we must neither fear nor sigh.

If some people have gone astray through damage to their mind, you must know that they have incurred this through self-will and pride. For if a man seeks God with obedience, questioning and wise humility, he will always be protected from harm by the grace of Christ, Who desires all men to be saved. If temptation assails such a man, this occurs to test and crown him, and is accompanied by speedy help from God Who has allowed this, since His ways are inscrutable. For, as the fathers say, he who lives rightly and is faultless in his behaviour with all men, holding himself from sycophancy and presumption, will not be harmed, even if a whole army of demons put innumerable temptations in his way. But those who act with self-will and self-confidence are easily subject to harm. Therefore the practiser of silence should always keep to the royal road. For excess in anything is usually accompanied by conceit, which is followed by prelest.

In keeping silence, there are three virtues we should practise strictly and verify each hour whether we constantly abide in them, lest we be robbed by forgetfulness, and move outside them. They are: abstinence, not talking, and self-belittlement, i.e. humility. They support and protect one another; prayer is born of them and grows without ceasing.

The beginning of the action of grace in prayer manifests itself differently, for, according to the Apostle, the Spirit divides his gifts severally 'as he will' (1 Cor. xii. 11). To some there comes the spirit of fear, rending the mountains of passions and breaking in pieces the rocks—hardened hearts—such fear that the flesh seems to be pierced by nails and numbed as in death. Others quake, being filled with joy—what the fathers called the leaping of joy. In yet others, pre-eminently in those who have achieved success in prayer, God produces a subtle and serene glow of light when Christ comes to dwell in the heart (Eph. iii. 17) and to shine mysteriously in the spirit. Therefore God spoke to

Elijah on the mount of Horeb (1 Kings xix. 12) and said that the Lord is not in this or that—not in some individual actions of beginners—but in a subtle glow of light [24] which shows the perfection of prayer.

### 8. Question:

What is a man to do when the demon takes the form of an angel of light and tries to seduce him?

#### Answer:

In this case a man needs great power of discernment to discriminate rightly between good and evil. So in your heedlessness, do not be carried away too quickly by what you see, but be weighty (not easy to move) and, carefully testing everything, accept the good and reject the evil. Always you must test and examine, and only afterwards believe. Know that the actions of grace are manifest and the demon, in spite of his transformations, cannot produce them, namely, meekness, friendliness, humility, hatred of the world, cutting off passion and lust— which are the effects of grace. Works of the demons are: arrogance, conceit, intimidation and all evil. By such actions you will be able to discern whether the light shining in your heart is of God or of Satan. Lettuce looks like mustard, and vinegar in colour like wine; but when you taste them the palate discerns and defines the difference between each. In the same way the soul, if it has discernment, can discriminate by mental taste the gifts of the Holy Spirit from the fantasies and illusions of Satan.

## On Silence and Prayer

### 2.[25] How to practise prayer

In the morning force your mind to descend from the head to the heart and hold it there, calling ceaselessly in mind and soul:

[24] The English version of 1 Kings xix. 12 has 'still small voice'; the nearest English equivalent to the Slavonic version is 'subtle and serene wafting of wind'. Although this text is under reference, the literal translation of the passage which has been rendered as 'subtle glow of light' would be 'subtle and serene wafting of light'. (Translators' note.)

[25] The numbering of sections in 'Dobrotolubiye' is not consecutive at this point. (Translators' note.)

'Lord Jesus Christ, have mercy upon me!' until you are tired. When tired, transfer your mind to the second half, and say: 'Jesus, Son of God, have mercy upon me!' Having many times repeated this appeal, pass once more to the first half. But you should not alternate these appeals too often through laziness; for, just as plants do not take root if transplanted too frequently, neither do the movements of prayer in the heart if the words are changed frequently.

When you notice thoughts arising and accosting you, do not look at them, even if they are not bad; but keeping the mind firmly in the heart, call to Lord Jesus and you will soon sweep away the thoughts and drive out their instigators—the demons— invisibly scorching and flogging them with this Divine Name. Thus teaches John of the Ladder, saying: with the name of Jesus flog the foes, for there is no surer weapon against them, either on earth or in heaven.

### 3. The need for watching oneself and for remembering God

Isaiah the Hermit says: 'Restrain the unrestrainable mind, scattered and dispersed as it is by the power of the enemy, who, through our negligence, has once again, since Baptism, returned to our slothful soul, along with other more evil spirits; as the Lord said: "the last state of that man is worse than the first" (Matt. xii. 45).' Another teaches: 'A monk should have memory of God in place of breath' or, as another says: 'One's love of God should run before breathing.' St. John of the Ladder advises: 'Let the memory of Jesus combine with your breath—then will you know the profit of silence.' The Apostle Paul asserts that 'nevertheless I live, yet not I, but Christ liveth in me', acting and breathing Divine life (Gal. ii. 20). The Lord also says: 'The wind bloweth where it listeth' (John iii. 8) taking his example from the blowing of the physical wind. Purified by baptism we have received the betrothal of the Spirit, which deifies those who share in it and increases their stature. But since we have neglected the commandments, the guardians of grace, we have once again fallen into passions and, instead of the breath of the Holy Spirit, have become filled with the wind of evil spirits, the cause of all our disorder. But he who has preserved the Spirit and has been purified by Him, is warmed by Him and inspired by Divine life, and then speaks by Him, thinks by Him and moves by Him, according to the words of the Lord: 'For it is not ye that speak, but the Spirit of your Father which speaketh in you' (Matt. x. 20). In the same way he who has in him a spirit opposed to the Lord and is possessed by it, speaks and acts against the Lord.

### 4. How hesychasts should psalmodise

'If a man be tired', says St. John of the Ladder, 'he should get up and pray, then sitting down again, should courageously resume his former doing' (27, 23). Although this was said about mental doing, that is for a man who has achieved the guarding of the heart, it would not be out of place to say the same of psalmody. Barsanuphius the Great, when asked about psalmody, namely, as to how one should psalmodise, replied: 'Hours and chanting are church traditions and are wisely given for bringing together those who gather for prayer. But Sketiotes[26] sing no hours, and have no chants, but only handicraft, training in solitude (mental prayer) and a little brief oral saying of prayers. Standing at prayer, you should recite the *Trisagion* and the Lord's Prayer, and ask God to deliver you from the old Adam' (21). One should not linger too long at this oral prayer; but your mind should remain in prayer throughout the day. By these words the staretz showed that training in solitude is prayer of mind or heart; and to a small degree prayer is also standing up to psalmodise. St. John of the Ladder says the same: 'The work of silence is detachment from everything, diligent prayer, that is psalmody, and thirdly, unrobbed doing of the heart' (27, 46). This is the seat of prayer, as well as of silence.

### 5. Question:

Why this difference, that some teach to psalmodise much, others—little, others again—not at all?

### Answer:

The solution of this question is as follows. Those who have acquired the action of grace by active life, through long years of

[26] Monks of Sketis (Translators' note.)

much labour, teach others in the same way as they have themselves learned. They do not believe those who say of themselves,
like St. Isaac, that, by the mercy of God, and through warmth
of faith, they have reached this attainment in a short time;
blinded by ignorance and self-esteem they censure such people and
assure others that if something happens differently from their
own experience, it is prelest and not an act of grace. They do
not know that 'it is an easy thing in the sight of the Lord on the
sudden to make a poor man rich' (Ecclus. xi. 21). The Apostle
also reproves the disciples of his day, who knew not grace, saying: 'Know ye not your own selves, how that Jesus Christ is in
you, except ye be reprobates?'[27] (2 Cor. xiii. 5), that is, men
who do not make progress, through laziness. This is why such
people, through unbelief and arrogance, do not accept (do not
recognise as true) the miraculous effects of prayer produced in
some by the action of the Holy Spirit.

6. Tell me, you judges, if a man fasts, abstains, keeps night
watches, stands in psalmody, executes bows and genuflections,
weeps, renounces all possessions, is not this doing? (But we
consider all this indispensable for one who practises silence.)
How then can you think and say that we assert that one can
succeed in prayer without a life of action?—It is not this that we
assert, but the fact that, besides a life of action, another, a mental
activity is required, without which it is impossible to succeed in
prayer.—Now listen. If a man prays with his lips while his mind
is wandering, what use is this? 'When one buildeth, and another
pulleth down, what profit have they then but labour?' (Ecclus.
xxxiv. 23). But as a man does to his body, so must he also do to
his mind, lest he appear righteous in the body, while his heart is
filled with untruth and impurity. The Apostle asserts the same
when he says: 'If I pray in an *unknown* tongue' (that is, with my
lips), 'my spirit' (or my voice) 'prayeth, but my understanding
is unfruitful. What is it then? I will pray with the spirit, and I
will pray with the understanding also.' And: 'Yet . . . I had rather
speak five words with my understanding . . . than ten thousand
words with my tongue' (1 Cor. xiv. 14, 15, 19). St. John of the

27 The Slavonic version has непскусный, that is 'unskilled'. (Translators'
note.)

Ladder, testifying that the Apostle speaks of mental prayer, says in his chapter on prayer (paragraph 21): 'The great doer of the great and perfect prayer says: "I had rather speak five words with my understanding", and so on.' Works are many but they are individual; prayer of the heart is great and all-embracing, as the source of virtues (John of the Ladder, on prayer, paragraph 1), because every good is acquired thereby. St. Maximus says: 'Nothing is more terrible than the thought of death, and nothing more glorious than remembrance of God', showing the supremacy of this doing. But in our times some people do not even want to hear about the existence of grace, because through their insensibility and ignorance they are blind and of little faith.

7. Those who do not psalmodise much, do right in my opinion, since they pay its due to moderation (for measure is good in all things); lest they exhaust all the power of their soul in the active labour of psalmody, and so leave the mind with little zeal or strength for prayer; but psalmodising a little, they spend most of their time in prayer. On the other hand, when the mind is exhausted by frequent mental calling and a ceaseless marshalling of attention in prayer, it is right to give it some rest by releasing it from the straitness of silent prayer into the freedom of psalmody. This is an excellent rule, this teaching of wise men.

8. Those too, do right who wholly abstain from psalmody, if they are making progress. Such people have no need of psalmody, but should remain in silence, constant prayer and contemplation, if they have attained enlightenment. For they are united with God and must not tear their mind away from Him and plunge it into turmoil (or a crowd of thoughts). St. John of the Ladder says: 'For a cenobite downfall is—to follow his self-will; but for a hesychast downfall is—to abandon and stop prayer.' For if he relinquishes remembrance of God such a man commits adultery, as if he were unfaithful to the bridegroom and lovingly seized the most unworthy objects.

It is impossible for all to be taught this discipline. Obedient illiterates and simples can be trained in it—yes—since obedience for the sake of humility is capable of all virtue. But the disobedient, whether simple or educated, are not taught this science lest they fall into prelest. For those who are a law unto themselves cannot escape conceit, which is usually followed by prelest as St. Isaac says. But some people, not thinking of the harm they may do, teach every newcomer the efforts they themselves make to keep remembrance of God, in order that the mind should become accustomed to this remembrance and begin to love it—which is impossible, especially for those accustomed to live as they choose. For, since their mind is impure owing to negligence and arrogance, and is not cleansed with tears, they mostly see images of shameful thoughts instead of prayer, while the impure spirits rooted in their hearts gnash their teeth, disturbed by the terrible name (of God), and strive to destroy the man who thus wounds them. Therefore, if a man, who acts on his own, hears or reads in books about this doing and wishes to practise it, he will suffer one of two things: if he forces himself to efforts he will fall into prelest and will remain uncured or, if he does not make efforts, he will remain unsuccessful his whole life.

9. I will add to this from my own small experience. When you sit in silence, by day or by night, without thought ceaselessly praying to God in humility, and your mind is exhausted with invocations, your heart and body ache from the continual alertness of calling on the name of Jesus, and when no feeling of warmth or joy comes to engender and encourage the zeal and patience of the struggler, then rise up and psalmodise, either by yourself or with a pupil who happens to be with you, or occupy yourself with reflections on some words of the Scriptures (or in general think of Divine things); or sink yourself into memory of death; or do some work with your hands; or listen to reading, preferably standing up to tire your body.—When you stand to psalmodise alone, recite the *Trisagion*, then pray with your soul or mind, making your mind pay attention to your heart. If you are weighed down by despondency, read two or three psalms, or moving troparions,[28] but not aloud; since, as St. John of the Ladder asserts, they are not recited aloud. For, as St. Mark says, here it is enough if the heart aches for piety and is filled with spiritual warmth to give them joy and gladness. After the psalm again pray in mind or soul, keeping your thoughts from wandering—and

[28] 'Troparion' is a hymn or prayer for a special occasion. (Translators' note.)

then Hallelujah.—Such is the order established by St. Barsanuphius, Diadochus and others. The divine Basil advises a change of
psalms each day, in order to stimulate zeal and to prevent the
mind losing its delight in psalmody through the monotony of
always repeating the same ones. The mind should be given freedom and it will grow stronger in its zeal and application.—If you
psalmodise with a trusted pupil, let him recite psalms, while you
guard yourself, secretly watching your heart and praying. With
the help of the prayer ignore all thoughts coming from the heart,
whether of the senses or the mind. For silence means cutting off
all thoughts except the most Divine which come from the Spirit,
lest, in accepting the former as good, we lose what is greater.

### 10. On prelest

Watch with care and intelligence, you lover of God. When,
while you work, you see within or without you a light or a flame,
or an image—of Christ, for example, or of an angel, or of someone else—do not accept it lest you suffer harm. And do not yourself create fantasies; nor pay attention to those that create themselves, nor allow your mind to take their impression. For all
those things, being impressed and imagined from without, aim at
seducing your soul.—The true beginning of prayer is warmth of
the heart, which scorches passions, fills the heart with the joy
and delight of unshakable love and strengthens it with sure conviction. The holy fathers teach that whatever enters the heart,
whether sensory or spiritual, if the heart doubts and refuses to
accept it, is not from God, but is sent by the enemy. Moreover,
if you see your mind being enticed by some invisible force to
come out or to soar aloft, do not trust it and do not let it be enticed, but immediately force it to continue its work. What is of
God comes of itself, says St. Isaac, without your knowing even
the time of its coming. Although the enemy tries to substitute
the imaginary for the spiritual in your loins, offering one thing
in place of another, bringing a disorderly burning instead of
warmth, exciting profane delight and the sweetness of the
humours instead of joy, and succeeds in hiding from the inexperienced behind these seductions, time, experience and feeling usually reveal him to those who are not without knowledge

of his evil wiles. The palate discriminates between different foods, say the Scriptures. In the same way spiritual taste clearly shows up everything as it really is and does not give way to seduction.

### 11. On reading

St. John of the Ladder says: If you are a doer (practising active life) read the writings of the fathers on doing. For, if you translate what you read into practice, other reading will be superfluous for you (27, 78). Always read about silence and prayer, namely—St. John of the Ladder, St. Isaac, St. Maximus, the New Theologian and his disciple Stethatos, Hesychius, Philotheus of Sinai and others who have written on this subject. Leave for a time all other writings, not as something inadmissible, but as something not corresponding to your aim at the moment (gaining experience in prayer); for the subjects they treat of may distract your mind from prayer. Let your reading be in solitude and not aloud, to avoid the temptation of boasting to yourself either about your voice, or about the refinement of your enunciation, or of imagining yourself reading to a gathering and entrancing everyone with your art. Let not your reading be insatiable—for in everything it is best to have a measure. Do not read either too fast, or too lazily or carelessly, but with reverence, attention and intelligence. Invigorated by reading that profits the soul, the mind acquires strength and prays firmly. Reading without order clouds the mind and weakens it, rendering it unfit for prayer.

12. Pay heed, also, to the intention of your will, watching which way it inclines: whether it is towards God, whether it is for the sake of good itself and for the benefit of your soul that you sit in silence, psalmodise, recite prayers or perform any other good works, lest you be imperceptibly robbed, and prove to be God's doer only according to the Schema,[29] while in your heart you remain a man, and not one who desires to please God. For the enemy has many wiles and secretly keeps an alert watch on the inclination of our will, striving in every way imperceptibly

---

[29] 'Schema.' The strictest rule of monkhood, comprising two degrees, the lesser and the great. Entry into each degree is marked by a special ritual and vows. The great Schema involves seclusion either in a monastery or hermitage. (Translators' note.)

to despoil our work, so that what is done is no longer a work of God.—But in spite of his ceaseless strivings and shameless attacks, you will not often be robbed by him if you keep to a firm determination to please God alone, though he may push your will reluctantly towards a trap and make it waver. Even if, through weakness, a man is overcome against his will, he is soon forgiven and praised by Him Who knows our intentions and our hearts.— This passion, I mean vainglory, prevents a monk from succeeding in virtue, so that he labours in vain and in the end remains barren. Vainglory steals up on all three—the beginner, the monk on the path and the perfect one—and despoils them of the fruit of their striving for virtues.

13. One thing more I have to add from my own experience: a monk can in no way succeed without the following virtues: fasting, abstinence, vigil, patience, courage, silence, prayer, not talking, tears, humility, which generate and preserve one another. Constant fasting withers lust, and gives birth to abstinence; abstinence to vigil; vigil to patience; patience to courage; courage to silence; silence to prayer; prayer to abstinence from talk; abstinence from talk to weeping; weeping to humility; humility again to weeping, and so on. Thus going backwards, you will see how daughters give birth to mothers.

14. It is necessary to enumerate here in their right order the painful labours of this struggle, and to show clearly how each work should be practised so that a man, proceeding not without pain on this path, according to what he has heard, and receiving no fruit from his labours, should not blame us or someone else because in actual practice things are not as we have shown. For grieving of the heart and bodily labour usually do the work as in truth it should be done. Through them is made manifest the action of the Holy Spirit, with which every believer is endowed at baptism but which, through neglect of commandments, becomes buried under passions. In His infinite mercy the Lord awaits our repentance, to save us from hearing in the end, for our barrenness: 'Take therefore the talent from him' (Matt. xxv. 28) and: 'Whosoever hath not (fruit), from him shall be taken even that which he seemeth to have' (Luke viii. 18), and from being cast down into hell and condemned to eternal torment in Gehenna.

No work, whether physical or spiritual, if it be devoid of labour or suffering, ever brings any profit to the doer, for the Lord says: 'The kingdom of heaven suffereth violence, and the violent take it by force' (Matt. xi. 12). By violence should be understood the most painful bodily sensation felt in all your efforts. Many have worked and work painlessly for long years but, since they have made and make efforts without suffering, have proved and prove to be devoid of purity and lacking the Holy Spirit, for they have not borne the acute suffering of painful labours. Since those who seem to labour much, but do it carelessly and lazily, never gather any fruit, for owing to the painlessness of their efforts they remain deeply insensible. A witness of this is he who says: 'Even if we perform all the great endeavours of our way of life, but have not acquired a grieving heart, they are all counterfeit and corrupt' (John of the Ladder 7, 64). St. Ephraim says the same: 'In labouring labour painfully, to avoid the pain of vain labours. For if, according to the Prophet, our loins are not filled with the pain of fasting; if the pangs of suffering do not take hold upon us, as the pangs of a woman that travaileth, we shall not conceive the spirit of salvation in the soil of our heart (Is. xxi. 3; xxvi. 18).' But all we boast about is long years, life in a barren desert and idly keeping silence, imagining that through this we are somebody. At our death we shall all know for certain what is the fruit of our life.

15. It is impossible for anyone to learn by himself the art of virtue, although some have used their own experience as a teacher. For acting by one's own inclination, instead of following the advice of those who have succeeded, leads to a high opinion of oneself. For if 'The Son can do nothing of himself, but what he seeth the Father do: for what things soever he doeth, these also doeth the Son likewise' (John v. 19), and the Spirit 'shall not speak of himself' (John xvi. 13), who can think that he has reached such heights of virtue that he has no need of someone's guidance amid mysteries? In his presumption such a man seems to be more mad than virtuous. Therefore one should listen to those who have themselves experienced the pains and labours of active virtue, and practise it under their guidance, that is, hungry fasting, bitter abstinence, patient vigils, painful

kneelings, standing still without moving, constant prayer, unfeigned humility, constant contrition and sighing, wise silence and patience in everything. 'Thou shalt eat the labour of thine hands' (Ps. cxxviii. 2) say the Scriptures, and also: 'The kingdom of heaven suffereth violence, and the violent take it by force' (Matt. xi. 12). Those who strive with all possible effort daily to carry out these practices, will with God's help gather the fruits of their labours at their appointed time.

# ST. SIMEON THE NEW THEOLOGIAN

## Short Biographical Note

St. Simeon, born in Paphlagonia, was brought up in Constantinople by his uncle, a courtier. On completing his education, he remained for a short time attached to the Court, but soon left and entered the Studit monastery to join his staretz, Simeon the Devout, whose guidance he had enjoyed even from his schooldays. The excessive strictness of his life incurred the displeasure of the brotherhood, and, on the advice of his staretz, he moved to the monastery of St. Mamas where, on the death of the Abbot, he was elected to take his place and was ordained into priesthood by the Patriarch Nicholas Chrysovergos. Having organised the monastery, St. Simeon went into silent retreat, putting in his place a worthy and well-tried successor—Arsenius. Not for long did he enjoy the peace of silence. A storm broke against him for instituting a remembrance day in honour of his staretz, Simeon the Devout, on the latter's death; and he was cast out of Constantinople. Not far from there he chose a spot where stood the dilapidated church of St. Marina. The owner of this place, one of the nobles, Christopher Fagura, who venerated him, ceded him the whole locality, and helped him to organise a monastery there. When he had ordered everything in the new monastery, St. Simeon once more went into retreat and after thirty years of peaceful life in silence, at the beginning of the eleventh century he died. His relics were revealed in A.D. 1050. His memory is celebrated on March 12th, the day of his death. . . .

St. Simeon left many writings. When he was head of the monasteries he often preached in church, and during his two retreats he wrote epistles and instructions, both general, for all Christians, and special, for those engaged in spiritual warfare.

The latter are mostly written in the form of short texts or articles.

His disciple, Nicetas Stethatos, who wrote his biography, collected his writings and began to make fair copies of them even before the death of the saint. . . .

# ST. SIMEON THE NEW THEOLOGIAN

## Practical and Theological Precepts

1. Faith is (readiness) to die for Christ's sake, for His commandments, in the conviction that such death brings life; it is to regard poverty as riches, insignificance and nothingness as true fame and glory and, having nothing, to be sure that you possess all things. But above all, faith is attainment of the invisible treasure of the knowledge of Christ, regarding everything visible as dust or smoke.

2. Faith in Christ is not merely neglect of the pleasures of life, but also a good and patient disposition of the soul in enduring all temptations, whether griefs, sorrows or unpleasant happenings, until God's favour looks down upon us; thus we would imitate David who says: 'I waited patiently for the Lord; and he inclined unto me, and heard my cry' (Ps. xl. 1). (In other words, I bore my sorrows in hope that the Lord would help me; therefore the Lord, seeing me await His help without wavering, looked down upon me and showed me His mercy.)

3. Those who in any way prefer their parents to the commandment of God, have no faith in Christ. Of course their own conscience also denounces them in this lack of faith, if conscience is alive in them. For the real mark of true believers is never to transgress in anything the commandments of the great God and of our Saviour Jesus Christ.

4. Faith in Christ, the true God, gives birth to desire for eternal blessings and to fear of torment. Desire for these blessings and fear of torment lead to a strict observance of the commandments, and a strict observance of commandments teaches men a deep realisation of their own weakness. This realisation of our

actual weakness gives birth to memory of death. He who has this memory for his constant companion, painfully seeks to learn what awaits him after departure from this life. He who tries painstakingly to learn about the future, must first of all deprive himself of the present (that is of the blessings and things of this world). For he who is attached to something of the latter, however small and insignificant, cannot acquire a perfect knowledge of the former. Even if God chooses to grant him some taste of this knowledge, if the man does not immediately renounce whatever he is attached to, and does not give himself up solely to the work of acquiring this knowledge, not allowing himself even to think of anything else—then he will be deprived even of the knowledge he thinks he has.

5. Renunciation of the world and complete withdrawal from it—if it includes complete withdrawal from all worldly things, habits, opinions and people, and the disowning of body and will —in a very short time will bring great profit to a man who is fired with such zeal.

6. If you intend to withdraw from the world, do not at the outset let your soul be plunged into carnal consolations, while you are still living and moving in the world, even if all your relatives and friends urge you to it. They are incited to this by the demons in order to extinguish the warmth of your heart, so that, even if they fail to break your resolution altogether, they may still manage to weaken and cool it.

7. If you refuse courageously all worldly pleasures and hold yourself aloof from every comfort, then the demons, inciting compassion in your relatives, will make them sob and weep over you in your presence. That this is truly so you will see from the fact that, if you remain undaunted by this temptation, you will immediately find your relatives filled with rage and hatred of you, turning their backs on you as on an enemy, and refusing even to look at you.

8. Seeing your parents, brothers and friends grieving over you, laugh at the demon who in such varied ways strives to fight against you; yet hasten to withdraw in fear and ceaselessly implore the Lord to allow you quickly to reach the harbour of the good Father, where He will give peace to your troubled and burdened

soul—for the sea of life contains much that is extremely dangerous and disastrous.

9. Whoever wants to hate the world must love God with the innermost depths of his soul, and acquire a constant memory of Him, for nothing can more strongly urge a man to renounce everything gladly and turn away from worldly things, as from dung.

10. Do not remain long in the world either from right-sounding or profane motives; but as soon as you are called, hasten to obey. For nothing pleases God more than when we hasten to obey His will. Speedy obedience, with poverty, is better than procrastination with many possessions.

11. Since the world and all in it is transitory, while God is incorruptible and immortal, rejoice all you who, for His sake, have abandoned the corruptible. Corruptible things are not only money and riches, but every sinful enjoyment and pleasure is corruption. God's commandments alone are light and life—and so are they called by all.

12. If, brother, fired by zeal for salvation, you have come in all haste to the monastery, or to your spiritual father, then, if he, or your brethren working with you, offer you a bath, or food, or some other physical comforts, do not consent. On the contrary, be always ready (desire, seek, strive) for fasting, sufferings (deliberate privations) and extreme abstinence. If your spiritual father orders you to give some comfort to your body, obey him, thus cutting off your own will. If not, do with patience and joy what you have chosen to do of your own free will (that is, to abstain in every way from everything). Observing this, you will always remain in everything as one who fasts and abstains and who has totally renounced his will. Moreover, you will thus preserve unextinguished the flame burning in your heart and urging you to despise everything.

13. When the demons fail, although they have done all they can to break our intention towards God or to interfere with its fulfilment, they enter into some brethren who pretend to be devout and, through them, try to hinder the good works of those who have already begun the path of spiritual struggle. To start with, as though moved by love and compassion, they advise them

not to shun physical comforts, so as not to exhaust the body (so they say) nor fall into despondency. Furthermore, engaging them in useless conversation, they force them to waste whole days in this way. Thereupon, if any of the zealous listen to their counsels and become like them, they begin to mock them, as though rejoicing in their downfall. But if a man refuses to listen to them and keeps aloof from it all, keeping his attention in himself, but without arguing (meek and humble with everyone), they become filled with envy and set against him, using all possible means, even to driving him out of the monastery. For infamous vanity cannot bear true humility being praised before its eyes.

14. A vain man suffers anguish when he sees a humble man, shedding tears, gain God's mercy and stir men to spontaneous praise.

15. When you have surrendered yourself to your spiritual father, know that thenceforth you are divorced from everything you have brought with you from outside, whether it be money or other possessions. Therefore do nothing with them without his orders and ask from him none of those things, either small or great, except only when he himself, on his own initiative, orders you to take something or gives it to you himself.

16. Without the will of your father in God, never arrange to give alms out of the money you have brought with you; do not even try to take some of it through the intermediary of some third person. For it is better to be regarded as a destitute tramp than to give and distribute money among the poor when you are still a beginner. To put everything in the hands of your spiritual father, as in the hand of God, is an act of perfect faith.

17. Do not even beg for a drop of water, though you may be tormented with thirst, until your spiritual father orders you to drink of his own will. Oppress and drive yourself in everything, admonishing yourself thus: if God wills and thinks me worthy of a drink He will suggest to my father to say to me 'Drink'. Then will you drink with a clear conscience, even though it may not be at the right time.

18. Someone who has acquired experience of spiritual profit and attained true faith, said, naming God as his witness: 'I made a decision never to ask my father for food or drink, and generally

never to accept anything until God suggested to him to order me to do so.' Acting thus, he said: 'I have never been frustrated in my hope.'

19. A man who has acquired active faith in his father in God, when seeing him thinks he sees Christ Himself; and being in his presence or following him, firmly believes that he is with Christ and follows Christ. Such a man will never wish to converse with anyone else, and will prefer no worldly things to the love and memory of the Lord. For what can be better or more profitable, both in the present and future life, than being with Christ? What can be sweeter and more beautiful than contemplation of Him? And if someone is vouchsafed converse with Him, then without fail he draws eternal life therefrom.

20. A man who is well disposed towards and loves those who revile and abuse him and cause him harm, and who prays for them, in a short time attains to great achievements. For if the feelings of his heart are so disposed, this good disposition leads a man to the abyss of humility and opens up the springs of tears, which flood all three parts of his soul (that is, the intellectual, the desiring and the excitable powers); it leads the mind to the heaven of passionlessness and renders it contemplative; and tasting the blessings of heaven, man is disposed to regard as dung all the blessings of the present life, and even to eat and drink less than his fill and not so often.

21. A man engaged in spiritual struggle should not only withdraw from all evil deeds, but should also try to be free from thoughts and ideas (opposed to the commandments and the will of God), and must always be occupied with salutary and spiritual recollections, remaining detached from all worldly cares.

22. As a man who has stripped his whole body but has left his eyes covered by a veil, and refuses to lift and throw off this veil, cannot see the light through stripping the rest of his body; so a man who has abandoned all his money and possessions, and has even freed himself from passions of that kind, can never see the spiritual light—our Lord Jesus Christ and God—if he does not also free the eye of his soul from worldly memories and wrong thoughts.

23. What a veil is for the eyes, so worldly thoughts and life recollections are for the mind, or the eye of the soul. So long as

we allow them to exist we shall see nothing; but when we banish them through memory of death, we shall see the true light which illumines every man coming into the world.

24. A man blind from birth cannot see the power of the written word or believe in it; but if his eyes become opened, he will testify that what is written and read is true.

25. A man who sees with his physical eyes knows when it is day and when night, but a blind man does not know one from another. So with a man whose spiritual eyes are opened and who has inner sight with them; if, once he has seen the true and ever-lasting light, he returns again to his former blindness and becomes deprived of light through carelessness and negligence, he feels deeply, when in a right state, the loss of this light and is not ignorant of the reason why he has suffered this deprivation. But a man blind from birth (spiritually) can know nothing of this either from experience or from its action. It is only by hearsay that he may learn of what he has never seen, and begin to tell others of it, although neither he nor his listeners have any true knowledge of the things they are discussing.

26. It is impossible to fill the body to satiety with food and at the same time have spiritual enjoyment of mental and Divine blessings. For inasmuch as a man panders to his belly, in the same measure he deprives himself of spiritual blessings; con-versely, in proportion as he keeps his body lean, he will be filled with spiritual food and consolation.

27. Let us abandon everything earthly—not only riches and gold or other worldly things, but let us drive out of our soul even the very desire of those things. Let us hate, not only the pleasures of the body, but even its uncontrolled movements and let us strive to mortify it by labours and ascetic privations. For it is through the body that lusts are excited and brought into action. So, while the body is full of life, our soul must of necessity be dead—unwieldy, or even quite immovable for any work on God's commandments.

28. As the flame always rises upwards, especially if the burn-ing matter is poked and turned; so the heart of a vain man cannot become humble. As soon as you say something to him for his own good, his heart exalts itself more and more; if he is denounced

and admonished, he argues heatedly; if he is praised and welcomed, he puffs himself up still more.

29. A man given to arguing becomes for himself a double-edged sword; he destroys his soul, without knowing it, and renders it alien to eternal life.

30. An argumentative man is like someone who deliberately gives himself up to his king's enemies. Argument is a fishing line baited with veracity (defence of truth, self-justification, self-defence) by which we are seduced into swallowing the hook of sin. In this manner, hooked by tongue and throat, the poor soul is wont to be ravished by evil spirits. Now rising upwards, now sinking in the chaotic abyss of sin, it is condemned with those cast down from heaven.

31. A man who is deeply wounded in his heart by provocation and abuse shows thereby that deep in himself he harbours the old serpent. If he bears the blows in silence or answers with great humility, he will render this serpent weak and powerless (or will kill it altogether). But if he argues with bitterness or speaks with arrogance, he will give the serpent an added strength to pour poison into his heart and mercilessly to devour his entrails. In this way, daily gaining strength, the serpent will finally devour the very intention of the poor soul to reform and to keep itself reformed by mending its ways of life, and will destroy its power to do so. Thereupon the man will live for sin and become totally dead to truth.

32. If you wish to renounce the world and learn to live according to the Gospels, place yourself under an experienced teacher with knowledge of the passions, lest instead of life according to the Gospels you are taught the life of the devil. For good teachers give good lessons, and bad teachers bad. A bad seed invariably produces a bad plant.

33. With prayers and tears implore God to give you a saintly instructor, free from passions. Study also yourself the Holy Scriptures, especially the practical writings of the holy fathers, in order to compare with them what you are being taught by your teacher and preceptor. Thus will you see, as in a mirror, how far they agree. Thereupon absorb and retain in your thoughts what corresponds to the holy writings, and after wise deliberation put

aside what does not correspond, lest you fall into prelest. For you should know that many false teachers and seducers have appeared in our days.

34. Every man who does not see (is spiritually blind), yet undertakes to guide others, is a seducer, throwing his followers into the moat of destruction, according to the words of the Lord: 'If the blind lead the blind, both shall fall into the ditch' (Matt. xv. 14).

35. A man who is blind in relation to one thing (to God) is totally blind in relation to all things; and a man who sees in the one (in God), has vision of all things. He is both removed from the vision of all things, and at the same time has vision of all things, and is outside all things visible. Thus being in the One, he sees all, and being in the all, sees nothing of the all. Seeing in the One, through Him he sees himself, others and all else; and being concealed in Him, he sees nothing of the all.

36. He who has not assumed the image of our Lord Jesus Christ, Divine man and God, in his inner or spiritual man, with perception and consciousness, is nothing but blood and flesh and cannot directly apprehend spiritual glory from words alone, just as those blind from birth cannot conceive what the light of the sun is, merely from hearing about it.

37. He who thus sees, hears and apprehends, knows the force of what is being said, since he has already assumed the image of heaven and has become 'a perfect man, unto the measure of the stature of the fulness of Christ' (Eph. iv. 13). Being such, he is also able rightly to guide Christ's flock on the path of God's commandments. But if a man knows it not and is not such, it shows that the senses of his soul are unenlightened and unhealthy; and it is far better for him to be guided than to guide others, to their danger and his own.

38. He who strains his attention to listen to his teacher and preceptor as though to God, cannot argue. A man who thinks and says that he can do both (that is, listen to his father as to God as well as argue), let him know that he is in error; for he does not know how the men of God stand in relation to God.

39. A man who believes that his life and death are in the hands of his shepherd will never argue. Argument is born of ignorance of this fact, which causes eternal spiritual death.

40. Until the verdict is pronounced, the prisoner is given the right to plead for himself, to tell the judge what he has done; but after his case has been examined, and the judge has pronounced the verdict, he may no longer dispute with those who execute the verdict.

41. Until a monk enters this court-house (of repentance— a monastery) and reveals what is in his heart, he may, perhaps, be allowed to contradict sometimes, either through ignorance or wishing to hide some of his deeds. But after his thoughts have been revealed and sincerely confessed, he can never contradict his lord and judge in God, even unto death. For a monk who has entered this court-house and has uncovered all the secrets of his heart, if he is a man of sense, becomes convinced from the very beginning of his life here that he deserves an infinite number of deaths, but believes that through obedience and humility he will escape all torment and punishment, provided, of course, he truly knows the power of this mystery.

42. A man who keeps this imprinted in his mind, will never have his heart incited to anything unseemly when he is being taught, admonished and exposed. For if a man, in this process, falls into the deadly sin of disputing with his spiritual father and teacher and of unbelief in him, he is cast, even while living, into ruin in the depths of hell and becomes the abode of Satan with all his unclean armies, an unruly son of perdition.

43. I implore you, who have undertaken the yoke of obedience, frequently to keep this in your thought and to strive to the utmost not to fall, in this way, into hell and eternal torment. Every day you should pray warmly to God, and say: 'God, Lord of hosts, Who hath power over every breath and every soul, Thou Who alone canst cure me, hear my prayer and send Thy Holy Spirit to kill and destroy the serpent nestling in this poor wretch. Teach and direct me, naked as I am and destitute of all virtue, to fall at the feet of my father and move his holy soul to mercy and compassion towards me. Grant, O Lord, humility to my heart and grant me the thoughts of a sinner who has resolved to bring his repentance to Thee. Abandon not utterly the soul which has once been united with Thee, which professed Thee and chose Thee, and preferred Thee over all the world. Thou

knowest, Lord, how I desire salvation, though my evil habits obstruct my way. But to Thee, Lord, all is possible that to men is impossible.'

44. Those who, with fear and trembling, have laid sound foundations of faith and hope in the courtyard of righteousness and who have planted their feet firmly on the rock of obedience to their spiritual fathers, listening to their teaching as though it came from the lips of God, and on this foundation of obedience unwaveringly and humbly practise what they are taught, speedily reach success. The first great work carried out in them is renunciation of themselves. For obedience to the will of another, instead of their own, not only strengthens their denial of their own soul, but renders the whole world dead for them.

45. The demons rejoice over a man who disputes with his father; but a man who humbles himself before him even unto death, arouses the wonder of angels. For such a man does the work of God, imitating the Son of God, Who obeyed His Father even unto death, death on the cross.

46. Long and excessive sorrowing of the heart for anything sensory darkens and disturbs the mind. It banishes pure prayer and tenderness from the soul and brings a painful pining of the heart. This leads to measureless hardness and insensibility; and thereby the demons usually bring despair upon those who have undertaken to lead a spiritual life.

47. When such a thing happens to you, brother, and at the same time you find zeal in your soul and a great longing for perfection, so that you strive with all your might to fulfil every commandment of God, and you are anxious not to sin even in some careless word and not to fall behind the ancient saints, in actions, knowledge, or contemplation, but you see the enemy hindering you in this, sowing tares of faintness in your soul and preventing you from soaring to such heights of sanctity, weakening you by stirring up fearful thoughts through these suggestions, and when you realise that it is impossible for you to gain salvation and to obey all God's commandments unswervingly in the midst of life, then, sit you down in a corner, in solitude, withdraw into yourself and collect your thoughts; and thereupon give good counsel to your soul, saying: ' ''Why art thou cast down, O

my soul? and why art thou disquieted in me? hope thou in God: for I shall yet praise him for the help of his countenance" (Ps. xlii. 5). Whose works can be justified in the sight of the law? The King and Prophet also says: "In thy sight shall no man living be justified" (Ps. cxliii. 2). But through the faith I have in my God I hope that in His infinite mercy He will grant me salvation. Out of my sight, Satan! I worship my Lord God, and from my youth serve Him Who alone can save me in His mercy. So leave me; may God Who has created me in His likeness and image annihilate you.'

48. The only thing God demands from us, mortals, is that we do not sin. But this is not the fulfilment of the law; it is merely keeping inviolate the image and high rank we possess by nature. Clothed thus in the radiant garment of the Spirit, we abide in God and He in us; through grace, we become gods and sons of God and are illumined by the light of His knowledge, according to the words: 'Lord, lift Thou up the light of Thy countenance upon us' (Ps. iv. 6).

49. Physical weakness and heaviness entering the soul through laziness and negligence divert us from practising the usual rule, cloud the mind and bring faintness of soul. Thereupon, thoughts of fear and blasphemy begin to appear more and more often in the heart, and a man tempted by the demon of weakness and despondency is often too timid to enter his usual place of prayer and so gives himself up to laziness, or at times experiences an attack of sundry unseemly thoughts about the Creator of all. Thus, knowing the cause from which all this arose, hasten to your usual place of prayer and, falling down before the all-merciful God, pray with a groaning heart, with contrition and tears, imploring God to lift from you the burden of weakness, despondency and evil thoughts. And soon you will be granted freedom from them, if you continue to knock painfully and unceasingly (at the doors of God's mercy).

50. He who has acquired purity of heart has conquered fear. But a man who is still in process of purification, at times is conquered by fear, and at times conquers it. A man, however, who does not strive at all after this purity, is either for ever sunk into a state of insensibility and, being a friend of passions and demons and filled with vanity and conceit, 'think(s) himself to be

something, when he is nothing' (Gal. vi. 3); or he is a slave, delivered into the hands of fear and, being of a childish mind, trembles and is afraid, where for those who fear God there is no fear or trembling.

51. He who fears God does not fear the onslaughts of the demons or their impotent attacks; neither does he fear the threats of evil men; but being like a flame or a blazing fire, even when traversing secret or unlit places, he routs the demons, who flee while he flees not, lest he scorch them with the tongue of the Divine fire he emits.

52. He who is permeated by fear of God is not afraid to be among evil men. Having the fear of God in him, and wearing the unconquerable armour of faith, he is strong in everything and can even do things which seem hard and impossible to others. He walks among them like a giant among young monkeys, or a roaring lion among dogs and foxes, and, putting his trust in God, fills them with wonder at the strength of his reasoning, brings awe to their understanding and strikes them down with words of wisdom, as with a rod of iron.

53. Not only one who practises silence or obedience, but also an abbot, in charge of many, while organising everything, must remain carefree, that is, free from cares and anxiety about everyday needs. For if we are full of cares we transgress God's commandment, which says: 'Take no thought for your life, what ye shall eat, or what ye shall drink; nor yet for your body, what ye shall put on. (For after all these things do the Gentiles seek)' (Matt. vi. 25, 32). And again: 'And take heed to yourselves, lest at any time your hearts be overcharged with surfeiting, and drunkenness, and cares of this life' (Luke xxi. 34).

54. A man whose thoughts are occupied with cares of this life is not free; for these cares hold him in their hands and make him their slave, whether he worries for himself or for others. But a man who is free from all this does not worry about things of this life either for himself or for others, be he bishop, deacon or abbot. Nor is he ever idle, and neglects nothing, however small and insignificant; thus, while doing and organising everything in a manner pleasing to God, he is free of all cares—and remains thus all his life.

55. Watch, lest you ruin your own house in trying to build the house of your neighbour. It is difficult work and hard to accomplish; therefore beware, lest it happen that you undertake this, but wreck your own house and can in no wise build another's.

56. If you have not acquired complete non-attachment to money and the things of this life, do not aspire to be entrusted with economy (with looking after these things and managing them in the monastery), lest you become their captive; and, instead of being rewarded for your labour in serving the monastery, are condemned for theft and sacrilege. If you are forced by the abbot to undertake this work, do it as though you had to deal with burning fire. Banish the very first suggestion of misappropriation by confession and repentance and, through the prayers of your abbot, you will remain unharmed.

57. A man who has not become free from passions, does not even know what passionlessness is, and does not believe there can be anyone like this on earth. For if a man has not first renounced himself and has not exhausted his blood for the sake of this truly blessed life, how can he imagine that anyone else has done this, to acquire passionlessness? In the same way, a man who imagines that he has the Holy Spirit in him, yet in reality has nothing, when he hears that the actions of the Holy Spirit are clearly recognisable in those who possess Him, refuses to believe it; neither does he believe that there can be in our generation men who are equal to the Apostles of Christ and to the saints of all ages, and are, like them, moved and influenced by the Divine Spirit, or consciously see and apprehend Him. For each man judges others by his own state, that is, by what he is himself—in virtues or sins.

58. Passionlessness of the soul is one thing and passionlessness of the body is another. The former (that of the soul) sanctifies also the body, both by its own radiance and by the light of the Spirit; while, by itself, the latter is useless even to those who have acquired it.

59. A man who from dire poverty has been raised to high rank by the king, enriched, clothed in glittering garments and ordained to stand in his presence, looks upon his king with devotion and loves him exceedingly as his benefactor, rejoices in his bright

garments, is conscious of his rank and knows the riches bestowed upon him. Likewise a monk who, having truly abandoned the world and all worldly things, has come to Christ and, incited by right emotional perception, has obeyed the commandments and thereby has risen to the heights of spiritual contemplation, contemplates God without prelest and sees clearly the transformation effected in him. For he is constantly aware of the grace of the Holy Spirit illumining him, which is called both a garment and royal purple. For believers, this garment is Jesus Christ Himself, since those who believe in Him are clothed in Him.

60. Many themselves read the Holy Scriptures, others hear them read. But few have the power rightly to understand the meaning and significance of what is read. Some think that what is written in the Holy Scriptures is impossible; others, considering the direct meaning of the writings difficult to accept, undertake to interpret them in their own way and interpret wrongly. What is said of the present must, in their opinion, refer to the future; and what is said of the future, they take as something which has already happened or is happening every day. Thus they have no right judgment or true discrimination for distinguishing between things human and Divine.

61. We should look upon every believer alike, and suppose that Christ abides in each; we must have such loving disposition towards him as to be ready to lay down our life for him. We should never think or say that someone is evil, but, as is said, should see everyone as good. If you see someone attacked by passions, hate not the brother but the passions attacking him. And when you see someone succumbing to the tyranny of lusts and bad habits, have a still greater compassion for him, lest you suffer a similar temptation—since you are changeable and under the influence of changeable matter.

62. If someone is false through hypocrisy, or is guilty of some bad deed, or is slightly touched by some passion, or is somewhat at fault in one respect or another through negligence; such a man is not accepted into the community of those who are faultless in everything, but he is swept away as useless and inept for good works; so that he may not disrupt a union which should remain unbroken, and not divide those who must remain indivisible,

thereby bringing sorrow to both alike. For those who are ahead (who make progress) would worry and sorrow for those who remain behind, while the latter would grieve at being parted from those who have outstripped them.[30]

63. As earth thrown over it extinguishes a fire burning in a stove, so worldly cares and every kind of attachment to something, however small and insignificant, destroy the warmth of the heart which was there at first.

64. A man who has renounced everything external with joy and perfect wholeness of feelings, I mean renounced things and people and has forgotten it all, leaving every attachment as beyond a wall, is alien to the world and to everything in it. Keeping his mind collected he trains himself always in one thing alone —the memory and thought of death. Therefore his care is always about things connected with judgment and reward. Totally imprisoned in this, and as it were chained and bound to it, he plants unspeakable fear in his heart by thinking and pondering these things.

65. A man who has planted the fear of judgment in his heart seems in the eyes of the world like a prisoner in irons. For he is constantly afraid of being seized by a merciless executioner and dragged to the place of execution. So he thinks of nothing but the sufferings and tortures he will have to endure in the eternal fire. This fear engenders and keeps the sense of torment ineradicably planted in his heart, and prevents him from caring about any human matters, for he constantly feels himself hanging on the cross and is acutely aware of the torment and pain of death on the cross—and this prevents him from paying attention to man's appearance, or thinking of human honour or dishonour. With all his soul he considers himself to deserve every contempt and

30 The translation is made from the Greek text of Philokalia. The passage is obscure. The modern Greek translation contains the following paraphrase: 'So as not to cause the links of the chain to be broken when it is stretched, i.e. not to disrupt the union of the brethren at a time when they undertake ever greater deeds of virtue, not to produce a division among the brethren who must remain indivisible, and not to be a cause of sorrow for either party; for those who walk ahead, i.e. who progress in virtue, will grieve for those who have remained behind, while those remaining behind will grieve at being parted from the former.' (Note from 'Dobrotolubiye'.)

dishonour, and pays no attention to the abuse and humiliations which he may suffer.

66. A man filled with the fear of death despises all food and drink or adornments, and neither eats nor drinks his fill of bread or water, allowing his body only the bare necessities to maintain its life. Like a sensible slave, he renounces all will of his own and executes all the orders he receives.

67. A man who has given himself up as a slave to his fathers in God, is prevented by fear of torment from choosing among the orders he receives that which would ease the sufferings of his heart or loosen the bonds of his fear; neither will he listen to those who may encourage him to do so out of friendship or flattery or by command. He will always prefer what increases this suffering, will wish his bonds to be tightened still more, and will welcome what strengthens his executioner. He will always keep this disposition, without hope of ever freeing himself entirely from the extremities he has deserved. For hope of liberation alleviates sufferings of the heart which at that stage is not good for the penitent.

68. Fear of torment and the sufferings of the heart it engenders are salutary to everyone who begins life in God. A man who hopes to lay the foundations of righteous life without such sufferings, or to free himself from the bonds of fear, lays the foundations of his work on sand and dreams to build his house in the air without groundwork, which is of course impossible. At the same time, very soon these sufferings turn to joy, these bonds sever the bonds of all sins and passions, and this executioner leads a man not to death, but to eternal life.

69. A man who, instead of avoiding and running away from sufferings of the heart produced by the fear of eternal torment, willingly accepts them in his heart (follows the right path with suffering, or follows by the decisions of his will, and with the acquiescence of his heart, that which the suffering and fear suggest) will be determined, as he progresses, to tighten this bond ever more and more, and will thus advance more quickly. It will lead him to the presence of the King of kings. When this comes to pass, then, as soon as he sees, however dimly, the glory of God, his bonds—fear—will at once fall off, his executioner

will hasten away and his heart's grief will turn into joy which will become in him a fountain of life or a spring for ever gushing forth: physically—rivers of tears; spiritually—peace, meekness and unspeakable delight, together with courage and free and unhindered readiness to strive towards every fulfilment of God's commandments. This latter is not yet possible for beginners, but only for those who are well on the way towards attainment. For those who are near to perfection, this spring becomes changed into light with a sudden change and transformation of the heart.

70. If a man who possesses within him the light of the Holy Spirit is unable to bear its radiance, he falls prostrate on the ground and cries out in great fear and terror, as one who sees and experiences something beyond nature, above words or reason. He is then like a man whose entrails have been set on fire and, unable to bear the scorching flame, he is utterly devastated by it and deprived of all power to be in himself. But, through constant watering and cooling by tears, the flame of Divine desire in him burns all the brighter, producing yet more copious tears, and being washed by their flow he shines with ever greater radiance. And, when the whole of him is aflame and he becomes as light, the words of John the Divine are fulfilled: 'God unites with gods and is known by them' (God becomes united with those who are deified by Him and who know Him), and this, maybe, (is fulfilled in him) in the degree that he is already united with Him who is conjoined with him, and has proved himself as knowing Him.

71. Let no one be misled or mislead himself with empty words —before we have mourned and shed tears we have no repentance, nor a true desire to change, nor fear of God in our hearts. For we have not yet become conscious of our guilt nor judged ourselves, nor has our soul had the foretaste of the last judgment and eternal torment. For if we had judged ourselves, if we had experienced such movements of the heart, if we had had such feelings, we would have shed tears forthwith. Without this the hardness of our hearts cannot be softened, nor can our souls acquire spiritual humility, nor have we ourselves the power to become humble. A man who is not such, cannot unite with the Holy Spirit; without this union brought about by purification from all

passions he cannot know and contemplate God, nor can he be worthy of the secret teaching of the virtues of humility.

72. The first effect of mourning in God is humility; but later it brings unspeakable joy and gladness. Round humility in God grows hope of salvation. For the more a man feels with his whole soul that he is the most sinful of men, the more strongly hope and humility grow and blossom in his heart, and fill him with the conviction that, through humility, he will surely gain salvation.

73. The more a man descends into the depths of humility and condemns himself as one not worthy of salvation, the more he mourns and sheds streams of tears. The more he mourns and sheds tears, the more spiritual joy flows into his heart, and with it flows increasing hope which gives him the most complete certainty of salvation.

74. Every man should examine himself and watch himself with good judgment, lest he rely on hope alone without mourning and humility in God; nor on humility and tears unless followed by hope and spiritual joy.

75. There is a false humility which comes from laziness and negligence and from strong reproaches of conscience. Those who possess it often regard it as a cause of salvation. But in reality it is not so, for it brings no joy-giving tears which should be joined with it.

76. Mourning can also come without spiritual humility and those who mourn thus also think that such mourning purifies them from sin. But they deceive themselves, for they are deprived of the delight mysteriously born of the Spirit in the spiritual treasure-house—the repository of the soul—and are not fed by the Lord's goodness. Therefore they are apt to be inflamed by anger and are incapable of complete detachment from the world and what is in the world. Those who are not completely detached from it and do not whole-heartedly hate it, can never acquire a firm, undoubting hope of salvation. Such people will always be pushed hither and thither by doubts, for they have not founded their hope on rock.

77. Mourning has a twofold action: like water tears extinguish all the fire of passions and wash the soul clean of their foulness; and, again, through the presence of the Holy Spirit, it is like

fire bringing life, warming and inflaming the heart, and inciting it to love and desire of God.

78. Watch yourself and learn in yourself the effects of humility and mourning, seeing how they benefit you every hour. Beginners receive yet another benefit from them, namely, withdrawal from all earthly anxieties and attachments and renunciation of all men—parents, relatives and friends—freedom from cares and detachment from all things—money and everything else, not only to the last thread but even to one's own body.

79. Many people, the eye of whose soul is not cleansed (to enable them to see them direct) and who are unable to recognise men by their fruits, regard some as passionless and saintly who pretend outwardly to be virtuous but are inwardly otherwise, and who are often filled with all kinds of unrighteousness, envy, and the tumult and stench of sensory lusts. Such people are unable to distinguish true saints living in devotion to God, virtue and simplicity of heart from the rest of mankind, pass them by with disdain and regard them as nothing.

80. Such people take a showy babbler for a spiritual man and teacher, while they regard as a dumb and illiterate savage a man who is silent and refrains from idle talk.

81. Presumptuous men, sick with pride born of the devil, turn their backs on a man who speaks from the Holy Spirit, accusing him of presumption and pride, since his words wound them, rather than produce contrition or move their hearts. Conversely, they accept and praise a man who talks like a windmill, either from his belly or according to mere learning, although he misleads them in everything concerning the work of salvation. Thus there is no one among such people who could rightly see and discriminate either between men or as regards the work for salvation.

82. 'Blessed are the pure in heart,' says the Lord, 'for they shall see God' (Matt. v. 8). Not one or two, or even ten virtues make the heart pure, but all of them together, merged as it were into a single virtuousness, which has reached the last degree of perfection. But even then virtues alone cannot make the heart pure without the action and presence of the Holy Spirit. As a blacksmith can do nothing without the help of fire, however

skilled he may be in wielding his tools, so a man should do everything he can on his side to purify his heart, using virtues as tools for this purpose; but without the fire of the Spirit, everything he does will remain inactive and useless for his aim, for by itself what he does is powerless to cleanse the soul of its dirt and foulness.

83. In holy baptism we receive remission of sins, are freed from the ancestral curse and are illumined by the descent of the Holy Spirit; but it is not then that we receive the perfect grace, spoken of by the Apostle: 'I will dwell in them, and walk in them' (2 Cor. vi. 16). For this belongs to men perfectly grounded in faith who have proved it in their deeds. But if after baptism we go astray and commit bad and evil deeds, we completely lose this sanctification, and it is only after repentance, confession and tears that we again receive, according to our works, first, remission of our sins and, later, the sanctification of higher grace.

84. Through repentance the filth of former bad deeds is washed off, after which comes communion with the Holy Spirit, not simply, however, but through the power of faith, through disposition (a firm resolution to stand without falling) and through the humility of those who repent with all their soul; and not merely through a manifestation of such dispositions, but after receiving absolution from one's spiritual father and sponsor. Therefore it is good to repent every day, as the commandment demands. For the words: 'Repent ye: for the kingdom of heaven is at hand' (Matt. iii. 2) impose upon us a practice not limited to a definite time but for always.

85. The grace of the Holy Spirit is given to souls who are the brides of Christ, as a sign or token of betrothal. As without betrothal a maiden cannot be sure that she will one day be united with her husband in bonds of matrimony, so a soul will never acquire a definite assurance of becoming for ever united with its Lord and God, or becoming mysteriously and ineffably married to Him and enjoying His inaccessible beauty, without first being granted betrothal, or a token of His grace, and without consciously possessing Him within itself.

86. As a betrothal cannot be firm until the marriage contract is signed by trustworthy witnesses, so the light of grace is not

secure before the practice of commandments and the acquisition of virtues. For this practice of commandments and virtues is to spiritual betrothal as the witnesses who sign the marriage contract. Through them every man who is to be saved acquires complete security in betrothal (that is, the grace of the Holy Spirit).

87. First the conditions of the marriage contract are, as it were, written down through the practice of commandments, then they are sealed and signed by virtues; and then Christ, the bridegroom, gives the bride—the soul—a ring, that is, the betrothal in the Spirit.

88. Just as before marriage the bride receives from the bridegroom only a token of betrothal, expecting to obtain the agreed settlement and other gifts only after the marriage, so the bride of Christ—whether the Church of the faithful or the soul of each one of us—first receives from Christ, the bridegroom, only the betrothal of the Spirit, and hopes to receive eternal blessings and the kingdom of heaven after leaving this world; and the soul is assured of this by the token of betrothal which reveals this to her as in a mirror and confirms the sure future acquisition of everything covenanted between itself and its Lord and God.

89. If, annoyed that the bridegroom stays away too long, or because he puts off the wedding for a time, being occupied with other business, the bride repudiates his love and the marriage contract, or cancels it, or tears it up, she immediately deprives herself of all the expectations which promised her so much from the bridegroom. The same thing is wont to happen with the soul. For if anyone engaged in spiritual struggle says to himself: 'How much more must I suffer (bear all kinds of privations)?' and begins to neglect spiritual struggle and labours, ceases to follow the commandments and abandons constant repentance, he will cancel and tear up his contract with the Lord. He will then be immediately deprived of the token of betrothal (grace) and will lose all hope in God.

90. A bride who gives to another man the love due to her betrothed and goes to live with him, openly or in secret, not only loses everything promised her by the bridegroom, but, according to law, must expect a rightful punishment and disgrace. So it happens with us. For if a soul openly or secretly transfers

its love for the bridegroom—Christ—to some other object and lets its heart be possessed thereby, it becomes hateful and distasteful to the Bridegroom and is unworthy of uniting with Him. For He said: 'I love them that love me' (Prov. viii. 17).

91. These are the signs by which each man should distinguish whether he has received the betrothal of the Spirit from the Bridegroom—our Lord Jesus Christ. If he has received it, he must strive to hold and preserve it; if he has not been granted it as yet, he must try to acquire it by right actions, useful works and warm repentance and later preserve it by obeying commandments and multiplying his virtues.

92. The betrothal of the Holy Spirit is inexplicable even for those who have been granted it, for it is comprehended incomprehensibly, is constrained unconstrainedly, is seen invisibly; it animates, speaks in and moves him who has acquired it; it flies away from its secret abode, wherein it is sealed, and is unexpectedly found there again. This proves that when it comes it is not permanently and for ever, and when it departs, it is not never to return. Therefore if a man who has acquired it does not have it (palpably present) it is as though he has it, and when he has it it is as though he has it not.

93. Like a man who, standing in a dark room with all windows and doors fastened, opens a window and the light streaming in suddenly envelops him in such a brilliant glare that, unable to bear it, he closes his eyes, wraps up his head and hides; so if a soul, totally imprisoned in the sensory world, lets its mind peep out into the supersensory world, as out of a window, it becomes bathed in the radiance of betrothal with the Holy Spirit, which is within it, and unable to bear the brilliance of the uncovering of Divine light, it immediately trembles in its mind, hides within itself and flees as though into a house, seeking cover in the sensory and the human.

94. 'Can a man take fire in his bosom, and his clothes not be burned?' (Prov. vi. 27) says the wise Solomon. And I say: can he, who has in his heart the Divine fire of the Holy Spirit burning naked, not be set on fire, not shine and glitter and not take on the radiance of the Deity in the degree of his purification and penetration by fire? For penetration by fire follows upon purification

of the heart, and again purification of heart follows upon penetration by fire, that is, inasmuch as the heart is purified, so it receives Divine grace, and again inasmuch as it receives grace, so is it purified. When this is completed (that is, purification of heart and acquisition of grace have attained their fulness and perfection), through grace a man becomes wholly a god.

95. A house roof is held up by the foundations and the rest of the building, and the foundations with the rest of the building are laid to hold the roof—since both are necessary and useful—and neither is the roof built without the foundations and the rest of the house, nor can foundations and walls without roof make a building fit to live in. So it is with the soul: the grace of the Holy Spirit is preserved by keeping the commandments, and the keeping of commandments is the foundation laid for receiving the gift of God's grace. Neither does the grace of the Holy Spirit remain in us without our obeying the commandments, nor can obeying the commandments be useful and salutary without Divine grace.

96. A house left without roof through the negligence of the builder is good for nothing, and causes the builder to be derided. In the same way a man who, through keeping the commandments, has laid the foundations and has built high walls of virtues, if he does not receive the grace of the Holy Spirit and does not see it and sense it in his soul, is still imperfect and is an object of pity to the perfect. The causes of his being deprived of grace may be twofold: either because he has neglected repentance or because, overawed by the prospect of completely acquiring all virtues as too great an undertaking, he has omitted some of them which, although apparently unimportant, are nevertheless quite essential for the final construction and completion of the house of virtues, for without them the house cannot be roofed in by the grace of the Holy Spirit.

97. If the Son of God and God came down on earth in order to reconcile us—His enemies—with His Father by His mediation, and to conjoin us with Himself palpably by means of His Holy and consubstantial Spirit, and if a man is deprived of this grace, what other can he receive? It is obvious that such a man is not reconciled with the Father, neither is he conjoined with the Son through the grace of the Holy Spirit.

98. A man who becomes a participant of the Divine Spirit is freed from all passionate lusts, but is not liberated from all natural bodily needs. Therefore, freed from the bonds of passionate lust, having tasted immortal glory and sweetness and being conjoined with it, he is constantly urged to soar on high and be with God, not allowing himself even for a moment to retreat from contemplation and insatiable enjoyment of Him. But being shackled by body and corruption, he is torn by the latter away from on high, is pulled down and returns to earth. Then he experiences the same grief at parting from what is on high as the soul of a sinner probably experiences at parting from the body.

99. As, for a man who loves life and his body, and is attached to lusts and the world, parting with these objects of his love is death; so for the lover of purity, of the incorporeal God and of virtue even a short separation of his heart from them is true death. A man who sees physical light, and then closes his eyes or has them closed by someone else, is annoyed and saddened and cannot bear it for long, especially if he was looking at some necessary and wonderful objects. It is much more so for a man who is illumined by the Holy Spirit and apprehends clearly, both directly and mentally, when awake and asleep, the blessings which the eye has not seen, the ear has not heard, the heart has not felt, and which God's angels themselves wish to penetrate. Will not he grieve and suffer if something tears him away from their contemplation? For it would truly mean death for him and deprivation of eternal life.

100. Some praise life in a desert, others life in monasteries, still others a place of authority among people, to instruct and teach them and organise churches where many may find food for body and soul. I would not wish to give preference to any of these, nor to say that one is worthy of praise and another of censure. In all ways of life, blessed is the life lived for God and according to God in all actions and works.

101. Ordinary human life is built up and maintained by an interaction between various life undertakings, crafts and arts—that is, one man does one thing, another does another and offers it for the use of his fellow men; thus people live by giving and taking and so satisfy their bodily needs. The same can be seen in

spiritual life: one practises one virtue, another another; one chooses one path of life, another a different one, but all of them together pursue one aim, mutually helping one another.

102. The aim of all those who live in God is to please our Lord Jesus Christ and become reconciled with God the Father through receiving the Holy Spirit, thus securing their salvation, for in this consists the salvation of every soul. If this aim and this activity is lacking, all other labour is useless and all other striving is vain. Every path of life which does not lead to this is without profit.

103. A man who has renounced the world and retired to a mountain to lead a life of silence, and who writes thence vain letters to those remaining in the world, pandering to some, flattering and cajoling others, is like a man who, having divorced his unfaithful, worthless and malicious wife and having gone far away in order to eradicate her from his memory, forgets the aim which made him go away to a mountain and, filled with desire, writes to those who hold concourse with or rather who are being defiled by his wife, and panders to them. Although such a man is not defiled in his body, he is polluted in his heart and mind, as though willingly lending his support to their liaison with his wife.

104. As men living in the world and purifying their senses and hearts from every sinful lust are worthy of praise and approbation, so men living in mountains and caves and yearning for praise and approbation of men are deserving of blame and abomination. In the eyes of God Who sees our hearts such men are equal to those who commit adultery. For a man who passionately wishes his life, name and works to be rumoured in the world commits adultery in the eyes of God just like the old people of Judea, according to David.

105. A man who has renounced the world and everything in it with unfailing faith, believes that the merciful and generous God will accept those who come to Him repentant; and he knows that from dishonour God leads His slaves to honour, from extreme poverty to riches, glorifies them through abuses and degradations, through death makes them heirs and participators of eternal life. Such a man strives to go forward by these means (that is, by means of dishonour, poverty and so forth), like a thirsty stag, towards the immortal spring; and by them to ascend

on high, as by a ladder. On this ladder angels ascend and descend to help the climbers, while God stands above it awaiting such labours and efforts as are within our power; not that God rejoices at seeing us labouring, but, being merciful, He wishes to give us our reward as if it were our due.

106. God does not allow those who strive towards Him with all their zeal to fall completely off this ladder, but seeing them exhausted, helps and supports them, stretching out the hand of His power and leading them to Himself. Thus He helps them, both openly and secretly, with and without their knowledge, until, having climbed the ladder, they approach Him and, totally uniting with Him, forget all earthly things and abide with Him— whether in bodies or without bodies I do not know—enjoying unspeakable blessings.

107. It is right that we should, *first of all*, bend our necks to the yoke of Christ's commandments, neither swerving aside, retreating nor lagging behind, but walking in them uprightly and zealously even unto death, for ever renewing ourselves and making of ourselves a fresh paradise of God, until, through the Holy Spirit, the Son and the Father enter into us, and dwell in us. It is only then, when we have thus acquired Him as our indweller and teacher, if He commands any of us (to undertake some service) and entrusts us with some task, that we should be committed to this service; and we must then perform it as the Lord wills. But it is wrong to aspire to this service prematurely, or to accept it when it is offered by people (of themselves); one should abide in the commandments of our Lord and God and await His command (to undertake one service or another).

108. If after being entrusted with some service in Divine things we perform it worthily, and are thereupon directed by the Spirit to pass to another service, or activity, or work, we must not resist. For God does not wish us either to be idle or always to keep to the activity with which we began. He wishes us, in our progress, to advance further and further towards attainment of perfection, but always guided by His will instead of our own.

109. He who wishes to kill his own will must do the will of God—instead of his own will introduce God's will into himself, inculcate and implant it in his heart. Moreover, he must watch

carefully to see whether what is inculcated and implanted is making good root and sprouting. If it has sprouted and has formed a stem, and the stem is cut for grafting, he must make sure that the scion grows on to the stock and the two become one tree, and that the scion blossoms and produces beautiful, sweet fruits. Neither must he be ignorant of the soil which has first received the seed, nor of the deep roots from which this ineffable and inscrutable life-giving plant firmly springs.

110. If a man cuts off his will through fear of God, then, without his being aware of it or knowing how it happens, God grants him His will and ineradicably plants it in that man's heart, at the same time opening the eyes of his heart so that he can know it (that is know that it is God's will), and gives him the power to fulfil it. This is done by the grace of the Holy Spirit, and without it nothing is done.

111. If you have received absolution from all your sins, whether simply through the mystery of repentance and confession alone, or whether you have taken on the holy angelic Schema at the same time; what love, what gratitude and humility must it not bring you, that, not only are you freed from the untold tortures you deserved, but are even granted sonship, glory and the kingdom of heaven?

Always turn this in your mind and remember it, watch and be ready lest you dishonour your Creator, Who has thus honoured you, and has forgiven you your countless sins, and strive to honour and glorify Him in everything you do, in order that He Who has thus honoured you above all visible creatures (by creating you man) should reward you with still greater honours (by grace), and should name you His true friend.

112. In as far as the soul is higher than the body, so is a wise man better and higher than the rest of the world. Look not at the mightiness of creations existing in the world, thinking that they are greater than you, O man; but seeing the grace bestowed upon you, and realising the rank of your intelligence and the glory of your soul, sing praises to God Who has honoured you above all visible creation.

113. Let us look and learn how to glorify God. The only way we can glorify Him is as the Son has glorified Him. But by that,

by which the Son has glorified His Father, was He also glorified by the Father. Let us then strive to do what the Son has done, so as to glorify our Father Who is in heaven, and Who deigned so to call Himself, and be ourselves glorified by Him through the glory of the Son 'which' the Son 'had with' Him 'before the world was' (John xvii. 5). This is the cross—to become dead to the whole world, to suffer sorrows, temptations and other passions of Christ; in bearing this cross with complete patience, we imitate Christ's passion and thus glorify our God the Father as His sons in grace and co-heirs of Christ.

114. A soul which is not completely freed of worldly habits and attachments to visible things in the very feelings and dispositions of the heart cannot be impervious to the sorrows, wrongful accusations and temptations which assail it from demons and from men. Shackled by attachment to human things, it is vulnerable to loss of money, grieves deeply when deprived of things, and suffers severely from bodily hurts.

115. A man who has wrenched his soul away from fondness and attachment to sensory things and has joined it closely to God, is not only indifferent to any things and money he has, and feels no grief at their loss, as though they were not his but someone else's, but gladly and thankfully suffers pain, even to his body, always realising, in the words of the divine Apostle, that 'though our outward man perish, yet the inward man is renewed day by day' (2 Cor. iv. 16). It is impossible to bear gladly the afflictions sent by God in any other way. This requires perfect knowledge and spiritual wisdom. Lacking these, a man always walks in the darkness of hopelessness and ignorance, having no means of seeing the light of patience and consolation (of prayer).

116. No man, wise in his own opinion, because he has studied all the sciences and is learned in external wisdom, will ever penetrate God's mysteries or see them unless he first humbles himself and becomes foolish in his heart, repudiating his self-opinion together with his acquirements of learning. For a man who acts thus and follows with undaunted faith those who are wise in things Divine, is guided by them and with them enters into the city of the living God, and, taught and enlightened by the Holy

Spirit, sees and knows things which no one else can see or know. Thus he becomes taught of God.

117. Pupils of the sages of this world consider those taught of God foolish, whereas it is they who are truly foolish, since they are trained only in external, distorted wisdom; they are those whom, according to the divine Apostle, 'God made foolish' (1 Cor. i. 20), and about whom it is said: 'This wisdom descendeth not from above, but is earthly, sensual, devilish' (James iii. 15). Being outside the compass of the Divine light, such people cannot see the miracles it contains, and regard those as beguiled who, dwelling in this light, see and teach what they see. But in reality it is the former who are beguiled and who have never tasted of Divine blessings.

118. Even now there live among us men who are free from passions, saintly and filled with Divine light, who have so mortified their earthly limbs, cleansing them of all impurity and passionate lust, that not only does no thought of wrong action ever enter their mind, but they even allow no interference with their passionless state when others incite them to wrong. Even those who treat them with contempt, and refuse to believe them when they hear them teach about Divine things in the wisdom of the Spirit, would have recognised them if they had clearly understood the Divine words they read and sing daily. For if they knew the Divine Scriptures perfectly, they would believe in the blessings promised and granted us by God. But since they do not participate in those blessings, owing to their self-opinion and negligence, they condemn and distrust those who have been granted participation in them and teach of them.

119. The only reason why men filled with Divine grace, and perfect in knowledge and higher wisdom, desire to go out into the world to meet people living there, is to dispose men towards good works by reminding them of the Divine commandments, thus giving them a chance of earning a certain reward; if, of course, people will hear them, listen and be convinced. For these others, not being guided by the Spirit of God, walk in the dark, not knowing whither they go and whether or not they make progress in practising one or another commandment; so, men who live in grace come to them with reminders, wishing

to help them and hoping that one day they will accept the true teaching of the Holy Spirit, will lift themselves out of the self-opinion which possesses them and, listening sincerely to the will of God, without hypocrisy or self-praise, will repent in order to obey it and, in this way, become participants in some spiritual gift. If a holy man fails thus to profit the laymen he visits, then, weeping over the hardness and blindness of their hearts, he returns to his cell and prays day and night for their salvation. For men who are constantly with God and are filled with every blessing can have no other care.

120. What is the aim of the incarnate dispensation of God's Word, preached in all the Holy Scriptures but which we, who read them, do not know? The only aim is that, having entered into what is our own, we should participate in what is His. The Son of God has become Son of Man in order to make us, men, sons of God, raising our race by grace to what He is Himself by nature, granting us birth from above through the grace of the Holy Spirit and leading us straightway to the kingdom of heaven, or rather, granting us this kingdom of heaven within us (Luke xvii. 21), in order that we should not merely be fed by the hope of entering it, but entering into full possession thereof should cry: our 'life is hid with Christ in God' (Col. iii. 3).

121. Baptism does not destroy our self-will and wilfulness but it frees us from the tyranny of the devil, who can no longer rule over us against our will. After baptism, it begins to lie within our will either of our own accord to obey the commandments of our Lord and God Jesus Christ, in Whose name we were baptised, or to deviate from the right path, and return again to the devil, our adversary and foe.

122. Those who, after holy baptism, obey the wishes of the evil one, and do what pleases him, are estranged from the womb of holy baptism, as David said: 'The wicked are estranged from the womb' (Ps. lviii. 3). For the nature of a man as he is created is not changed or transformed into something different. Being created good by God (for God created nothing evil), and remaining unchanged in nature and substance as he was created, man does what he wishes and desires according to his free will, whether it be good or evil. As a knife does not change its nature

but remains steel whether it is used for good or evil, so a man acts and does what he wills, without stepping out of his nature.

123. A man is not saved by having once shown mercy to someone, although, if he scorns someone but once, he merits eternal fire. For 'hungred' and 'thirsty' is said not of one occasion, not of one day, but of the whole of life. In the same way 'ye gave me meat', 'ye gave me drink', 'ye clothed me', and so on, does not indicate one incident, but a constant attitude to everyone. Our Lord Jesus Christ said that He Himself accepts such mercy from His slaves (in the person of the needy).

124. A man who gave alms to a hundred of the needy but, while able to help others too, and to give food and drink to many, denied it to some who begged and implored him, will be judged by Christ as one who refused Him food. For, in all these, it is still Him Whom we feed in every beggar.

125. If a man has one day provided for all the bodily needs of the poor, but, being able to do so on the next day, neglects some of his brethren and leaves them to die of hunger, thirst and cold —then he has neglected and left to die Him Who said: 'Inasmuch as ye have done it unto one of the least of these my brethren, ye have done it unto me' (Matt. xxv. 40).

126. Our Lord was pleased to assume the likeness of every poor man and compared Himself to every poor man in order that no man who believes in Him should exalt himself over his brother, but, seeing his Lord in his brother, should consider himself less and worse than his brother, just as he is less than his Creator; and should take the poor man in and honour him, and be ready to exhaust all his means in helping him, just as our Lord Jesus Christ exhausted His blood for our salvation.

127. A man who is commanded to love his neighbour as himself should of course do so not for one day, but for his whole life. Likewise a man commanded to give to everyone who asks is under this commandment for his lifetime. In the same way, he who wishes good from others, is required to do the same to them.

128. A man who loves his neighbour as himself cannot allow himself to possess anything more than his neighbour; so that, if he has possessions, and does not distribute them without envy until he becomes poor and is himself like his neighbours, he does

not fulfil the Lord's commandment exactly. In the same way, a man who has a mite or a piece of bread and who sends away a beggar empty-handed, or who, refusing himself to do for his neighbour what the latter wants, sends him to someone else, is not a man who wants to give to everyone who asks. Thus, a man who gave food, drink and clothes to every poor man and helped him in all other ways, but who disdained and refused only one of them, will still be regarded as one who has disdained Christ our Lord when He hungred and thirsted.

129. How can some men confine Christ our Lord to one poor man when He is indivisibly divided and exists totally in every poor man? Let us suppose that a hundred beggars are as one Christ, for Christ remains perfectly indivisible. Then if a man gives a coin to ninety-nine poor men, but reviles, chastises and sends away one other empty-handed, to whom do you think he does this? Of course to Christ Himself Who has said, says and will always say: 'Inasmuch as ye have done it unto one of the least of these my brethren, ye have done it unto me' (Matt. xxv. 40).

130. It is clear from the aforesaid that the Lord accepts and takes everything done for our poor neighbours as done for Him Himself. And His words 'ye have done it unto me' are not limited only to those to whom we were unkind, or whom we wronged, or whose possessions we have appropriated, or to whom we have done other harm, but include also those whom we have disdained.—This latter is alone sufficient for our condemnation for, in disdaining them, we disdain Christ Himself.

131. All this may appear too hard to people and they may think it right to say to themselves: 'Who can strictly follow all this, satisfying and feeding everyone and leaving no one unsatisfied?' Let them listen to Paul who says clearly: 'For the love of Christ constraineth us; because we thus judge, that if one died for all, then were all dead' (2 Cor. v. 14).

132. As the principal commandments embrace all the particular commandments included in them, so the principal virtues contain in themselves all the particular virtues they embrace. For example, a man who sells his possessions and distributes them among the poor, thus becoming poor himself, has fulfilled

at one stroke all the particular commandments relating to this. Therefore he no longer needs to give to him who asks or to refrain from turning his back on him who wants to borrow from him. In the same way a man who has achieved constant prayer has thereby fulfilled all the commandments referring to prayer and no longer needs to praise the Lord seven times a day, or in the evening and morning and at midday, for he has already fulfilled all the rule of singing and saying prayers at definite times and hours. Likewise a man, who consciously possesses in himself God the Giver of knowledge to men, has already studied all the Holy Scriptures and has collected, like fruit, all the benefit their reading can afford. So he no longer needs to read books. For what need can a man have of reading books, if he is in converse with Him Who has inspired the writers of Holy Scriptures, and if all His ineffable mysteries are indelibly inscribed within him? On the contrary, he himself will be for others an inspired book containing mysteries both old and new, inscribed in him by the finger of God, since he has accomplished everything and in God is at rest from all his works—this is the height of perfection.

134. Repentance is not fitting to one who has the Word of God, neither is having the Word of God fitting to a penitent. For having the Word of God is as far removed from penitence as east is from west. A man in a state of repentance, if he performs in truth the works of penitence, is like a sick man who lives day after day in his ailments, or like a beggar clothed in tatters and begging for alms. But one who has the Word of God is like a man, who spends his days in the king's palace, clothed in bright princely garments, is always near to his king, speaks with him and hears from him clearly and directly his wishes and commands. (Having the Word of God means the state of contemplation and not abstract theology.)

135. Increasing knowledge of God decreases knowledge of all else. In other words, the more a man knows God the less he knows of other matters. And not only this, but he begins to realise more and more clearly that neither does he know God. The more radiantly God shines in a man's spirit, the more He becomes invisible, and the more a man's senses soar above the senses, the less he can sense all that is without. But how can one

call 'sense' a sense which knows not wherein it resides—neither where nor what it is—and is utterly incapable of learning or understanding it? And indeed how can the senses know what the eye has not seen, nor the ear heard, and what never entered a man's heart?

136. He Who gives us that which is above the senses, also endows us, through the grace of the Holy Spirit, with another sense which is above the senses, in order that we may clearly and purely apprehend His gifts and blessings, which are above the senses.

137. A man who is deaf to the Word of God is altogether deaf to His voice; and conversely, a man who hears the words of God is capable of hearing any word of God. Such a man hears no one except those who speak (teach) by the grace of the Word, and it is not them he hears, but only the word which their voice utters voicelessly.

138. When you are down—in earthly things, do not investigate what is on high—heavenly things; and ascending on high do not be curious about things below before you have reached the summit, lest you slip and fall down, or rather, lest you remain below imagining that you are moving upwards.

139. A man enriched by heavenly treasure, namely the advent of Christ Who makes His abode in him, as He said: 'My Father will love him, and we will come unto him, and make our abode with him' (John xiv. 23), knows in his soul (by experience, by consciousness, by feeling), what joy he has received and what great treasure he possesses in the royal treasure-house of his heart. Speaking with God as friend with friend, he stands daringly in the presence of Him Who abides within him in unapproachable light.

140. Blessed is the man who believes what I have said. Thrice blessed is he who strives by holy works to gain this knowledge (to know it by experience). A man who, by action and contemplation, has attained to the height of such a state and has reached God Himself as a son, is, to say no more, an angel.

141. A man standing on the seashore sees the immense expanse of water, but his eye can embrace only a small part and cannot reach its limit. In the same way a man who, through con-

templation, is given to see the limitless ocean of Divine glory and to see God Himself with the eyes of his mind, sees God and the infinite vastness of His glory, though not the whole as it really is, but only as much as is possible for him.

142. As a man standing on the seashore not only sees the sea but can also walk into it as often as he likes; so is it with men who have reached spiritual perfection: they can also enter the Divine light when they wish, contemplating it and participating in it consciously in proportion to their works, their efforts and the aspirations of their desire.

143. While a man standing on the seashore is on dry land, he can see around him and encompass with his eyes the expanse of the sea. But if he begins to wade into the waters and to plunge into them, the more deeply he enters the less he sees what is outside. So it is with the participants of Divine light: the greater the knowledge of God they attain, the greater, correspondingly, becomes their nescience (of everything outside God).

144. A man who wades into the sea to his knees or to his waist can clearly see everything outside the water; but when he goes into the depths and becomes submerged he can no longer see things outside and knows only one thing, that the whole of him is in the water. The same happens to those whose spiritual achievement grows, and who ascend towards perfect vision and contemplation.

145. When men progressing in spiritual perfection are enlightened and illumined in their minds, they have inward vision of the glory of the Lord and are inwardly taught by Divine grace knowledge after knowledge, ascending from contemplation of existing things to knowledge of things which are indeed above everything existing.

146. Men approaching perfection, who as yet see only partially the infinity (of spiritual things) and are aware of the incomprehensibility of what they see, are filled with awe and wonder. But the more they mysteriously enter into the light of knowledge, the more they are aware of their own weakness. What appears to them somewhat darkly, as in a mirror of divination, only partially illumines the mind so occupied. But when it is pleased to reveal itself in a fuller light and unites, through

participation, with the man it illumines, drawing him completely into itself, so that the whole of him is in the depths of the Spirit as in the depths of a measureless sea of light, then the man is ineffably plunged into total nescience as one who has ascended to a place where all is beyond knowledge.

147. Our mind is pure and simple, so when it is stripped of every alien thought, it enters the pure, simple, Divine light and becomes quite encompassed and hidden therein, and can no more meet there anything but the light in which it is. It finds there nothing to move it to thought of aught else, but abides within the Divine light, and may not look out. This is shown by the saying that God is light—the highest light. Therefore when the aforesaid comes to pass, it is followed by a quietude which contemplates all.

148. The mobile mind becomes motionless and unthinking—without thoughts—when it is entirely encompassed by the Divine cloud and light, at the same time remaining in conscious contemplation and apprehension, feeding on the blessings which surround it. The depths of the Holy Spirit are not as the depths of the sea; they are the living waters of eternal life. Everything in these depths of the Holy Spirit is beyond understanding or explanation. The mind enters therein after relinquishing everything visible and mental, and moves and turns motionlessly among those incomprehensible things, living a life more than life, being a light while yet in the light, though no light when in itself. Then it sees not itself but Him Who is above it and, being inwardly transformed by the glory surrounding it, loses all knowledge of itself.

149. A man who has attained the final degree of perfection is dead and yet not dead, but infinitely more alive in God with Whom he lives for he no longer lives by himself, as the Apostle says: 'I live; yet not I, but Christ liveth in me' (Gal. ii. 20). He is also blind, yet not blind: he sees not with his natural eyes, for he is above all natural vision, receiving new eyes, infinitely better than his natural eyes, and through these he looks above nature. He is inactive and at rest, as one who has come to the end of all action of his own. He is without thought, since he has become one with Him Who is above all thought, and has come

to rest where movement of mind can have no place, that is, movement of recollection, thought or reflection. He can neither know nor understand the incomprehensible and the miraculous, yet he finds perfect rest therein through this blessed stillness of the senses; unquestioning, he enjoys ineffable blessings, but with sure, definite apprehension.

150. A man who has not been granted such measure of perfection and has not attained to such blessings, should blame himself alone and not say in self-justification that such a thing is impossible, nor that it is possible for us to have perfection, but a perfection of which we are unaware. He should know from the testimony of the Holy Scriptures that such a thing is possible, that it actually occurs in its full force and is accompanied with perfect awareness and consciousness, but that, through neglect and the transgression of God's commandments, every man deprives himself of these blessings according to the degree of his negligence.

151. From the first God created two worlds, the visible and the invisible, and has made a king to reign over the visible who bears within himself the characteristic features of both worlds—one in his visible half and the other in his invisible half—in his soul and his body. Two suns shine in these worlds, one visible and another intellectual. In the visible world of the senses there is the sun, and in the invisible world of the intellect there is God, Who is and is called the sun of truth. The physical world and everything in it is illumined by the physical and visible sun; but the world of the intellect and those who are in it are illumined and enlightened by the sun of truth in the intellect. Moreover, physical things are illumined by the physical sun, and things of the intellect by the sun of the intellect separately from one another, for they are not mixed with or merged into one another —neither the physical with the intellectual nor the intellectual with the physical.

152. Of all visible and invisible creation man alone is created dual. He has a body composed of four elements, the senses and breath; and he has a soul, invisible, unsubstantial, incorporeal joined to the body in an ineffable and unknown manner; they interpenetrate and yet are not compounded, combine and yet do

not coalesce. This is what man is: an animal both mortal and immortal, both visible and invisible, both sensory and intellectual, capable of seeing the visible and knowing the invisible creation. As each of the two suns influences his own world separately, so they affect separately each side of a man: one illumines the body and the other the soul, each giving of its own light to its own side, whether richly or sparingly according to what it can receive.

153. The physical sun is seen but does not see; the sun of the intellect is seen by the worthy and itself sees everyone, especially those who look upon it. The physical sun does not speak and endows no one with the gift and power of speech; but the sun of the intellect both speaks to its friends and endows everyone with the gift and power of speech. The physical sun, illumining the physical garden, merely dries the moisture of the soil by the warmth of its rays, but does not fertilise the soil or feed the seeds and plants. The sun of the intellect, when it shines in the soul, does both these things: it dries the moisture of passions, at the same time cleansing the soul from the filth and stench they have produced, and fertilises the inner soil of the soul (making it rich) with Divine grace, and feeds the plants of the virtues so that they gradually grow and prosper.

154. On rising, the physical sun lights up the physical world and everything in it—people, animals and the rest—pouring its light equally over all; it reigns at midday and then hides again, leaving in darkness the places over which it shone. But the sun of the intellect, once it begins to shine, shines always, totally and immaterially contained in everything and at the same time remaining apart from its creatures, inseparably separated from them, since it is wholly in everything and at the same time is in none of the creatures exclusively (for at the same time it is elsewhere also). The whole of it is in the visible and the whole of it is in the invisible; it is totally present everywhere and yet exclusively present nowhere.

155. Christ is the beginning, the middle and the end. He is in those who are the first, in the middle and the last, and as He is in the first, so He is in all. For Him there is no difference between them, as there is for Him 'neither Jew nor Greek, there

is neither bond nor free, there is neither male nor female: for ye are all one in Christ Jesus' (Gal. iii. 28).

156. Sacred love, permeating all from first to last, from head to foot, joins all to itself, links them up, ties together and unites, renders them strong and unshakable. In experience, it reveals itself to each man as one and the same. It is God with Whom the last may be first and the first may be as the last.

157. As the immaterial hierarchies of heavenly powers are illumined by God in just sequence, so that the Divine light penetrates from the first hierarchy to the second, from the second to the third and so to them all; so the saints, illumined by holy angels, are linked together and united by the bond of the Holy Spirit and thus become akin to them and of equal rank. Moreover, the saints—those who appear from generation to generation, from time to time, following the saints who preceded them— become linked with their predecessors through obedience to Divine commandments and, endowed with Divine grace, become filled with the same light. In such a sequence all of them together form a kind of golden chain, each saint being a separate link in this chain, joined to the first by faith, right actions and love; a chain which has its strength in God and can hardly be broken.

158. A man who does not express desire to link himself to the latest of the saints (in time) in all love and humility owing to a certain distrust of him, will never be linked with the preceding saints and will not be admitted to their succession, even though he thinks he possesses all possible faith and love for God and for all His saints. He will be cast out of their midst, as one who refused to take humbly the place allotted to him by God before all time, and to link himself to that latest saint (in time) as God had disposed.

159. Inasmuch as God wishes to be known by us, so He reveals Himself; and inasmuch as He reveals Himself, so is He seen and known by those who are worthy. But no one can be worthy of this experience until he unites with the Holy Spirit, having previously acquired by labour and sweat a heart that is pure, simple and contrite.

160. A man who offers to teach rhetoric and philosophy to someone who is only learning his alphabet, far from doing him

any good, will only distract him from what he is learning, and make him forget what he has learned, for his mind will be unable to cope with these subjects. In the same way, a man who discourses about the last degrees of perfection to beginners, and especially to the more lazy ones, far from bringing them any profit will only make them lose ground. For as soon as they look up at the heights of virtue and see how far they are from the summit, they will think it impossible for them to reach it, and will give up even the few useful works they had already begun, as being useless, and be plunged into hopelessness.

161. When men, ruled and swayed by passions, hear that a man who is perfect in God considers himself more impure than any man, any animal or any beast and that he rejoices at being defamed, blesses and praises those who slander him, bears persecutions with patience and prays God with tears and heart-felt sorrow for his enemies, they refuse at first to believe it, pretending and imagining themselves to be like him. Then, being refuted by the Holy Scriptures, and disproved by the saints, who had demonstrated all this in practice, they confess they cannot reach such a degree of perfection. But when they hear that if they do not behave thus they cannot be saved, then, unwilling to relinquish sinful habits and repent of their sins, they fall into hopelessness.

162. Where there is deep humility, there also are copious tears; and where these are, thither too comes the Holy Spirit. When the grace of the worshipful Spirit comes, the man under its influence is filled with all purity and saintliness; then he sees God and God too looks on him. For the Lord says: 'To this man will I look, even to him that is poor and of a contrite spirit, and trembleth at my word' (Is. lxvi. 2).

163. A man may conquer passions but he cannot uproot them. He is given the power not to do evil, but not the power not to think of it. Yet real righteousness not only means not doing evil, but also not thinking of it. He who thinks of evil has no purity. For how can a heart be pure in a man who is defiled by unclean thoughts, as a mirror is dimmed by dust?

164. In my opinion, a man has a pure heart, if he is not only untroubled and unburdened by any passion but even cannot think of anything evil or worldly, supposing he wished to, and only

holds on to remembrance of God with irresistible love. For if nothing interferes with its contemplation, the mind—the eye of the soul—sees God purely in a pure light.

165. I call a man passionless when he not only refuses to follow the dictates of passions, but is even a stranger to lusting after them. And not only that, but when his mind is stripped of the very thought of them, and freely soars above the heavens as it wills, reaching beyond the limits of the visible and the sensory, it is as though the senses were completely closed and the mind were floating in the domain of the supersensory, but yet keeping its senses just as the eagle keeps his feathers (when floating in the sky).

166. The mind does not manifest its actions without the senses, nor the senses without the mind.

167. A heart is and is called pure when it finds in itself no worldly thought, but wholly cleaves to God, and is so united with Him that it no longer remembers anything worldly, either sad or joyful, but remains in contemplation, soaring up to the third heaven, enters paradise and sees the blessings promised to the saints as their inheritance; and then accordingly it reflects eternal blessings as far as is possible for human weakness. This serves as a true sign of purity of heart, by which every man can determine the degree of his purity and see himself as in a mirror.

168. As a man who is outside cannot see people inside a house, so a man who has crucified himself and died to the world has no feelings for the things and doings of the world.

169. As a dead body has no feelings either for the living or for the dead lying with it, so a man who by the grace of the Holy Spirit has left the world, and is with God, has no feelings for the world nor attachment to worldly things, although he is subject to the needs of his body.

170. There is a death which precedes physical death and a resurrection of souls which precedes the resurrection of bodies —by means of deeds, experience, power and truth. For when mortal wisdom is destroyed by immortal mind and death is banished by life, then the soul, as it were risen from the dead, sees itself clearly, as one awakened from sleep, and knows the true God Who has resurrected it. Thinking of Him and giving thanks to Him it rises above the limits of the senses and of the

whole world, filled with unspeakable delight, and thus stills every mortal movement.

171. Some things are brought (into the life of salvation) by ourselves, others are given us by God. The more we are purified by our own sweat and efforts after God, the more we shine with Divine light, and the more we are cleansed by our own tears, offering the tears from ourselves and receiving from God the light of contrition in their place.

172. Many who have brought in what is from themselves have not received what is wont to be given by God. This is clear from what Cain and Esau did and had to suffer. For if a man does not bring in what is his own with right thought, with righteous disposition, with faith and great humility, he cannot expect God to look on him with kindness, and accept his offering; and having refused the offering, it is impossible to expect Him to grant what He is wont to grant in such a case.

173. For the saints, the world and the people in it are dead. Therefore, just as people of the world, seeing, do not see the good works of saintly men, and, hearing, can in no way understand the Divine words offered them by the grace of the Holy Spirit, so spiritual and saintly men cannot see the evil deeds of evil men of the world, or understand their passionate speech. In other words, seeing, they also do not see what is in the world and, hearing about people in the world, are as if they did not hear, since in such a Divine state and disposition they have no organ of sense for it. Thus there is no communication between the spiritual and the worldly, or between the worldly and the spiritual.

174. Just as the division between light and darkness is clear and to mix them is impossible: 'What communion hath light with darkness? . . . or what part hath he that believeth with an infidel?' (2 Cor. vi. 14, 15), so is there a division between those who possess the Holy Spirit and those who do not possess it. For the former have their lives in heaven, having become angels rather than men, whereas the latter (who have not the Spirit) still sit in ancestral darkness and in the shadow of death, chained to the earth and to earthly things. The former are richly illumined by the inner light which has no eventide, and the latter by physical light alone. The former see themselves and their neigh-

bours—but the latter, seeing every day themselves and their neighbours dying the death of the soul, do not know and do not believe that there is a resurrection of the dead, judgment and reward to each man according to his deeds.

175. You can see with certainty from its actions in you whether you possess the Holy Spirit or not; as the Apostle Paul says: 'Where the Spirit of the Lord is, there is liberty' (2 Cor. iii. 17) and: 'The body is dead because of sin; but the Spirit is life because of righteousness' (Rom. viii. 10) and: 'They that are Christ's have crucified the flesh with the affections and lusts' (Gal. v. 24). For those baptised in the Holy Spirit are wholly clothed in Christ, have become sons of light and walk in the light that has no eventide, seeing the world they see not, and hearing worldly things they hear not. It is written of fleshly men that seeing they see not and hearing of Divine things they do not understand and cannot absorb spiritual things because to them they seem utter madness. Think in the same way of men who possess the Spirit in themselves, for although they have bodies they are not in the flesh as the Apostle says: 'But ye are not in the flesh, but in the Spirit, if so be that the Spirit of God dwell in you' (Rom. viii. 9). They are dead to the world and the world is dead to them, as he says of them, in speaking of himself: 'The world is crucified unto me, and I unto the world' (Gal. vi. 14).

176. As man is dual, consisting of soul and body, so, similarly, the world is dual—the visible and the invisible; each has its own affairs, corresponding to its spirit, and its own cares that go with them. I find the same in visions and dreams. Whatever occupies the soul and whatever it talks about in day-time is the subject of its dreams and philosophisings in sleep. If it has spent the day in activities concerned with human affairs, it worries over them in dreams; if its time was wholly occupied in studying Divine and heavenly things, it has visions of them in sleep and is taught wisdom by these visions, as the prophet says: 'Your young men shall see visions' (Joel in Acts ii. 17). Such a man is not misled by false dreams, but has dreams that are true and learns from revelations.

177. When the desiring part of the soul is moved to passions, amusements, pleasures and diversions of this world, it has corresponding dreams. And again, when the excitable part of the soul

rages like a wild beast against others of its kind, a man dreams of attacks of animals and reptiles, of wars and strife, dissensions and wranglings in lawsuits with people with whom he has quarrelled. When the thinking part of the soul swells with conceit and pride, a man dreams of flying high on wings, of sitting in the high chairs of judges and potentates, of ceremonial receptions and welcomes, and so on.

178. Only those can have true visions in sleep (they should not be called dreams but visions), whose mind has been made simple by the grace of the Holy Spirit, and freed from the pressure of passions and from slavery to them. These are men whose only care is things Divine, whose only thought is of future rewards and blessings, whose life is above ordinary life, free of care, not dispersed, serene, pure, full of mercy, wisdom, heavenly knowledge and other good fruits tended in them by the Holy Spirit. In people who are not like this, dreams are disorderly and false, and everything in them is sheer deceit and prelest.

179. A man who does his will to death is thereby left completely without will. Yet no living and moving creature is without will, but only those that have neither senses nor power to move. Plants possess a certain inner movement and growth; but it cannot be said that this movement and growth are the result of their natural will—for they have no soul. But every creature with a soul by nature possesses a will. Thus, whoever kills his will by effort, with attention and zeal specially directed towards this end, and becomes devoid of will, has obviously transcended his nature and is outside it. Such a man no longer himself wishes anything, since he has no wishes of his own, and does nothing of himself, either good or evil.

180. Those who with the help of the Holy Spirit have been vouchsafed union with God and have tasted of His ineffable blessings, no longer delight in empty—I would even say dishonourable and worthless—glory had from men. Neither do they wish for money, costly garments, or precious stones, as the foolish call them: they do not love to be attached or to cleave with their hearts to transitory and inconstant riches, passing from one man to another; they do not love to be known to kings and potentates who are not true princes, lords and rulers, since they are pos-

sessed and ruled by many passions. Such men do not regard them as high and mighty and do not think that they bestow any special glory on their familiars. Neither do they aspire to be close to any other famous or renowned men of the world, since no man cares to exchange riches for poverty or to become dishonoured, bereft of glory, despicable and lowest of all, instead of being a great and powerful lord covered in glory.

181. It is difficult for a man who says many things with his lips in prayer to be conscious of all he says. But a man who prays with few words can be conscious of what he says in prayer. Those who are not properly conscious of all they say are instructed to say many things. But a man who has learnt to be conscious of what he says in prayer cannot say many things, lest his mind become dispersed. There is no need to say much to God, but a man should be intelligently conscious of the little he does say, that is, should understand it. But to be intelligently conscious in prayer without the participation of the Holy Spirit is by no means possible. If a man has not become a friend of God through our Lord Jesus Christ in the Holy Spirit, his soul cannot pray with intelligent consciousness, as one of the great fathers said: 'when we pray as we ought we pray by the force of the Holy Spirit.' Thus the prayer of a man who imagines he prays in a proper manner without the Holy Spirit, even if he sings praises to God, is the same as blasphemy, since he is impure and has not yet become a friend of God.

182. If a man constantly looks at the physical sun, he involuntarily suffers a change in his vision, for he can no longer see anything else of the visible, and sees nothing but the sun in everything. It is the same with a man who is always looking at the sun of truth with mind and heart: involuntarily he will suffer a change in his mental vision, for he will be unable to imagine anything earthly and will see only God in all things.

183. This holy and blessed Simeon[31] was once asked what a priest should be like. He answered: 'I am unworthy of being a

---

[31] It is not clear from the text whether the Simeon here referred to is the teacher of Simeon the New Theologian or is the latter himself, in his capacity of teacher to his pupil Stethatos, who collected his sayings (see Introduction). (Translators' note.)

priest, but I know exactly what a priest should be like. First of all, he must be pure not only in his body but also in his soul, and devoid of all sin. Secondly, he must be humble not merely in his external behaviour and his habitual actions, but also in his inner disposition. Furthermore, standing before the altar and seeing the holy Eucharist with his eyes, he must always inwardly contemplate the Deity. More than that, he must acquire Him Who is invisibly present in the Eucharist and be conscious of Him dwelling in his heart, to enable him daringly to send his prayers to God and, speaking with Him as friend with friend, to say: "Our Father, Which art in heaven, hallowed be Thy name"; for this prayer shows that the man who utters it has present within him Him, Who by His nature is the Son of God, with the Father and the Holy Ghost. I have seen such priests, forgive me, fathers and brethren.'

184. He also said the following, as though speaking of someone else, in order to cover himself and avoid men's praise; but once he was forced by love of his neighbours to speak out for the general good as follows: 'I heard from a priest-monk, who confided in me as in a friend and said: "I have never celebrated the Liturgy without seeing the Holy Spirit as I had seen Him descending upon me while I was being ordained, when the Metropolitan was reading over me the prayer of priestly ordination and the Omophor was reposing on my unworthy head." I asked him, how he had seen Him then and in what form. He replied: "Simple and without form, and yet like light. And when I saw what I had never seen before, I was at first surprised and asked myself what it could be. Thereupon He said to me secretly but in a clear voice: 'I descend thus upon all prophets, Apostles and the present saints and chosen of God; for I am the Holy Spirit of God.'"' To Him be glory and power, for ever and ever. Amen.'

# ST. SIMEON THE NEW
# THEOLOGIAN

## On faith; and to those who say that those living in the world cannot attain perfection in virtues. To start with, a most profitable tale

It is good to preach God's mercy before all men and to reveal to one's brethren His great compassion and ineffable grace shed on us.—I know a man who kept no long strict fasts, no vigils, did not sleep on bare earth, imposed on himself no other specially arduous tasks; but, recollecting in memory his sins, understood his worthlessness and, having judged himself, became humble—and for this alone the most compassionate Lord saved him; as the divine David says: 'The Lord is nigh unto them that are of a broken heart; and saveth such as be of a contrite spirit' (Ps. xxxiv. 18).[32] In short, he trusted the words of the Lord and for his faith the Lord received him. There are many obstacles obstructing the way to humility; but no obstacles bar the way to belief in the words of God. As soon as we wish with all our heart, straightway we believe. For faith is a gift of the all-merciful God, which He gave us to possess by nature (infused in our nature), subjecting its use to the authority of our own will. Consequently, even the Scythians and barbarians have natural faith and believe one another's words. But to show you an actual example of whole-hearted faith, listen to a tale, which will confirm this.

There lived in Constantinople a young man by the name of

[32] The quotation in the Slavonic is not to be identified but has the same sense as the above quotation. (Translators' note.)

George, about twenty years old. All this happened in our life-time, in our own memory. He had a handsome face and in his walk, his bearing and his manner there was something osten-tatious. Owing to this, people, who see only what is on the surface and, ignorant of what is hidden inside each man, come to mistaken conclusions about others, made various evil suppositions about the youth. He made the acquaintance of a certain monk, who lived in one of the monasteries in Constantinople, a man of holy life. Revealing to this monk the innermost secrets of his heart, he also told him of his ardent desire to save his soul. The good father, after some needful words of direction, gave him a small rule to follow and a book of St. Mark the Wrestler in which he writes on spiritual law. The young man accepted the book with as much love and reverence as if it had been sent to him by God Himself, and conceived a strong faith in it, hoping to gain from it great benefit and much fruit. He read it through with much zeal and attention and received great help from it all. But three paragraphs made a particularly deep impression on his heart. The first was: 'If you seek to be healed, take care of your conscience (listen to it), and do what it tells you: this will profit you' (Para. 69). The second: 'He who seeks (hopes to receive) active grace of the Holy Spirit before practising the command-ments, is like a slave bought for money who, the moment he is bought, expects his freedom to be signed, together with the payment of his purchase price' (Para. 64). The third: 'He who prays physically, without having yet acquired spiritual reason, is like the blind man who cried: "Son of David, have mercy on me" (Mark x. 48). But another man who had been blind, when his eyes were opened and he saw the Lord, no longer called Him son of David, but worshipped Him as the Son of God (John ix. 35, 38)' (Para. 13, 14 on spiritual law). These three paragraphs pleased him greatly and he believed that, as the first paragraph asserts, by attention to his conscience the ills of his soul would be cured; that he would be made active by the Holy Spirit through obedience to commandments, as the second paragraph teaches; and that, by the grace of the Holy Spirit, his inner eyes would be opened and he would see the ineffable beauty of the Lord, as the third paragraph promises.—And so he became

wounded by love for this beauty and, though as yet he did not
see it, conceived a strong longing for it and sought it assiduously,
in the hope of finding it in the end.

In spite of all this, he did nothing special (as he assured me on
oath), except that every evening without fail he practised the
small rule given him by his staretz, and never went to bed to
sleep without performing it. But after some time his conscience
began to urge him: Make a few more prostrations, recite a few
extra psalms, repeat 'Lord Jesus Christ, have mercy on me!' as
many more times as you can. He willingly obeyed his conscience
and did all it suggested without thought, as though it were a command of God Himself. He never went to bed with his conscience
reproaching him: why did you not do this or that? Thus he
always listened to his conscience, never leaving undone whatever
it suggested to him. And every day his conscience added more
and more to his usual rule, and in a few days his evening prayers
swelled to great proportions. His days were spent in the house
of a certain Patriky, his work being to cater for the needs of all
the people living there. But every evening he went away, and no
one knew what he did at home. What he actually did was to shed
copious tears, to make a great many genuflexions, prostrating
himself with his face to the ground. When he stood at prayer he
always kept his feet tightly pressed together and stood without
moving; with a grieving heart, with sighing and tears he recited
prayers to the Holy Virgin; addressing himself to our Lord Jesus
Christ, he fell at His immaculate feet as if He had been there in
the flesh, and implored Him to have mercy on him, as He once
had on the blind man, and to open the eyes of his soul. Each
evening his prayers grew longer and longer so that, at last, he
stood at prayer till midnight. Yet he never permitted himself
when at prayer, either slackness or negligence, or easy postures;
never let his eyes turn to the right or left or upwards to look at
something, but stood motionless, like a pillar or as though he
had no body.

Once, when he was thus standing at prayer, saying more in his
mind than with his lips: 'God, have mercy on me, a sinner,' a
brilliant Divine radiance descended on him from above and filled
all the room. Thereupon the young man forgot that he was in a

room, or beneath a roof, for on all sides he saw nothing but light; he was not even aware of standing on the ground. All worldly cares left him, and there came to his mind no thoughts common to men clothed with flesh. He became wholly dissolved in this transubstantial light and it seemed to him that he himself became light. So he forgot the whole world and was filled with tears and unspeakable joy. Thereupon his mind rose upwards to heaven and there he saw another light, brighter than the light which surrounded him. And to his surprise it seemed to him that on the edge of this light stood the holy and angelic staretz who had given him the small precept on prayer and the book of St. Mark the Wrestler.

On hearing this from the young man, I thought that he had been greatly helped by the prayers of his staretz, and that God had granted him this vision to show the high level of virtue on which this staretz stood. As the young man said later, when the vision vanished and he came to himself, he found himself filled with joy and wonder, shedding copious tears, his heart filled with great sweetness. Finally he went to bed, but immediately a cock began to crow, showing that it was already past midnight. A little later he heard the church bells ringing for matins; so the young man got up, according to his custom, to read the early morning service. Thus he never slept that night—the thought of sleep never entered his mind.

How all this came to pass, only the Lord knows, for it was all His inscrutable work. Yet this youth did nothing in particular, except always to adhere firmly to the rule given him by the staretz, and to follow the instructions contained in the little book, with unshakable faith and undaunted hope. Let no one say that he did all this as a test. Such a thing never even entered his mind. He who makes tests does not possess firm faith. But, brushing aside every passionate or self-indulgent thought, this youth was so anxious to perform exactly what his conscience suggested, that he no longer had any feeling for the things of this world, finding no pleasure even in eating and drinking his fill.

Have you heard, brethren, what faith in God can do, when it shows in right actions? Have you understood that youth does not hinder, nor old age help, if a man lacks reason and the fear of God? Have you realised that the world and worldly cares do not hinder in fulfilling God's commandments, when there is zeal and attention? That silence and retirement from the world are useless, if laziness and negligence prevail? Hearing of David with wonder, we all say: there was only one David and there is no one else like him. But here you see that something greater than in David was manifested in this youth. David received testimony from God, was anointed king and prophet, received the Holy Spirit and had many assurances of God. Therefore, when he sinned and lost the grace of the Holy Spirit and his prophetic gift, and became cut off from his usual converse with God, is it surprising that, remembering the grace he had forsaken, he once more sought his lost blessings from God? But this youth had nothing of the kind; he was tied to worldly affairs, cared only for the temporal, had no time even to think of anything higher than earth, and yet—wonderful are the ways of the Lord!—as soon as he heard a few words from that holy staretz and read three paragraphs of St. Mark's, he immediately believed what he heard and read and, without the shadow of doubt and with unshakable hope, put it into practice. Thus, through the little work he did, and by the intercession of the Holy Virgin, he was found worthy of raising his mind to heaven. With the help of Her prayers he gained God's mercy and drew to himself the grace of the Holy Spirit, which pervaded him with such force that he was able to see that light to which many aspire, but which few are given to see. This youth kept no long fasts, did not sleep on bare earth, did not wear a hair shirt, had not left the world in body but only in spirit—by the disposition of his soul—kept only short vigils, and yet became higher than the wonderful Lot of Sodom, or rather became an angel in human flesh—externally a man, but inwardly an angel. Therefore he was given to see the most sweet light of the spiritual sun of truth, our Lord Jesus Christ, which light convinced him that he would be granted the light of the life to come. And so it was in truth, for love and the cleaving of his heart to God brought him into ecstasy, tore his spirit away from this world, out of his own self and all else, and transformed him wholly into the light of the Holy Spirit. Yet he lived in a city, was steward to a large house and looked after the needs of freemen and slaves, performing all that was due in this life.

Enough has been said in praise of the youth, and to stimulate you to similar love, in imitation of him. Or do you wish me to tell you something else, something much greater, which, maybe, your ear cannot hear? But, after all, what can be greater and more perfect than the fear of God? Nothing, of course. St. Gregory the Theologian said: 'The beginning of wisdom is the fear of the Lord. For where there is fear, there the commandments are kept; where the commandments are kept, there is the flesh purified—that cloud which envelops the soul and prevents it from seeing clearly the Divine ray; where the flesh is purified, there light springs forth, and the shining of the light fulfils desire above all desires.' In these words, he showed that illumination by the Spirit is the endless end of every virtue and that whoever attains this illumination by the Spirit has finished with everything sensory and has begun to live with his consciousness in spiritual things alone. These, my brethren, are the wonders of God. And God leads out His secret slaves into the open, so that lovers of the good and the righteous should imitate them, while the evil-minded are left without excuse. For even those who move among crowds and spend their life in the vicissitudes of the world, gain salvation, if they lead their lives as is needful. For the sake of the faith they show in God, He endows them with great blessings, so that those who have failed to attain salvation, through their laziness and negligence, may have nothing to say in their own justification on the day of judgment. True is His word Who promised to grant us salvation for the sake of belief in Him! So, my beloved brethren, have concern for yourselves and for me, who love you and constantly shed tears for you. For the merciful and compassionate God commanded that we too should be merciful and compassionate and should have concern alike for ourselves and for each other. With your whole heart have faith in the Lord, hate this world as you should hate it and care not about its temporal and insecure blessings, but strive towards God and cleave to Him. For in a little while the end of the world and of this life will come, and woe to those who fall away from the kingdom of God. Tears suffocate me, I weep and grieve with my whole heart when I reflect that—though we have the bountiful and charitable Lord Who, merely for sincere faith in Him, grants us such great and wonderful blessings, exceeding all imagination, hearing or expectation—yet we are unthinking, like dumb animals, and prefer the earth and earthly things which, in God's compassion, were given us for the use of our body in order that, while it is fed by them in moderation, the soul should pursue unhampered its ascent towards the primordial, fed by the mental food emanating from the grace of the Holy Spirit, according to the soul's own measure of purification and regeneration. For God has created us intelligent beings so that we may glorify, thank and love Him for the lesser blessings given us for the needs of our present life, and become worthy to gain great and eternal blessings in the life to come. But woe to us, that we have no care whatever for the future, but remain ungrateful to God even for what we have, thus being like the demons, or, rather, worse. Therefore it is just that we should be subjected to greater torment than they. For we are more favoured than they: we have become Christians, we have had so many spiritual gifts, we believe in God Who became man for our sake, suffered such tortures and died on the Cross to free us from the errors of prelest and sin. But what can I say to all this? Woe to us! Only in words do we believe in God, but in our deeds we turn away from Him. Is not Christ's name uttered everywhere—in towns and villages, in monasteries and on the mountains? Are there not Christians everywhere? But if you find it expedient, investigate and examine carefully whether they fulfil Christ's commandments; and indeed among thousands and myriads you will with difficulty find one, who is a Christian both in word and in deed. Did not our Lord Jesus Christ say: 'He that believeth on me, the works that I do shall he do also; and greater works than these shall he do' (John xiv. 12)? But which of us will dare to say: 'I do the works of Christ and truly believe in Christ'? See you not therefore, my brethren, how in the day of judgment we are in danger of being adjudged unfaithful and may be condemned to a worse torment than the unbelievers, that is, those who are altogether ignorant of Christ? One of two things is certain: either we must suffer a worse punishment than the unbelievers, or Christ must be false to His word—which is impossible.

I have written this, not to prevent anyone from renouncing the world and not to make anyone prefer life in the world to silence, but to assure all who read these writings that a man who wishes to act rightly receives from God the power to act, no matter where he is—whether in the world or in a silent retreat. On the contrary, the tale I have related should inspire an even greater desire for retiring from the world. But if a man living in the world and never thinking of renouncing the world or possessions, or of obedience, has received such mercy from God only because he believed and called to Him with his whole soul, then what blessings are in store for those who, renouncing the whole world and all men, give up their very life unto death for the sake of God's commandment, as He has ordained? Moreover, if any man starts to act rightly with unshaken faith and great zeal, and begins to experience the profit which comes from it, he will by himself realise that worldly cares, and living and moving in the world, are a great obstacle to those who wish to live in God. As we have said, what happened to this youth is something marvellous and extraordinary; and we have heard of no other case like it. But if such a thing has happened or happens to any-one else, they should know that if they do not abandon the world, they will soon lose what they have received.

About this youth I later learned from him the following. I met him when he was already a monk, three or four years after he had taken monastic vows. He was then thirty-two. I knew him very well: we had been friends from childhood and were brought up together. So he told me the following. 'A few days after this miraculous vision and the change that happened in me, I was assailed by many worldly temptations so that I saw myself gradually losing this blessing through them when performing my secret works of God. So I conceived a strong desire to abandon the world and in solitude to seek Christ Who had appeared to me. For I believe, brother, that He deigned to appear to me in order to take me to Himself, unworthy as I am, separating me from the whole world. But since I was unable to do this at once, I gradually forgot everything I told you about and fell into utter darkness and insensibility, no longer remembering anything I related to you, either big or small, remembering not even the slightest movement of thought or feeling. Upon which I was plunged into evils greater than before and ended in such a state, as if I had never heard the words of Christ, or understood them. Even the saint who had been so kind to me, and had given me that small rule and the book of St. Mark's, became for me one of the people one has met accidentally, for I no longer thought of what I had seen concerning him.—I am telling you all this in detail,' he continued, 'so that you should realise the depths of perdition into which I, an impious wretch, fell, through my negligence, and that you should be filled with wonder at the ineffable mercy shown me later by God. I cannot tell you how it happened that, unknown to myself, love and belief in that saintly staretz had remained in my poor heart, but I think that, for the sake of this love and belief, God in His loving kindness listened to his prayers and, even after this long time, had mercy on me and, again through him, drew me out of prelest and dragged me up from the depths of evil. Unworthy as I am, I did not completely break with the staretz, but when in town, frequently called on him in his cell, and confessed to him all that was happening to me, although I shamelessly neglected to follow any of his precepts. But now, as you see, the merciful God has overlooked the multitude of my sins and, through this same staretz, has arranged for me to become a monk, allowing me to be constantly with him, truly unworthy as I am. After great labours and copious tears, with the strictest withdrawal and retirement from the world, total obedience and renunciation of my will, many other acts and methods of rigorous self-mortification and an irresistible yearning for all that is good, I was once more granted, although somewhat darkly, the vision of a small ray of this most sweet Divine light. But even to this day I have never been given to see again the vision I had before.'

This and many other things he told me with tears. And I, poor man, while listening to these holy words thought that he was wholly filled with Divine grace and was wise, despite his not having studied external wisdom. Drawing his knowledge from practice and experience, he had acquired the most subtle understanding of spiritual things. Therefore I asked him to tell me what kind of faith it was that could produce such marvellous phenomena, and to expound it to me in writing, like a teacher. He immediately began to tell me of this, and readily wrote down what he said. Not to make the present chapter too long, I shall relate elsewhere what he said, for the enjoyment and delight of those who like to read such writings with faith.

So, I beg you, brethren, let us also proceed with zeal on the way of Christ's commandments—and our faces will not be covered with shame. Let us be like those who knock patiently and to whom the Lord opens the doors of His kingdom, according to His promise, and like those who seek and are given the Holy Spirit. It is impossible for a man, who seeks with all his soul, not to find Him and be enriched by His gifts. So will you indubitably receive His Divine blessings, prepared by Him for those who love Him—partly here, as spiritual wisdom will show, and wholly in the life to come, in company with the saints of all ages, in Jesus Christ our Lord, to Whom be glory for ever and ever. Amen.

# Three methods of attention and prayer

1. There are three methods of attention and prayer, by which the soul is uplifted and moves forward, or is cast down and destroyed. Whoever employs these methods at the right time and in the right way, moves forward; but whoever employs them unwisely and at the wrong time is cast down.

Attention should be linked to prayer as inseparably as body is linked to soul. Attention should go on ahead, spying out the enemy, like a scout. It should be the first to engage sin in combat, and to oppose evil thoughts entering the soul. Prayer should follow in its wake, instantly exterminating and destroying all the evil thoughts with which attention has been battling beforehand; for attention alone cannot destroy them.

On this warfare against thoughts by attention and prayer hangs the life and death of the soul. If by means of attention we keep prayer pure, we make progress; if we have no attention to keep it pure but leave it unprotected, it becomes soiled with bad thoughts and we remain futile failures.

Thus, since there are three methods of attention and prayer, we must explain the distinctive features of each, so that he who loves salvation should choose the best.

### 2. *On the first method of attention and prayer*

The distinctive features of the first method are as follows: if a man stands at prayer and, raising his hands, his eyes and his mind to heaven, keeps in mind Divine thoughts, imagines celestial blessings, hierarchies of angels and dwellings of the saints, assembles briefly in his mind all that he has learnt from the Holy Scriptures and ponders over all this while at prayer, gazing up to heaven, and thus inciting his soul to longing and love of God, at times even shedding tears and weeping, this will be the first method of attention and prayer.

But if a man chooses only this method of prayer it happens that, little by little, he begins to pride himself in his heart, without realising it; it seems to him that what he is doing comes from God's grace, sent as a solace to him, and he prays God to grant him always to remain in this doing. But this (that is, to think in this way of this method of prayer) is a sign of prelest; for the good is no longer good if it be not rightly done.

If then such a man gives himself up to utter silence (that is, becomes a hesychast, an anchorite) he can scarcely avoid going out of his mind (he will be in extreme danger of suffering this). If by any chance he is not driven out of his mind, it will in any case be impossible for him to acquire virtue or passionlessness. This method contains another danger of going astray; namely, when a man sees light with his bodily eyes, smells sweet scents, hears voices and many other like phenomena. Some have become totally possessed, and in their madness wander from place to place; others have been led astray, mistaking the devil for an angel of light, in the guise of which he appeared to them without their recognising him. Thus they remained incorrigible to the end, refusing to listen to any brother's advice. Some of them, instigated by the devil, have committed suicide: have thrown themselves over a precipice, or have hanged themselves. Who could enumerate the various forms of prelest by which the devil seeks to seduce, since they are innumerable?

From what we have said, it is not difficult for a man of sense to understand what harm comes from this first method of attention and prayer (if it is taken as the final perfection in prayer). If however someone avoids incurring these evils while practising the first method, because he lives in a community (for it is the solitary who is especially subject to them), he will still remain all his life without success (in spiritual life).

### 3. On the second method of attention and prayer

The second method is this: a man tears his mind away from all sensed objects and leads it within himself, guarding his senses and collecting his thoughts, so that they cease to wander amid the vanities of this world; now he examines his thoughts, now ponders over the words of the prayer his lips utter, now pulls back his thoughts if, ravished by the devil, they fly towards something bad and vain, now with great labour and self-exertion strives to come back into himself, after being caught and vanquished by some passion. The distinctive feature of this method is that it takes place in the head, thought fighting against thought.

In this struggle against himself, a man can never be at peace in himself, nor find time to practise virtues in order to gain the crown of truth. Such a man is like one fighting his enemies at night, in the dark; he hears their voices and suffers their blows, but cannot see clearly who they are, whence they come and how and for what purpose they attack him; because he himself remains in the head, whereas evil thoughts are generated in the heart. He does not even see them, for his attention is not in his heart. The darkness enveloping his mind and the storm raging in his thoughts are the cause of this defect (for they prevent him from seeing this), and it is impossible for him to slip away from the demons, his enemies, and to avoid their blows. But if, together with all this, a man is overcome by vainglory and imagines he has attention on himself as he should, the unhappy man works in vain and will even lose his reward for ever. In his pride, he despises and criticises others and praises himself, deeming himself worthy to be a shepherd of human sheep and to guide others—and so he is like a blind man who undertakes to lead the blind.

Such is the second method of attention and prayer. Every man striving after salvation should know the harm it does to the soul and should carefully watch himself. Still, this method is better than the first, just as moonlight is better than a dark night without moon.

### 4. *On the third method of attention and prayer*

Truly the third method is marvellous and difficult to explain; and not only hard to understand but even incredible for those who have not tried it in practice. They even refuse to believe that such a thing can actually be. And, indeed, in our times, this method of attention and prayer is very rarely met with; and it seems to me that this blessing has deserted us in company with obedience.—If someone observes perfect obedience towards his spiritual father, he becomes free of all cares, because once and for all he has laid all his cares on the shoulders of his spiritual father. Therefore, being far from all worldly attachments, he becomes capable of zealous and diligent practice of the third method of prayer, provided he has found a true spiritual father, who is not subject to prelest. For if a man has given himself up entirely to God and has shed all his cares on to God and his spiritual father, so that, in his obedience, he no longer lives his own life or follows his own will, but is dead to all worldly attachments and to his own body—what accidental thing could ever vanquish and enslave such a man? Or what worry or care can he have? Therefore all the wiles and stratagems used by the demons to entice a man towards many and varied thoughts are destroyed and dispersed by this third method of attention and prayer, conjoined with obedience. For then the mind of such a man, being free from all things, has the necessary leisure to examine, unhindered, thoughts introduced by the demons, and can readily repel them and pray to God with a pure heart. Such is the beginning of true (spiritual) life! And those who do not begin in this way, labour in vain without realising it.

The beginning of this third method is not gazing upwards to heaven, raising one's hands or keeping one's mind on heavenly things; these, as we have said, are the attributes of the first method and are not far removed from prelest. Neither does it consist in guarding the senses with the mind and directing all one's attention upon this, not watching for the onslaughts of the demons on the soul from within. (They look and struggle, but all this is in the head, so they are unguarded.) This is the attribute of the second method and those who practise it become enslaved by the demons, and cannot take revenge, for the enemies both constantly attack them, openly and secretly, and render them proud and vain.

But you, beloved, if you want to be saved, begin to work thus: having established perfect obedience in your heart, which, as we have said, you must have towards your spiritual father, act in everything else with a pure conscience, as though in the presence of God; for it is impossible to have a clear conscience without obedience. You must keep your conscience clear in three respects: in relation to God, in relation to your spiritual father and in relation to other men, as well as to things and objects of the world (of life).

In relation to God it is your duty to keep your conscience clear, permitting yourself no action which, to your knowledge, is distasteful and unpleasing to God.

In relation to your spiritual father do only what he tells you, allowing yourself to do nothing either more or less, and proceed guided solely by his will and intention.

In relation to other people, you will keep your conscience clear if you refrain from doing to them anything you yourself hate or dislike being done to you

In relation to things, your duty is to keep your conscience clear by always using them rightly—I mean food, drink and clothes.

In brief, do everything as though in the presence of God and so, in whatever you do, you need never allow your conscience to wound and denounce you, for not having done your work well.

Proceeding in this way you will smooth for yourself a true and straight path to the third method of attention and prayer which is the following: the mind should be in the heart—a distinctive feature of the third method of prayer. It should guard the heart while it prays, revolve, remaining always within, and thence, from the depths of the heart, offer up prayers to God. (Everything is in this; work in this way until you are given to taste the Lord.) When the mind, there, within the heart, at last tastes and sees that the Lord is good, and delights therein (the labour is ours, but this tasting is the action of grace in a humble heart), then it will no longer wish to leave this place in the heart (then it will say the words of the Apostle Peter: 'It is good for us to be here' [Matt. xvii. 4]), and will always look inwardly into the depths of the heart and will remain revolving there, repulsing all thoughts sown by the devil. (This is the third method of attention and prayer, practised as it should be.) To those who have no knowledge of this work and no experience of it, it mostly appears difficult and oppressive. But those who have tasted its sweetness and have enjoyed it in the depths of their heart, cry with the divine Paul: 'Who shall separate us from the love of Christ?' (Rom. viii. 35).

Therefore our holy fathers, harkening to the Lord Who said: 'For out of the heart proceed evil thoughts, murders, adulteries, fornications, thefts, false witness, blasphemies' and: 'These are the things which defile a man' (Matt. xv. 19, 20), hearing also that in another place of the Gospels we are instructed to 'cleanse first that which is within the cup and platter, that the outside of them may be clean also' (Matt. xxiii. 26), have renounced all other spiritual work and concentrated wholly on this one doing, that is on guarding the heart, convinced that, through this practice, they would easily attain every other virtue, whereas without it not a single virtue can be firmly established. Some of the fathers called this doing, silence of the heart; others called it attention; yet others—sobriety and opposition (to thoughts), while others called it examining thoughts and guarding the mind. They all practised it pre-eminently and, through it, received Divine gifts. Ecclesiastes means the same thing when he says: 'Rejoice, O young man, in thy youth . . . and walk in the ways of thine heart' (Eccles. xi. 9) in purity, withdrawing the heart from evil thoughts. In another place he speaks of the same: 'If the spirit of the ruler rise up against thee, leave not thy place' (Eccles. x. 4)—by place, meaning the heart. The Lord too tells us in the Gospels: 'Neither be ye of doubtful mind' (Luke xii. 29)—do not dart about like meteorites, do not rush hither and thither with your mind. And again in another place He says: 'Blessed are the poor in spirit' (Matt. v. 3), that is, blessed are those who have no attachment to the world in their heart, but are destitute of all worldly thought. All the holy fathers wrote much about this. Those who wish may read their writings and see what St. Mark the Wrestler has written, or St. John of the Ladder, Hesychius of Jerusalem, Philotheus of Sinai, Abba Isaiah, Barsanuphius the Great, and many others.

In a word, he who does not have attention in himself and does not guard his mind, cannot become pure in heart and so cannot see God. He who does not have attention in himself cannot be poor in spirit, cannot weep and be contrite, nor be gentle and meek, nor hunger and thirst after righteousness, nor be merciful, nor a peacemaker, nor suffer persecution for righteousness' sake. Speaking generally, it is impossible to acquire virtue in any other way, except through this kind of attention. Therefore you should try to gain this more than anything else, so as to learn what I tell you in your own experience. If you wish also to learn how it should be done, I will tell you of this.

You should observe three things before all else: *freedom from all cares*, not only cares about bad and vain but even about good things, or in other words, you should become dead to everything; *your conscience* should be clear in all things, so that it denounces you in nothing; and you should have complete *absence of passionate attachment*, so that your thought inclines towards nothing worldly. Keep your attention within yourself (not in your head but in your heart33). Keep your mind there (in the heart), trying by

33 Here St. Simeon describes certain external methods by which some fall into temptation and relinquish their work, and others distort the work itself. Since, owing to scarcity of instructors, these methods may lead to evil effects, while in themselves they are nothing more than external adaptations for inner doing and have no essential value, we omit them. The essential thing is to acquire the habit of making the mind stand on guard in the heart—in this physical heart, but not physically. It is necessary to bring the mind down from the head to the heart and to establish it there or, as one of the fathers said, to join the mind with the heart. How to attain this? Seek and you will find. The best way is by walking in God's presence and by the work of prayer, especially by going to church. But it should be remembered that ours is only the labour,

every possible means to find the place where the heart is, in order that, having found it, your mind should constantly abide there. Wrestling thus, the mind will find the place of the heart. This happens when grace produces sweetness and warmth in prayer. From that moment onwards, from whatever side a thought may appear, the mind immediately chases it away, before it has had time to enter, and become a thought or an image, destroying it by Jesus' name, that is, Lord Jesus Christ, have mercy upon me! Moreover, from that moment, a man conceives hatred of the demons and anger against them, constantly battles with them and vanquishes them. As to other results which usually come from this work, with God's help, you will learn them from your own experience, by keeping your mind attentive and in your heart holding Jesus, that is, His prayer—Lord Jesus Christ, have mercy upon me! One of the holy fathers says: 'Sit in your cell and this prayer will teach you everything.'

*Question.* But why cannot the first and second methods of attention and prayer produce this?

*Answer.* Because we use them wrongly. St. John of the Ladder, likening these methods to a ladder with four rungs, says: 'Some tame passions and become humble; others psalmodise, that is, pray with their lips; yet others practise mental prayer; others rise to contemplation. Those who undertake to climb by these rungs do not begin with the top and then go down, but start from the bottom and go upwards—stepping first on the first rung, then on the second, then on the third and, finally, on the fourth. The method by which he who wishes it may raise himself from off the earth and rise to heaven is as follows: first, he must wrestle with his mind and tame his passions; second, he must practise psalmody, that is, pray with the lips, for, when passions are subdued, prayer quite naturally brings sweetness and enjoyment even to the tongue and is accepted by God as pleasing to Him; third, he must pray mentally; fourth, he must rise to contemplation. The first is appropriate to beginners; the second, to those who have already achieved some measure of success; the third to those

---

while the object itself, that is the joining of mind and heart, is a gift of grace which the Lord grants to us as and when He chooses. The best example is Maximus Kapsokalivitos. (Footnote in 'Dobrotolubiye'.)

drawing nigh to the last rungs of achievement, and the fourth—
to the perfect.'

Thus the only possible beginning is the diminishing and taming
of passions. This can only be achieved in the soul by guarding the
heart and by attention, for, as the Lord says, out of the heart
proceed evil thoughts which defile a man. So it is there that
attention and guarding are needful. When, through the heart's
opposition to them, passions are completely subdued, the mind
begins to long for God, seeking to get close to Him, for which
purpose it increases its prayer and spends most of its time praying. From this longing for God and praying, the mind acquires
strength and chases away all thoughts which circle round the heart
seeking entry, and strikes them down with prayer. Then warfare
begins: with a great roar the evil demons arise, and through the
passions raise mutiny and storm in the heart. But by the name of
Jesus Christ all this is dissolved and vanishes, like wax in a flame.
Yet, even when banished and driven out from the heart, the
demons are not quelled, but make other attempts to disturb the
mind, from without, through the senses. But here again the mind
very soon restores, and begins once more to feel its usual quiet;
for they have no power to disturb its depths but can manage only
to ruffle its surface. But the mind is not yet able to free itself
from warfare completely, and to be untroubled by attacks of the
evil demons. This is the attribute only of the perfect—of those
who have completely renounced everything and whose attention
remains ceaselessly in the heart.

Thus, if a man practises all this in due order, doing each thing
at its appointed time, then, when his heart is purified from
passions, he will be able to give himself up entirely to psalmody,
to struggle with thoughts, to look up at heaven with his bodily
eyes, or to contemplate it with the inner eyes of his soul, and to
pray in true purity, as he should.

Still, it is advisable to gaze up at heaven with bodily eyes as
seldom as possible, for fear of the evil demons which are to be
found in the air. They are called spirits of the air because they
produce in the air various forms of prelest—so we must take
care. God demands only one thing from us—that our heart be
purified by means of attention. As to the rest, it will be as the

Apostle said: 'If the root be holy, so are the branches' (Rom. xi. 16). But if a man begins to lift his eyes and his mind to heaven and imagine something in his mind, doing it not in the order we have indicated, he will see dreams, something false instead of true, because his heart is not pure. Thus, as we have said more than once, the first and second methods of attention and prayer do not lead a man to achievements. When we wish to build a house we do not put on the roof before building the foundations, for to build a house this way is impossible; first lay the foundations, then build the house and only then put on the roof. So also must we do in relation to spiritual things: first lay the foundations, that is, start to guard the heart and cleanse it from passions; then build the spiritual house, that is, repulse the insurrection against us, raised by evil spirits through the outer senses, and learn to cut off such attacks as quickly as possible; and only then should we put on the roof, that is, complete renunciation of everything in order to give ourselves up entirely to God. In this way we shall complete our spiritual house in Jesus Christ, to Whom be glory for ever. Amen.

# THE PATRIARCH CALLISTUS
and his fellow-worker
# IGNATIUS, OF XANTHOPOULOS
Short Biographical Note

Callistus of Xanthopoulos, the holy Patriarch of Constantinople, lived in the reign of Andronicus, the second of the Paleologoi (A.D. 1360). He was the pupil of St. Gregory of Sinai, whose life he later described in detail, and led a life of spiritual struggle on the Holy Mount Athos, in the Magul skete, opposite the monastery of St. Philotheus. He lived there with his fellow anchorite Mark for twenty-eight years. At the same time, he was also united in such close friendship with Ignatius of Xanthopoulos that it was as though they had but one soul between them. Later becoming Patriarch, he undertook a journey to Serbia, accompanied by his attendant clergy, to pacify their church. On his way there he journeyed by way of the holy mountain, where Maximus Kapsokalivitos foretold his early death, saying: 'This staretz will not see his flock again, for the funeral dirge sounds behind him: "Blessed are the sinless on the way".' On reaching Serbia he exchanged corruptible life for incorruptible.

Simeon of Salonika, speaking of the Prayer of Jesus, says the following of those two great spiritual workers: 'In our times Father Callistus, Patriarch of New Rome, and his intimate fellow-worker Father Ignatius, bearing God in their hearts and moved by the Holy Spirit, have left most excellent writings in a book composed with all their wisdom of God, giving full and perfect knowledge of the Jesus Prayer. They were offspring of the Imperial city, but having renounced everything, first led the chaste life of monks in obedience (in a monastery) and later lived together a truly heavenly life of spiritual struggle, abiding as one in Christ, as Christ Himself prayed for us of His Father (John xvii. 11). Having kept to perfection the peace which St. Paul wished for his disciples (Phil. iv. 7), they passed peacefully to another life where they enjoy higher peace, in purity contemplating Jesus, Whom they loved and sought whole-heartedly, being as one with Him and insatiably tasting the sweetness of His light. They had acquired a pledge of this, even while in this life, being purified by contemplation and doing, and having been granted Divine illumination, the reflection of which was seen in their faces, as in the face of Stephen.'

# THE MONKS CALLISTUS AND IGNATIUS, OF XANTHOPOULOS

## Directions to hesychasts, in a hundred chapters

1. *On the need to teach each other good*

As children of light, heirs of God and co-heirs of Christ, according to the Divine promise, we should be taught by God Himself (John vi. 45) and should have the New Testament ineffably inscribed in our hearts, in letters brighter than flame, and be governed by the gracious and true Spirit. We should be like the angels, with no need of being taught by anyone to 'know the Lord' (Jer. xxxi. 34). But, on the one hand, from our very childhood, we have strayed from the good and inclined towards evil, and, on the other hand, the seduction and undying enmity towards us of the redoubtable *Belial* teach us to turn away from the soul-saving commandments of God, and to be tossed hither and thither in rapids which wreck the soul. Moreover, what is still more lamentable, they incite us to think and act against ourselves, so that, in the words of God, 'there are none that do understand, and seek God' (Ps. xiv. 2). Thus we have all gone aside from the true way, all become filthy, carnal and devoid of grace. Therefore we are in dire need of mutual help in directing and assisting each other towards good.

2. *Shows that the present directions are written at the request of a certain brother and in obedience to the precept of the fathers; asks God's help for the writers in their work, and for readers in their understanding and practice of what is written*

Since, in accordance with the word of the Lord, you were moved by a desire to search into the Divine life-giving Scriptures and to be initiated into their mysteries without error, and so have often begged us wretches for a word, and a written rule for your own good and also, possibly, for others', as you yourself say: we have deemed it our duty, with God's help, to satisfy at last your laudable desire, our most beloved spiritual child; and so, in our love to you and for the sake of your good, we forget our companion—laziness, and imitate your zeal towards good and your untiring labours, and this, above all, through fear of God's condemnation, which threatens every man who buries his talent. Moreover, we wished thus to obey the precepts which our fathers and spiritual teachers have given us, enjoining us to transmit, to other God-loving men, that which we learnt from them. May God, the Father of love, the generous bestower of all blessings, Who granted speech even to senseless beasts, grant us helpful words and open our slow, dumb lips for those who can hear. May He give you and your companions a wise ear to hear rightly what we have to say, and to live unswervingly in the way which pleases Him. For it is written that without Him we can do nothing good or salutary for the soul (John xv. 5), and 'Except the Lord build the house, they labour in vain that build it' (Ps. cxxvii. 1).

## 3. Programme of the present directions

Since every work is governed by its aim, and our aim is to say everything which may help you to succeed, as far as is in our powers, while your aim is strictly to conform your life to what will be said, it is first of all necessary to look at Christ's economy as a whole, so as to find what can serve as a right foundation to the house of life, how to build this house, and how in due time, or as God helps, to cover it with a fitting roof—having in all this the Spirit as architect.[34]

## 4. The fundamental principle of the directions

With God's help, the fundamental principle of our directions is briefly reduced to the following proposition: it is necessary to try in all ways and with all effort to live in accordance with the laws laid down in Christ's Divine Commandments—so that

34 Paraphrase, for the passage is obscure. (Footnote in 'Dobrotolubiye'.)

through keeping them we should once more ascend to that perfect refashioned and re-created image freely bestowed on us by the grace of the Spirit in the holy font of baptism. Or, if it pleases you so to define this gift—so that, casting away the old Adam with his works and lusts, we should be clothed in a new spiritual man, which is our Lord Jesus Christ, as the divine Paul says: 'My little children, of whom I travail in birth again until Christ be formed in you' (Gal. iv. 19); and 'For as many of you as have been baptised into Christ have put on Christ' (Gal. iii. 27).

5. *The glory of the grace of holy baptism, what dims and what restores it*

What this grace is and how we acquire it, what dims and what purifies it, will be explained to you better than all gold by St. John Chrysostom, shining in word and soul, who says: '"But we all, with open face beholding as in a glass the glory of the Lord, are changed into the same image" (2 Cor. iii. 18). This was more clear for believers in the times of the Apostles when miraculous gifts occurred. Still, it is not hard, even now, for a man who has the eyes of faith to understand it. When we are being baptised, our soul, purified by the Spirit, becomes brighter than the sun; not only are we then able to look at the glory of God, but we ourselves take on something of its radiance. As polished silver, illumined by the rays of the sun, radiates light not only from its own nature but also from the radiance of the sun, so a soul, purified by the Divine Spirit, becomes more brilliant than silver; it both receives the ray of Divine glory, and from itself reflects the ray of this same glory. Therefore the Apostle says: "But we all, with open face beholding as in a glass the glory of the Lord, are changed into the same image from glory to glory" (2 Cor. iii. 18), that is, from the glory of the Spirit to our own glory, which fills us and which should be "even as by the Spirit of the Lord".'

A little later he continues: 'If you wish, I will show you this more clearly and palpably in the Apostles. Think of Paul, whose very garments had a miraculous effect. Remember Peter, whose very shadow manifested miraculous power. Had they not borne within them the image of the King of heaven and their radiance been beyond our attainment, their garments and their shadows would not have had such power: for the garment of the King is terrible even for robbers. Do you wish to see how their inner light penetrates even through their bodies? ''And looking steadfastly on Stephen, they saw his face as it had been the face of an angel'' (Acts vi. 15). But this is as nothing compared with the glory which shone within him. For what Moses showed in his face, they carried in their souls. And much more than that, for what Moses had was more physical, whereas this was spiritual. Just as bodies which can receive and reflect light, when illumined by self-radiant bodies, themselves pour their reflected light on other bodies close to them, so it is with believers. This is why those with this experience become detached from the earthly and think only of heavenly things.—But alas! we ought to groan bitterly; for, though granted such noble rank, we do not even understand what is said about it, because we quickly lose it and incline to the sensory. This ineffable and terrible glory remains in us one or two days, after which we extinguish it, bringing in the storm of worldly affairs and their thick clouds which repulse its rays.' (Seventh discourse, on the 2nd Epistle to the Corinthians.)

In another place he says: 'The bodies of men who have pleased God will be vested in such glory as our present eyes cannot even see. Certain signs and vague traces of this were graciously given by God both in the Old and the New Testaments. There the face of Moses shone with such glory as the eyes of the Israelites could not bear; while in the New Testament the face of Christ shone with a still greater light.'

Have you heard now the words of the Spirit? Have you realised the power of this sacrament? Have you understood the travail of our complete spiritual regeneration after we leave the holy font, its fruits, its fullness and the honours of victory? Do you see how much it lies in our power to increase or to diminish this super-natural grace, that is, to show it forth or to obscure it? What obscures it is the storm of worldly cares, and the ensuing dark-ness of passions which attack us like a whirlwind, or a wild torrent and, flooding our soul, give it neither rest nor possibility to look at the truly good and blessed things for which it was created. Instead, it is mauled and tortured by the waves and smoke of sensory lusts, it is plunged into darkness and dissoluteness. Conversely, grace is manifested by that which is reflected from the Divine commandments, in the souls of those who walk not in the flesh, but in the Spirit; for it is said: 'Walk in the Spirit, and ye shall not fulfil the lust of the flesh' (Gal. v. 16). Grace leads such souls towards salvation and raises them, as by a ladder, to the very summit of perfection, to its very highest degree—love, which is God.

### 6. *In holy baptism we freely receive Divine grace. When we cover it over with passions, we cleanse it again by obedience to commandments*

In the Divine womb, that is, in the holy font, we freely receive perfect Divine grace. If after this we cover it over with the fog of passions, either through abuse of temporal things, or through excess of cares for worldly activities, it is possible, even after this, to regain possession of it, to restore its supernatural brightness and to see quite vividly its manifestation, by repentance and the fulfilment of commandments whose action is Divine. Grace manifests in proportion to each man's zeal in remaining faithful to faith, but above all through the help and benevolence of our Lord Jesus Christ. St. Mark says: 'Christ, as perfect God, gave to those baptised the perfect grace of the Holy Spirit, which receives no increase from us, but merely reveals itself and manifests in us in accordance with our keeping the commandments, and gives us increase in faith "till we all come in the unity of the faith, and of the knowledge of the Son of God, unto a perfect man, unto the measure of the stature of the fulness of Christ" (Eph. iv. 13).' Therefore, whatever we may bring after our regeneration in Him, must previously have been concealed in us by Him and of Him.

### 7. *A man living in God should follow all the commandments, but devote the greater part of his activity to the foremost of them as the parents of others*

As we have said, the principle and root of all activity natural to us is to live in accordance with the saving commandments, while the fruit and the end (expected from this) is to recapture the perfect grace of the Holy Spirit, granted us from the first through baptism, which still remains in us (for 'the gifts and calling of God are without repentance', as the Apostle says [Rom. xi. 29]), although, being buried under passions, it reveals itself only through our fulfilling the commandments given by God. Therefore it behoves us to try with all zeal to fulfil all these commandments, and by this purification to reveal the grace of the Spirit existing in us, making it manifest and clearly seen. 'Thy word is a lamp unto my feet', says the blessed David to God, 'and a light unto my path' (Ps. cxix. 105), and: 'The commandment of the Lord is pure, enlightening the eyes' (Ps. xix. 8), and: 'I esteem all Thy precepts concerning all things to be right' (Ps. cxix. 128). He who lay on the Lord's breast says: 'He that keepeth his commandments dwelleth in him, and he in him' (1 John iii. 24), and: 'And his commandments are not grievous' (1 John v. 3). And the Lord Himself teaches: 'He that hath my commandments, and keepeth them, he it is that loveth me: and he that loveth me shall be loved of my Father, and I will love him and will manifest myself to him' (John xiv. 21), and: 'If a man love me, he will keep my words: and my Father will love him, and we will come unto him, and make our abode with him' (John xiv. 23), and: 'He that loveth me not keepeth not my sayings' (John xiv. 24).

Most of all is it necessary to keep the first and original commandments which are, as it were, the mothers of the rest, and to consecrate to them the greater part of one's activity. For in this way, with God's help, we shall attain without stumbling both the aim of the right action we have undertaken in the beginning, and the end of our strivings, that is, the manifestation in us of the grace of the Holy Spirit.

8. *The beginning of every action pleasing to God is calling with faith on the name of our Lord Jesus Christ, together with the peace and love radiating from this*

The beginning of every action pleasing to God is calling with faith on the life-saving name of our Lord Jesus Christ, as He Himself said: 'Without me ye can do nothing' (John xv. 5), together with the peace and love which accompany this calling. Peace, for as the Apostle says: 'I will therefore that men pray . . . without wrath and doubting' (1 Tim. ii. 8); love, for 'God is love; and he that dwelleth in love dwelleth in God, and God in him' (1 John iv. 16). These two, peace and love, not only make the prayer propitious, but are themselves reborn and shine forth from this prayer, like inseparable Divine rays, increasing and coming to perfection.

9. *Each of these three and all three together bestow upon us an abundance of all blessings*

Each of these three and all three together bestow on us and multiply in us an abundance of all blessings. For, by calling on the name of our Lord Jesus Christ with faith, we firmly hope to obtain mercy and the true life concealed in Him, which spring forth from Him as from some Divine and ever-flowing source, when within our hearts we pronounce in purity the name of our Lord Jesus Christ. With boundless peace passing all understanding, we are granted reconciliation with God and with each other. By love, which is above all praise, for it is the end and the beginning of the law and the prophets, since God is called love—we wholly unite with God. Then our sin is abolished by God's truth, and the sonship of grace acts in us miraculously through love. 'For charity shall cover the multitude of sins' (1 Peter iv. 8). Charity 'beareth all things, believeth all things, hopeth all things, endureth all things. Charity never faileth' (1 Cor. xiii. 7, 8).

10. *In the days of His passion for our salvation, our Lord Jesus Christ gave them to His disciples as final commandments and Divine heritage. He did likewise after resurrection*

Therefore the all-merciful and most sweet Lord Jesus Christ, when approaching His voluntary passion for our sakes, and when later He appeared to the Apostles after the resurrection, and also when He was about to ascend to God (His Father by nature and ours by grace), Himself like a true Father, who loves his children, left, to all who are His own, His last commandments and sweet consolations, as precious and sure pledges, so to speak, or rather as a heritage given by God. At the time of His passion for our salvation, He revealed them in the following words, spoken to His disciples: 'If ye shall ask any thing in my name, I will do it' (John xiv. 14) and: 'Verily, verily, I say unto you, Whatsoever ye shall ask the Father in my name, he will give it you. Hitherto have ye asked nothing in my name: ask, and ye shall receive, that your joy may be full' (John xvi. 23, 24). Again after resurrection He said to them: 'And these signs shall follow them that believe; In my name shall they cast out devils; they shall speak with new tongues', and so on (Mark xvi. 17). St. John says the same in his Gospel: 'And many other signs truly did Jesus in the presence of his disciples, which are not written in this book: But these are written, that ye might believe that Jesus is the Christ, the Son of God; and that believing ye might have life through his name' (John xx. 30, 31). St. Paul the Apostle says: 'At the name of Jesus every knee should bow', and so on (Phil. ii. 10). And in the Acts of the Apostles it is written: 'Then Peter, filled with the Holy Ghost, said unto them, Ye rulers of the people, and elders of Israel, If we this day be examined of the good deed done to the impotent man, by what means he is made whole; Be it known unto you all, and to all the people of Israel, that by the name of Jesus Christ of Nazareth, whom ye crucified, whom God raised from the dead, even by him doth this man stand here before you whole' (Acts iv. 8, 9, 10). And a little further: 'Neither is there salvation in any other: for there is none other name under heaven given among men, whereby we must be saved' (Acts iv. 12). And again the Saviour: 'All power is given unto me in heaven and in earth' (Matt. xxviii. 18). The same is clear from what our Lord, God and Man, said to the Apostles before the cross: 'Peace I leave with you, my peace I give unto you' (John xiv. 27); and: 'These things I have spoken unto you, that in me ye might have peace' (John xvi. 33); and: 'This is my commandment, That ye love one another, as I have loved you' (John xv. 12); and: 'By this shall all men know that ye are my disciples, if ye have love one to another' (John xiii. 35); and: 'As the Father hath loved me, so have I loved you; continue ye in my love. If ye keep my commandments, ye shall abide in my love; even as I have kept my Father's commandments, and abide in his love' (John xv. 9, 10). Then, after the resurrection He often appeared at different times to those who were His own, giving them peace and saying: 'Peace be unto you' (John xx. 21). To Peter the Apostle, to whom He gave precedence over the disciples, He said three times: 'Simon . . . lovest thou me more than these? . . . Feed my sheep' (John xxi. 15, 16), thus showing that entrusting him with the care of the flock is a certain reward for a most fervent love for Lord Jesus Christ Himself. It would not be far from our aim or our subject if someone says that the three virtues we have shown by themselves give birth to other three miraculous fruits, namely: purification of the soul, enlightenment and spiritual ripeness.

11. *All the virtues are contained in these three*

If a man undertakes an exact investigation with all his attention, he will find that the whole royal mantle of virtues woven by God hangs on this triple, unbreakable cord. For life in God is like a precious chain, rich in gold, in which one virtue is closely linked with another, and all are harmonised into one whole. This must be so, since they all constitute one body—namely, they deify a man who sincerely lives by them, as it were enriching him with their connected links. A man is enriched by the faith, and if you will, by the hope and humility, with which he calls on the most sweet name of our Lord Jesus Christ; and he is enriched also by peace and love. For these are truly a three-stemmed life-giving tree planted by God. A man touching it in due time and eating of it, as is fitting, shall gather unending and eternal life instead of death, like Adam.

12. *The gift and advent of the Holy Spirit is given to the faithful from God the Father through Christ Jesus and His holy name*

The gift and advent of the Holy Spirit is given to the faithful from God the Father through Christ Jesus and His holy name, as the most Divine and compassionate Lord Jesus Christ said to the Apostles: 'It is expedient for you that I go away: for if I go not away, the Comforter will not come unto you; but if I depart, I will send him unto you' (John xvi. 7); and: 'But when the Comforter is come, whom I will send unto you from the Father, even the Spirit of truth, which proceedeth from the Father . . .' and so forth (John xv. 26); and again: 'But the Comforter, which is the Holy Ghost, whom the Father will send in my name . . .' (John xiv. 26).

13. *The holy fathers and the Holy Spirit living in them have directed us to pray to Lord Jesus Christ and ask His mercy*

Our glorious teachers and preceptors, in whom liveth the Holy Spirit, wisely teach us all, especially those who have wished to embrace the field of Divine silence and consecrate themselves to God, having renounced the world to practise hesychasm with wisdom, and to prefer prayer to the Lord above any other work or care, begging His mercy with undaunted hope. Such men should have, as their constant practice and occupation, the invoking of His holy and most sweet name, bearing it always in the mind, in the heart and on the lips. They should force themselves in every possible way to live, breathe, sleep and wake, walk, eat and drink with Him and in Him, and in general so to do all that they have to do. For as in His absence all harmful things come to us, leaving no room for anything to profit the soul, so in His presence all evil is swept away, no good is ever lacking and everything becomes possible, as the Lord Himself says: 'He that abideth in me, and I in him, the same bringeth forth much fruit: for without me ye can do nothing' (John xv. 5). Thus, unworthy as we are, we too call with faith on this most terrible and most worshipful name; and with His aid daringly set sail and launch forth on these writings.

14. *For a man who wishes to walk in the Lord without stumbling on the path of silence, it is most necessary to choose perfect obedience, together with complete renunciation of everything*

In the name of our great God and Saviour Jesus Christ, Who said: 'I am the light of the world.' 'I am the way, the truth, and the life: no man cometh unto the Father, but by me' (John viii. 12; xiv. 6); and: 'I am the door: by me if any man enter in, he shall be saved, and shall go in and out, and find pasture' (John x. 9), that is, of course, salvation: hear what we say and sincerely advise. First of all choose for yourself, according to the Divine word, complete renunciation and perfect and sincere obedience. To this end, spare no effort in trying to find a teacher and guide, free from prelest (let his freedom from prelest be proved by testimonies from the Divine Scriptures confirming his words); he should be a man bearing the Spirit within him, leading a life corresponding to his words, lofty in vision of mind, humble in thought of himself, of good disposition in everything and generally such as a teacher of Christ should be, according to Divine words.

Having found such a man, cleave to him with body and spirit like a devoted son to his father and from then onwards obey all his commands implicitly, accord with him in everything, and see him not as a mere man, but as Christ Himself. Casting out all doubt and unbelief, as well as all thoughts and desires of your own, follow your teacher step by step, as though you were a mirror; follow him as your own conscience, observing total and unquestioning obedience. If the devil, the enemy of all good, suggests to you something contrary to this, flee from it as from lust or from fire, wisely admonishing yourself in opposition to the seducer, who put such thoughts into your head. Speak thus to yourself: 'It is not the guided who leads the guide, but the guide leads the guided; it is not I who have shouldered the verdict (the guilt) of my master, but he has done this for me; it is not I but he who is my judge, according to St. John of the Ladder', and so on.

He who wishes to tear up the account of his sins and to be inscribed in the Divine book of the saved, can find for this purpose no better means than such a mode of life, that is, obedience. For, according to St. Paul, the Son of God, our God, Lord Jesus, Who for our sake assumed our likeness, and in His wisdom obtained His Father's mercy for us, Himself followed this path of obedience, and, in His form of man thereby pleased God and was glorified, for: 'Being found in fashion as a man, he humbled himself, and became obedient unto death, even the death of the cross. Wherefore God also hath highly exalted him, and given him a name which is above every name' (Phil. ii. 8, 9). Who then would dare to hope presumptuously, if not to say foolishly, to gain the glory of our Lord and Saviour Jesus Christ and the blessings of the fathers, without choosing to follow the path of our Leader and Teacher, Jesus Christ. For if a pupil wants to become like his teacher, he must take every care to look on the life and works of his guide as an example, and as the best possible prototype, and must follow it unswervingly with all the zeal of his soul, forcing himself to imitate his teacher always and in everything. The same is written of our Lord Jesus Christ Himself, that He 'was subject unto' His father and mother (Luke ii. 51). Our Saviour says of Himself: 'The Son of man came not to be ministered unto, but to minister' (Matt. xx. 28). Is it therefore possible to think that a man leads a Divine life, in accordance with the word of God, if he lives without a guide, pandering to himself and obeying his own self-will? Naturally not. St. John of the Ladder says: 'As a man travelling without a guide easily loses his way and goes astray, so a man leading a monastic life guided by self-will easily perishes, even if he possesses all worldly wisdom.' Consequently a great many, if not to say all, of those who proceed without obedience and advice, although in their labours and sweat they dream, as in sleep, that they sow much, in truth reap but very little. Alas, some of them reap tares instead of wheat, having organised their life according to their own discretion and pleasure—which is worst of all. St. John of the Ladder says the following on this subject: 'You who have resolved to enter the path of this mental profession of faith; you, who wish to put your necks under the yoke of Christ; you who desire, from now onwards, to place your burden on the neck of another, who strive to sell yourselves voluntarily into slavery, to obtain true freedom in exchange; you who swim across this vast sea, supported by the hands of others; know that you are attempting a short but hard way which has only one road leading into error, called self-will. He who entirely renounces self-will has already attained everything he deems to be good, spiritual and pleasing to God, even before he has entered a life of spiritual struggle, for obedience means not believing that anything good comes from oneself, even to the end of life.'

Therefore you also, having wisely understood this, and wishing to learn that good part which shall not be taken away from you, that is, the heavenly path of silence, follow strictly the established laws, as is indicated, and first embrace obedience, and then silence. For as doing is a step towards contemplation, so obedience is a step towards silence. 'Remove not the ancient landmark, which thy fathers have set' (Prov. xxii. 28), and remember that 'woe to him that is alone' (Eccles. iv. 10). Thus making a good start with the laying of the foundations, you will in due time put a glorious roof on your spiritual building. For if the start lacks skill, the whole thing is futile, as someone has said. And conversely, if the start is skilful, everything is harmonious and well ordered, although at times the reverse may occur. This, however, is due to our own will.

15. *Signs of true obedience, enabling a true monk to practise obedience without downfalls*

Since there are many things to say about this mode of life which are 'hard to be uttered' (Heb. v. 11), and consequently people practise it differently, it is necessary to point out to you certain distinctive features of it which can serve as marks; if you keep to these as to a rule and plumb-line, you will be able to lead an irreproachable and sinless life. Therefore we say to you that, in our opinion, it is all-important for a true monk to keep the following *five virtues*. First of all *faith*—a pure and sincere faith in his teacher, to the extent of regarding him as Christ Himself, and obeying him as he would obey Christ. Our Lord Jesus says: 'He that heareth you heareth me; and he that despiseth you despiseth me; and he that despiseth me despiseth him that sent me' (Luke x. 16). And as the Apostle teaches: 'Whatsoever is not of faith is sin' (Rom. xiv. 23). Secondly—*truth*, that is, he must be truthful in word, deed and an exact confession of his thoughts, for it is written: 'Thy word is true from the beginning' (Ps. cxix. 160); and: 'Thou desirest truth' (Ps. li. 6). And Christ says: 'I am the truth' (John xiv. 6)—and so is called self-truth. Thirdly: *not to do his own will*, for it is said that for a monk to do his will is a great loss and great harm; he should always cut off his will, and do so voluntarily, that is, without being compelled by his father. Fourthly: *he must never contradict or be contentious*; for contradiction and contentiousness are not seemly for the righteous. The blessed Paul writes: 'But if any man seem to be contentious, we have no such custom, neither the churches of

God' (1 Cor. xi. 16). If this is quite simply forbidden to all Christians in general, how much more so to monks, who have taken a vow of complete obedience in everything. Contradiction and contentiousness come from conceit, a companion of unbelief and haughtiness; and conversely, absence of contradiction and contentiousness come from a right and wisely humble disposition. Fifthly, he should practise the following virtue: *he must confess everything to his teacher, sincerely* and exactly; since in taking our monastic vows, when we stood as it were before the terrible throne of Christ in the presence of God and His holy angels, we vowed, with our other vows and covenants with the Lord, to confess the secrets of our hearts (thoughts and desires), as the beginning and end of our actions and strivings. The divine David also says: 'I acknowledged my sin unto thee, and mine iniquity have I not hid. I said, I will confess my transgressions unto the Lord; and thou forgavest the iniquity of my sin' (Ps. xxxii. 5). St. John of the Ladder also says: 'Sores, when revealed, do not get worse but are cured.'

If a man wisely and sensibly keeps these five virtues, let him know with certainty that from then onwards he has received a pledge of future participation in the bliss of the righteous. Such are the characteristics of this ever to be remembered obedience, as it were its root, and its foundation. Now hear about its branches, its fruit and its canopy.

St. John of the Ladder says: 'Obedience gives birth to humility; humility—to the gift of good judgment; good judgment—to discernment; discernment—to pre-vision,' which is the work of God alone and a precious supernatural gift, which He bestows only on those whom He deifies. Moreover, let it be known to you, that in proportion to the sincerity and thoroughness of your obedience, humility will be born in your heart; and again in proportion to humility—good judgment. The same can be said about the whole sequence of virtues. Therefore, strain to the utmost to walk without stumbling on the path of obedience, and you will move forward without error. If, however, you stumble at the stage of obedience, then know that you will not successfully complete the course which is before you, that is, life in Christ, and will not be crowned with the victor's wreath. So let obedience, with these attributes, be your guide, or your compass, such as mariners use for plotting their course; so that, keeping your eyes steadfastly on them, you may cross the great sea of virtues without disaster, and so reach the untroubled harbour of passionlessness. If some storm or agitation attack you, this too will be in proportion to your obedience. Even the devil himself can do no harm to a truly obedient monk, as the holy fathers have said. But to show you briefly the glorious loftiness of obedience, let us again recall the words of St. John of the Ladder.

This brightest light of life in Christ, this new Bezaleel of the heavenly ladder, says: 'The fathers call psalmody a weapon; prayer—a wall; pure tears—a bath; and the blessed obedience—the profession, without which none of the passionate will see the Lord.' This inimitable simile seems to us sufficient as a most effective demonstration and glorification of thrice-blessed obedience. But we can also see from experience what a great work obedience is, if we cast our eyes on the past, both to examine the cause of our deterioration and mortality, for we were not originally created such as we are now, and again in order to discover the cause of our renewal and immortality. We find that the cause of the former, that is, of our deterioration, was the self-assurance, self-will and disobedience of Adam, which led to his abandonment and transgression of the Divine commandment; while the source of the latter, that is, of renewal and incorruptibility, is the second Adam, our Lord and God, the Saviour Jesus Christ, being of one mind with God the Father, and obedience to Him, whence comes the keeping of His commandment. 'I have not spoken of myself;' says the Lord, 'but the Father which sent me, he gave me a commandment, what I should say, and what I should speak. And I know that his commandment is life everlasting: whatsoever I speak therefore, even as the Father said unto me, so I speak' (John xii. 49, 50).

Thus, as in our forefather, and in those in his likeness, the root and mother of all evil is arrogance; so in the new God-man, Jesus Christ, and in those who resolve to live in His image, the origin, source and foundation of all blessings is humility. We see that this order and canon is observed in the holy and heavenly world of Divine angels, above us, as also in our Church on earth.

From this we learn to believe that those, who deviate from this fundamental law and insolently choose to live according to their self-will, fall away from God, from the heritage of Divine light and from the universal Church; and so are banished utterly and cast into outer darkness and the fire of hell. The same fate, we presume, awaits the deceitful evil-mongers who have taken the side of the fallen star of dawn, and the evil-minded heretical babblers who have appeared from time to time, as we read in the Scriptures. For their self-will and pride they are fatally cut off from the Divine glory and the holy community of those who please God.

One of the wise men said, that a thing is cured by its opposite. So, since the cause of all evil for us lies in disobedience and pride, whereas the source of all joy is submission and contrition: a man, who wishes to live without sin, must remain for a time in obedience to an experienced father, free from prelest, who by long and arduous work has acquired knowledge of things Divine, and whose life is adorned by all the virtues, and he must regard every command or advice of his father as the voice and advice of God Himself. For the wise Solomon says: 'In the multitude of counsellors there is safety'35 (Prov. xi. 14); and: a man without counsel is his own enemy. If some of the holy fathers succeeded in acquiring Divine silence and perfection in God without this task of obedience, it was due to special Divine revelation and was a very rare happening. And what is rare (as is written somewhere) is not the law of the Church, just as one swallow does not make the spring. But you, believing that true obedience is a certain preparatory education for the blessed silence, leave the rare cases which happened by special dispensation, and conform to what is general and established for all by the holy fathers. Thus you will gain the reward reserved for those who live according to law.

What then? If a man is unlikely to take an unexplored path without a true guide; if no one will risk going to sea without a skilful navigator; if no man will undertake to learn a science or an art without an experienced teacher, who will dare to attempt

35 The Slavonic text reads: 'In the multitude of counsels . . .'. (Translators' note.)

a practical study of the art of arts and the science of sciences, to enter the mysterious path leading to God, and venture to sail the boundless mental sea, that is monastic life, akin to the life of the angels, and be sure of reaching his goal without a guide, a navigator and a true and experienced teacher? Whoever such a man may be, he is deceiving himself indeed, and has gone astray even before starting, as one who does not conform to the law. On the contrary, a man who submits to the statutes of the fathers, reaches his goal before he has made a single step. For how else can we know how to battle against the flesh and how to arm ourselves against passions and demons? How, without such help, can we learn to discriminate between good and evil, when bad passions cling to virtues and for ever stand at their door? How shall we contrive, without their help, to curb our bodily senses and harmoniously tune the powers of our soul, like strings in a harp? Above all, how can we, without these statutes, discriminate between voices, revelations, suggestions, Divine visions, and snares, prelest and illusions of the demons? In a word, how can we attain union with God and learn the celebrations and sacraments, whose action is Divine, without being initiated into these mysteries by a true and enlightened guide? In no way is this possible—in no way—when we see that even the blessed Paul, this chosen vessel, this mouth of Christ, this light of the world, this universal sun, this teacher of the whole world, hastens to his fellow-apostles to examine with them his preaching. Why does he do it? 'Lest by any means I should run, or had run, in vain', he says (Gal. ii. 2). We see that wisdom itself, our Lord Jesus Christ, says: 'For I came down from heaven, not to do mine own will, but the will of him that sent me' (John vi. 38), and says of the holy life-giving Spirit that 'he shall not speak of himself; but whatsoever he shall hear, that shall he speak' (John xvi. 13).

Looking at this beneficial order, embracing all things of heaven and earth, we are filled with trembling, amazement and horror at the thought of our weakness and laziness, and the dangerous position of those who, through thoughtlessness and conceit, dare to be a law unto themselves or, what is the same, live with no law and order, to their own loss and destruction. Truly frightening is this undertaking, the robbers on the way are innumerable, the ambushes of pirates endless, shipwrecks are without number. And so, out of many, very few are saved.—But those, as they wish, so let them go, for it is written that 'the fire shall try every man's work of what sort it is' (1 Cor. iii. 13); and: 'For thou renderest to every man according to his work' (Ps. lxii. 12). Or rather not simply as they wish, but let them both wish and live as they must. May 'the Lord give . . . understanding in all things' (2 Tim. ii. 7). Having understood from these Scripture texts, as if from a fringe, the whole golden spiritual texture of blessed obedience, you and every other man wishing to live in God must, as has been said earlier, try to find for himself a teacher who is perfect and without error. According to the divine Paul: 'Strong meat belongeth to them that are of full age, even those who by reason of use have their senses exercised to discern both good and evil' (Heb. v. 14). Seeking thus, with all zeal and faith, you will reach your aim without going astray. 'For every one that asketh receiveth; and he that seeketh findeth; and to him that knocketh it shall be opened' (Matt. vii. 8), says the Gospel. He (the teacher you will find) will then teach you, in right order and sequence, all that is suitable and pleasing to God. Furthermore, if he sees that you willingly observe moderation, simplicity and abstinence in everything, in food and drink, dress and coverings, content with what circumstances require and what is seemly and necessary, seeking nothing superfluous, nothing that coddles the body and is merely a delight to the senses—as those who live unwisely do, thus drawing the sword against themselves and their own salvation—he will lead you towards things still more pleasing to God and more spiritual; such things as are beyond the strength of many and are not within all men's reach. For the great Apostle says: 'Having food and raiment let us be therewith content' (1 Tim. vi. 8).

But you also wish to learn from us, and to have our written exposition of everything concerning the beginning, the middle and the end of life in Christ. The question is praiseworthy but difficult to answer quickly. However, Christ will stretch out His helping hand and we shall find the solution of your question, building complete the oft praised house of spiritual architecture, that is, Divine silence, on the firm and immovable foundation of blessed obedience. So, basing our words on the sayings of the fathers inspired by the Spirit, we proceed thus:

16. *A man who sincerely wishes to embrace a life of silence in God should, together with orthodox faith, strive to be filled too with good works, and so forth*

(a) The Saviour says: 'Not every one that saith unto me, Lord, Lord, shall enter into the kingdom of heaven; but he that doeth the will of my Father which is in heaven' (Matt. vii. 21). Therefore you also, well-beloved, if your desire for Divine silence is not just bare words, but you love it in deed and in truth, strive not only to have orthodox faith but also to be filled with good works. (To those who approach it with sincerity, this Divine silence even here brings clear manifestations of the kingdom of heaven, which in the world to come will be still fuller and more perfect.) Moreover, live peaceably with all men, as much as lieth in you (Rom. xii. 18); do not get distracted by anything, do not be full of cares, that is, do not allow yourself to be possessed by vain worries, be quiet and sparing of speech, grateful for everything and conscious of your own weakness. Keep an unsleeping eye over all this, wakefully attentive to all the numerous and varied temptations which assail you every day, fighting with patience and an untroubled heart every tribulation and sorrow that may come to you.

As regards the first and the second, that is, orthodox faith and good works, you will find clear teaching on this in the words of the glorious brother of God, who says: 'Faith without works is dead' (James ii. 26), just as works without faith are dead, and: 'Show me thy faith without thy works' (James ii. 18). Before him the Teacher and Preceptor of all, our Lord Jesus Christ, said to His disciples: 'Go ye therefore and teach all nations, baptising them in the name of the Father, and of the Son, and of the Holy Ghost: teaching them to observe all things whatsoever I have commanded you' (Matt. xxviii. 19, 20). And St. Gregory the Theologian says: 'God demands the following three virtues from every man who is baptised: from the soul—true faith; from the body—chastity; from the tongue—truth.'

## (b) *Faith is of two kinds*

Note that, according to Divinely inspired words, faith is of two kinds: one, common to all orthodox Christians, the faith into which we were originally baptised, and in which we shall go out of this world; and another which belongs to very few. These latter are men who, by keeping all the Divine commandments, have reached the state of being fashioned in God's image and likeness. Being thus enriched with the Divine light of grace, they have put all their hope in the Lord to such measure that, in accordance with the word of our Lord (Mark xi. 23), when they pray they do not think in their heart about their petitions to God, but with faith both ask and readily receive what is needful. But these blessed men acquired such firmness of faith through pure works, because they had steadfastly renounced all knowledge, speculation and hesitation, had freed themselves of all cares and were totally absorbed in the Divine rapture of faith, hope and love of God, thus, according to divine David, undergoing a change to a better and more blessed state by the 'right hand of the Most High' (Ps. lxxvii. 10).

It is not timely to speak now in detail about the first faith. But it is most timely to speak of the second which springs from the first, blossoms and bears Divine fruit. This faith is, as it were, the root and beginning of Divine silence. St. John of the Ladder says: 'If the hesychast has no faith, how will he lead a life of silence?' (27, 68). The divine David also says: 'I believed, therefore have I spoken' (Ps. cxvi. 10). And the great Apostle Paul says: 'Faith is the substance of things hoped for, the evidence of things not seen' (Heb. xi. 1); and: 'The just shall live by faith' (Heb. x. 38). And the Lord, when the disciples asked Him to increase their faith, said: 'If ye had faith as a grain of mustard seed, ye might say unto this sycamine tree, Be thou plucked up by the root, and be thou planted in the sea; and it should obey you' (Luke xvii. 6); and on another occasion: 'If ye have faith, and doubt not, ye shall not only do this which is done to the fig tree, but also if ye shall say unto this mountain, Be thou removed, and be thou cast into the sea; it shall be done. And all things, whatsoever ye shall ask in prayer, believing, ye shall receive'

(Matt. xxi. 21, 22). St. Isaac also writes: 'Faith is more subtle than knowledge, as knowledge is more subtle than sensory things. All the saints who have embraced this life of awe-inspiring veneration of God, by the power of their faith remain in enjoyment of this supernatural life. By faith we mean here, not faith in the three distinct Divine hypostases we worship, nor in the one all-supreme nature of the Deity; nor faith in the miraculous dispensation of incarnation through assuming our nature—although this faith is also extremely lofty—but that faith which is ignited in the soul by the light of grace; which, through the evidence of the mind, fortifies the heart in sureness of hope remote from all self-opinion, which shows itself not in inclining the ear of hearing but in contemplating with spiritual eyes the mysteries hidden in the soul, those riches of grace, concealed from the eyes of the sons of the flesh, and revealed by the Spirit to those who feed at the feast of Christ by practising His laws, as He said: If you keep my commandments, I shall send you a Comforter, "the Spirit of Truth; whom the world cannot receive . . . he shall teach you all things" (John xiv. 17, 26). He reveals to man this holy force, which dwells in him for all times, ever protecting him and driving all harm away from him. This force the spiritual mind senses with the eyes of faith. It is that same Comforter, Who ignites the forces of the soul with the force of faith, as with a flame, and the soul soars on high, oblivious of all danger through its hope in God. On the wings of faith, it rises above all visible creation and forever remains in a state of rapture in wonder at the Divine solicitude for us, and in pure contemplation of Divine Being. For until this consummation of the mysteries comes and we are vouchsafed their clear revelation, it is faith that ministers the ineffable mysteries between God and the saints (that is, receives, maintains and contemplates these mysteries). By the grace of Christ, may we too be vouchsafed these mysteries, here as a token, and in the kingdom of heaven in actual truth' (Ch. 28).

### (c) *You should be at peace*

Concerning the third thing, that you should be at peace with all men, you find a strong admonition in the saying of the blessed David and a word, louder than the trumpet-call, from Paul the

Christ-bearer. The first says: 'Great peace have they which love thy law: and nothing shall offend them' (Ps. cxix. 165); and: 'My soul hath long dwelt with him that hateth peace' (Ps. cxx. 6); and: 'Seek peace and pursue it' (Ps. xxxiv. 14); and the second announces: 'Follow peace with all men, and holiness, without which no man shall see the Lord' (Heb. xii. 14); and: 'If it be possible, as much as lieth in you, live peaceably with all men' (Rom. xii. 18).

### (d) *You should not be distracted*

St. Isaac admonishes you on the fourth, that is, the necessity of not being distracted, saying: 'If lusting is engendered by the senses, let them finally hold their tongue who assert that they preserve peace of mind even amid many vain distractions. Have no intercourse with such restless people.'

### (e) *You must not be engrossed in worries and cares*

As to the fifth, that is, that you must not be engrossed in worries and cares about things whether of good or evil report, you will find a lesson in the words of the Lord in the Gospels: 'Therefore I say unto you, Take no thought for your life, what ye shall eat, or what ye shall drink; nor yet for your body, what ye shall put on. Is not the life more than meat, and the body than raiment? Behold the fowls of the air: for they sow not, neither do they reap, nor gather into barns: yet your heavenly Father feedeth them. Are ye not much better than they? Which of you by taking thought can add one cubit unto his stature? And why take ye thought for raiment?—Therefore take no thought, saying, What shall we eat? or, What shall we drink? or, Wherewithal shall be be clothed? (For after all these things do the Gentiles seek:) for your heavenly Father knoweth that ye have need of all these things. But seek ye first the kingdom of God, and his righteousness; and all these things shall be added unto you. Take therefore no thought for the morrow: for the morrow shall take thought for the things of itself. Sufficient unto the day is the evil thereof' (Matt. vi. 25-8, 31-4). And St. Isaac says: 'Without freedom from cares do not expect to find light in your soul, nor peace and silence with your senses at large' (Ch. 69, 1). And John of the

Ladder says: 'A small hair worries the eye and a small care destroys silence, for silence means laying aside of all thoughts not bearing on the work of salvation, and renunciation of all cares, even for matters of good report. Nor will a man who has attained true silence worry about his body for He Who promised to care for it is not false' (Ch. 27, 51, 52).

### (f) *You should be abstinent in speech*

According to the order of our directions, we must now speak of the sixth, that is, that you should be abstinent in speech. St. Isaac says: 'Above all love abstinence in speech, for it brings you nearer to the fruit. The tongue cannot express it. First of all let us force ourselves to abstain from speech; then from this abstinence will be born in us something which leads to silence itself. May God grant you the experience of this something, born of this abstinence. But if you embrace this life, I cannot tell you how much light it will bring you. When you put on one side of the scales all the works of this life (life of a monk, of a hesychast), and on the other silence, you will find that the latter outweighs the former' (Ch. 41, p. 250). 'Silence is the mystery of future life, whereas words are the instrument of this world' (Ch. 42, p. 263). 'He who forbids his lips to gossip (to speak much), preserves his heart from passions. He who preserves his heart from passions, sees God every hour' (Ch. 8, from the beginning). To St. Arsenius also the Divine voice spoke thus the second time: 'Arsenius! flee, speak not, abide in silence, for in that are the roots of sinlessness' ('Sayings about St. Arsenius', 2).

### (g) *You should practise silence (love solitude)*

About the seventh, that is the necessity to lead a solitary life of silence, you will find authentic indications in Basil the Great and again in St. Isaac. The first says: 'Silence is the beginning of purification of the soul,' and the second: 'The end of silence is stillness from all things.' With these words the former describes in brief the beginning of silence, and the latter its end. In the Old Testament it is also written: 'Be still, and know that I am God' (Ps. xlvi. 10). And St. John of the Ladder says: 'The first work of silence is freedom from cares for all things, whether of good or evil report, for he who opens the door to the former is sure to fall into the latter. The second work is prayer free from laziness; and the third—unrobbed doing of the heart. Just as in the natural order of things it is impossible to read books if one does not know the alphabet, even more impossible is it to practise the last two works of silence with understanding, without having acquired the first' (Ch. 27, 46). And again St. Isaac writes: 'The constant welcome expectation of death should be a necessary practice of silence. A man who embraces silence without this thought, cannot endure what we have to bear and suffer at all costs' (Ch. 41, p. 255).

#### (h) *You should give thanks to God for everything*

As to the eighth, that is the necessity to give thanks to God for everything, the teaching of the divine Apostle Paul should suffice you, when he says: 'In every thing give thanks' (1 Thess. v. 18). Add to this also St. Isaac who writes: 'Gratitude from the receiver incites the giver to bestow gifts greater than before. He who is ungrateful in lesser things, is false and unjust in greater' (Ch. 2, from the beginning). Again: 'The transmitter of Divine gifts to man is the heart, continually moved to gratitude, and the transmitter of temptations to the soul is discontented thought for ever moving in the heart.' Again: 'Lips forever giving thanks receive God's blessing, and a heart filled with gratitude unexpectedly receives grace.'

#### (i) *You should be conscious of your own weakness*

You will understand the ninth, that is, what great good is gathered in a man who has reached the understanding of his own weakness, if you ponder over the sixth psalm of divine David, which says: 'Have mercy upon me, O Lord; for I am weak' (Ps. vi. 2); and in another place: 'I am a worm, and no man; a reproach of men, and despised of the people' (Ps. xxii. 6). And St. Isaac says: 'Blessed is the man who realises his weakness, for this knowledge becomes the foundation, the root and the beginning of every boon. For as soon as a man understands and truly feels his weakness, he immediately puts a restraint on the vain pride of his soul which obscures reason, and thus he gains protection' (Ch. 61, from the beginning); and: 'A man, who has reached an understanding of his own measure, has attained perfect humility.'

### (j) *You must valiantly endure temptations*

The last paragraph of this chapter, which completes the ten we planned, shows that it is necessary valiantly to endure the many and varied temptations which may assail you and to resist them with patience and courage. So listen to the words of the Holy Scriptures about this. Here is what Paul the Christ-bearer says: 'For we wrestle not against flesh and blood, but against principalities, against powers, against the rulers of the darkness of this world, against spiritual wickedness in high places' (Eph. vi. 12); and: 'But if ye be without chastisement, whereof all are partakers, then are ye bastards, and not sons' (Heb. xii. 8); and: 'For whom the Lord loveth he chasteneth, and scourgeth every son whom he receiveth' (Heb. xii. 6). The meaning of the first chapter of the epistle of James, the brother of God, is the following: 'A man who has not endured temptations has not been tried.' St. Elias Ekdikos says: 'No Christian, believing in God, should be careless, but should always expect temptation and be ready for it, so that, when it comes, he may not think it strange and be confused by it, but suffer the burden of affliction with gratitude, remembering the words of the prophet: "Examine me, O Lord, and prove me" (Ps. xxvi. 2); and: "Your chastisement will correct me in the end" (quotation not identified); he does not say, Your chastisement will destroy me, but that it will correct me in the end.'

Do not seek to find the causes of temptations or whence they come; only pray to suffer them with gratitude, as St. Mark says: 'When a temptation assails you, do not seek to understand why and wherefore it comes; your only care should be to bear it gratefully and without rancour' (St. Mark on exculpation by deeds, Ch. 198). Again: 'Since there is no man who could please God without temptations, one should give thanks to God for every sorrowful occurrence' (ibid., Ch. 200); and: 'Every affliction reveals the disposition of our will, whether it inclines to the right or to the left. An affliction is therefore called temptation, because it puts to the test the man afflicted by it, proving his inner disposition' (ibid., Ch. 204). St. Isaac also says, among other things: 'Temptation is useful for every man. For if temptation was useful to Paul, then "every mouth may be stopped, and all the world may become guilty before God" (Rom. iii. 19). Spiritual doers are tempted, that they may add to their riches; the weak—that they may protect themselves from harm; those who are asleep—to prepare them for awakening; those far away —to bring them nearer to God; those who are of God's own household (who dwell in His house)—that they may abide in Him with daring. A son who is not made to practise (carrying burdens) cannot profitably inherit the riches of his father's house. Therefore God first tempts and oppresses, and then reveals the gift of grace. Glory be to the Lord, leading us to the sweetness of health by bitter remedies! No man can pass the time of his education without affliction; and no man, while drinking the poison of temptations, can fail to find it bitter. Yet without them it is impossible to acquire a strong constitution (of the soul). But again, to withstand them is not in our power. How could perishable clay withstand the action of water unless the Divine fire make it strong? If we submit to the yoke of God's will and pray with constant desire in humility, then, through patience, we also shall receive everything from our Lord Jesus Christ' (Ch. 37, pp. 231-2). In the book of the Wisdom of Jesus the Son of Sirach it is also said: 'My son, if thou come to serve the Lord, prepare thy soul for temptation. Set thy heart aright, and constantly endure, and make not haste in time of trouble' (Ecclus. ii. 1, 2).

*You should put your hope in God and expect all good things from Him*

Firmly place the anchor of hope (Heb. vi. 19) in God, Who can save men, and expect from Him the ceasing of temptations in due time. For the Apostle says: 'But God is faithful, who will not suffer you to be tempted above that you are able; but will with the temptation also make a way to escape' (1 Cor. x. 13). Hear what more the Scriptures have to say: 'Tribulation worketh patience; And patience, experience; and experience, hope; And hope maketh not ashamed' (Rom. v. 3-5). 'But he that shall endure unto the end, the same shall be saved' (Matt. xxiv. 13). 'In your patience possess ye your souls' (Luke xxi. 19). 'My brethren, count it all joy when ye fall into divers temptations; Knowing this, that the trying of your faith worketh patience. But let patience have her perfect work, that ye may be perfect and entire, wanting nothing. . . Blessed is the man that endureth temptation: for when he is tried, he shall receive the crown of life, which the Lord hath promised to them that love Him' (James i. 2–4, 12). 'The sufferings of this present time are not worthy to be compared with the glory which shall be revealed in us' (Rom. viii. 18). 'I waited patiently for the Lord; and He inclined unto me, and heard my cry. He brought me up also out of an horrible pit, out of the miry clay, and set my feet upon a rock, and established my goings. And He hath put a new song in my mouth, even praise unto our God' (Ps. xl. 1–3). The blessed Simeon Metaphrastes writes: 'A soul bound by the bonds of love to God, regards sufferings as nothing, takes joy in sorrows and blossoms in grief. When it suffers nothing for the sake of its Beloved, it thirsts still more for sufferings and flees from consolation as from torment.'

### 17. Of the fear of God, which is twofold: in beginners, and in the perfect

Let us not be slow now in mentioning the twofold fear of God, since the holy fathers place fear of God after faith in the order of virtues.

#### Of the first fear of God—in beginners

Know, beloved, that the fear of God is twofold; in beginners; and in the perfect. The following is written of the first fear: 'The fear of the Lord is the beginning of wisdom' (Ps. cxi. 10; Prov. i. 7). 'Come ye children, hearken unto me: I will teach you the fear of the Lord' (Ps. xxxiv. 11). 'By the fear of the Lord men depart from evil' (Prov. xvi. 6), and where there is fear, there the commandments are kept. The blessed Isaac says: 'Fear of the Lord is the beginning of virtue. It is regarded as the offspring of faith, and is sown in the heart when the mind becomes estranged from worldly vanity, and collects its dispersed thoughts by constant absorption in the coming regeneration of all things' (Ch. 1, from the beginning); and: 'The beginning of true life in man is—fear of God: but it cannot bear to remain in the soul in company with dispersed thoughts' (ibid., p. 4); and: 'Strive to make fear of God serve as the foundation of your progress, and in a few days you will find yourself at the doors of the kingdom, without wandering on the way' (ibid., p. 7).

### On the second, the perfect fear of God

The following is said of the second or the perfect fear of God: 'Blessed is the man that feareth the Lord, that delighteth greatly in his commandments' (Ps. cxii. 1). 'Blessed is every one that feareth the Lord; that walketh in his ways' (Ps. cxxviii. 1). 'O fear the Lord, ye his saints: for there is no want to them that fear him' (Ps. xxxiv. 9). 'Behold, that thus shall the man be blessed that feareth the Lord' (Ps. cxxviii. 4). 'The fear of the Lord is clean, enduring for ever' (Ps. xix. 9). St. Peter of Damascus writes: 'The sign of the first fear is hatred and anger against sin, like the anger of a man mauled by a wild beast. The sign of the perfect fear is love of virtue and fear of changeability; for no man is safe from changing. Therefore in this life we should always fear falling down in whatever work we do' (Book 2, Ch. 3, p. 14, in the Russian). Therefore you too, who hear all this with understanding, strive duly to preserve in yourself also the first fear, together with all the other virtues mentioned above. For it is the strongest treasure-house for all good works. If you keep to this, you will always have your steps directed towards doing all the commandments of our Lord Jesus Christ. As you progress further on this path, you will acquire also perfect fear in its purity, through love of virtues and through the mercy and loving kindness of our Lord.

18. *When the time comes we should not spare our life itself for the commandments and for faith in our Lord Jesus Christ*

You should know, too, that for the sake of the life-giving commandments and faith in our Lord Jesus Christ we must, if needs be, be ready willingly to lose our very soul, that is, not spare our life, as the Lord Jesus Christ Himself says: 'For whosoever will save his life shall lose it; but whosoever shall lose his life for my sake and the gospel's, the same shall save it' (Mark

viii. 35), believing without doubt or wavering that our Saviour, God and Man, Jesus Christ is Himself the resurrection and the life, and everything that leads to salvation, as He Himself said: 'I am the resurrection, and the life; he that believeth in me, though he were dead, yet shall he live: and whosoever liveth and believeth in me shall never die' (John xi. 25, 26); and: 'For God so loved the world, that he gave his only begotten Son, that whosoever believeth in him should not perish, but have everlasting life' (John iii. 16); and also: 'I am come that they might have life, and that they might have it more abundantly' (John x. 10). So abiding in this disposition, 'forgetting those things which are behind, and reaching forth unto those things which are before' (Phil. iii. 13), press forward with our Lord Jesus Christ, without 'looking back' (Luke ix. 62).

At this point it seems to us suitable to expound a certain natural method of the blessed Nicephorus of entering the heart by attention through breathing, which contributes to the concentration of thoughts. After quoting the evidence of many holy fathers concerning inner life, this holy man says the following from his own experience:

19. *The natural method of entering the heart by attention through breathing, together with saying the prayer: Lord Jesus Christ, Son of God, have mercy upon me. This method contributes greatly to the concentration of thoughts* [36]

'You know, brother, how we breathe: we breathe the air in and out. On this is based the life of the body and on this depends its warmth. So, sitting down in your cell, collect your mind, lead it into the path of the breath along which the air enters in, constrain it to enter the heart together with the inhaled air, and keep it there. Keep it there, but do not leave it silent and idle; instead give it the following prayer: "Lord, Jesus Christ, Son of God, have mercy upon me." Let this be its constant occupation, never to be abandoned. For this work, by keeping the mind free from dreaming, renders it unassailable to suggestions of the enemy and leads it to Divine desire and love. Moreover, brother, strive

[36] This text differs somewhat from that given in 'Nicephorus', pp. 31–34 above. (Translators' note.)

to accustom your mind not to come out too soon; for at first it feels very lonely in that inner seclusion and imprisonment. But when it gets accustomed to it, it begins on the contrary to dislike darting about among external things. For the kingdom of God is within us, and for a man who has seen it within, and having found it through pure prayer, has experienced it, everything outside loses its attraction and value. It is no longer unpleasant and wearisome for him to be within. Just as a man who has been away from home, when he returns is beside himself with joy at seeing again his children and wife, so the mind, after being dispersed, when it reunites with the soul, is filled with unspeakable sweetness and joy' (an abbreviated quotation). These are the words of this blessed father, uttered for the purpose of teaching the mind, under the influence of this natural method, to abandon its usual circling, captivity and dispersion and to return to attention to itself; and through such attention to reunite with itself and in this way to become one with the prayer and, together with the prayer, to descend into the heart and to remain there for ever. Another father filled with Divine wisdom, and experienced in this sacred doing, says the following in explanation of what has been said:

20. *More about the natural method of calling on Lord Jesus Christ in conjunction with breathing*

A man who wishes to learn this doing should know that, when we have accustomed our mind to enter within while inhaling, we shall have learnt in practice that at the moment when the mind is about to descend within, it forthwith rejects every thought and becomes single and naked, freed from all memory but that of calling on our Lord Jesus Christ. Conversely, when it comes out and turns towards the external, it immediately becomes distracted by varied memories.

21. *St. John Chrysostom also teaches praying in the heart with the words: Lord Jesus Christ, Son of God, have mercy upon me*

The great Chrysostom also says: 'I implore you, brethren, never to break or despise the rule of this prayer.' And a little further: 'A monk when he eats, drinks, sits, officiates, travels or does any other thing must continually cry: "Lord, Jesus Christ,

Son of God, have mercy upon me!'' so that the name of Lord Jesus, descending into the depths of the heart, should subdue the serpent ruling over the inner pastures and bring life and salvation to the soul. He should always live with the name of Lord Jesus, so that the heart absorbs the Lord and the Lord the heart, and the two become one.' And again: 'Do not estrange your heart from God, but abide in Him and always guard your heart by remembering our Lord Jesus Christ, until the name of the Lord becomes rooted in the heart and it ceases to think of anything else. May Christ be glorified in you.'

### 22. *Evidence of the same from St. John of the Ladder and St. Hesychius*

St. John of the Ladder says: 'May the memory of Jesus combine with your breathing; then will you understand the use of silence' (Ch. 27, 61). Hesychius says: 'If you truly wish to cover thoughts with shame, to keep silence as you should and to be sober in your heart without effort, let the Jesus prayer cleave to your breath—and in a few days you will see it in practice' (Ch. 182).

### 23. *Every man who wishes to practise mental sobriety—especially a beginner—should, for the sake of better training in prayer, live in a quiet, dimly lit cell; for, through this, mind and thoughts naturally become collected into one*

What we have described is the main thing, long ago ordained by the great holy fathers, as is seen from the evidence we have mentioned concerning the method by which we should descend with the breath into the heart with our Lord Jesus Christ, Son of God, and there pray, reflect and practise sobriety and seek His help in His holy and life-saving name. In addition we add the following: every man striving to practise mental sobriety in his heart, and especially a beginner, should always, and particularly at the appointed time of prayer, seek refuge in his cell, quiet and dimly lit, as the divine fathers and teachers, experienced in this blessed doing, direct and advise. For sight, seeing with the eyes, usually distracts and disperses thoughts; but if a man be shut up in a quiet and dimly lit room, as is said, thoughts cease to dart about and multiply, and thus the mind, whether it likes it or not, little by little grows more still and collected within itself; as St. Basil says: 'A mind undistracted by external things and not dispersed through the senses among worldly things, returns to itself.'

24. *Collectedness is given to the mind above all by our Lord Jesus Christ when we call on His holy name in our heart with faith. This natural method of descending into the heart by way of breathing, and seclusion in a quiet dimly lit place, as well as all other similar things, are merely certain aids to this*

The first, or rather the greatest and most important, thing on which the success of this mental doing depends is the help of the Divine grace, together with a heart-felt, pure and undistracted calling to our Lord Jesus Christ; and it can in no way be achieved solely by this natural method of descent into the heart by way of breathing, or by seclusion in a quiet and dimly lit place. This can never be!

For the only reason why this method was invented by the holy fathers was to help to collect thoughts, and to bring the mind from its usual dispersed flitting back to itself and to concentrate its attention, as has been said earlier.

Collected thoughts and concentrated attention make the mind pray unceasingly, purely and undistractedly, as St. Nilus says: 'Attention seeking prayer will find prayer; for what most naturally follows upon attention is prayer, and it is upon prayer that our greatest efforts should be directed' (Ch. 179). This is how one should look upon this doing. But you, my child, although of the flesh, are moved by love for a better life and a desire to live in your body as though free from it; so you should live according to the following rule and statute.

25. *How the hesychast should spend his time from evening to the time he wakes up from sleep*

After sunset, having asked the help of the all-merciful and all-powerful Lord Jesus Christ, sit you down on a low stool in your quiet and dimly lit cell, collect your mind from its customary circling and wandering outside, and quietly lead it into the heart by way of breathing, keeping this prayer: 'Lord, Jesus Christ,

Son of God, have mercy upon me!' connected with the breath. In this way, in conjunction with breathing, you introduce into the heart the words of the prayer, as Hesychius says: 'Connect with your breathing sobriety, the name of Jesus, an unfailing memory of death and humility; for all these bring great profit' (189). In addition to this, connect with this prayer memory of judgment and reward for good and evil deeds and, with all your soul regarding yourself the most sinful of all men and more despicable than the demons, have in mind that you are due to be eternally tormented in hell. If one of these thoughts brings contrition, tears and weeping, pause at this thought until the tears cease of themselves. If you are not yet granted the gift of tears, take on this doing and pray with humble thoughts to acquire them. For by them we are purified from passions and filth, and by them also we gain good and saving dispositions, as St. John of the Ladder says: 'As fire consumes wood, so pure tears consume every filth both visible and mental' (Ch. 7, 31). And another father says: 'A man who wants to strip himself of what is bad, let him do so through tears, and he who wants to acquire virtues let him acquire them through weeping. If you have no contrition, know that you are possessed by vanity, for it prevents the soul from being contrite.' If tears do not come, having sat thus praying and paying attention to such thoughts for about an hour, get up and sing with attention the small compline. Then sit down again and keep to the same prayer as much as you can, purely and without distraction, with no cares or thoughts or dreaming, but with complete sobriety, for about half an hour. Finally, crossing yourself and your bed with the sign of the holy and life-giving cross, sit down on it and ponder over future bliss and torment, over the transitory and deceptive nature of everything temporal, over the sudden coming of death—due to us all —and over the terrible torture of cross-examination after and before death. Remember briefly all your trespasses and warmly beg forgiveness for them. Having examined in detail how you have spent the day, lie down on your bed, keeping the prayer, as someone said: 'Go to sleep and sleep with the prayer of Jesus.' Sleep for about five or six hours; in general regulate your sleep by the length of the night.

### 26. *How, upon awakening, to spend time till the morning*

Upon awakening, first give praise to God and, having asked His intercession, begin your most important work, that is, to pray in the heart, purely and without distraction. Pray thus for about an hour. At this time the mind is usually quiet and serene by itself. We are commanded to bring the first and the best as offering to God, that is our first thought which we must direct straight to our Lord Jesus Christ in a pure prayer of the heart, as St. Nilus says: 'He who always brings all his first thoughts like ripe fruit to God makes his prayer heard' (Ch. 126). Then sing the midnight service.

You may not be well grounded in perfect silence and so cannot begin as we have said for one reason or another, as often happens with beginners in this doing, and at times, though rarely, with those who have achieved some success in it but have not yet reached perfection, for only the perfect 'can do all things through Christ which strengtheneth them' (Phil. iv. 13); in that case, rise up from sleep and, having re-established wakeful sobriety as far as is in your power, first sing the midnight service with attention and understanding of what is sung.

After this sit down and pray in your heart, purely and without distraction, as has been shown, for about an hour, or better still for as long as you are granted by the Bestower of bounty. St. John of the Ladder says: 'During the night spend more time in prayer and less in psalmody. During the day arrange your work to correspond with your strength' (Ch. 27, 77).

If after thus forcing yourself you are still weakened by sleep and laziness, get up and tense yourself, always keeping to the prayer and trying with every possible effort to bring yourself to an awakened state (St. Isaac says: 'Go out and walk for a short time'). Then sit down and pray, as is written, always taking the greatest care to converse with the Pure God with pure prayer.

Then get up, sing with understanding the sextet of psalms, Psalm li, and some canon of your own choice. Then sit down once more and again pray for half an hour with sincere sobriety. Then again get up, sing praises to God, the usual doxology and the first hour. Thereupon recite the dismissal.

Utter with your lips what you read in a voice barely loud enough for your own ears to hear, since we are also commanded to offer to the Lord the fruit of our lips. With all your soul and all your thought give thanks to the all-wise God for His loving kindness and solicitude for us, in allowing us, in His infinite mercy, to cross safely the abyss of the past night and to see the bright scene of the day. Moreover, pray warmly for strength safely to weather the ominous raging tempest of passions and demons.

### 27. *How to pass the time from morning to dinner-time*

Relying entirely on God alone, and praying to Him with contrition to implore His help in your weakness, laziness and thoughtlessness, try to spend all the time from morning till dinner-time in prayer of the heart, pure and undistracted, as much as your strength allows you, and in reading. When reading the allotted Psalms, the Apostle and the Holy Gospels, read them standing; do the same in reciting prayers to our Lord Jesus Christ and the Holy Mother of God. Read the other Scriptures sitting down. When the appointed time comes sing with attention the usual hours, wisely established by the fathers, straining with all the strength of your soul to banish idleness, this mentor of evil, and avoiding passions as well as their causes, no matter how small and innocent they may appear.

### 28. *About the necessity of avoiding idleness and the need for the hesychast to keep the traditions of the Church*

St. Isaac says: 'Beware of idleness, well beloved, for it conceals certain death; and it is idleness alone that delivers a monk into the hands of enemies striving to capture him. On that day God will condemn us not for psalms nor for omitting prayers, but for the fact that by omitting them we opened the door to the demons. When those latter find a way in, they enter and close the doors of our eyes. Then they fill us tyrannically with all manner of filth which will bring Divine condemnation and most severe punishment. Thus, for a small omission in a thing which, for Christ's sake, is considered worthy of the greatest care, we become like those of whom it is written: "Whoever does not submit his will to God will fall under the yoke of His adversary.'' Therefore you should do in your cell the work wisely established by those in charge of the statutes of the Church, based on the revelation of the spirit for the purpose of preserving our life; and you should regard this work as a wall protecting you from those who aim at capturing us, no matter how small this work may seem to you. It looks small only to the unwise who do not take into consideration the harm that comes from this. But for such men both the beginning and the middle of the way is unrestrained freedom, which is the mother of passions. Therefore it is better to exert oneself not to omit this little, lest by this omission one makes room for sin. For the end of such disastrous freedom is cruel slavery' (Ch. 71, p. 519).

A little further he says: 'How enticing are impulses to passions! A man may sometimes cut off passionate actions and install a certain measure of peace in himself by withdrawing from their objects, thus enjoying rest from them. But he cannot stop passionate impulses. This is why we experience temptations even against our will; and we grieve over passions (when they arise), yet we love to prolong their impulses and their sweetness. Sins we do not desire; yet we accept with enjoyment the impulses which lead us to them. So in practice the latter become for us the cause of the former. He who enjoys the sweetmeats of passions becomes involuntarily subjected to them and is a slave to his passions against his will. He who hates his sins will cease to commit sins, and he who confesses them will receive absolution. But it is impossible for a man to be freed from the habit of sin before he hates it, just as it is impossible to receive forgiveness before confessing his trespasses; the one is the cause of true humility, and the other—of contrition born in the heart from shame' (ibid., p. 529). And: 'There is no unforgivable sin, except the sin that is not repented' (Ch. 2, p. 12). But enough of that.

After singing the said hours you should sit down and eat, keeping the prayer while you eat your food, in order by so doing to acquire, by God's grace, the practice of praying without ceasing, as we are commanded. Directions about food which, in the infinite wisdom of the Creator, maintains the body, must wait a while, for first we must speak about the food which gives life and force to the soul, which, according to the holy fathers, is sacred and Divine prayer. This is only just, for the soul is more precious than the body.

### 29. *More about prayer and the need to pray always*

As when the soul leaves, the body becomes dead and stinking; so the soul not urging itself to prayer is dead, damned and fetid. The great prophet Daniel, who chose death rather than being without prayer for a single moment (Ch. 9), teaches us that we should regard being deprived of prayer as worse than any death. St. John Chrysostom too speaks well on this: 'Every man', he says, 'when praying converses with God. Each of us understands how great a thing it is, being man, to converse with God; but I doubt if anyone can express this honour in words, for it is higher even than the station of angels.' And: 'Prayer is a doing common to both angels and men; and no wall divides the two kinds of being in this doing. Prayer separates you from those who lack the Word and unites you with the angels. A man who strives all his life to practise praying and serving God, speedily becomes akin to angels in life, honour, estate, wisdom and understanding.' Again: 'When the devil sees a soul protected by virtues, he dare not come near it, fearing the strength and power given to it by prayer, which feeds the soul more richly than food feeds the body.' And: 'Prayers are the nerves of the soul. By nerves the body is kept in order, lives, moves and remains stable; but when the nerves are cut the whole harmony of the body is destroyed; in the same way souls are kept in order by holy prayers, acquire stability and move smoothly and easily in the way of righteousness. If you deprive yourself of prayer, it is like taking a fish out of water. For as water means life to a fish, so prayer means life to you. As a fish through water, so the soul can rise through the air to heaven and stand in the presence of God.' Again: 'Prayer and praying make men temples of God. As gold, precious stones and marble adorn the palaces of kings, so do prayers adorn the temples of Christ—the souls of believers. What greater praise can there be for prayer than that it makes us temples of God, and that He Whom the heavens cannot contain yet enters into the living soul in prayers?' And: 'The power of holy prayers can be seen from how Paul, who traversed the whole universe as on wings, lived in prisons, endured floggings, was put in chains, lived among blood and suffering, cast out demons, raised the dead, cured diseases, yet put his trust in none of these in building the salvation of men, but kept his soul safe by prayers and, when he had performed miracles and raised the dead, hastened to prayer as to the supreme doing, crowning all endeavour—for it is prayer that bestows the power of raising the dead and of all else. For prayers have the same power in the lives of saints as water in the life of trees.' Again: 'Prayer is the cause of salvation, the source of immortality, the indestructible wall of the Church, the unassailable fortress, which terrifies the demons and protects us in the work of righteousness.' And: 'As a queen entering a town is attended by all kinds of riches, so prayer, entering a soul, brings every virtue in its train.' And: 'Prayer in the soul is as the foundation to a house. Setting it in the soul, as root and foundation, we must zealously build thereon chastity, care of the poor and the fulfilment of all the laws of Christ.' And again: 'Zealous prayer is the light of mind and soul, a constant, inextinguishable light. Therefore during prayer our bitter enemy floods our mind and drenches our soul with a measureless filth of thoughts and collects together quantities of things which had never entered our heads.' And: 'Prayer is a great weapon, a great protection.' The Theologian also says: 'It is more essential to remember God than to breathe.' And: 'You must think of God more often than you breathe.' And St. Isaac says: 'You cannot approach God without constant prayer.' And: 'Placing some other care in the mind, after the work of prayer, brings dispersal of thoughts.' And: 'Every prayer which does not tire the body, and make the heart contrite is like an abortive child: for such a prayer is without soul.' And St. John of the Ladder says: 'In quality prayer is communion ($\sigma\upsilon\nu\upsilon\upsilon\sigma\acute{\iota}\alpha$, co-existence, merging into one being) and union of man with God. In action, it is what the world stands by, reconciliation with God, the mother of tears and again their daughter, propitiation for sin, a bridge over temptations, a wall against sorrows, the cessation of warfare, the doing of angels, the food of all incorporeal spirits, the future bliss, a doing without end or limit, the source of virtues, the seeker and finder of gifts, invisible achievement, food of the soul, light of the mind, the sword cutting off despair, the evidence of hope, the loosing of the bonds of sorrow, the riches of monks, the treasure of hesychasts, the gradual decrease of anger to nought, the mirror of achievement, the measure of a man's degree, the evidence of spiritual state, the foreteller of the future, the sign of glorification. For a man who truly prays, prayer is the torture chamber, the court of justice and the throne of the Lord even before the throne of the future' (Ch. 28, 1). And: 'Prayer is estrangement from the world both visible and invisible.' And St. Nilus says: 'If you wish to achieve prayer, renounce all to inherit all.' And: 'Prayer is ascent of the mind to God.' Again: 'Prayer is converse of the mind with God.' And: 'Bread is food for the body, virtue—for the soul: prayer is spiritual food for the mind.'

So think thus of prayer (as of food of the soul).

Now it is timely to speak briefly, as far as is in our power, of physical food, its measure, quality and quantity.

### 30. On diet for a hesychast

It is written: Son of man, thou shalt eat bread and drink water by measure (Ezek. iv. 9–11), as much as is needful to keep alive a man struggling for God. For, as one of the fathers says, if you do not give of your blood, you will not receive the Spirit. And the great Paul says: 'But I keep under my body, and bring it into subjection: lest that by any means, when I have preached to others, I myself should be a castaway' (1 Cor. ix. 27). The divine David says the same: 'My knees are weak through fasting; and my flesh faileth of fatness' (Ps. cix. 24). And the Theologian: 'Nothing pleases God more than sufferings or bodily privations for His sake; and nothing attracts His loving kindness more than tears.' And St. Isaac says: 'As a mother cares for her child, so Christ cares for the body of the sufferer (one who endures bodily privations for His sake), and is always close to his body' (Ch. 58). Again: 'A satiated body has no vision of the mysteries of God' (ibid.). And: 'As those who sow tears reap joy, so sufferers for God's sake (who voluntarily suffer bodily privations) are filled with gladness.' And: 'Blessed is he who has barred the door to all

sensory delights which draw him away from his Creator'
(Ch. 75).

Again: 'As one who for long was subjected to temptations,
both from the right and the left, and who has thus had many
occasions to study himself by those two means, having endured
innumerable blows from the foe and having received great help
in secret, in the course of many years I have acquired experience
and, with the help of God's grace, I have learnt the following:

'The foundation of all good, escape of the soul from enemy
bondage, the way leading to light and life—all this is included in
the following methods: gathering oneself to singleness and observing continuous fast; that is, subjecting oneself to a wise and
sensible rule of abstinence in food, and constantly abiding in one
place, continually thinking of God.

'Hence, subjugation of the senses; hence, sobriety of the
mind; hence, taming of the ferocity of passions aroused in the
body; hence, peace of thoughts; hence, luminous movements of
thoughts; hence, zeal in practising virtues; hence, high and
subtle conceptions; hence tears without measure, flowing at any
time; and memory of death; hence, pure chastity, totally removed from all dreaming which may tempt the thought; hence,
perspicacity and far-sightedness; hence, deep and mysterious
ideas which the mind understands with the help of Divine words,
inner movements occurring in the soul, and division and discrimination between, on the one hand, spiritual things coming
from holy powers and true visions, and on the other, vain fantasies.

'Hence, that fear on the highways and tracks of the mental sea
which cuts off laziness and carelessness; that flame of zeal which
disregards all danger and overcomes all fear; that fire which dis-
dains all desire to possess and effaces it from the mind, and
together with the rest, leads to forgetfulness of all memory of the
temporal. Hence, in brief, a true man's freedom, joy of the soul
and resurrection with Christ in His kingdom.

'If a man neglects these two means, let him know not only that
he will harm himself in all we have spoken of, but also that by
neglecting these two virtues he will undermine the foundations of
all virtues. As in a man, who keeps them in himself and abides in

them, these two virtues are the head and beginning of Divine doing in the soul, the way and the door to Christ; so a man who neglects them and withdraws from them is led to the two opposite vices, namely, bodily tramping and dishonourable gluttony. These are the starting point of everything opposed to what was said earlier and give rise to passions in the soul' (Ch. 75).

In another place he writes: 'Those who are weak and lacking in zeal at the beginning of their work are thrown into panic and confusion not only by those and similar attacks,37 but merely by a rustle of leaves and are made to turn back abandoning their work by any small need, hunger in case of want, or a slight illness. But true and experienced doers refrain from over-satiation by cereals and vegetables, feeding even on dry herbs, refuse to eat anything before the appointed hour but lie on bare earth in bodily exhaustion. Their eyes can hardly see from inanition of the body, and if from want they come near to parting with the body, they refuse to cede victory over themselves and to abandon their firm resolution, for they prefer and desire to bear hardships and work for virtue from love of God, rather than have temporary life with every ease. When temptations assail them, they rejoice greatly and become more perfect through them. Even amidst the hardest labours they never waver in their love for Christ, but ardently wish to withstand attacks with courage so long as they live, and not to retreat, because through this they gain perfection' (Ch. 60).

Adapting our words to these and similar lessons, as well as obeying him who says: 'Turn not to the right hand nor to the left: remove thy foot from evil' (Prov. iv. 27), we expound to you a moderate rule concerning food, as follows:

31. *How a spiritual doer should feed on Monday, Wednesday and Friday*

On the second, fourth and sixth day of the week observe the 'niners', that is always take food only once a day (at nine o'clock). Eat about six ounces of bread, of dry food not to satiation, and

37 The temptations of the enemy described above. (Footnote in 'Dobrotolubiye'.)

drink three or four cups of water following the 69th rule of the Apostles which says: 'If a bishop, or a priest, or a deacon, a reader or a singer [38] does not fast during the Holy forty days before Easter, or on Wednesday or Friday, let him be cast out, unless he does this through bodily illness. If he be a layman, let him be excommunicated.' Fast on Mondays was established later by the holy fathers.

### 32. *How to feed on Tuesdays and Thursdays*

On two days, Tuesdays and Thursdays, take food twice a day. Eat again six ounces of bread, some kind of cooked food in moderation and a certain amount of dry food; drink three or four cups of wine diluted with water (if you take wine). In the evening eat half the quantity of bread, some dry food or some vegetables, and drink some watered wine, one or at most two cups, if you are very thirsty.

Thirst, however, helps greatly in producing tears, and vigil does the same. St. John of the Ladder says: 'Thirst and vigil render the heart contrite, and a contrite heart produces tears' (Ch. 6, 13). And St. Isaac says: 'For the sake of God suffer thirst, so that He may quench it with His love.'

If on those two days you prefer to eat only one meal a day, you will do well, for fasting and abstinence is the first virtue—the mother, root, source and foundation of all good. A wise layman says: 'Choose the best life; thereupon habit will make it pleasant.' And Basil the Great: 'There are no obstacles where there is will with firm determination.' And another holy father says: 'The beginning of fruit is blossom; and the beginning of active life is abstinence' ('Nilus', Part I).

To some people this and what follows may seem difficult or even impossible. But a man who takes into consideration the resultant profit and keeps before his mental vision the glorious state born of this, will not consider it difficult; and with the help of our Lord Jesus Christ, combined with his own utmost efforts, he will show by word and deed that such a thing can be accomplished with ease and will corroborate by sealing it (by his words and deeds). St. Isaac says: 'Meagre fare at the table of the pure

[38] Ascetics are counted as clergy. (Footnote in 'Dobrotolubiye'.)

cleanses the partaker's soul of all passions. Borrow the cure for your life from the table of those who fast, keep vigil and labour for the Lord, and thus quicken your deadened soul. For the Beloved reclines at their table, sanctifying their food and transforming the bitterness of their meagre fare into ineffable sweetness, while His spiritual heavenly servants encompass them and their holy fare' (Ch. 8). And: 'The breath of a man who fasts is very sweet and a meeting with him gladdens the heart of the wise. The behaviour of an abstainer is pleasing to God.'

### 33. *The fare for Saturday. Also about vigils and how to partake of food during them*

Every Saturday, except on Easter eve, you should have two meals a day, the same as on Tuesdays and Thursdays. This you should do as laid down by the sacred rules and also because on every Lord's day, except the week before great Lent, you should keep vigil, unless some great holy day or a saint's day falls on that week, in which case you should keep vigil on that day and omit it on the Lord's day. Still, in either case take food twice a day on Saturday. Yet, as it is always useful to force yourself to keep night vigil, it is better for you always to keep vigil on Sundays, in spite of the additional vigils which may occur during the week on the above-mentioned days. You will soon see for yourself the great profit this brings you, for in the words of the prophet Isaiah: 'Then shall thy light break forth like the morning, and thine health shall spring forth speedily' (Is. lviii. 8).

St. Isaac says: 'The work of fasting and vigil is the beginning of every endeavour directed against sin and lust, especially in the case of a man who fights against the sin which is within. This practice shows hatred of sin and lust in the doer of this invisible warfare. Almost all passionate impulses decrease through fasting. The next thing which specially helps in spiritual doing is night vigil. He who keeps these two as his companions through life is a friend of chastity. As pandering to the belly and excessive sleep, which weakens a man and incites the lust of fornication, are the beginning of all evil; so fasting, vigil and sobriety in serving God are the sacred way of God and the foundation of all virtue.' And: 'In a soul radiant through memory of God and through unceasing vigil by day and night, the Lord produces a cloud to shade it by day and a light of fire to illumine it at night, to keep it firm and safe' (Ps. lxxviii. 14). And: 'Choose for yourself a sweet doing, continual practices of night vigil, by which all the fathers freed themselves of the old Adam and had their mind renewed. During those hours the soul feels the immortal life, its senses are freed from the darkness of passions and it receives the Holy Spirit.' Again: 'Honour the keeping of vigils and your soul will find consolation.' And: 'Do not think, O man, that the work of a monk has any doing greater than night vigil.' And: 'Do not look upon a monk, who keeps vigil with understanding, as on a man clothed in flesh, for this doing is truly that of the angels.' Again: 'A soul striving in this angelic doing of vigil will have the eyes of a cherubim and with them will continually see and contemplate heavenly visions.'

Pass those vigils in prayer, psalmody and reading, purely, without distraction and with contrite warmth of feeling, either alone or with a dear friend of like mind. After every vigil allow yourself a small consolation for the labour endured and eat during the evening meal about three ounces of bread and enough dry food to satisfy your needs; drink about three cups of wine with water. Note that if your vigil falls on a 'niners' day, do not break the 'niners' for the sake of this vigil. For you should observe the one, and not neglect the other. The above-mentioned relief is prescribed after the end of the vigil.

### 34. *Sunday fare and other things—also about work and humility*

Take two meals a day on Sundays, as you do on Saturdays. This rule should be strictly observed except in case of sickness. Do the same on all other days as regards which the holy fathers have given permission, or when for some reason it has become established by long custom. On such days we do not partake of food only once, do not keep solely to dry food, but eat all good things that are not forbidden; we also eat vegetables, if there are any, but sparingly and not exceeding a definite amount, for abstinence is good in everything and at all times. In bodily sickness, as we have said, we can eat without shame everything that is good for us and allowed, in order to sustain the body. For the holy fathers taught us to be killers of passions and not killers of body. By things that are allowed, we mean not things allowed to all Christians but to us, monks. Partake of all this thankfully, to the glory of God and to avoid arrogance, but refrain from excesses. St. Isaac says: 'Meagre fare involuntarily teaches a man abstinence, even against his will; if, on the contrary, things are plentiful and access to them easy, it is hard for us to abstain.' Do not love comforts for the flesh, for, according to St. Isaac, 'a soul which loves God finds comfort in God alone.' It is better for you to choose labour and poor living—and humility. For one of the saints writes: 'Labour and humility acquire Christ.'

### 35. How to live and what diet to keep during Lent, especially the great Lent

I think it is superfluous to talk in detail about the diet and mode of life during holy Lents. For as you are ordained to behave during 'niners', so must you behave during the holy Lents, except Saturdays and Sundays. But, if you can, be even more strict, more sober during them, especially during the great forty days Lent which is as it were the tithe paid to God for the whole year, which brings to conquerors in Christ rewards for their efforts on the bright day of Divine resurrection.

### 36. About good judgment in particular and the fact that moderation in doing is above all price; also about obedience

Yet you should practise all these and similar things with careful judgment, so as to preserve peace in your heart together with satisfying the needs of your dual nature. 'Through wisdom is the house builded,' says Solomon; 'and by understanding it is established: And by knowledge shall the chambers be filled with all precious and pleasant riches' (Prov. xxiv. 3, 4). The divine Thalassy writes: 'Well-judged scarcity and straitness is the royal road; ill-judged austerity and unreasonable self-indulgence are harmful, since they are equally senseless.' And St. Isaac says: 'Weakening of the members leads to frenzy and ferment of thoughts; excessive work leads to despondency and despondency leads to frenzy. But one kind of frenzy differs from another: one leads to attacks of lusts; another—to abandoning one's silent abode and tramping about from place to place. But moderate work, performed with patience, although with difficulty, is beyond price. A slackening of self-exertion in a monk's life multiplies sinful lust, and excess of it leads to frenzy' (Ch. 71). St. Maximus the Confessor says: 'Do not give all your care to the body, but having allotted to it work commensurable with its strength, turn all your attention to what is within. "For bodily exercise profiteth little; but godliness is profitable unto all things" (1 Tim. iv. 8)' (On love, the fourth hundred, 63). 'When the body outweighs the soul on the scales, it tortures and burdens the soul, driving it towards unseemly and corrupt desires and impulses, as is written: 'The flesh lusteth against the Spirit, and the Spirit against the flesh' (Gal. v. 17). Then, having curbed it by the curb of abstinence, you should yourself mortify it until, even though unwillingly, it becomes obedient to the ruler and submits to the best, remembering the words of the great Paul: 'Though our outward man perish, yet the inward man is renewed day by day' (2 Cor. iv. 16). St. Isaac also says: 'Let yourself die in striving, rather than live in sloth; for not only those are martyrs who died for Christ's faith, but also those who die for the sake of keeping the commandments.' And: 'It is better for us to die in endeavours than to live in downfalls.' Again: 'The main thing is to do everything with asking and taking advice from your spiritual father in Jesus Christ; for in this way all unbearable things and all pitfalls become easy and you will feel as if you were being carried over an even, slightly sloping field.' But it is time we should return to our subject from which we have digressed.

37. *How a striver should spend time from meal time to sunset; also on the need to believe that Divine blessings increase in the measure of our doing*

Having fortified yourself with food, according to the words of the divine Paul who says that 'every man that striveth for the mastery is temperate in all things' (1 Cor. ix. 25), sit down and read sufficient of the writings of the holy fathers, especially those which teach sobriety. Then sleep for about an hour, if the days are long. After getting up, do some work with your hands, keeping the prayer; then pray as was shown before . . . then read again, think and exercise your mind, trying in every possible way to be humble and to regard yourself lower than all other men.

For the Lord says: 'Every one that exalteth himself shall be abased; and he that humbleth himself shall be exalted' (Luke xviii. 14). And: 'Let him that thinketh he standeth take heed lest he fall' (1 Cor. x. 12); and: 'God resisteth the proud, but giveth grace unto the humble' (James iv. 6; Prov. iii. 34). Again: 'The beginning of pride is when one departeth from God' (Ecclus. x. 12). And: 'The proud have had me greatly in derision: yet have I not declined from thy law' (Ps. cxix. 51). And: 'Mind not high things, but condescend to men of low estate' (Rom. xii. 16). And the divine Chrysostom says: 'He knows himself best who thinks that he is nothing; and nothing pleases God more than counting oneself the last of all.' St. Isaac says: 'Mysteries are revealed to the humble.' And: 'Where humility flourishes, the glory of the Lord springs forth.' Again: 'Grace is preceded by humility, and chastisement is preceded by self-esteem.' And St. Barsanuphius says: 'If you truly wish to be saved, show obedience in deed. Lift your feet off the earth, lead your mind to heaven and there remain in your thoughts day and night. At the same time strive with your whole strength to consider yourself despicable, endeavouring to see yourself in every way lower than all men. This is the true way; there is none other for a man who wants to be saved "through Christ which strengtheneth" him (Phil. iv. 13). "So run" ye who wish, run ye who wish, run ye who wish, "that ye may obtain" (1 Cor. ix. 24). This I testify before the living God, desirous to grant eternal life to everyone who desires it' (Answer 477). And St. John of the Ladder: 'I have not fasted, nor kept vigils, nor slept on bare earth, but I humbled myself, seeking above all to regard myself as nothing, and the Lord soon saved me.' Again St. Barsanuphius says: 'Freedom from all cares brings you near to the city; regarding yourself as nothing among men installs you in the city; and being dead to all men makes you heir to the city and its treasures.' And: 'If you wish to be saved, regard yourself as nothing and move forward.' According to St. John, a disciple of this saint: 'Regarding oneself as nothing means not comparing oneself to anyone and not saying about some good deed: "I too have done that".'

After this, pray again, purely and without distraction, until evening. Then sing the usual evening service and read the dismissal, trusting with a pure heart that in proportion to our labours and sufferings for the sake of virtue, and generally in the measure of our endeavours, God adjudges to us gifts, crowns and comforts as the divine David says: 'In the multitude of my thoughts within me thy comforts delight my soul' (Ps. xciv. 19). And the Saviour Himself says: 'Come unto me, all ye that labour and are heavy laden, and I will give you rest' (Matt. xi. 28). And the great Paul says: 'If so be that we suffer with him' (Christ), 'that we may be also glorified together. For I reckon that the sufferings of this present time are not worthy to be compared with the glory which shall be revealed in us' (Rom. viii. 17, 18). St. Maximus, wise in understanding of Divine things, says: 'The cause of bestowal of one or another Divine gift is in the measure of every man's faith. For as much as we believe, so have we the power of zeal to act according to our belief. Therefore a man acting according to faith, reveals by his actions the measure of his faith and receives grace in proportion to his faith. And a man who does not act according to faith reveals the measure of his unbelief in proportion to his idleness and thus, owing to his lack of faith, is deprived of grace. So a man, who envies those who make progress, behaves wrongly, since it is in his power and no one else's to apply his faith and act in accordance with faith so as to receive grace which is in the measure of faith.'

Finally, entreat the Lord with your whole heart to pass the remainder of your life in peace and repentance, to be granted a Christian death, without torment, blameless and peaceful, and that you may have a good defence before the fearful judgment-seat of our Lord God and Saviour Jesus Christ.

## 38. *Pure prayer is greater than all doing*

In addition to what was said above you should know, brother, that every means or method, every rule and, if you like, all these various practices are established and legalised because we cannot as yet pray purely and without distraction. Therefore when through the benevolence and grace of our Lord Jesus Christ this comes to pass in us, then, abandoning the many and the varied, we shall unite with the One, the Single and the Unifying, directly in a union which transcends reason, as the glorious Theologian says: 'When God unites with gods (that is, god-like men) and is known by them, then the heart is filled with radiance by the penetration of the Holy Spirit.' It is born from the pure and undistracted prayer of the heart such as we have spoken of. Very few, maybe one in thousands, are granted the attainment of this state by the grace of Christ. To rise still higher and attain spiritual prayer and be granted the revelation of the mysteries of future life is given to very few, who appear maybe once in several generations through the benevolence of grace. St. Isaac writes: 'As out of many thousands barely one can be found who has fulfilled the commandments and all that is lawful and has attained to purity of soul; so among thousands hardly one can be found who through great efforts of preserving prayer pure, has been given to achieve it, to break the bounds of this life and to gain possession of that mystery, for many have failed to achieve pure prayer, and only few have reached it. But a man who has reached the mystery which comes after it and is beyond it, through the grace of Christ, can hardly be found in many generations' (Ch. 16).

So you too, if you wish to attain to such new mysteries in deed and in fact, that is by experience in Jesus Christ, strive to pray in your heart purely and without distraction at all times and all hours in everything you do. Continuing in this practice you will come from a sucking babe 'unto a perfect man, unto the measure of the stature of the fulness of Christ' (Eph. iv. 13) and together with the faithful and wise builder (steward) will receive your reward and spoken praise, as being one who speaks wisely in the court of justice, that is, whose life corresponds to his words and who therefore will never waver. Philemon writes thus about it: 'Brother, if God grants you pure and undistracted prayer, whether in the day-time or at night, pay no attention to this rule of yours, but strive with your whole strength to cleave to God, and He will enlighten your heart in your spiritual doing.' One of the wise fathers also said: 'If you wish while yet in your body to serve God as an incorporeal being, attain to constant secret prayer of the heart and your soul will become angelic even before death.' St. Isaac writes the same in answer to a question about what is the most important thing in this work, that is, the work of silence, which would enable a man to realise that he has reached perfection in this mode of life. He answered: 'When a man has been granted constant prayer. For when he attains it, it will mean that he has reached the summit of all virtues, and has become the abode of the Holy Spirit; for a man who has not wholly received this grace of the Comforter cannot keep this prayer in his heart with joy. Therefore it is said that when the Holy Spirit comes to live in a man, he never ceases to pray, for then the Holy Spirit Himself constantly prays in him (Rom. viii. 26). Then prayer never stops in a man's soul, whether he is asleep or awake. In eating or drinking, sleeping or doing something, even in deep sleep his heart sends forth without effort the incense and sighs of prayer. Then prayer never leaves him, but at every hour, even if externally silent, it continues secretly to act within. This is why someone has called the silence of the pure bearers of Christ—prayer; for their thoughts are Divine movements, and the movements of mind and heart which are pure are meek voices by which they secretly sing praises to the One Who is in secret' (Ch. 21). Many other holy men, secretly taught by grace itself, have spoken words worthy of wonder which we omit so as not to make our writing too long.

### 39. On the number of genuflexions in the course of day and night

As regards the number of genuflexions, we know that according to the ruling of holy fathers they should be three hundred, which we must practise on every day and night of the five weekdays. For we have been commanded to refrain from them on Saturdays and Sundays as well as on some other days and weeks established through custom for certain mysterious and secret reasons. However, some people make a greater number of genuflexions and others less: every man according to his strength and determination. So also must you do according to your strength. Yet truly blessed is he who drives himself in all godly works and does the same in this. For 'the kingdom of heaven suffereth violence, and the violent take it by force' (Matt. xi. 12).

40. *The distribution of Divine gifts is not only according to the measure*
    *of our striving and doing, as was said, but also according to our*
    *experience and capacity, our faith and our natural predisposition*

You should know that the distribution of Divine gifts is not only according to the measure of our striving and doing, as we have said earlier, but also according to our experience in this mode of life, our capacities, our faith and our natural disposition. St. Maximus says: 'The mind is the organ of wisdom; reason is the organ of knowledge; natural conviction derived from both is the organ of faith formed in accordance with both of them; natural love of men is the organ of the gift of healing. For, for each Divine gift of grace there is a corresponding natural organ capable of receiving it, as experience, or as power or as predisposition. Namely: a man who has purified his mind of all sensory fantasies receives wisdom; a man who has established his reason as master of passions inherent in us, that is, of anger and lust, receives knowledge; a man who by his mind and reason becomes firmly convinced of Divine things receives all-powerful faith; a man who has progressed in natural love of men, when completely freed from self-love, receives the gift of healing.' And all this is so.

Take care that no one knows what you do except your teacher, and pray assiduously also for us, worthless men, who speak but do not practise good, so that we may first do what is pleasing to God and only then teach and advise others. For, in the words of the Lord: 'Whosoever shall do and teach' (the commandments) 'the same shall be called great in the kingdom of heaven' (Matt. v. 19). May the Almighty God in His munificence give you strength and help you to hear all this with understanding and practise it with all zeal. For, according to the divine Paul: 'Not the hearers of the law are just before God, but the doers of the law shall be justified' (Rom. ii. 13). May He lead you to all good and saving deeds, and by the prayers of the saints may His Spirit guide you in the sacred mental work which is before you. Amen.

Since we have already said a little about active good judgment, it is now timely to speak, as far as we can in brief, about perfected and all-embracing good judgment, for on the testimony of our great fathers it is greater than all other virtues.

41. *On the most perfect and all-embracing judgment; and about who lives unnaturally and according to the flesh; who lives naturally according to the soul, and who lives supernaturally and according to the spirit*

A man who lives and acts carnally and unnaturally has utterly lost his good judgment. A man who is resolved to shun all evil and do good (as is written: 'Depart from evil, and do good' [Ps. xxxiv. 14]), and who is but newly introduced to the domain of good and to lending his ear to teaching, acquires to a certain small degree a sense of judgment, such as is appropriate to a beginner. A man who lives and acts according to his soul and nature, that is, with good sense and judgment, and is therefore called intermediate, sees and judges, according to his capacity, what concerns him, and what concerns other men like him. Finally, a man who lives according to the spirit and above nature, sees himself and judges himself most clearly as one who has transcended the limits of the passionate state, the beginner's state and the intermediate state and through the grace of Christ has attained perfection, that is, transubstantial enlightenment and most perfect judgment. Such a man also sees and judges others rightly and with complete precision, while he himself, although in full view of others, is neither rightly seen nor judged. For the Apostle says: 'He that is spiritual judgeth all things, yet he himself is judged of no man' (1 Cor. ii. 15).

42. *More about judgment; some similes*

The first is like a traveller in deepest night and impenetrable darkness. Wandering in unrelieved blackness, which envelops him on all sides, he neither sees himself nor judges himself; he does not even understand where he is going nor where he puts his foot. As the Saviour says: 'He that walketh in darkness knoweth not whither he goeth' (John xii. 35). The second is like a man walking in a clear night lit by stars. In their feeble glimmer he walks slowly, often stumbling against the stones of injudiciousness and constantly falling down. This man sees himself and judges himself a little but as in deep shadow, as is written: 'Awake thou that sleepest, and arise from the dead, and Christ shall give thee light' (Eph. v. 14). The third is like a man walking in a calm night when the moon is full. Guided by the light of the moon he walks more surely and moves forward—he sees himself as in a mirror and judges himself as well as his fellow-travellers, as it is said: 'Ye do well that ye take heed' (to the word of prophecy), 'as unto a light that shineth in a dark place, until the day dawn, and the day star arise in your hearts' (2 Peter i. 19). The fourth is like a man who walks at clear noontide, in bright sunshine. Such a man sees himself clearly, as in the light of the sun, and judges with full truth both himself and many others. In other words he judges all things he meets with according to the words of St. Paul quoted above, whatever and wherever they may be; and he himself goes not astray and leads his followers without stumbling to real Light, life and truth. Of such men it is written: 'Ye are the light of the world' (Matt. v. 14). And the divine Paul says: 'For God, who commanded the light to shine out of darkness, hath shined in our hearts, to give the light of the knowledge of the glory of God in the face of Jesus Christ' (2 Cor. iv. 6); and the blessed David says: 'Lord, lift thou up the light of thy countenance upon us' (Ps. iv. 6) and 'in thy light shall we see light' (Ps. xxxvi. 9). And again the Lord Himself: 'I am the light of the world; he that followeth me shall not walk in darkness, but shall have the light of life' (John viii. 12).

43. *Of the alterations and changes which occur in every man and about the high rank of humility*

We wish you to know also that even those who have reached perfection through self-purification and enlightenment, as far as this is possible (for in our imperfect age there is no perfect perfection but only partial perfection)—even those do not always remain unchanged. Owing to natural weakness or through self-aggrandisement which at times steals in, such men occasionally suffer a change and are robbed of their gains as a test, but later are again granted the most powerful intercessions. For stability and unchangeableness is a property of the future life; in the present life, there may be a time of purity, peace and Divine comfort, and times when impure agitation and sorrow become mixed with them. This happens according to the life and progress of each man, and according to the Lord's own inscrutable ways, so that we may realise our weakness (for blessed is he who is aware of his weakness, as someone says); and, according to St. Paul, we 'should not trust in ourselves, but in God which raiseth the dead' (2 Cor. i. 9). St. Isaac says: 'Some transgress the law time and time again, and heal their souls by repentance, and grace receives them; for every sentient being changes times without number and every man alters hourly. A man of good judgment has many occasions to understand this. But his trials, day by day, have special power to make him wise in this, if he watches over himself with sobriety; so that, among other things, he may observe himself with his mind and learn what changes his soul undergoes every day, how it departs from meekness and its peaceful disposition and is suddenly thrown into confusion, and what unspeakable danger threatens him at such times. The blessed Macarius, moved by his great care and concern for his brethren, has written about this for their edification and remembrance; he advised them not to fall into despair at the vicissitudes of adversity (or battles); because downfalls constantly occur even to those who have attained purity, just as air at times becomes cooler. Such downfalls, opposed to the aim of their efforts, may come without any laziness or carelessness, but, on the contrary, when they are moving in accordance with their degree of attainment' ('St. Isaac', Ch. 46).

A little further St. Macarius says: 'Changes occur in everyone just as they do in the atmosphere.' Take note that he says *in everyone*, for by nature men are the same. He adds this 'in everyone' so that you should not think that he refers only to the lowest and weakest and that the perfect are free from changes and always remain firmly established on one and the same degree, without passionate thoughts, as the Euchites say. What do you mean, blessed Macarius? You say that as the weather changes, now cold, now hot, now hail, now fine again; so it happens in our life of striving: now we are attacked, now grace protects us; at one moment the soul is beset by cruel waves; at another it changes again with the coming of grace and the heart is once more filled with joy and God's peace, with chaste and serene thoughts. He mentions here these chaste thoughts, implying that before them thoughts were bestial and unclean and appears to admonish us, saying: 'If these chaste and modest thoughts are followed by an onslaught of bad ones, let us not grieve and despair. And let us never puff ourselves up in self-praise in times of grace-given quiet; but in time of joy let us be ready for sorrow' (ibid.).

Further on he says: 'You should know that all the saints have endured this. So long as we are in this world, sorrow is accompanied by a secret overflowing comfort. For every day and at every hour we are required by struggle and endeavour against temptations, to gain experience in our love of the Lord. This is what not grieving and not despairing in our struggle means; and thus our progress is corrected. He that wishes to step aside or deviate from this path becomes a prey to the wolves.' How wonderfully this holy father has in a few words corroborated this thought, proving it to be full of wisdom and silencing all doubt in the mind of the reader. He says: 'A man who has deviated and has become a prey to the wolves does not wish to follow the right road but is resolved in his mind to attain his aim by following a way of his own, a way which the steps of the holy fathers have not trodden' (ibid.).

Still further he says: 'Even without deeds humility obtains forgiveness of many sins; but deeds without humility are useless. What salt is for food, this humility is for every virtue, and it can destroy the power of many sins. Consequently our constant care should be to acquire it, belittling our own understanding. If we acquire humility, it will make us sons of God and will lead us to the presence of the Lord even without good deeds. But lacking it, all our deeds, all virtues and every endeavour are useless. It is sufficient by itself to bring us face to face with God without any extraneous help, and to plead for us' (ibid.). And: 'One of the saints said: "When a proud thought comes to you saying:— Remember your virtues, answer it by saying:—Look, old man, at your lechery"' (ibid.).

### 44. *On repentance, purity and perfection*

St. Isaac says: 'The perfection of our whole progress consists of the following three things: repentance, purity and perfection.

What is repentance? Abandoning what has been and grieving over it. What briefly is purity? A heart filled with compassion for every creature. What is perfection? The depth of humility which means renunciation of everything visible and invisible; by visible—meaning all sensory things, and by invisible—all creations of the mental world' (Ch. 48, 298).

Again: 'Repentance is a complete and voluntary dying to everything. A compassionate heart is a heart burning for every creature, for men, birds, animals, for demons and all creation' (ibid.).

Again: 'So long as we are in this world and remain in the flesh, even if we rise up to the very vault of heaven, we cannot live without works and labour and without concern. All perfection is in this, forgive me. Above this there is a secret education of the heart without thoughts or mental prayer' (Ch. 47, towards the end).

St. Maximus says: 'Wise love of virtue usually produces passionlessness of will, and not passionlessness of nature. Through this passionlessness of will the mental grace of Divine bliss enters the soul.' And again: 'A man who has experienced bodily grief and joy may be called experienced, since he has learnt by experience the pleasantness and unpleasantness of bodily things. A man who by force of reason has conquered bodily joys and sorrows may be called perfect. A man who preserves unaltered his habits of thought and action through steadfast striving towards God may be called whole. This is the reason why good judgment is considered to be the highest of all virtues; for those in whom it is born through God's grace are illumined by Divine light and thus can discern with the utmost precision things both human and Divine as well as mysterious and secret visions.'

But the time has now come to expound to you, as far as we can, all that refers to the beginning of sacred and Divine silence. May God guide us in what is to be said.

45. *The five activities of preliminary, or introductory silence to be practised by beginners, namely: prayer, psalmody, reading, thinking on Divine things and work with one's hands*

A beginner just starting the practice of silence should spend every twenty-four hours, that is, the hours of day and night, in five activities pleasing to God, namely: *in prayer*, that is, in constant remembrance of our Lord Jesus Christ, quietly led into the heart by way of breathing, as was described above, and again led out, with closed lips, without any extraneous thought or imagining. This prayer is practised in the cell and should be accompanied by all-round abstinence, that is control of belly, sleep and the senses, together with sincere humility. In addition to this prayer, a beginner should spend his time in *psalmody*, in *reading* the holy Apostle, the Gospels, and the writings of the holy fathers, especially chapters on prayer and sobriety and other Divine words of the Spirit; in *remembrance of his sins* with heartfelt pain; in *meditating* on the day of judgment, or on death, or eternal torment, or on participation in eternal bliss and other such things, and to a small extent in *work with his hands*, to banish despondency. (But after these activities, especially work with his hands) he should again return to prayer, however difficult this work may be and however hard he must push himself until the mind learns by experience easily to suppress its wanderings by all-embracing diligence (or undivided attention) to our Lord Jesus Christ, by constant memory of Him, by frequent penetration into the inner chamber or the hidden region of the heart and firm rooting of attention there. St. Isaac writes: 'Strive to enter within your inner chamber and you will see the chamber of heaven. For the two are the same and one entrance leads to both.' And St. Maximus says: 'The heart governs all the organs and when grace fills all the pastures of the heart it governs all thoughts and all members. For there are to be found the mind and all the thoughts of the soul; therefore it is there that one must look to see whether the grace of the most holy Spirit has inscribed therein its laws.' There; where? In the ruling organ, the throne of grace where the mind and all the thoughts of the soul are to be found, that is, in the heart.

46. *How those who desire to practise wise silence should begin; the beginning of this practice, its growth, progress and perfection*

The first and as it were introductory work of novices who have undertaken to practise silence wisely is as follows: they *begin* with the fear of God, a constant fulfilment of all Divine commandments and unconcern with all things, whether of good or evil report; above all they begin with faith, complete withdrawal from everything opposed to their undertaking and a sincere inclination towards what in truth really exists, as has been said earlier. They *grow* by unashamed trust, stretching themselves forward towards the measure of the stature of the fulness of Christ by abiding in prayer of the heart, pure and undistracted and wholly cleaving to God. In this way they *enter into perfection* through constant, unceasing spiritual prayer, and from perfect love there issue ecstasy, rapture and union with the one God, the focus of all their desires. Such is sinless progress towards contemplation, through work. When our Lord's forefather David had experienced this and been transformed by this blessed transformation, he loudly exclaims 'I said in my haste,39 All men are liars' (Ps. cxvi. 11). Another who had attained to this degree said: 'Eye hath not seen, nor ear heard, neither have entered into the heart of man, the things which God hath prepared for them that love him' (1 Cor. ii. 9); and then added: 'But God hath revealed them unto us by his Spirit; for the Spirit searcheth all things, yea, the deep things of God' (1 Cor. ii. 10).

### 47. *On the practice of silence by beginners*

Thus, as has been said above, a beginner should not leave his cell too often and should avoid meetings and conversations with all men, except in the case of direst need. Even then he should do it rarely and with attention and restraint, as the divine Isaac says: 'In all works this memory (about guarding oneself) should be with you, for the help which comes from guarding yourself is greater than the help which comes from works.' Such meetings and conversations produce dispersion and distraction of thoughts, not only in the case of beginners but also in the advanced. As St. Isaac says again: 'Pandering to the flesh brings harm only to the young, but lack of control brings harm both to young and old;' and: 'Silence kills the outer senses, but brings inner movements to life; external contacts produce the opposite effect, that is, they bring to life the outer senses and kill inner movements.' St. John of the Ladder writes: 'A hesychast is a bodiless being—

39 The Slavonic text reads: 'In my folly . . .'. (Translators' note.)

striving to keep his soul within the limits of its carnal abode, which is a most marvellous thing.' And: 'A hesychast is he who says: "I sleep, but my heart waketh" (Song of Songs, v. 2).' And again: 'Close the door of your cell to the body, the door of your lips to conversation and the inner door of your soul to evil spirits' (Ch. 27).

### 48. *On attentive and sober prayer of the heart and how to practise it*

Prayer practised within the heart, with attention and sobriety, with no other thought or imagining, by repeating the words 'Lord Jesus Christ, Son of God,' silently and immaterially leads the mind to our Lord Jesus Christ Himself. By the words 'have mercy upon me,' it turns it back and moves it towards him who prays, since he cannot as yet not pray about himself. But when he gains the experience of perfect love, he stretches out wholly towards our Lord Jesus Christ alone, having received actual proof of the second part (that is, of mercy). (Therefore, as someone has said, a man calls only: 'Lord Jesus Christ!' his heart overflowing with love.)

### 49. *How the holy fathers teach us to say the prayer*

Therefore not all the holy fathers teach us always to say the whole prayer, but some teach us to say the whole of it, others only half, perhaps, according to the strength and the state of him who prays. Thus the divine Chrysostom teaches us to say the whole of it in the following words: 'I implore you, brethren, never to abandon the rule of prayer or neglect it. For I heard some of the fathers say: "What monk is this if he neglects a rule or disregards it? Eating and drinking, at home or on a journey, or whatever else he does, a monk should constantly call: 'Lord, Jesus Christ, Son of God, have mercy upon me!'"' in order that this remembering of the name of our Lord Jesus Christ should incite him to battle with the enemy. By this remembrance a soul forcing itself to this practice can discover everything which is within, both good and bad. First it will see within, in the heart, what is bad, and later—what is good. This remembrance is for rousing the serpent, and this remembrance is for subduing it. This remembrance can reveal the sin living in us, and this remembrance can destroy it. This remembrance can arouse all the enemy hosts in the heart, and little by little this remembrance can conquer and uproot them. The name of our Lord Jesus Christ, descending into the depths of the heart, will subdue the serpent holding sway over the pastures of the heart, and will save our soul and bring it to life. Thus abide constantly with the name of our Lord Jesus Christ, so that the heart swallows the Lord and the Lord the heart, and the two become one. But this work is not done in one or two days; it needs many years and a long time. For great and prolonged labour is needed to cast out the foe so that Christ dwells in us.'

And again: 'It is necessary to lock oneself up within oneself, to curb and control one's mind and to chastise every thought or action of the evil one by calling on the name of our Lord Jesus Christ.' And: 'Where the body stands, there the mind should be, so that nothing exists between God and the heart as a dividing wall or a partition to screen off the heart and separate the mind from God. If the mind happens to be ravished by something, it is necessary not to let the thoughts dwell on it, lest identification with thoughts is counted as sin on judgment day in the presence of the Lord, when God will judge the secrets of men. Always free yourselves and remain with our Lord and God until He gives you of His bounty. Seek nothing from the Lord of glory except this one mercy; and seek this mercy with a humble and warm heart, calling to Him from morning till evening and if possible all night: "Lord Jesus Christ, have mercy upon me," and forcing your mind to this work until death itself. For this work demands great forcing, since "strait is the gate, and narrow is the way, which leadeth unto life" (Matt. vii. 14), and only those who force themselves enter the kingdom of heaven, for the "violent take it by force" (Matt. xi. 12). I implore you therefore not to withdraw your hearts from God, but to watch them and guard them by constant remembrance of our Lord Jesus Christ, until the name of our Lord is deeply rooted in your heart and you cease to think of aught but glorifying the Lord in you.'

Before St. John Chrysostom, St. Paul said in one of his Epistles: 'If thou shalt confess with thy mouth the Lord Jesus, and shalt

believe in thine heart that God hath raised him from the dead,
thou shalt be saved. For with the heart man believeth unto
righteousness; and with the mouth confession is made unto
salvation' (Rom. x. 9, 10). And again: 'No man can say that
Jesus is the Lord,[40] but by the Holy Ghost' (1 Cor. xii. 3). By
'by the Holy Ghost' he means when the heart is made active by
the Holy Ghost and prays through Him: which is the attribute of
those who have succeeded in their work and have been actively
enriched by Christ dwelling in them. St. Diadochus expresses the
same idea: 'When by remembrance of God we close all the exits
of our mind it has need of some obligatory work to satisfy its
restlessness. The only thing it should be given is the sacred name
of our Lord Jesus; let this wholly satisfy its zeal to attain the aim
it has set itself. But it should be realised that, as the Apostle says:
"No man can say that Jesus is the Lord, but by the Holy Ghost."
On our side it is demanded that the aforesaid prayer ("Lord
Jesus Christ, and so on") should be uttered by a mind imprisoned
within itself and should be repeated continuously in its fastnesses,
so that it may not stray into any foreign dreamings. Those who
mentally keep this holy and most glorious Name unceasingly in
the depth of their heart, can see too the light of their mind
(clarity of thought or a definite consciousness of all inner movements).' And again: 'When this wonderful Name is kept in
thought with intense care it very effectively scorches every filth
which appears in the soul. "For our God is a consuming fire"
scorching all evil, says the Apostle (Heb. xii. 29). Out of the fire
the Lord finally brings the soul into a great love for His glory.
For the glorious and most coveted Name, becoming established
in the warmth of the heart through the mind's remembrance of
it, gives birth to the habit of unhampered love of His goodness,
since nothing then remains to hinder this. This is the precious
pearl which a man acquires having sold his possessions and
rejoices greatly in acquiring Him' (Ch. 59). Hesychius speaks
thus of it: 'When after death the soul soars into the air to the
gates of heaven, it will not be shamed by its enemies even there,
if it has Christ with it and for it; but then, as now, it will boldly

---

40 The Slavonic text reads: 'No man can say Lord Jesus . . .'. (Translators'
note.)

"speak with the enemies in the gate" (Ps. cxxvii. 5). So long as it does not grow weary of calling to our Lord Jesus Christ, the Son of God, day and night till death itself, He will avenge it speedily according to His true promise, given in the parable of the unjust judge: "I tell you that he will avenge them speedily" (Luke xviii. 8) both in this life and after leaving the body' (Ch. 149). St. John of the Ladder says: 'Flog the foes with the name of Jesus; for there is no stronger weapon against them either in heaven or on earth' (Ch. 21). In another place he adds: 'Let the memory of Jesus combine with your breathing; then will you know the profit of silence' (Ch. 27).

50. *Not only in the holy fathers but also in the holy Apostles can the words of this sacred prayer be found, uttered by the spirit as a secret guidance*

You will find the words of the sacred prayer not only in the holy fathers and similar writings, but even before them in the very first and foremost Apostles—Peter, Paul and John. As we have mentioned, one of them says: 'No man can say that Jesus is the Lord, but by the Holy Ghost' (1 Cor. xii. 3); another: 'Grace and truth came by Jesus Christ' (John i. 17), and: 'Every spirit that confesseth that Jesus Christ is come in the flesh is of God' (1 John iv. 2). He who was preferred among the disciples of Christ, in answer to a question of the Saviour addressed to all Apostles: 'Whom do men say that I the Son of man am?' replied on behalf of all, introducing this most blessed profession: 'Thou art the Christ, the Son of the living God' (Matt. xvi. 13, 16). Therefore those who came after them, our glorious teachers, and particularly those who without constraint embraced the path of silent life in the desert, have collected these sayings which were uttered by those three pillars of the Church fragmentarily and in parts, and put them together as Divine words, lawfully established by the Holy Spirit through revelation. With the help of the Holy Spirit abiding in them, they combined and harmonised them in a wonderful manner and thus evolved our sacred prayer, naming it the pillar of prayer and passing it on to their followers to keep and preserve it in the same form.

Look now at its marvellous order and sequence, clearly bearing the seal of heavenly wisdom! One utters the name of 'Lord Jesus'; another of 'Jesus Christ'; the third of 'Christ, Son of God', as though following one another and attentively holding on to one another, in the harmony and accord of these divinely acting words. Do you see how each of them takes the word standing at the end of the previous saying and places it at the head of his? The blessed Paul said: No one can say *Lord Jesus*. The last word 'Jesus' is taken up by St. John and placed first in his saying: that confesseth that '*Jesus Christ*'. His last word *Christ* is put in th : first place by St. Peter: 'Thou art *Christ*, the *Son of God*'. Thu. was our Divine prayer composed, plaited and woven with wisdom and good judgment, like a three-stranded and unbreakable rope. So it has reached us and so it is observed by us and will pass in the same form to those who come after us. As regards the words: 'Have mercy upon me' added to the salvation-working words of the prayer 'Lord Jesus Christ, Son of God', it was added by the holy fathers chiefly for those who are still infants in the work of virtue, the beginners and the imperfect. For the advanced and the perfect in Christ are content with any one of those forms: 'Lord Jesus'; 'Jesus Christ'; 'Christ Son of God!' or even with one word 'Jesus', which they kiss and embrace as the complete doing of the prayer, sufficient to fill them with ineffable bliss and joy exceeding all mind, all vision and all hearing. As sure evidence and testimony of this, our sweetest and loving Lord Jesus Christ, Son of God, Whose words are deeds and Whose sayings are Spirit and life, said clearly: 'Without me ye can do nothing' (John xv. 5); and: 'Whatsoever ye shall ask in my name, that will I do' (John xiv. 13, 14).

51. *On how beginners too may sometimes say the whole prayer and sometimes only part of the words, but always within the heart and without ceasing. The words of the prayer must not be changed often*

Beginners may at times say all the words of the prayer and at times only part of them, but must pray constantly and within the heart. For, according to St. Diadochus: 'A man who always remains in his heart is far from all the allurements of this life.

Walking in the spirit, he cannot experience carnal lusts. Such a man proceeds under the protection of virtues, having these virtues as guards posted at the doors of his city of purity; so all the wiles of the demons fail against him' (Ch. 57). St. Isaac writes: 'A man who keeps hourly watch over his soul has his heart gladdened by revelations. A man who concentrates the vision of his mind within himself sees there the dawn of the Spirit. A man who abhors all dispersion of the mind sees his Lord in his own heart' (Ch. 8).

Moreover, one should refrain from changing the words of the prayer too often lest this frequent chopping and changing (of attention from one thing to another) should accustom the mind not to concentrate on one thing but to deviate from it and so remain for ever not firmly planted in itself; and thus it will bear no fruit, like a tree which is many times transplanted from place to place.

### 52. On how the fruit of inner prayer of the heart requires long work and forcing oneself; and in general, how everything good is attained by long and strenuous effort

Incessant prayer within the heart and all that follows beyond this is not reached by simple happening or by short and easy work. Although God in His inscrutable ways accords this achievement to some, it requires long time and much effort and labour both of body and soul, and a long and intense forcing of oneself. The excellence of the gift and of the grace, in which we seek to participate, require us to make corresponding efforts within our powers, and to establish the hours and limits of this work, the purpose of which, according to our holy teachers, is to cast the enemy out of the pastures of the heart and to have Christ actively abide there instead. Thus St. Isaac says: 'He who wishes to see the Lord within himself must use every effort to purify his heart by constant remembrance of God; in a mind thus illumined he will see the Lord at all hours' (Ch. 8). And St. Barsanuphius says: 'If inner doing with God does not help a man, his external efforts are in vain. For inner doing with a contrite heart brings purity; purity brings true silence of the heart; this silence brings humility; humility prepares man to be the abode of God. By the power of God dwelling in a man, all demons and passions are cast out and man becomes a temple of God, full of sanctity, light, purity and grace. Blessed is he who contemplates the Lord in the innermost recesses of his heart and pours out his prayer with mourning to the loving kindness of the Lord' (Answer 210). St. John of Karpathos says: 'Long labour in prayer and considerable time are needed for a man with a mind which never cools to acquire a new heaven of the heart where Christ dwells, as the Apostle says: "Know ye not your own selves, how that Jesus Christ is in you, except ye be reprobates?" (2 Cor. xiii. 5).' And the great Chrysostom: 'Abide constantly with the name of our Lord Jesus, so that the heart swallows the Lord and the Lord the heart and the two become one. But this work is not done in one or two days; it needs long effort and a long time. For much labour and time are needed before the enemy is cast out and Christ comes to dwell in us.'

### 53. On impure prayer of the heart and on how to attain pure and un-distracted prayer

Continuity in applying this method or means to acquire pure and undistracted prayer, together with overcoming all obstacles in thoughts and external contacts, finally lead the struggler to the habit of praying truly, without forcing himself, purely and un-distractedly, or to a state in which the mind is always in the heart. It no longer needs effort to bring it there through breathing against its will, so that it immediately jumps out again, but now it loves to remain there and to pray without ceasing. Hesychius says: 'He who has no prayer free from thoughts has no weapon for battle. By prayer I mean the prayer which is constantly active in the innermost secret places of the heart, so that the enemy in his secret onslaughts is invisibly flogged and scorched by calling on the name of our Lord Jesus Christ' (Ch. 21). And: 'Truly blessed is he who cleaves with his thought to the prayer of Jesus, constantly calling to Him in his heart, just as air cleaves to our bodies or the flame to the candle. The sun, passing over the earth, produces daylight; and the holy and worshipful name of our Lord Jesus, constantly shining in the mind, produces a measure-less number of sunlike thoughts' (Ch. 196).

*54. On pure and undistracted prayer of the heart and the warmth born thereof*

That prayer is and is called prayer of the heart, pure and undistracted, which gives birth in the heart to a certain warmth which is sung in the psalms: 'My heart was hot within me, while I was musing the fire burned' (Ps. xxxix. 3); this is the fire which our Lord Jesus Christ came to send on the earth of our hearts, where formerly grew the tares of passions but which now through grace brings forth spiritual fruit. As our Lord Jesus Christ says: 'I am come to send fire on the earth; and what will I, if it be already kindled?' (Luke xii. 49). In the past this same fire warmed and made burn the hearts of Cleopas and his companion and made them cry out in ecstasy one to another: 'Did not our heart burn within us, while he talked with us by the way, and while he opened to us the scriptures?' (Luke xxiv. 32). St. John of Damascus says in one of his troparions to the immaculate Mother of God: 'The fire in my heart of love for the Virgin drives me to song.' And St. Isaac writes: 'Intense doing gives birth to measureless heat intensified in the heart by flaming thoughts, which arise anew in the mind. And this doing and guarding refine the mind by their heat and endow it with vision. This heat produced by the grace of contemplation gives birth to the flow of tears. Constant tears still the thoughts in the soul and purify the mind, and with a pure mind a man comes to the vision of Divine mysteries. After this the mind attains vision of revelations and symbols such as the prophet Ezekiel saw' (Ch. 59). And again, 'Tears, striking oneself on the head during prayer, casting oneself on the ground produce the sweet warmth of tears in the heart, and with marvellous ecstasy the heart soars to God, with the cry: "My soul thirsteth" for Thee "the living God: when shall I come and appear before God?" (Ps. xlii. 2).' And St. John of the Ladder says: 'When (spiritual) fire comes into the heart, it resurrects prayer; after its resurrection and ascension on high, Divine fire descends to the chamber of the soul' (Ch. 28). And: 'He is the true and wise monk who has kept his warmth unextinguished and to his death never ceased to add fire to fire, warmth to warmth, desire to desire, zeal to zeal.' And

St. Elias Ekdikos writes: 'When the soul becomes freed from everything external and is united with prayer, then prayer like a flame envelops it, as fire envelops iron and makes it all fiery. Then the soul, though still the same soul, like red hot iron, can no longer be touched by anything external' (Ch. 103). And: 'Blessed is the man who, while still in this life, has been granted this appearance and who himself sees his image, perishable by nature, become fiery through grace.'

### 55. Warmth has different origins; but warmth which comes from pure prayer of the heart is the most true of all

You should know that this warmth in us may have different and varied origins and natures. This is clear from the sayings of holy fathers quoted above, though we dare not speak of it from our own experience. Of these, the most genuine warmth is that which comes from pure prayer of the heart, with which it is always born, grows and in essential enlightenment comes to rest on its Sabbath, that is, according to the fathers, it makes a man essentially filled with enlightenment.

### 56. Direct effect of warmth of the heart

The direct effect of this warmth is to drive away everything which prevents perfect practice of pure prayer. For our God is fire, a fire which burns the evil wiles of the demons and of our passions. St. Diadochus says: 'When the heart receives, with burning pain, the shooting of the demons, so that the victim seems to feel the very piercing of the arrows, this is the sign that the soul has begun to hate passions acutely. This is the beginning of its purification. For if it does not suffer great pain from the shamelessness of sin, it cannot later fully enjoy the beneficence of truth. A man who thereupon wishes to cleanse his heart should constantly inflame it by memory of our Lord Jesus, having this (that is, memory of the Lord) as the sole object of his thoughts and his constant spiritual doing. For a man who wishes to rid himself of his rot should not now pray and now not pray, but must constantly exercise himself in prayer with sobriety, even if he lives far away from the houses of prayer. A man wishing to refine gold must not leave his furnace without fire for however short a time, lest the ore hardens again. In the same way, a man who now remembers God, now not, loses by stopping prayer whatever he appears to have gained by its practice. A man who is a lover of virtue makes constant memory of God consume the earthiness of his heart, so that under the action of the fire of this blessed remembrance evil may gradually evaporate, and the soul may fully attain its natural radiance and glory' (Ch. 97). This is how the mind abides in the heart unhindered and prays purely and without wandering; as a certain saint says: 'Prayer is pure and free from wandering when the mind guards the heart during prayer.' Hesychius also writes: 'He is a true monk who keeps sobriety, and he is truly sober who is a monk in heart (in whose heart there is only himself and God)' (Ch. 159).

### 57. On desire and turning towards God, born of warm attention and prayer

This warm and attentive prayer, that is, prayer that is pure, gives birth in the heart to desire, to turning towards God and to love towards the ever-remembered Lord Jesus Christ, as is written: 'Thy name is as ointment poured forth, therefore do the virgins love thee' (Song of Songs i. 3); and: 'I am sick of love' (Song of Songs ii. 5). And St. Maximus says: 'All the virtues assist the mind to turn towards God, but most of all pure prayer; for soaring through prayer to God, the mind is outside all.'

### 58. On tears of the heart and more about desire and turning towards God

Such a heart often sheds tears, which purify and enrich rather then exhaust and dry up the man whom they endow. For the latter comes from fear of God and the former from turning towards God with strong and irresistible desire and love of the ever-remembered Lord Jesus Christ. Thus enraptured, the soul cries: 'Thou hast given me the delight of desire, O Christ, and hast changed me by turning me towards Thee.' And: 'Thou art all sweetness, O my Saviour, all desire and yearning, Thou art all insatiable, all beauty beyond thought.' And together with Paul the preacher of Christ, it exclaims: 'The love of Christ constraineth us' (2 Cor. v. 14). 'Who shall separate us from the love of Christ? shall tribulation, or distress, or persecution, or famine, or nakedness, or peril, or sword? . . . For I am persuaded, that neither death, nor life, nor angels, nor principalities, nor powers, nor things present, nor things to come, Nor height, nor depth, nor any other creature, shall be able to separate us from the love of God, which is in Christ Jesus our Lord' (Rom. viii. 35, 38, 39).

### 59. Admonition not to seek what is beyond one's measure; also guidance in the constant remembrance of our Lord Jesus Christ in the heart

If a man is desirous of attaining what comes after this—about which it is not timely to speak at present—he must adhere strictly to the following rule: 'Not to seek before its time that which will come in its own time: for the good is no longer good if it be not rightly done.' And St. Mark says: 'It is not profitable before working at the first practices to know about the second; for knowledge without doing puffeth up, but charity edifieth, for it beareth all things' (1 Cor. viii. 1; xiii. 7). As was said, no efforts should be spared in striving always to keep the remembrance of our Lord Jesus Christ in the depths of the heart—in the depths and not outside or on the surface; as St. Mark says: 'If full spiritual hope does not open up the innermost secret repository of our heart, it is impossible truly to know what dwells therein and to see whether our verbal offerings are accepted or not.'

### 60. On warmth of zeal: on the appearance of God in us and on the light of grace wholly imbuing man

In this way a man zealous for perfection in spirit will easily turn aside not only from evil deeds but also from passionate thoughts and unseemly imagination, as it is written: 'Walk in the Spirit, and ye shall not fulfil the lust of the flesh' (Gal. v. 16). More than this, he will withdraw from all thought and all imagination in general, as one whose fervent zeal for virtue scorches and destroys every evil influence, which was formerly active both in his senses and his mind, together with all the malevolent demons, instigators of all evil, as St. Isaac says: 'He who uproots with flaming zeal the thorns which the enemy fosters in him, inspires fear in the demons and pleases God and His angels' (Ch. 8). Such a man will attain to that degree of achievement where he will receive the testimony of God's love for him and will be granted an active manifestation of the light of grace, wholly imbuing the man, and an indwelling of Divine grace. With great rejoicing he will return again to the noble rank and spiritual sonship mysteriously imparted to him by the grace of holy baptism. St. Isaac speaks of it in these words: 'This is Jerusalem and the kingdom of God, concealed within us according to the word of the Lord (Luke xvii. 21). This region is the cloud of Divine glory which only the pure in heart enter, to contemplate the face of their Lord' (ibid.). But let no man himself seek the appearance of God in himself, lest he mistakes for light that which in reality is darkness and only a travesty of light.

### 61. On active influences of God and of the enemy

Therefore if a man's mind sees light when he does not seek it, let him neither accept nor reject it; as St. Mark says: 'There is an action of grace unknown to those who are still infants in Christ; and there is another action, that of an evil power, which bears a resemblance to truth. It is best not to dwell too much on such a phenomenon, for fear of prelest; neither should one curse it, lest one offends truth. In all circumstances it is best to have recourse to God, Who alone knows what is useful in either case. However, one should ask advice of him who is endowed with grace and the power to teach and to judge according to God.'

### 62. On the enlightened teacher who is not in error

If a man finds someone capable of teaching him, not only because he has learned from the Divine Scriptures, but also because he has himself had blessed experience of Divine enlightenment—glory be to God. If not, it is better for a man not to accept these things, but to have recourse to God with a humble and sincere heart, regarding and calling himself unworthy of such honour and vision: by Christ's mercy, we had this advice mysteriously from the unlying lips of men moved to speak by the Holy Spirit, as well as from the Divine Scriptures; and partly we learnt it from experience.

63. *On true and false illumination, that is, on Divine light and the deceptive light of the enemy*

In some of their writings, our glorious fathers point out the signs of illumination, free from prelest, and the signs of illumination which is prelest. This was done by the thrice blessed Paul of Latros when, in answer to a question of his disciple he said: 'The light of the enemy power is like the smoky flame of physical fire. When a soul which has subdued passions and is cleansed sees it, it abhors and abominates it. The light of the Spirit of good is good, pure and joy-giving; its coming illumines a man with its light and fills the soul with gladness and peace, making it gentle and compassionate.' The others say the same.

64. *On improper and proper imagination and the right attitude to them*

Since a little earlier we mentioned imagination, and in particular wrong imagination, it would be very useful, it seems, to say as much more as we can about it, and also to speak about imagination in general. For this accursed imagination is a great obstacle to pure prayer of the heart and to single undistracted work of the mind. Therefore the holy fathers have much to say about it and against it. Taking many forms, this imagination, according to the holy fathers, serves as a bridge for the demons, over which these murderous miscreants cross and recross, commune and mix with the soul and make of it a hive of drones —the abode of barren and passionate thoughts. This imagination must be firmly swept away, even if sometimes one does not so wish, for the sake of penitence and contrition, of mourning and humility, and especially for the sake of putting this chaotic imagination to shame; and one must attract and oppose to it well-ordered imagination, and by mixing the two together incite them to battle with one another, and so strike down the former as dishonourable and shameless, and triumph over it. Acting thus, instead of suffering harm you will gain much profit, since, through managing your affairs with faultless good judgment, you will annihilate chaotic imagination by well-ordered imagination and thus deal a mortal blow to the enemy with his own weapons, like David and Goliath (1 Sam. xvii. 49).

65. *Not only improper but also proper imagination is considered by the holy fathers unseemly in pure prayer and in simple, single-minded doing*

Such a method of struggle, however, is appropriate only for infants or beginners. After many years of struggle the advanced sweep away all imagination, both proper and improper, so that no trace of it remains. As wax melts in the fire, so does imagination disperse and disappear under the action of pure prayer through simple, imageless cleaving of the mind to God, self-abandonment to Him and a most sincere union with Him. Hesychius says: 'Every thought reproduces in the mind the image of some sensory object; for the Assyrian (the enemy) being a mental power, can seduce us only by using something sensory to which we are accustomed' (Ch. 180). And again: 'Since every thought enters the heart through imagining something sensory (and, moreover, the sensory hinders the mental); so the light of the Deity begins to illumine the mind when it is freed of everything and totally empty of form (without representation of shape or form). For this illumination is manifested in a mind already pure, on condition that it is free of all thoughts' (Ch. 89). Basil the Great says the same: 'As the Lord dwells not in temples built by human hands, neither does He dwell in any imaginings or mental structures (fantasies) which present themselves (to the attention) and surround the corrupt soul like a wall, so that it is powerless to look at the truth direct but continues to cling on to mirrors and fortune-telling.' And the divine Evagrius says: 'Where God is recognised as abiding, there He is known; this is why a pure mind is called the throne of God. The thought of God is not to be found in those thoughts which imprint images in the mind, but in the thoughts which make no imprints. Therefore a man who prays must strive in every possible way to repulse thoughts which imprint images in the mind.' And St. Maximus in his commentaries on the great Dionysius says: 'Imagination is one thing, thinking or thought is another. They are produced by different forces and differ in the qualities of their movements. For thought is the action or the production of mind, and imagination is the fruit of passion, the imprint of an image representing something that is or seems to be sensory. Therefore no imagination can be admitted in relation to God, for He exceeds all mind.' And Basil the Great: 'A mind not dispersed among external objects, and not carried about the world by the senses, returns to itself and from itself rises to thoughts of God; illumined by this beauty it forgets nature itself.' Knowing this, you too must compel yourself with God's help to pray purely every hour, without fantasies, imaginings or images, with your whole mind, whole soul and whole heart. St. Maximus also speaks of it thus:

### 66. *On purity and perfection of mind, of soul and of heart*

*On purity of mind:* 'That mind is pure which, freed from ignorance, is illumined by Divine light.'

*On purity of soul:* 'That soul is pure which, freed from passions, is ceaselessly made glad by Divine love.'

*On purity of heart:* 'That heart is pure which, always presenting to God a formless and imageless memory, is ready to receive nothing but impressions which come from Him, and by which He is wont to desire to become manifest to it.'

*On perfection of mind:* 'That mind is perfect which, having received through faith the knowledge of Him, Who is above all knowledge, and having surveyed all His creatures, has received from God an all-embracing knowledge (in its general features) of His Providence, and His judgment manifested in them—naturally as much as a man can understand.'

*On perfection of soul:* 'That soul is perfect whose desiring power is wholly directed towards God.'

*On perfection of heart:* 'A heart is called perfect when it is devoid of all natural impulse towards any thing or any image; a heart like a well polished tablet on which, being clean, God inscribes His laws.'

Let us add to this the following:

*On purity of mind:* According to St. Diadochus: 'To purify the mind is the work of the Holy Spirit alone.' According to St. John of the Ladder: 'To make the mind refrain from wandering is also the work of the Holy Spirit alone.' St. Nilus says: 'He who wishes to see what his mind really is, must free himself of all thoughts; then he will see it like a sapphire or the hue of heaven.' And: 'Mind is a sublime height of the hue of heaven in which, during prayer, there appears the light of the Holy Trinity.' And St. Isaac says: 'When mind abandons the old Adam and becomes clothed in the new man of grace, it will see its purity like the hue of heaven, which the elders of the children of Israel called the place of God (Exod. xxiv. 10), when God appeared to them on a mountain' (Ch. 16).

Proceeding as has been described above, that is, praying purely, without fantasies or images, you will press forward in the footsteps of the saints. Otherwise you will be a dreamer instead of a hesychast and instead of grapes will gather thorns, from which God preserve you!

### 67. How the prophets saw visions by images

If anyone assumes that visions, images and revelations of the prophets were fantasies and belonged to the natural order, let him realise that he is far from the right mark and truth. For the prophets of old and the holy recluses of our times had visions such as they had, not according to some natural order or law, but in a manner which is Divine and above nature. Their visions were created and imprinted in them by the ineffable power and grace of the Holy Spirit, as Basil the Great says: 'The prophets received images in their mind through a certain ineffable power, when they had their mind pure and undistracted; and they heard the word of God as though uttered within them.' And: 'Prophets saw visions by the action of the Spirit, Who imprinted images in minds sovereign over themselves.' And Gregory the Theologian says: 'The Holy Spirit acted first in angelic and heavenly powers; then in the fathers and prophets some of whom saw God or knew Him; others foresaw the future when their sovereign mind received such images from the Spirit, as made them contemporaries of the future as though it were the present.'

### 71. On purity of prayer

St. Nilus says: 'Strive to render your mind deaf and dumb during prayer: then you will be able to pray as you should' (On prayer, Ch. 11). And: 'Blessed is the mind which during prayer keeps itself wholly without image or fantasy' (ibid., Ch. 117). And Philotheus says: 'Men with a silent mind are very rarely found. This is the attribute only of those who use all means in their power to attract to themselves Divine grace and to be filled with the spiritual comfort flowing from it.' And Basil the Great says: 'Right prayer is that which actively implants the memory of God in the soul. The dwelling of God in the heart means to have God planted firmly in oneself by memory, when this memory is never interrupted by worldly cares, and the mind is not troubled by accidental passionate impulses. A lover of God flees all things and goes to God.'

72. *Passionlessness of mind is one thing and true prayer is another—the latter being higher than the former*

It should be realised that, although according to St. Maximus, 'the mind cannot be freed from passions solely through right activity, if it does not at the same time receive many and varied contemplations:' none the less, according to the divine Nilus, it is possible to be free from passions and still not to have true prayer, but to be distracted by various thoughts and remain far from God. For this father speaks on this as follows: 'Not every man who has achieved passionlessness has true prayer; for such a man can still be occupied with simple thoughts (about things, without passionate movements being attached to them) and be distracted by their stories (perhaps their pictures and their various connections) and thus be far from God' (Ch. 56). And again: 'But even when a mind does not tarry on simple thoughts of things, it still does not mean that it has yet found the place of prayer. For it may be occupied with (philosophical) speculation concerning these things and pondering over their causal relationships. Although all these are abstractions, yet, since they are speculations about things, they imprint on the mind their images and lead it far away from God (The mind philosophises instead of praying:—this is the state of the savant.)' (Ch. 57). St. John of the Ladder says: 'Men, whose mind has truly learned to pray, indeed converse with the Lord face to face, as those who have the ear of the king (that is, his most close and trusted servants).'

You can understand from these sayings the exact difference between the two modes of life and activity and make an incomparable comparison between them: one—a life led under influence from above, and the other—life organised by man's own powers. The activity of one is—learning and various mental speculations; the activity of the other is—true prayer. Moreover, remember that passionlessness of mind is one thing and true prayer is another; and also that, as the holy fathers point out, a man who possesses true prayer of necessity possesses a passionless mind, but it cannot always be said that a man possessing a passionless mind has true prayer.

73. *More on imaginings and fantasies of the mind, and on the distinctive signs of prelest and of truth*

### The signs of prelest

Keeping silence and wishing to be alone with the one God, if you see something sensory or mental, whether within or without —such as the face of Christ, or of an angel, or the image of a saint, or some radiant image dreamed of by the mind—never accept it, but indignantly refuse to believe in it, even if it is good, until you have questioned someone with experience. Such behaviour is the most practical, profitable and pleasing to God. Always keep your mind empty of colour, image, form, appearance, quality or quantity, solely listening to the words of the prayer, learning from them and pondering over them in an inner movement of the heart, thus following St. John of the Ladder who says: 'The beginning of prayer is to banish oncoming thoughts as soon as they appear. Its middle stage is to keep the mind contained in the words we say or think. The perfection of prayer is ravishment to the Lord' (Ch. 28). St. Nilus speaks of it thus: 'The highest prayer of the perfect is the ravishment of the mind and its total transcendence of everything sensory, when "the Spirit itself maketh intercession for us with groanings which cannot be uttered" (Rom. viii. 26), before God, Who sees our heart like an open book, intimating its desire by the soundless signs written therein. Thus St. Paul was "caught up to the third heaven", "whether in the body, I cannot tell; or whether out of the body, I cannot tell" (2 Cor. xii. 2). Thus "Peter went up upon the housetop to pray'' and saw a vision (Acts x. 9). The stage of prayer which comes second to this higher prayer, is when the words are pronounced with a contrite mind following the words, conscious of Him to Whom it sends its prayer. But a prayer interrupted by cares of the flesh and mixed with them is far from a level becoming to one who prays.' Abide in this and accept nothing else until your passions are subdued, always questioning the experienced, as has been said.

These are the signs of prelest. Now hear of

### The signs of truth

The signs of truth and of the good and life-giving Spirit are: 'love, joy, peace, longsuffering, gentleness, goodness, faith, meekness, temperance' (Gal. v. 22, 23) as the divine Apostle says, calling these virtues the fruit of the Spirit. In another place he says: 'Walk as children of light: (For the fruit of the Spirit is in all goodness and righteousness and truth)' (Eph. v. 8, 9). Everything opposed to it is the attribute of prelest. One with God's wisdom says in answer to a question: 'Concerning the right road to salvation about which you ask, my beloved one, know that many ways lead to life and many lead to death. One way leading to life is keeping Christ's commandments. In these commandments you will find every kind of virtue, especially these three: humility, love and mercy, without which no one will see the Lord. These three are unconquerable weapons against the devil; the Holy Trinity has given us, I repeat—humility, love and mercy—upon which the demons' hosts cannot even bear to look. For they have no trace of humility, and because they are blackened by vainglory, the eternal fire awaits them. How can there be in them even a shadow of love or mercy when they bear an undying enmity towards the human race, never ceasing to attack it day and night? Let us then put on these weapons, for he who wears them cannot be caught by the enemy. We see that this three-stranded rope, woven and plaited for us by the Holy Trinity, is both three and one: three in name and, if you like, in form; and one in power and action, and in drawing us near to God, in giving us élan towards Him and in aiding our surrender to Him. The Lord said of them (humility, mercy and love): ''My yoke is easy, and my burden is light" (Matt. xi. 30). And His beloved disciple said: "His commandments are not grievous" (1 John v. 3). Therefore the soul, merged with God by purity of living, by keeping of commandments and by these three weapons, which are God Himself, becomes clothed in God, and in a certain way itself becomes god through humility, mercy and love. Transcending material duality and rising above the summit of the law, that is, love, it unites with the transubstantial and life-giving Trinity and converses directly with It, by light receiving light, and rejoicing in constant and eternal joy.' But enough of that. Having thus partially pointed out to you the signs and fruits of prelest and truth, let us now speak a little of the comforts brought by these two, using, as we should, the sayings of the fathers; speak, that is, of Divine comfort which truly comes from grace, and the counterfeit comfort which comes from the enemy. The divine Diadochus speaks of them thus:

### 74. On Divine and false comfort

'When the mind begins to feel the blessed comfort of the Holy Spirit, then Satan too slips his own comfort into the soul in a seemingly sweet feeling during the night rest, at the moment when sleep is lightest (or at the moment of falling asleep). If at that moment the mind keeps a warm memory of the holy name of our Lord Jesus and uses it as a sure weapon against prelest, the wily seducer immediately retreats, but instead finally attacks the soul with his person (instead of with thoughts). Thus discriminating exactly among the deceitful prelests of the evil one, the mind acquires an ever greater experience in the discrimination of spiritual things' (Ch. 31).

And again: 'Blessed comfort comes either when the body is awake or when it is falling asleep while a man with warm memory of God cleaves, as it were, to Him in love. But false comfort, which is prelest, always comes, as we have said, at times when a struggler is in a state of light slumber or drowsiness and his remembrance of God is not strong. The first, coming from God, obviously moves the souls of strugglers for righteousness towards love of God, in an abundant outpouring of feeling of the soul; but the second fans the soul with a breeze of deceitful prelest, and during physical sleep strives to capture the feelings by a taste of something pleasant, notwithstanding that the mind is to some extent awake to the memory of God. Thus, as I have said, if at such a time the mind proves to be remembering our Lord Jesus with sobriety, this breath of the enemy, deceitfully pleasant as it seems, is at once dispersed and the mind gladly comes to grips with it, endowed by grace with a ready weapon against it in its praiseworthy spiritual experience' (Ch. 32).

And again: 'If the soul is inflamed by Divine love without wavering or dreaming, drawing even the body into the depths of its ineffable love, if it thinks of nothing except that for which it aspires, whether the man under the influence of the holy grace is awake or, as I said, is dropping asleep, you must know that it is the action of the Holy Spirit. Filled to overflowing with the blissful sense of this ineffable Divine sweetness, it can then think of nothing, but only rejoices with inexhaustible gladness. If, being thus excited, the mind is visited by a wavering of doubt or by some impure thought, and if thereupon it uses the holy name of the Lord as protection against evil, instead of being impelled solely by love of Him, you should know that such comfort comes from the seducer and is only an illusion of joy. Such joy comes from without, and is not a quality and abiding disposition of the soul. It is thus clear that the enemy wants to make the soul commit adultery. If he sees that the mind begins to display a sure experience of its own feeling, he attempts to comfort the soul with his own comforts which appear good, in the hope that, distracted by this happy physical sweetness, it will not discern its being mingled with the seducer. By these signs we can discern "the spirit of truth and the spirit of error" (1 John iv. 6). However, no one can taste the feeling of Divine goodness, nor can experience palpably the gall of the demons, unless he has come to know in himself that grace has made itself an abode in the depths of his mind, whereas evil spirits are nesting somewhere round the members of the heart. The demons, however, are strongly opposed to a man's acquiring this knowledge, lest the mind should possess it with certainty and so stand for ever armed against them by memory of God' (33).

Now that you have enough information about this, rest content with it according to the advice of the Wise One: 'Hast thou found honey? eat so much as is sufficient for thee, lest thou be filled therewith, and vomit it' (Prov. xxv. 16).

## 75. Of Divine sweetness pouring from the heart

It would be nearer to the essence of the matter to say: who will explain the sweetness of honey to those who have not tasted it? It is incomparably harder to explain to those, who have not tasted it, that sweetness which is Divine and that transubstantial spring of living joy, which ever flows from true and pure prayer of the heart, of which Jesus, God and Man says: 'But whosoever drinketh of the water that I shall give him shall never thirst; but the water that I shall give him shall be in him a well of water springing up into everlasting life' (John. iv. 14). And again: 'If any man thirst, let him come unto me, and drink. He that believeth on me, as the Scripture hath said, out of his belly shall flow rivers of living water (But this spake he of the Spirit, which they that believe on him should receive)' (John vii. 37–9). And the great Paul corroborates: 'God hath sent forth the Spirit of his Son into your hearts, crying, Abba, Father' (Gal. iv. 6).

## 76. This spiritual sweetness has many signs but no name

This spiritual sweetness, this transubstantial spring of life, is at the same time essential radiance and light, inconceivable beauty, the last desire of desires, knowledge of God and mysterious deification, which remains inexpressible even after some expression of it, unknowable in part even after some knowledge of it, incomprehensible in part even after some comprehension of it. St. Dionysius speaks thus of it: 'We pray to come into this darkness which is above light and, through non-vision and non-knowledge, to see and to know Him Who is above vision and above knowledge, (that is to see and to know) His very invisibility and unknowableness. For this is to see and to know the transubstantial and to sing Him transubstantially, through denying any created quality in Him.' And again: 'Divine darkness is the unapproachable light, in which God is professed to live, invisible because immeasurably manifest and unapproachable because transubstantially radiant. Every man granted the sight and knowledge of God is in this darkness, for the very reason that he does not truly see or know, when he finds himself in Him Who is above vision and knowledge and realises that He is beyond the limits of everything cognisable by mind and senses (or everything sensory and mental).' And Basil the Great says: 'Utterly inexpressible and indescribable is Divine beauty blazing like lightning; neither word can express nor ear receive it. If we name the brightness of dawn, or the clearness of moonlight, or the brilliance of sunshine, none of it is worthy to be compared with the glory of true light, and is farther removed therefrom than the deepest night and the most terrible darkness from the clear light of midday. When this beauty, invisible to physical eyes and accessible only to soul and thought, illumined some saint, wounding him with unbearable yearning desire, then, disgusted by earthly life, he cried: "Woe is me, that I sojourn in Mesech, that I dwell in the tents of Kedar!" (Ps. cxx. 5). "When shall I come and appear before God?" (Ps. xlii. 2). And: I have "a desire to depart, and to be with Christ; which is far better" (Phil. i. 23). And again: "My soul thirsteth for God, for the living God" (Ps. xlii. 2). And: "Lord, now lettest thou thy servant depart in peace" (Luke ii. 29). Oppressed by this life, as by a prison, how irresistible was the striving towards God of those whose soul was touched by Divine yearning. Owing to their insatiable desire to contemplate Divine beauty, they prayed that the sight of God's beauty should last for all eternity' (Vol. 5, p. 100).

And the Theologian says: 'Where there is fear, there the commandments are kept; where the commandments are kept, there is the flesh purified — that cloud which envelops the soul and prevents it from seeing clearly the Divine ray; where the flesh is purified, there light springs forth, and the shining of the light fulfils desire above all desires'. And St. Gregory of Nicaea says: 'When by zeal for a good life you wash away the filth stuck to your heart, then godly beauty will once more shine forth in you. Just as blackened iron, when the grinding stone strips it of rust, begins to shine and glitter, reflecting the rays of the sun, so, too, with our inner man, whom the Lord calls our heart, when a man has cleaned off the rusty dirt, formed on the pupil of his eye from the impurities of the evil one, he once more takes on his original image and becomes blessed.' And St. Nilus: 'Blessed is he who has comprehended (God's) incomprehensibility, inseparable from prayer.' And St. John of the Ladder: 'The abyss of mourning gives birth to comfort; purity of heart receives enlightenment. This enlightenment is the ineffable action of the Spirit which gives one to see without seeing and to know without knowing' (Ch. 7, 55).

Therefore thrice-blessed are those who, like Mary of old, have chosen the better part, this spiritual way of life, and who were thus granted a Divine lot so blessed and so full of great rapture and joy that they can cry with the divine Paul in ecstasy: 'But after that the kindness and love of God our Saviour toward man appeared, not by works of righteousness which we have done, but according to his mercy he saved us, by the washing of re-generation, and renewing of the Holy Ghost; which he shed on us abundantly through Jesus Christ our Saviour; that being justified by his grace, we should be made heirs according to the hope of eternal life' (Tit. iii. 4–7). And again: 'Now he which stablisheth us with you in Christ, and hath anointed us, is God; Who hath also sealed us, and given the earnest of the Spirit in our hearts' (2 Cor. i. 21, 22). Also: 'But we have this treasure in earthen vessels, that the excellency of the power may be of God, and not of us' (2 Cor. iv. 7). Thus speak men enlightened by God. With the help of their prayers, may we also live at least in part as they did by the mercy and grace of God.

### 77. Those who wish to practise silence as they should must of necessity have a meek heart

Now, our son, it is timely for you to know before all else, or rather together with all else, that just as a man wishing to learn to shoot does not bend his bow without a definite target, so a man who wishes to learn the practice of silence should have as his target—always to be meek in heart. St. Isidore speaks thus: 'It is not enough to struggle for virtue, but in this struggle it is necessary to observe also a proper measure (or to proportion and correlate one kind of works and doings with others). For example, if, while practising meekness, we interrupt it by some movements of revolt, this will mean that while we wish to gain salvation we have no wish to do what leads to it.' And still earlier than this saint, the most divine David, said: 'The meek will he guide in judgment: and the meek will he teach his way' (Ps. xxv. 9). And Sirach: 'Mysteries are revealed unto the meek' (Ecclus. iii. 19). And the most sweet Jesus: 'Learn of me; for I am meek and lowly in heart: and ye shall find rest unto your souls' (Matt. xi. 29). And: 'To this man will I look, even to him that is poor and of a contrite spirit, and trembleth at my word' (Is. lxvi. 2). Also: 'Blessed are the meek: for they shall inherit the earth' (Matt. v. 5)—or the heart, which will bring forth fruit by God's grace (in some thirty, in some sixty, in some an hundred-fold, according to their rank as beginners, more advanced, or perfect men); never troubling nor being troubled except about righteousness.

78. *How to acquire meekness; also about the three powers of the soul:
the excitable, the desiring and the reasoning*

You will easily succeed in meekness and absence of anger if you repulse everything from yourself, and press your soul forward towards love; if you speak less, are abstinent in food and are always praying; as the holy fathers said: 'Curb the excitable part of the soul by love; subdue the desiring by abstinence and give wings to the reasoning part by prayer. Then the light of your mind will never be dimmed.' And: 'The curb of anger is timely silence; of foolish desires—meagre fare; of uncontrolled thoughts —single-minded prayer.' And again: 'Three virtues invariably bring light to the mind: never to see evil intentions in anyone; to suffer everything that befalls without being troubled, and to do good to evil-doers. These three virtues give birth to yet three others, greater than they: not seeing evil intentions gives birth to love; untroubled bearing of what befalls gives birth to meekness; doing good to evil-doers brings peace.' And again: 'There are three principal requirements for monks: the first —to commit no sin in deed; the second—not to let passionate thoughts linger in the soul; the third—without passion to look in the mind on the faces of women and of those who have offended you.'

### 79. The need to repent quickly after downfalls, thus wisely strengthening oneself against further temptations

If at times you happen to be disturbed, or allow some impulse to enter, or fail to do something you should, you must immediately put it right; and if someone has offended you or you have offended someone, you must speedily make peace. For this purpose you must wholeheartedly repent, weep and shed tears, blaming yourself in everything; having thus fortified yourself for the future, you must thereupon wisely keep attention on yourself. Our Lord Jesus Christ teaches us thus, saying: 'If thou bring thy gift to the altar, and there rememberest that thy brother hath ought against thee; leave there thy gift before the altar, and go thy way; first be reconciled to thy brother, and then come and offer thy gift' (Matt. v. 23, 24). And the Apostle says: 'Let all bitterness, and wrath, and anger, and clamour, and evil speaking be put away from you, with all malice: and be ye kind one to another, tenderhearted, forgiving one another, even as God for Christ's sake hath forgiven you' (Eph. iv. 31, 32). And: 'Be ye angry, and sin not: let not the sun go down upon your wrath' (Eph. iv. 26). And again: 'Avenge not yourselves, but rather give place unto wrath'; and: 'Be not overcome of evil, but overcome evil with good' (Rom. xii. 19, 21). This is how the Scriptures speak of reconciliation with one another.

### 80. About slipping and repentance

St. Isaac speaks thus about slipping: 'Let us not grieve when we make a slip, but when we become hardened in it. For even the perfect often slip, but to be hardened in the same slip means utter death. The sorrow we experience at our slips is counted, through grace, as a pure deed. But he who slips a second time, relying on repentance, is being dishonest with God. Death strikes him down without warning, leaving him no time to fulfil the works of virtue as he had hoped' (Ch. 90). Again: 'We should constantly realise that in every one of these twenty-four hours of day and night we have need of repentance. The meaning of the word *repentance*, as we have learned from the true quality of things, is the following: it is an unflagging petition to God.

addressed to Him in prayer full of contrition, begging Him to overlook the past; it is also concern about protecting the future' (Ch. 47). And again: 'As a grace added to the grace of baptism men were given repentance; for repentance is a second birth from God. That gift, the pledge of which we received by faith, we obtain by repentance. Repentance is the door to mercy, open to those who seek it diligently; by this door we enter into Divine mercy and by no other entrance can we find this mercy. "For all have sinned, and come short of the glory of God; being justified freely by his grace" (Rom. iii. 23, 24) say the Divine Scriptures. Repentance is second grace and is born in the heart from faith and fear. Fear is the rod of the Father, which governs us until we have attained spiritual paradise. When we have attained this, fear will leave us and turn away. Paradise is the love of God, which holds the enjoyment of all bliss' (Ch. 83). Again: 'Just as it is impossible to cross a vast sea without a ship or a boat; so no one can attain love without fear. The fetid sea which lies between us and inner paradise can be crossed only by the boat of repentance in which fear is at the oars. If fear does not drive the boat of repentance across the sea of this world to approach God, we sink in this fetid sea' (Ch. 83).

81. *On repentance, fear, love, mourning, tears and self-reproach*

(Continuing the words of St. Isaac): 'Repentance is the ship and fear is its helmsman; love is the Divine harbour. Fear sets us aboard the ship of repentance, carries us across the fetid sea of life and brings us into the Divine harbour, which is love. All those that labour and are heavy laden with repentance come to this harbour. When we have attained love, we have reached God and our journey is over, for we have come to the island of the other world where dwell the Father, the Son and the Holy Ghost' (Ch. 83).

Of sorrowing after God the Saviour says: 'Blessed are they that mourn: for they shall be comforted' (Matt. v. 4). Of tears, St. Isaac writes: 'Tears during prayer is a sign of God's mercy, granted to the soul in its repentance. It is a sign that prayer is accepted and through tears has begun to enter the field of purity. If men are not freed from temporal thoughts, if they do not renounce worldly hope and do not scorn the world; if they have not begun to prepare for a righteous departure from this world and do not nourish in the soul thoughts of what awaits them beyond; then eyes cannot shed tears, because tears come from pure and undistracted thinking of God, of many, frequent and firmly abiding thoughts, of memory of something subtle which takes place in the mind, a memory which brings sorrow to the heart, whereupon tears flow more copiously and freely' (Ch. 30). And St. John of the Ladder: 'As fire burns wood, so pure tears burn every visible and mental filth' (Ch. 7). And: 'Let us try to attain pure tears, free from prelest which are born from pondering over our exit into eternity. For with such tears there is no despoiling and no self-exaltation, but only purification, progress in love of God, cleansing from sin and passionlessness' (ibid.). And: 'Do not trust your sources of tears before you are totally purified of passions, for the wine which has only just come out of the winepress is not reliable' (ibid.). And: 'Tears which come from fear are preserved by fear; but of tears born of love some men are easily despoiled, unless at the time the heart is lit by that great fire, which is ever to be remembered. It is truly surprising that the lesser in its own time endures better than the greater'[41] (Ch. 66).

Of *self-reproach*, Antony the Great says: 'A great work for a man is repenting of his sins before God and expecting temptations to his last breath.' And another holy father in answer to the question: 'What special thing have you found, father, on your path?' said: 'That one should reproach oneself in everything,' which the questioner praised saying: 'There is no other way but this.' And Abba Pimen said with a groan: 'All virtues enter into this world. But take one virtue—without which a man can hardly hold his ground.' He was asked what virtue it was, and he answered: 'That a man should always reproach himself.' He also said: 'He who reproaches himself will never be troubled, no matter what happens to him: whether it is loss, or dishonour, or sorrow, for he considers himself in advance as deserving it.'

[41] i.e. tears inspired by fear endure better than tears inspired by love. (Footnote in 'Dobrotolubiye'.)

82. *On attention and on the need to keep firmly to one's path with wise circumspection*

St. Paul also writes of *attention* and circumspect firmness: 'See then that ye walk circumspectly, not as fools, but as wise, Redeeming the time, because the days are evil' (Eph. v. 15, 16). And St. Isaac says: 'O wisdom! how wonderful thou art. How far-seeing and provident! Blessed is he who has acquired thee, for he is freed from the carelessness of youth. He who buys a cure for great passions at a low price does well. Love of wisdom means always to be watchfully attentive in small, even the smallest, actions. Such a man gains the treasure of great peace; he is unsleeping so that nothing adverse may befall him, and cuts off its causes beforehand; he suffers a little in small things, thus averting great suffering.' And further: the Wise One therefore says: 'Be sober and watch over your life; for sleep of the mind is akin to real death and is its image.' And the blessed Basil says: 'He who is careless in small things cannot be trusted to be zealous in great things' (Ch. 75).

83. *One who practises silence should be careful in all the aforesaid, but above all should be meek and quiet and strive by all means to call to our Lord Jesus Christ with purity from within the heart*

Therefore take zealous care in all this, and especially strive to remain quiet and meek and call to our Lord Jesus Christ in the depths of your heart with a pure conscience, as we have said. For, if you press forward in this way, Divine grace will repose in your soul. St. John of the Ladder says: 'Let no man addicted to irritation and conceit, hypocrisy and rancour ever dare to touch even the fringe of silence, lest he be driven out of his mind. But a man pure of these passions will finally learn himself what is useful. Yet I think that even he will not learn by himself' (Ch. 27). Not only will Divine grace repose in your soul, but your soul too will be in repose, freed from all that troubled and burdened it before—from demons and passions. For even if they continue to pester it, there will be no consequences; for the soul will no longer take their side and yearn for the pleasures they contain.

**84.** *On genuine and ecstatic love of God, and on Divine beauty*

In such a man all desire, all his heart-felt ecstatic love and every tendency is directed towards the transubstantial and most blessed Divine beauty, which the holy fathers call the highest of all objects of desire.

Thus Basil the Great says: 'When righteous love (that is love of God) envelops the soul, it laughs at all forms of warfare (that is, at attempts to entice it away) and torture is more joy than pain for the sake of the Lord it desires.' And: 'What is more wonderful than Divine beauty? What thought is more joyful than the thought of the splendour of God? What desire of the soul is as fervent, as insatiable, as that which God implants in a soul cleansed of all evil, which cries in all sincerity from its depths: "I am sick of love" (Song of Songs ii. 5).'

**85.** *On warfare, on being left by God to learn, and on being forsaken by God's turning away*

Yet even such a man may be subjected to warfare, being left by God to learn, though not forsaken by God's turning away. Wherefore? In order that his mind should not be puffed up, because of blessings he has acquired; but that, being attacked and so taught he should always keep humility, by which alone he can always not only overcome those who attack him in his pride, but also receive still greater blessings, advancing as much further as is possible for human nature; and so he can press forward towards perfection in Christ and passionlessness, in spite of being bound and held down by the inevitable shackles and weight of the flesh. St. Diadochus speaks thus: 'The Lord Himself says that Satan fell from heaven (Luke x. 18), to prevent this monster from seeing the abodes of the holy angels. How then can he, who has been deemed unworthy of communion with the good servants of God, share with God the dwelling place of the human mind? Even if anyone says that this can be so by God's will, such an argument cannot be regarded as valid. For being left by God to learn in no way deprives the soul of Divine light. As I have said already, the only thing that happens when the soul is subjected to this evil influence of the mind is that grace conceals its presence from the mind, in order to incite the soul experiencing the gall of the demons to seek God's help in all fear and great humility. Thus, when a babe misbehaves, and refuses to submit to the proper rules of suckling, its mother puts it down for a short time, so that it should be frightened of the strange ugly people or animals around it, and in great fear should again stretch its arms towards her and beg with tears to be taken up again. But the soul, which does not wish to have God in itself, is forsaken by God's turning away, and is delivered, as it were bound, to the demons. But we believe that we are not foundlings but true children of Divine grace. Fed by the milk of this grace, rarely left and often consoled, let us under the influence of such bounty come ''unto a perfect man, unto the measure of the stature of the fulness of Christ'' (Eph. iv. 13)' (Ch. 86). Thereupon he continues: 'At first, being left to learn strikes the soul down with great sorrow, a sense of debasement and a certain measure of hopelessness, in order to kill in it all vanity and desire, to impress and to bring it to a suitable state of humility. Then it immediately brings into the soul a fond fear of God, tearful confession of sins and a great desire for the most excellent silence. But when God forsakes a soul, turning away from it, He leaves it to itself, and the soul is filled with despair and unbelief, arrogance and anger. Knowing both cases, that is, when God leaves the soul to learn and when He forsakes it, we must attempt to approach God in accordance with the character of each. In one case, we must bring to God our thanks and vows, since He has mercifully chastised the unruliness of our disposition, by depriving it of comfort, in order to teach us, in His fatherly solicitude, sanely to discriminate between good and evil. The other case requires a constant confession of sins, ceaseless tears and much solitude, in the hope that through these labours we may succeed in gaining God's mercy and make Him take care of our hearts, as before. Moreover, it is necessary to realise that when God suffers the soul to enter into single combat with Satan for its edification, although grace conceals itself, it helps the soul secretly in order to show its enemies that victory over them is due to the soul alone' (Ch. 87). St. Isaac says: 'It is impossible for a man to become wise in spiritual warfare, to know God's Providence, to sense his God and to be secretly strengthened in his faith in Him, except in proportion to the severity of the trial he has endured. As soon as grace notices a trace of self-opinion beginning to appear in a man's thoughts, as soon as it sees that a man begins to think highly of himself, it immediately allows temptations to grow and gain strength against him, until he realises his weakness, and runs to clutch God in all humility. Thus a man comes to the measure of manhood by perfect faith and trust in the Son of God, and is elevated to love. For the wonderful love of God for man becomes manifest when he finds himself in circumstances which destroy his hope. It is here that God shows His power in saving him. For man can never learn the power of God in ease and freedom, and nowhere has God palpably manifested His action so much as in the land of silence and in the desert, in places devoid of crowds and rumours, which are always present when living with people' (Ch. 49).

### 86. *On passionlessness; what is human passionlessness?*

We should add to the aforesaid a word about passionlessness and perfection; then say a little more and end our present writing. St. Basil the Great says of passionlessness: 'He who has become a lover of God and is wishing to participate, however imperfectly, in the passionlessness of God, in spiritual sanctity, serenity, quietness and meekness, and to taste the joy and gladness born of them, must strive to lead his thoughts far away from every material passion which may trouble the soul, and to contemplate Divine things with a clear and unshaded eye, insatiably enjoying the Divine light. A man who has implanted this habit and disposition in his soul becomes akin to God, in as far as it is possible for him to be like God, and is loved and welcomed by Him as one who has courageously undertaken this great and difficult work, and has become capable of conversing with God in spite of his nature being compounded with matter, by sending to Him his thought pure and stripped of any admixture of carnal passions.' This is on passionlessness.

As regards human passionlessness St. Isaac writes thus: 'Passionlessness does not mean not feeling passions, but not accepting them. Thanks to the many and varied virtues, both evident and hidden, acquired by the saints, passions lost power in them and so could not be easily roused to attack the soul. So thought need no longer keep its attention on passions; for all its time is filled with thinking, studying and investigating the most perfect contemplations, which are consciously set in motion in the mind. Whenever passions begin to move and be excited, the mind is suddenly lifted away from them by some realisation of Divine things which has entered it, and passions remain without effect, as St. Mark said: 'When by the grace of God the mind practises works of virtue and comes near to knowledge, it is little capable of feeling what comes from the worst and unwise part of the soul. For this knowledge makes it soar on high and estranges it from everything that is in the world. By their chastity, by the subtlety, lightness and sharpness of their mind, as well as by their deeds, the mind of saints becomes purified and filled with light, for their flesh has withered through practising works of silence and their long abiding in it. Therefore contemplation comes easily and swiftly to each one of them and, abiding in them, leads them in wonder to the depths of the object of their contemplation. In this state contemplations richly multiply in them, and their thought never lacks subjects of the higher understanding. Thus they are never left without that which constitutes in them the fruit of the Spirit. Long experience of this kind erases from their heart such memories as incite passions in the soul; and it weakens the power of the devil's rule. For when the soul does not make friends with passions by thinking about them, then, since it is constantly occupied with another concern, the power of passions is unable to hold spiritual feelings in its grip' (Ch. 48).

And divine Diadochus says: 'Passionlessness does not mean not being attacked by the demons, for in that case we should, according to the Apostle, "go out of the world" (1 Cor. v. 10); but it means remaining unconquered when attacked; as warriors who, clothed in armour, are shot at by the enemy, hear the sound of flying arrows, see the arrows themselves directed against them, but remain impervious to them through the strength of their armour. Those warriors, protected by steel, remain immune in battle; as to ourselves, clothed through right doing in the armour of the holy light and in the helmet of salvation, we shall disperse the dark ranks of the demons. For refraining from doing evil in the future is not enough to bring purity; it is even more important totally to uproot evil in oneself by a whole-hearted zeal for good' (Ch. 98).

St. Maximus points to four kinds of passionlessness. He says: 'I call the first passionlessness when the carnal impulse towards sin is not translated into action. I call the second passionlessness a complete renunciation of passionate thoughts of the soul, whereby passionate impulses wither, since they are not instigated to action by passionate thoughts. I call the third passionlessness a total immobility of passionate lust, which usually has place also in the second, which is purity of thoughts. I call the fourth passionlessness a complete renunciation of passionate imaginings in thought, which also engenders the third, since it is devoid of sensory imaginings which present passionate images.' And: 'Passionlessness is a peaceful disposition of the soul, through which it is not easily moved to evil.'

## 87. On passionlessness and perfection

Here also are the words of St. Ephraim, who says of passionlessness and perfection: 'Insatiably pressing forward towards the highest desired good, the passionless render perfection imperfect and incomplete, since eternal blessings have no end. Perfection is finite or perfect when judged according to human powers: it is infinite and imperfect, as for ever exceeding itself by daily increase and rising ever higher and higher through ascents towards God.' St. Nilus says the same of perfection: 'Two kinds of perfection should be accepted: one temporal, another eternal, of which the Apostle writes: "But when that which is perfect is come, then that which is in part shall be done away" (1 Cor. xiii. 10). The words "when that which is perfect is come" show that we cannot contain Divine perfection here.' Again, 'the divine Paul knows two kinds of perfection and considers one and the same man both perfect and imperfect, calling him perfect in relation to the present life, and imperfect in relation to the true perfection inherent in him. Thus he says: "Not as though I had already attained, either were already perfect: but

I follow after, if that I may apprehend"; and a little further: "Let us therefore, as many as be perfect, be thus minded" (Phil. iii. 12, 15).'

### 88. *On passion, voluptuousness, attachment and passionlessness*

St. Elias Ekdikos says: 'Evil or sinful matter of the body is passion, of the soul voluptuousness, of the mind attachment. They are revealed or displayed—the first by touch, the others (voluptuousness and attachment) by the other senses. The opposite of them all (that is passionlessness) is revealed by an opposite disposition.' Again: 'The voluptuary is close to the passionate; the attached to the voluptuary. The passionless man is far removed from them all' (Ch. 71).

### 89. *The passionate, the voluptuary, the attached and the passionless and how to treat each of them*

The same saint says: 'A passionate man is a man in whom the attraction of sin is stronger than thought, although he does not as yet sin externally; a voluptuary is a man in whom sinful action (desire to commit sin) is weaker than thought, although he passionately savours it inwardly; a man is attached when he is freely or rather servilely bound to the one and the other. A man would be passionless if such varied impulses and states were unknown to him (a man who does not experience them).' Moreover he clearly indicates methods of treating them, saying: 'Passion is banished from the soul by fasting and prayer; voluptuousness by vigil and by refraining from speech; attachment by silence (solitude) and attention; passionlessness is established through remembrance of God' (Ch. 72, 73).

### 90. *On faith, hope and love*

Faith, hope and love are the beginning, middle and end and, if you like, the leaders and chief musicians among all blessings and virtues. They constitute a divinely woven three-stranded rope, especially love, for God is, and is called, love (1 John iv. 8). Therefore it would be wrong not to fill in what is lacking in this writing by mentioning them, especially since, according to St. Isaac: 'The fruit of the Holy Spirit comes to maturity when a man acquires perfect love' (Ch. 21). Let us then speak of them in the words of the holy fathers. St. John of the Ladder says: 'And now, linking and holding together everything in closest union "abideth faith, hope and charity, these three; but the greatest of these is charity" (1 Cor. xiii. 13); for God's name is love (1 John iv. 8). As I understand it, the first of them is a ray, the second light, the third a disc; but all three together are one brilliant radiance. The first can do all and build all; God's mercy encompasses the second and makes it unashamed; the third never falls, its flow never ceases, nor has a man sick of love any respite from its blessed intoxication' (Ch. 30). And: 'The word of love is known to the angels; but to them too it is known by the action of illumination. "God is love", and he who seeks to establish its bounds is like a blind man attempting to count the grains of sand in the deeps of the sea. In quality, love is the likeness of God, as far as this is possible to mortals; in action, it is intoxication of the soul; in its properties, it is the source of faith, the abyss of long-suffering, the sea of humility. Love is real renunciation of every contrary thought, for it "thinketh no evil" (1 Cor. xiii. 5). Love, passionlessness and sonship differ only in name. As light, fire and flame are combined in one single action, so is it with these three' (Ch. 5-9).

St. Diadochus says: 'Let faith, hope and love stand foremost in your spiritual contemplation, brother, but most of all love; for the other two (faith and hope) teach one only to despise visible blessings, whereas love unites the soul itself with God through virtues, comprehending the Invisible One by mental perception' (Ch. 7). And: 'One love is the love natural to the soul; the other is the love which is poured into it by the Holy Spirit. The first is moved by our desire and is in proportion to it; so it is easily despoiled by evil spirits when we do not constrain our will to abide in it. But the second so inflames the soul with love of God, that all parts of the soul cleave to the ineffable delight of this Divine love with utter simplicity of purpose. For then the mind, made pregnant by the action of spiritual grace, sends forth a rich torrent of love and joy.' And St. Isaac: 'Love incited by something external is like a small lamp whose flame is fed with oil, or like a stream fed by rains where flow stops when the rains cease. But love, whose object is God, is like a fountain gushing forth from the earth. Its flow never ceases, for He Himself is the source of this love and also its food which never grows scarce' (Ch. 30). In answer to the question: 'What constitutes the coming to maturity of the many fruits of the Spirit', St. Isaac said: 'When a man attains perfect love'. When he was asked: 'How to know if anyone has attained it?' he replied: 'When memory of God comes to life in his mind, man's heart is immediately set aflame by love of God and his eyes shed copious tears. For remembrance of loved ones is wont to bring tears and so tears never cease to flow in such a man, for that which moves him to remember God never stops working in him. Therefore even in sleep he converses with God, since it is natural for love to produce this effect and love is the perfection of men in this life' (Ch. 21). And: 'Love for God is naturally ardent and when it fills a man to overflowing, leads the soul to ecstasy. Therefore the heart of a man who experiences it cannot contain or bear it, but undergoes an extraordinary change according to its own quality and the quality of the love which fills him. Its sensible signs are the following: man's face becomes joyous and aflame and his body is warmed. Shame and fear leave him and he becomes like one in ecstasy. The force which keeps his mind collected flees from him and he is as one out of his mind. A terrible death is for him a joy, and his mental contemplation of heavenly things is never broken. Even when absent, he converses as if present though unseen. His knowledge and sight naturally cease, and he no longer feels his movements among sensory objects. Even if he does something, he is not aware of it, for his mind is on high in contemplation, and his thought always seems to be conversing with someone else. This spiritual intoxication was experienced of old by Apostles and martyrs. The first travelled far and wide over the whole world, working and suffering persecutions; the latter had their limbs cut off, shed blood like water, but, suffering the most terrible tortures, never lost courage and valiantly bore everything; being wise they were considered foolish. Yet others wandered among deserts, mountains, caves and precipices of the earth, remaining well-ordered amongst all disorder. May God grant us such disorder!' (Ch. 73).

**91.** *On holy communion and the blessings brought us by frequent communion with a clear conscience*

The greatest help and assistance in purification of the soul, illumination of the mind, sanctification of the body and a Divine transformation of the two, as well as in repulsing passions and demons and, above all, in transubstantial union with God, in joining and merging with Him, is frequent communion in the holy, pure, immortal and life-giving Mysteries—the precious body and blood of our Lord Jesus Christ, Our God and Saviour.—approached with a heart and disposition as pure as is possible for man. Therefore it is necessary to speak specially of this, and then to put an end to our writing.

About the extreme need for communion in the Holy Mysteries of Christ we have very clear words of the fathers; moreover the Life and the Truth Himself speaks most clearly of this, saying: 'I am that bread of life. . . . This is the bread which cometh down from heaven, that a man may eat thereof, and not die. I am the living bread which came down from heaven: if any man eat of this bread, he shall live for ever: and the bread that I will give is my flesh, which I will give for the life of the world' (John vi. 48, 50, 51). And: 'Except ye eat the flesh of the Son of man, and drink his blood, ye have no life in you. Whoso eateth my flesh, and drinketh my blood, hath eternal life; and I will raise him up at the last day. For my flesh is meat indeed, and my blood is drink indeed. He that eateth my flesh, and drinketh my blood, dwelleth in me, and I in him. As the living Father hath sent me, and I live by the Father: so he that eateth me, even he shall live by me. This is that bread which came down from heaven: . . . he that eateth of this bread shall live for ever' (John vi. 53–8). And St. Paul says: 'For I have received of the Lord that which also I delivered unto you, That the Lord Jesus the same night in which he was betrayed took bread: And when he had given thanks, he brake it, and said, Take, eat: this is my body, which is broken for you: this do in remembrance of me. After the same manner also he took the cup, when he had supped, saying, This cup is the new testament in my blood: this do ye, as oft as ye drink it, in remembrance of me. For as often as ye eat this bread, and drink this cup, ye do shew the Lord's death till he come. Wherefore whosoever shall eat this bread, and drink this cup of the Lord, unworthily, shall be guilty of the body and blood of the Lord. But let a man examine himself, and so let him eat of that bread, and drink of that cup. For he that eateth and drinketh unworthily, eateth and drinketh damnation to himself, not discerning the Lord's body. For this cause many are weak and sickly among you, and many sleep. For if we would judge ourselves, we should not be judged. But when we are judged, we are chastened of the Lord, that we should not be condemned with the world' (1 Cor. xi. 23–32).

92. *It is necessary to know the miracle of the Holy Mysteries—what they are, why they were given and what profit comes from them*

St. John Chrysostom writes: 'It is necessary to know the miracle of the Holy Mysteries—what it consists of, for what purpose it was given and what profit it brings. "There is one body," it is said, "For we are members of his body, of his flesh, and of his bones" (Eph. iv. 4; v. 30). Let the initiated hearken to these words! Thus, in order to be members of the body of Christ not only in love but in actual fact, let us unite with this body. This is done through the food which Christ gave as token of His great love for us. For this purpose He joined Himself with us and merged His body with us, so that we should form one with Him, as body and head are joined into one. This is the sign of the greatest love. Job pointed to this in speaking of the men of his tabernacle who loved him so much that they desired to be joined to his flesh: "Oh that we had of his flesh! we cannot be satisfied" (Job. xxxi. 31). They spoke thus, wishing to express their great love for him. Christ acted with the same purpose: to lead us to a greater union with Him and show His love for us. He gave to those who wished it not only to see Him, but also to touch, to taste, to bite His flesh, to unite with Him and through Him to satisfy every desire' (Discourse on John, 46). And: 'Those who partake of this blood stand together with the angels, the archangels and other high powers, clothed in the kingly garments of Christ and armed with spiritual weapons. But there I have said nothing great enough: they are clothed in the King Himself. Inasmuch as this mystery is great and marvellous, so is it certain that if you approach it in purity, you approach it for your salvation; but if your conscience be evil, you will reap punishment and torment. For it is said: "He that eateth and drinketh unworthily (of the Lord), eateth and drinketh damnation to himself" (1 Cor. xi. 29). If those who defile the King's purple have the same punishment as those who rend it, it is not surprising that people who partake of Christ's body with an impure soul will be subjected to the same punishment as those who tortured Him with nails. See of what terrible punishment St. Paul speaks: "He that despised Moses' law died without mercy under two or three witnesses: Of how much sorer punishment, suppose ye, shall he be thought worthy, who hath trodden under foot the Son of God, and hath counted the blood of the covenant, where-with he was sanctified, an unholy thing, and hath done despite unto the Spirit of grace?" (Heb. x. 28, 29).' And: 'In partaking of the body of the Lord and in drinking His blood let us firmly remember that we are partaking of that body which sits on high and which the angels worship, a body which stands nearby the imperishable power—that very body we eat. Oh, how many roads to salvation are open to us! He made us His body, He gave us His body, yet all this does not divert us from evil! O blindness! O insensibility!' (3rd Discourse on the Epistle to the Ephesians). And again: 'A certain marvellous elder told me that he had been given to see and hear that if those about to leave this world receive the communion of the Holy Mysteries with a clear conscience, then, after death, because of this communion, the angels receive them and carry them up on high.'

And the divine John of Damascus says ('On Orthodox Faith', Vol. IV, Ch. 13): 'Since we are dual and twofold, our birth must also be twofold, and our food complex. Birth is given us by water and Spirit, our food is the bread of life, our Lord Jesus Christ, descended from heaven.' And, much further on: 'Just as in baptism, since it is usual for men to wash with water and to anoint themselves with oil, He combined with oil and water the grace of the Spirit and made it the bath of eternal life; in the same way, since it is usual for us to eat bread and drink wine and water, He combined with them His divinity and made them His body and His blood, in order that we should attain a state which is above nature, through that which is usual and natural for us. The body is truly united with the Deity—that body which is of the Holy Virgin, not because the body which ascended to heaven itself comes down, but because bread and wine become transformed into the body and blood of our Lord God. If you wish to know how this happens, it is enough for you to hear: by the Holy Spirit, just as the Lord made His own body by the Holy Spirit from the Holy Virgin for Himself and in Himself. We know nothing more, except that the word of God is true, effective and all-powerful. Of the means we can know nothing.' And a little further: 'To those who partake of it worthily and with faith, the Holy Communion is for the remission of sins, and eternal life, and the preservation of soul and body. But to those without faith who partake of it unworthily, it is for damnation, and torment like the Lord's death. Bread and wine are not merely symbols of the body and blood of Christ. May this never be so! It is His Divine body itself, and His very blood. For He says: "For my flesh is meat indeed, and my blood is drink indeed".' Still further: 'The flesh and blood of Christ serve to strengthen our soul and body; but they do not get exhausted and are not subject to corruption, and they are to protect and cleanse us of all filth. Being purified by Him, we unite with Christ's body and His Spirit and become the body of Christ. This bread is the beginning of that future bread which is supersubstantial. For "*supersubstantial*" either indicates the bread of the future, that is the bread of future life, or the bread we now receive to preserve our being. For the flesh of the Lord is the life-giving Spirit, since it was conceived from the life-giving Spirit. And what is born of the Spirit is spirit. I say this, not to deny the nature of the body, but in order to show that it is life-giving and Divine.' And at the end of the chapter: 'This body and this blood in the mystery are called symbols of those to come, not because they are not truly body and blood of Christ, but because now we participate in Christ's Divinity through them, whereas in the other life we shall do so mentally, solely by contemplating Him.'

And the divine Macarius says: 'As wine courses through all the members of the body, so that the wine is in man and man is in the wine; so a man who drinks Christ's blood is filled with the Spirit of the Deity, Who spreads through the whole soul, so that the soul is totally in Him and, thus sanctified, becomes worthy of Christ our Lord. For the Apostle says: "We have been all made to drink into one Spirit" (1 Cor. xii. 13). In the same way those who truly partake of bread in the Eucharist are granted participation in the Holy Spirit, and thus worthy souls can have life in the ages. Just as the life of the body does not come from itself but from without, that is from the earth, so God has arranged for the soul to have meat, drink and garments, which truly give life to the soul, not from its own nature but from His Own Divinity, from His Own Spirit and Light. For the Divine Nature contains the Bread of life, Who said: "I am the bread of life" (John vi. 35) and living water, and joy-giving wine, and the oil of gladness.'

And St. Isidore says: 'Communion means partaking of the Divine Mysteries, because it gives us union with Christ and makes us participants in His kingdom.' And St. Nilus: 'It is impossible for a believer to be saved, to receive remission of sins and be admitted to the kingdom of heaven, unless in fear, faith and love he receives communion of the pure Mysteries of the Body and Blood of Christ.'—St. Basil the Great writes equally in his letter to the noble Cesarea: 'It is good and most useful to have communion every day and to partake of the Body and Blood of Christ, for Christ Himself says clearly: "Whoso eateth my flesh, and drinketh my blood, hath eternal life" (John vi. 54). For who can doubt that to participate constantly in life, means to have the most abundant life. We take communion four times every week: On Sunday, Wednesday, Friday and Saturday, as well as on other days if commemoration of some saint falls on them' (Vol. VI, letter 89).

I believe that this saint celebrated liturgy on these days, because, being burdened with many cares, he could not do so every day. And St. Apollos said: 'Monks should, if they can, have communion of the Holy Mysteries every day, since he who withdraws from the Holy Mysteries withdraws from God, and he who constantly receives communion, always receives the Saviour into himself. For the Saviour Himself says: "He that eateth my flesh, and drinketh my blood, dwelleth in me, and I in him'' (John vi. 56). Thus this practice is most useful for monks, for by this means they are constantly commemorating the passion of Christ for our salvation. Moreover they must each day be ready and so prepare themselves as always to be worthy to partake of the Holy Mysteries and receive remission of sins.' This order of life was always observed in the brotherhood of St. Apollos.

St. John of the Ladder says: 'If a body coming into contact with another body undergoes a change under its influence, how can a man not change if he touches the body of God with pure hands?' (Ch. 28). It is also written in the Hierondic: 'John of Vostros, a holy man, who possessed power over impure spirits, asked the demons who lived raging in some possessed maidens saying: "What are the things you fear in Christians?" They answered: "Truly you possess three great things: the first is what you wear round your neck; the second is what you wash with in Church; the third is what you partake of in community." Thereupon he asked them: "Of these three which do you fear most?" They answered: "If you guarded well that of which you partake, none of us could ever offend a Christian." These things which our deadly enemies fear most are: the cross, baptism and communion.'

93. *The end of all detailed expositions and a personal admonition to him who begged for them*

Thus, our beloved child, with God's help your request is granted. Maybe we were unable to do it exactly as you wished and expected; still we have done it to the limit of our powers. But work performed to the limit of one's powers is pleasing to God. Take care not only to love learning and labour in it, but also to prove your love and zeal for wisdom in actual deeds. For the illustrious brother of God says: 'Be ye doers of the word, and not hearers only, deceiving your own selves. For if any be a hearer of the word, and not a doer, he is like unto a man beholding his natural face in a glass: For he beholdeth himself, and goeth his way, and straightway forgetteth what manner of man he was. But whoso looketh into the perfect law of liberty, and continueth therein, he being not a forgetful hearer, but a doer of the work, this man shall be blessed in his deed' (James i. 22–5).

### 94. *How to hear and absorb the spiritual words of the fathers*

Most of all you must understand how you should hear and absorb the laying down of the Divine and spiritual laws by the fathers, rightly and with due reverence. For St. Macarius says: 'Spiritual subjects cannot be grasped by those who have not experienced them. But a saintly and faithful soul is helped in its understanding by the participation of the Holy Spirit. Then the heavenly treasures of the Spirit become clear only to a man who experiences them, but a man not initiated into them is wholly unable even to think of them. Thus hear of them with reverence until, for the sake of your faith, you are granted the same. Then you will know, from the experience of the eyes of the soul, in what blessings and mysteries the souls of Christians can participate even in this life.'

Remaining in this state you will very soon reap a rich increase and receive much help both from what you read and what you may hear. Combining with your knowledge the practice of what you have learnt you will achieve much, and will be able to guide and admonish others from your own experience of Divine things, which are inaccessible to many. God grant that you achieve this, held and guided by the almighty hand of our Lord Jesus Christ. Amen.

Since a surfeit of words is unpleasant to the ear, just as a surfeit of food is to the body, and since moderation is best in everything, we too should avoid excesses and embrace moderation as the best course and thus, after saying a little more about our subject and having made a brief résumé of the present writing, we must drop anchor.

### 95. *The principal matter—how one should pray—and on true illumination and Divine power*

The fathers say that a man desirous of practising wise sobriety should descend into the heart by way of breathing, and constantly compel himself to pray purely and undistractedly, listening only to the words of the prayer and going deep into them, namely: 'Lord, Jesus Christ, Son of God, have mercy upon me!' until the mind becomes illumined in the heart; as St. Diadochus says: 'Those who constantly keep this holy and glorious name mentally in the depths of the heart are able, in the end, to see the light of their mind' (Ch. 59). From the moment this comes to pass by a gesture of God's hand, the whole course of our life in God will be free from error or stumbling, since we shall then walk in the light and be of the children of light. The Giver of light Himself says: 'While ye have light, believe in the light, that ye may be the children of light' (John xii. 36); and: 'I am the light of the world: he that followeth me shall not walk in darkness, but shall have the light of life' (John viii. 12). And David calls thus to the Lord: 'In thy light shall we see light' (Ps. xxxvi. 9). And the divine Paul: 'For God who commanded the light to shine out of darkness, hath shined in our hearts' (2 Cor. iv. 6). For the truly faithful are guided by Him as if by a bright inextinguishable lamp and look beyond the limits of the sensory; and to the pure in heart He opens the door of heaven which leads to all lofty and angelic manner of life and disposition. Thus, light springs forth for them, as from the sun's disc, and enables them spiritually to reason, judge, see, foresee and the like. In general, through Him all showing and revelation of unknown mysteries shines forth for them; and they become filled with supernatural and Divine power in the Holy Spirit. This supernatural power renders their flesh lighter or rather finer and makes them soar on high like a meteor. By this power of light in the Holy Spirit some of the holy fathers, while still in their bodies, traversed wide rivers and deep seas dry-footed, as though immaterial and incorporeal. They covered in a moment great distances, requiring many days of travel and performed many other marvellous deeds in heaven, on earth, in the sun, on the seas, in deserts, in cities, in every place and country, in beasts, in reptiles and generally in every creature and every element—and they were glorified. When they stood at prayer, their holy and precious bodies were lifted off the ground as though on wings; after death they remained uncorrupted and performed signs and miracles; and after resurrection they 'shall be caught up together with them in the clouds, to meet the Lord in the air; and so shall we ever be with the Lord' (1 Thess. iv. 17); as St. Paul asserts. And St. Macarius says: 'Every soul which by faith and zeal in all virtues has been clothed in Christ even in this life, authentically and effectively, always receives a concrete knowledge of heavenly mysteries, since it is united with the heavenly light of its own incorruptible image. But in the day of resurrection for the sake of the same glorious heavenly image, the body will equal the soul in glory and will be caught up by the Spirit to meet the Lord in the air, since it has become conformable to the body of His glory.'

### 96. *Another summary*

The beginning and origin of these new things and understandings, impossible to describe in words, is the aforementioned silence, combined with total non-attachment, attention and prayer, firmly based on and invincibly protected by the fulfilment of Divine commandments. These, that is, non-attachment, silence, attention and prayer, set the heart in motion and produce in it heat, which scorches passions and demons and purifies the heart as in a furnace. This brings an insatiable desire and love of our Lord Jesus Christ; this opens the fountain of sweet tears in the heart which, like hyssop, cleanse and enrich both soul and body in repentance, love, thankfulness and profession of faith. From these comes boundless peace and quietness of thoughts, passing all understanding; and from this comes bright illumination, brilliant as snow. The end of it all is passionlessness, as far as is possible for man, resurrection of the soul before the body, assumption of the image and likeness of God and our return to that state by means of doing and contemplation, faith, hope and love, as well as a total striving upwards towards God, direct union with Him, ecstasy and rest in Him, and dwelling in Him. In this life, this dwelling in Him is but a token, as though in a mirror or by divination; but in the future life it means seeing God face to face, wholly communing with Him and enjoying Him for ever.

### 97. *This mode of life in God is indeed true and unerring, as handed down to us by the fathers, that is, silence following obedience, which the saints justly called secret life in Christ*

This way, this spiritual life in God, this sacred practice of true Christians is the true, unerring and genuine secret life in Christ.

Sweetest Jesus, God and Man Himself, laid this path and gave it His mysterious guidance; the divine Apostles trod it, as well as those who came after them. From the very beginning, from the first coming of Christ on earth up to our times, our glorious teachers who followed Him, shining like lamps in the world with the radiance of their life-bearing words and wonderful deeds, have transmitted to one another right up till to-day this good seed, this sacred drink, this holy germ, this inviolate token, this grace and power from above, this precious pearl, this Divine inheritance of the fathers, this treasure buried in the field, this betrothal of the Spirit, this kingly symbol, this running water of life, this Divine fire, this precious salt, this gift, this seal, this light, and so on. This inheritance will continue to be so transmitted from generation to generation, even after our time up to the very second coming of Christ. For true is the promise of Him Who said: 'I am with you alway, even unto the end of the world. Amen' (Matt. xxviii. 20).

98. *Although there are other ways leading to salvation, this is the royal way, leading to sonship*

Although there are other ways and modes of life and, if you like, other practices which have been and are traditionally regarded as righteous, leading to salvation and giving peace to those who follow them, this one is pre-eminently the royal way, surpassing all other practices as soul surpasses body, since it renews the man completely and leads him to sonship of God, miraculously deifying in the Spirit him who follows it as he should. Basil the Great says: 'In entering the soul, the Holy Spirit gave life, gave immortality, raised up the prostrate. That which was moved by the everlasting movement of the Holy Spirit became alive, holy; and through the Spirit entering him, man received the rank of prophet, apostle, angel, God, having formerly been dust and ashes.

99. *Owing to the loftiness of this practice, its names are many*

The holy fathers call this mode of life by many glorious names. They have called it the sane way, praiseworthy doing and true contemplation, most spacious prayer, sobriety of mind, mental doing, activity of the life to come, angelic life, heavenly life, Divine conduct, the land of the living, mysterious vision, most complete spiritual feast, paradise created by God, heaven, kingdom of heaven, kingdom of God, the darkness beyond light, secret life in Christ, vision of God, the most supranatural deification, and many other similar names.

Imitating these Divine fathers, we too decided carefully to grant your request, our beloved, and, although living in impure thoughts, words and deeds, have diligently done what you have asked, even beyond our measure, for the sake of our love for you, and in obedience to the commandments of the fathers, as we have said in the preface to this work. Our Leader in this angelic life is the Son of God, God the Word, in the ineffable new dispensation He built on earth through incarnation by the good will of the immortal Father and the assistance of the Holy Spirit.

100. *Conclusion:—that with God's help and grace we too should strive and do as much as we can; may we be granted even here as a token the same great and supernatural gifts; may we not lose them through petty laziness. May this never be!*

When such and similar blessings are in store for us, beloved ones, not only as a hope of things promised in the future, but even now, in reality and practice, let us strive to attain them while we have time. Let us press forward and struggle to obtain them, in return for small and temporary zeal and brief labour, but most of all as a gift of God's grace. 'For I reckon that the sufferings of this present time are not worthy to be compared with the glory which shall be revealed in us' (Rom. viii. 18) says St. Paul, the Divine preacher. Let us then listen to him; and if we try from now on, then, according to his assurance, we shall acquire them as a beginning and a betrothal (Rom. viii. 23; 2 Cor. i. 22). So let us persevere. For people of low estate, when invited to kinship and union with the reigning house, set in motion everything to this end—words, deeds and thoughts; they seize even upon the most inaccessible things, often risking their very life; and all this for the sake of temporary and transitory glory and honour, which often leads not to gain but to perdition. How much more effort and zeal should we use, then, when called to union and marriage with God, the King and Master of all kings, Who abides for ever and grants to His kin the most brilliant and everlasting glory and honour; and, more than that, when we are given the power to become children of God, as the Gospel says: 'But as many as received him, to them gave he power to become the sons of God, even to them that believe on his name' (John i. 12). He gives the power, but does not tyrannically drag or compel us against our wish. For tyrannical compulsion always provokes resistance against the compeller, to repay evil for evil. In this way He honours our ancient sovereignty, so that when some good deed is done entirely by His will and grace, its achievement should be ascribed entirely to our own zeal and labour. Although God and Master, He has performed all His work: He has equally created all and has died for all in order to save all equally. But He left us the power to come to Him, to believe, to become His kin, to serve with fearlessness, zeal and love our truly loving Master and Protector, Who loved us enough willingly to accept death, and a degrading death, for our sakes, in order to free us from the tyranny of the devil, father of evil and our enemy, to reconcile us with God the Father, and make us heirs of God and His own co-heirs; which is most wonderful and blessed. Let us then refrain from casting aside such blessings, honours and joys for the sake of some petty and short-lived self-pandering negligence and laziness or counterfeit pleasure. Let us zealously do all that we should and bear all kinds of labours, if necessary not even sparing our life, for the sake of pleasing our Lord Who did not spare His for our sakes, although He was God. Let us thus win crowns and blessings now and in the future. May we all win them by the mercy and grace of our Lord God, our Saviour Jesus Christ, Who has so humbled Himself for us, and through this humility has richly endowed us even in this life with His transubstantial and Divine grace. To Him belong all glory, honour and worship, with His eternal Father and His all-holy righteous and life-giving Spirit, now and for ever and from all ages to all ages. Amen.

# THE BLESSED CALLISTUS
# PATRIARCH
## Texts on Prayer

1. If you wish to pray as you ought, imitate the dulcimer player; bending his head a little and inclining his ear to the strings, he strikes the strings skilfully, and enjoys the melody he draws from their harmonious notes.

2. Is this example clear to you? The dulcimer is the heart; the strings—the feelings; the hammer—remembrance of God; the player—mind. By remembrance of God and of Divine things the mind draws holy feelings from the God-fearing heart, then ineffable sweetness fills the soul, and the mind, which is pure, is lit up by Divine illuminations.

3. The dulcimer player perceives and hears nothing but the melody he enjoys. So the mind, during active prayer, descends into the depths of the heart with sobriety and can no longer listen to aught but God. All his inner being speaks to God with the voice of David: 'My soul followeth hard after thee' (Ps. lxiii. 8).

4. If we do not bar our bodily senses, the fountain of that water which the Lord promised to the woman of Samaria will not gush forth in us. This woman, seeking physical water, found the water of life flowing within her. For, as the earth by nature contains water which it pours forth as soon as an outlet is opened, so the earth of the heart by nature contains this spiritual water which gushes forth as soon as this becomes possible, like the light which our forefather Adam lost through transgression.

5. As physical water flows continually from its source, so the living water, gushing forth from the soul as soon as it is opened, never ceases to flow. Flowing in the soul of the holy man Ignatius, it urged him to say: 'There is in me no matter-loving fire (feeding on matter), but water acts and speaks in me.'

6. This blessed or rather thrice-blessed water, I mean, mental sobriety of the soul, is like water gushing forth from the bowels of the earth. Water flowing from the source of the stream fills the stream; the water which gushes forth in the heart and is always, as it were, moved by the Spirit, fills the whole of the inner man with Divine dew and renders the outer man fiery.

7. Purified of everything external and having entirely mastered the senses by active virtue, the mind rests unmoving within the heart, its vision established in the centre. There it receives mental illuminations, like flashes of lightning, and thus collects Divine understandings.

8. If they hear of this, let none of the uninitiated or those who still 'have need of milk' (Heb. v. 12) touch it, for this is something that it is forbidden to touch before its time. The attempts of those who try to obtain before its time that which comes in its own time, and who strive to force their way into the harbour of passionlessness without due preparation, are called by the holy fathers madness. For he who knows no letters cannot read books.

9. Movements produced in the soul by the Divine Spirit as a result of efforts make the heart quiet and urge it to call out constantly: 'Abba Father!' This is not accompanied by any imaginings but is devoid of all images. But we ourselves become then transformed by the dawning of Divine light, which endows us with an image in keeping with the burning of the Divine Spirit. More than that, it changes and alters us by Divine power. How—He alone knows.

10. If a mind, purified by sobriety, is not freed from everything external by constant memory of Jesus, it is easily darkened. Equally, a man who has joined contemplation, or guarding the mind, with active practice, does not refute rumours about himself, nor turn away from talk about himself, whether open or hidden. For only a soul sick with Divine love for Christ (Song of Songs ii. 5) follows hard after Him alone, like a brother.

11. According to the prophet: 'Be still and know' (Ps. xlvi. 10); it is possible to curb carnal passions and their upsurgings, and to become wisely still from them, even while living in the world. But to wipe them out and annihilate them is impossible. Life in the desert, however, manifestly has the power to uproot them.

12. Some living or running waters flow fast, others are slow and calm. The former, flowing swiftly, cannot remain muddy for long, and even if at times they become slightly muddied, their movement soon clears them again. But if the flow of water changes and becomes very slow, it is easily muddied and remains largely so, through its immobility; and the only way to clear it is to make it flow faster.

13. The devil approaches beginners, those who are training in virtues and those who are active, with clear or unclear sounds. He approaches contemplatives by producing certain fantasies, at times colouring the air to resemble light, at others producing flame-like forms, in order thus to tempt the worker in Christ.

14. If you wish to learn how to pray, keep your gaze fixed on the end of attention or of prayer. This end is adoration, contrition of the heart, love of neighbour. It is self-evident that lustful thoughts, whisperings of slander, hatred of one's neighbour and similar things are opposed to it. All this is incompatible with the work of prayer.[42]

42 Evidently this text is only a fragment. (Footnote in 'Dobrotolubiye'.)

# PART TWO

# HESYCHIUS OF JERUSALEM
## Short Biographical Note

Hesychius was born in Jerusalem and in his youth was a pupil of St. Gregory the Theologian. After the death of this great teacher he spent his life in one of the hermitages in Palestine, where he continued to study the spirit of Christianity from books, from conversations with other contemporary spiritual workers in Palestine, and from his own experiences and researches. In A.D. 412 the Archbishop of Jerusalem ordained this enlightened monk as a priest and thenceforth, as priest and preacher, he appears in the history of the Church as one of its most famous teachers. 'The great Euthymius', writes Cyril of Scythopolis (in the life of his teacher St. Euthymius), 'was greatly pleased when St. Juvenal, Patriarch of Jerusalem, brought with him the enlightened Hesychius, priest and teacher of the Church, when he came to Euthymius' monastery in 429 to consecrate the Church'.

Theophan in his Chronography puts his death at the twenty-sixth year of the reign of Theodosius the Youngest, which corresponds to the year A.D. 432-3. In the almanack of the Emperor Basil his memory is celebrated on March 28. Throughout the Eastern Church his memory is now celebrated with all the holy ones on Shrovetide Saturday. In the Canon of Theodore the Studite he is included on that day among the number of the great teachers: Basil the Great, Gregory the Theologian, John Chrysostom, Athanasius the Great, the two Cyrils—of Jerusalem and of Alexandria—St. Epiphanes, and Gregory of Nyssa; and he is also called theologian, naturally after Gregory the Theologian.

In his learned writings Hesychius was a worthy pupil of St. Gregory the Theologian. The almanack of the Emperor Basil singles out Hesychius as preacher and interpreter of the Holy

Scriptures and says: 'He expounded and interpreted all the Holy Scriptures with great clarity for the benefit of all, and thus was renowned and admired by all.'

Imitating the Greek 'Philokalia', we have chosen out of his many writings that addressed to Theodulus, divided into 203 texts, as being the most helpful for those who wish to learn sobriety, attention and guarding of the heart. The blessed Photius, in his 'Philokalia', says of this writing that 'more than any other writings it is suitable for those who lead a life of striving for the sake of the kingdom of heaven. His exposition is clear and it is in every way suitable for men who do not go in for abstract researches but direct all their zeal and labour to the practical works of active life.'[43]

43 In translating, the Greek 'Philokalia' was amplified in some places from Migne's 'Patrologiae', vol. 93. (Footnote in 'Dobrotolubiye'.)

# HESYCHIUS OF JERUSALEM
## TO THEODULUS
### Texts on Sobriety and Prayer, for the saving of the soul

1. Sobriety is a spiritual art, which, with long and diligent practice and with the help of God, releases man completely from passionate thoughts and words and from evil deeds. And as it proceeds, it gives a sure knowledge of God the Incomprehensible, as far as this can be reached; and it gives in secret a solution of Divine and secret mysteries. It is the doer of every commandment in the Old and the New Testament; and the giver of every blessing in the life to come. In itself it is, in essence, purity of heart; which on account of its greatness and its high qualities, or to speak more exactly, on account of our inattention and our carelessness, is very rare among monks to-day; it is this which Christ calls blessed, saying: 'Blessed are the pure in heart: for they shall see God' (Matt. v. 8). Being then such as it is, it is bought for a great price. Sobriety, if it be constant in a man, becomes his guide to a righteous and God-pleasing life. It is also a ladder towards contemplation; and it teaches us to govern rightly the movements of the three parts of the soul (that is, the three powers—the thinking, the excitable and the desiring), and to guard the senses securely, and increases daily the four great virtues (that is, wisdom, courage, abstinence and justice).

2. The great lawgiver, Moses, or rather the Holy Spirit, showing the perfect and pure and comprehensive and elevating nature of this virtue, and teaching us how we must begin and complete it, says: 'Beware that there be not a thought in thy wicked heart' (Deut. xv. 9), by thought meaning any mental image of some sinful thing abhorrent to God. And this the fathers also

call suggestion, which is brought against the heart by the devil, and which our thoughts follow after as soon as it presents itself to the mind, and with which they passionately hold converse.

3. Sobriety is the way of every virtue and every commandment of God. It is also called silence of the heart, and is the same as guarding the mind, kept perfectly free of all fantasies.

4. He who was born blind does not see the light of the sun; so he who does not live in sobriety will not see in its richness the brightness of the grace which comes from above. Neither will he be freed from evil deeds and words and thoughts which are hateful to God; and not being free from them, when he departs, he will not pass unhindered by the rulers of Hell (whom he must meet).

5. Attention is unceasing silence of the heart, free of all thoughts. At all times, constantly and without ceasing, it breathes Christ Jesus, the Son of God and God, and Him alone, it calls upon Him, and with Him bravely fights against the enemies, and makes confession to Him Who has power to forgive sins. Such a soul, through continual calling on Christ, embraces Him Who alone searches the heart; and it seeks to hide its sweetness and its inner attainment from all men in every way, lest the evil one should have an easy entrance for his wickedness and destroy its excellent working.

6. Sobriety is the steadfast setting up of the thought of the mind and posting it at the door of the heart, so that it sees alien thoughts as they come, those thieves and robbers, and hears what these destroyers say and do; and sees what is the image inscribed and figured in them by the demons, who are trying thus to seduce the mind by fantasy. For this work, when it is done with loving effort, reveals to us very fundamentally and clearly, by experience, the art of mental war and brings skill in it.

7. The times of desertion by God and the occurrences of external temptations for our instruction bring great fear, which engenders a constancy of attentive observation in the mind of a man who is trying to seal up the fountain of evil thoughts and deeds. It is for this very purpose that times of desertion occur, and unexpected temptations are sent us from God, forcing us to correct our life, especially if a man has tasted the sweet peace

resulting from this excellence (attention and sobriety) and has become negligent. Constancy engenders habit; and this in its turn a kind of natural continuity of sobriety; and this, in the nature of things, gradually leads to the power of seeing the warfare, upon which follows a continuous praying to Jesus, and a sweet stillness of mind, free from fantasies and that wonderful state which comes from union with Jesus.

8. When the mind stands upright and calls upon Christ against its enemies, and runs to Him for refuge, it is like some wild animal, surrounded by many hounds, courageously facing them from the cover of its shelter. It discerns mentally from afar the mental ambushes of its unseen enemies, and remains unwounded by them, for it continually prays the peace-giving Jesus for His help.

9. If you know, and if it has been given to you in the morning to stand in the sight of the Lord, and not only to be seen but also to see (Ps. v. 3, 5), then you understand what I say. But if not, be sober, and you will receive.

10. The seas are compounded of many waters. Resolute sobriety—wakefulness and profound silence of the soul, as well as the depth of miraculous and ineffable contemplations and of wise humility, righteousness and love—all these are compounded of supreme sobriety and ceaseless prayer to Jesus Christ with sighs and without thoughts; with the utmost effort but without despondency or fainting (Luke xviii. 1).

11. 'Not everyone that saith unto me, Lord, Lord, shall enter into the kingdom of heaven;' says the Lord, 'but he that doeth the will of my Father' (Matt. vii. 21). And the will of the Father is this: 'Ye that love the Lord, hate evil' (Ps. xcvii. 10). So then, with prayer to Jesus Christ, let us hate evil thoughts—and the will of God is done.

12. Our Lord and God made flesh has offered us the image of all virtue, as an example to the human race; and to recall us from the ancient fall, has set before us, as in a picture, His all-virtuous life in the flesh. Among many other good examples, He has shown us how, after His baptism, when He went out into the wilderness, it was with fasting that He began His mental wrestling with the devil, who came against Him as against an ordinary man. And

through this manner of His victory, our Lord has taught us, His unprofitable servants, how we must practise our wrestling against the spirits of evil, that is with humility and fasting and prayer and sobriety: which He observed though He Himself had no need of such things, being God and God of Gods.

13. But how many ways of sobriety there are, in my belief, ways of cleansing the mind little by little from passionate thoughts, behold! I will not delay to reveal to thee in unadorned and simple language. For I have not thought it right in this discourse to do what is done in accounts of external wars, that is, by a stream of words, to conceal what is useful—especially from those who are simple. And do thou, my son Timothy, 'give attendance to reading', as the Apostle says (1 Tim. iv. 13).

14. One way of sobriety then is to watch closely imagination or suggestion; for without imagination Satan cannot form thoughts and exhibit them to the mind to seduce it by deceit.

15. And another way is to keep the heart always deeply silent, all thought stilled, and to pray.

16. Another is to call humbly and unceasingly on our Lord Jesus Christ for help.

17. And another way is to have remembrance of death unceasingly in the soul.

18. All these doings, beloved, keep off evil thoughts like doorkeepers. But of the need to look only on heaven (always occupying the mind with contemplation of heavenly things) and to regard as nothing the earth (and all earthly things), which also is one of the practical methods of sobriety, I will, if God grants it, set forth a more complete account in another place.

19. If we cut off the causes of the passions (occasions for their excitement), and busy ourselves with spiritual works only for a short time, but do not continue in them and persist in this same work for the rest of our life, we easily return to the passions of the flesh, having gained no other fruit than final darkening of the mind, and the deepest plunge into materiality.

20. He who struggles inwardly must practise at every moment these four (doings): *humility*, extreme *attention*, *resistance* (to thoughts) and *prayer*. *Humility*, so that, since this struggle is against proud demons, a man may have the help of Christ always

in the hand of his heart; for the Lord abominates the proud. *Attention*, that he may allow his heart to entertain no thought, even though it seems good. *Resistance*, so that, distinguishing clearly who it is that comes to him, he may at once with anger contradict the wicked one; as it is said: 'So shall I have wherewith to answer him that reproacheth me' (Ps. cxix. 42). And again: 'Truly my soul waiteth upon God' (Ps. lxii. 1). And *prayer*, that after resistance he may immediately cry from the depths of his heart to Christ, with groaning that cannot be uttered. Then he that struggles will see how the enemy with his imaginings is scattered by the worshipful name of Jesus, as dust by the wind, or as smoke that is dispersed and driven away.

21. He who has no prayer free from thoughts has no weapon for battle. By prayer I mean the prayer which is constantly active in the innermost secret places of the soul, so that the enemy in his secret onslaughts is invisibly flogged and scorched by calling on the name of our Lord Jesus Christ.

22. You should look within with a keen and intense look of the mind so as to perceive those who enter; and when you perceive them, you should at once crush the head of the snake by resistance; and along with this call on Christ with groaning. And then you will gain the experience of unseen Divine intercession; and you will see clearly what is rightness of heart (whether it works rightly and in what its right work consists).

23. As he who holds a mirror in his hands, and is standing amongst others as he looks into it, sees his own face, and what it is like, and sees too the faces of the others looking in the same mirror; so he who is looking into his own heart with complete attention, sees his own state in it, and sees too the dark faces of the Ethiopians of the mind.

24. But the mind cannot conquer evil imagination through itself alone, and let it never undertake it. For so cunning are our enemies, they pretend to be worsted, and from another side they trip up our heels by means of vanity. But against the invocation of Jesus they will not endure to stand and beguile you, even for a moment.

25. Take heed lest you should think highly of yourself in the manner of Israel of old (and invent your own methods of struggle),

and thyself too be delivered over to the mental enemies; for he, after he had been delivered from Egypt by the God of all, devised a molten image as a help for himself.

26. And you should understand that the molten image is our weak reason, which as long as it calls on Jesus Christ against the spirits of evil easily drives them away, and with skilful art routs the unseen hostile forces of the enemy. But whenever in its folly it trusts wholly to itself, like the bird called swift-winged, it falls down to its death.44 He who trusts in the Lord professes: 'The Lord is my strength and my shield; my heart trusted in him, and I am helped' (Ps. xxviii. 7). And again: 'Who', beside the Lord, 'will rise up for me against the evil-doers? or who will stand up for me against the workers of iniquity?'—'the multitude of my thoughts' (Ps. xciv. 16, 19). But he who trusts in himself and not in God shall fall with a grievous fall.

27. If you wish to struggle as you ought, beloved, let that little creature the spider be a pattern to you, showing you the way and order of silence of the heart. The spider seizes and kills small flies; like the spider (sitting in the middle of its web) may you too keep silence in the soul with the utmost effort, and never cease killing the children of Babylon; for such slaughter you would be called happy by the Holy Spirit through the mouth of David (Ps. cxxxvii. 9).

28. As it is not possible for the Red Sea to be seen in the firmament in the middle of the stars, and as it is not possible for a man walking on the earth not to breathe this air, so it is impossible to purify our heart from passionate thoughts, and to drive out our mental enemies, without constant calling on Jesus Christ.

29. If with humility of thought and remembrance of death, and with self-reproach and resistance (to thoughts) and calling on Jesus Christ, you remain constantly within your heart, and if you journey soberly with these weapons day by day on that way of the mind, which is narrow, but sweet and gladdening, you will come to the holy contemplation of holy things, and you will be enlightened by knowledge of the deep mysteries by Christ, 'In

---

44 A breed of pigeons which rise high, then fold their wings and drop down. If they have no time to unfold their wings they hit the ground and are killed. (Footnote in 'Dobrotolubiye'.)

whom are hid all the treasures of wisdom and knowledge' (Col. ii. 3). 'For in him dwelleth all the fullness of the Godhead bodily' (Col. ii. 9). For you shall feel in Jesus, that into your heart has leapt the Holy Spirit, by Whom the minds of men are illuminated 'and with open face beholding . . . the glory of the Lord' (2 Cor. iii. 18). It is said: 'No man can say that Jesus is the Lord, but by the Holy Ghost' (1 Cor. xii. 3) Who thus secretly affirms the seeker of the Lord (of the truth about Him).

30. And this too must be known to those who wish to learn, that the evil demons envying us, often hide and calm down the mental war, for they grudge us the great help it brings us in ascent to God and the knowledge we gain through it. And this is in order that when (forgetting the dangers of their attacks) we become negligent, they may again suddenly seize the mind (with imagination) and that they may again make some of us inattentive to our heart. For but one aim and one struggle occupies them ceaselessly: totally to prevent our hearts from being attentive, knowing as they do the wealth that is brought to the soul from the daily practice of attention. The more then should we (at times of lull in warfare), with remembrance of our Lord Jesus Christ, exert ourselves to spiritual contemplation, and war return to our mind. Only let us do everything with the advice, if I may so speak, of the Lord Himself; and with great humility.

31. It is right for us who live in a community to submit to him who is in authority over us, and to cut off every wish of our own with willing decision and a zealous heart, thus becoming, with God's help, as it were, wilfully will-less. Moreover we must endeavour not to be disturbed by irritability or allow unreasonable and unnatural movements of anger, for otherwise, in the hour of spiritual battle, we may prove to be without courage. For it is the way of our will, if it is not cut off by us with our consent, to be irritated against those who seek to cut it off by force (without our consent). And for this reason anger arises and, barking fiercely, obscures our understanding of the warfare (of skill in waging it), which was so difficult, almost impossible, to obtain. For the nature of anger is to be destructive. If it is moved against evil thoughts, it destroys and exterminates them; but if it is moved against men, it destroys in us good thoughts

towards them. Thus it is evident that anger is destructive of all kinds of thoughts, either evil thoughts or, as it may happen, good thoughts too. For it is given us by God as a shield and a bow and is such if it does not deviate from its function. But if it begins to act contrary to its function, it becomes destructive. I have seen a dog, at times a brave fighter of wolves, attack and rend sheep.

32. We ought to flee from overboldness (unguarded freedom of behaviour towards others) as from the poison of a snake and to avoid frequent conversation as we would serpents and the brood of vipers. For these things have great power to bring us quickly into complete forgetfulness of the inner warfare and to draw the soul down from the joyful heights reached by purity of heart. This accursed forgetfulness is opposed to attention as water is to fire; and every hour is violently hostile to it. For from forgetfulness we come to negligence, and from negligence to contempt (of the rules of spiritual life), and to despondency and lusts that have no place; and so we turn again to the things that are behind us, like a dog to his vomit (2 Peter ii. 22). Let us flee then from wilfulness as from the poison of death. And let us cure the evil mischief of forgetfulness and what springs from it by a most strict guarding of the mind, and by constant calling on Our Lord Jesus Christ; for without Him we can do nothing (John xv. 5).

33. It is not normal, it is not possible, to be friends with a snake and to carry it in your bosom; neither is it possible to indulge the body in all sorts of ways, to pamper it and love it beyond what is useful and necessary, and at the same time to have a care for heavenly virtue. For the nature of the one (the snake) is to wound him who warms it; and the nature of the other (the body) is to defile by movements of lusts him who pampers it. And in as much as the body sins, let it be beaten with whips to the drawing of blood, like a runaway slave who has drunk himself full with wine. Let him be aware that he has a master (mind) ready to punish him if he gets drunk with lust as with wine in a tavern. Let not this mortal clay, this daughter of darkness, also be ignorant of her immortal mistress (the soul). Until your very departing trust not in the flesh. It is said: 'The carnal mind is enmity against God: for it is not subject to the law of God'

(Rom. viii. 7). And again: 'The flesh lusteth against the Spirit' (Gal. v. 17). And again: 'They that are in the flesh cannot please God. But ye are not in the flesh, but in the Spirit' (Rom. viii. 8, 9).

34. The work of *good sense* is always to stir up our excitable power to fight in the battle within, and to reproach ourselves. And the work of *wisdom* is to stir up our thinking power to strict and continual sobriety and to spiritual contemplation. And the work of *justice* is to direct our desiring power towards virtue and towards God. And the work of *courage* is to guide and control the five senses, so that the inward man, or heart, may not be defiled by them, nor the outward man or body.

35. 'His excellency is over Israel'—that is, over the mind which sees as far as is possible the beauty of the glory of God Himself, 'and his strength is in the clouds' (Ps. lxviii. 34)—it is in souls shining like the light and looking up into the dawn; and it reveals in all His beauty Him Who sits on the right hand of the Father, sending forth light to them, as the sun sends forth rays to the pure clouds, and gives them loveliness.

36. 'One sinner destroyeth much good' (Eccles. ix. 18), says the Holy Scripture. And the mind by sinning destroys the meats and drinks of heaven, that we have just described.

37. We are not stronger than Samson; nor wiser than Solomon; nor have we more knowledge of Divine things than David; nor do we love God more than did Peter, the chief of the Apostles. Let us not then trust in ourselves; for the Scripture says, he who trusts in himself shall fall with a grievous fall.

38. Let us learn from Christ humility of heart, and from David to be humble, and from Peter to weep for the downfalls which occur. But let us not despair, as did Samson and Judas and Solomon, the wisest of men.

39. 'The devil, as a roaring lion, walketh about', with his hosts, 'seeking whom he may devour' (1 Peter v. 8). Let then continual attention of the heart, sobriety, resistance to thoughts, and prayer to Jesus Christ, our Lord, never be idle; for you will never find a better help than Jesus in your whole life. For the One Lord, Who is God, alone knows the villainies of the demons, their tricks and their wiles.

40. Let then the soul daringly trust in Christ, and call on Him and have no fear at all of enemies. For it does not fight alone, but with the help of its Terrible King, Jesus Christ, the Maker of all things bodiless and embodied, visible and invisible.

41. For as the more the rain pours down upon the earth, the more it softens the earth; so too the holy Name of Christ, when it is invoked by us without thoughts, the more constantly we call upon it, the more it softens the earth of our heart, and fills it with joy and delight.

42. And it is good that the inexperienced should know this too—that we, who are heavy and weighed down to the earth by body and discursive thought, have enemies who are bodiless and invisible, malicious and clever at harming us, skilful, nimble and practised in warfare waged all the years from Adam even until now. By no other means have we the possibility to conquer them except by continual sobriety of the mind, and calling on Jesus Christ, our God and Creator. May prayer to Jesus Christ be for the inexperienced an incentive and guide to experience and knowledge of good. But for the experienced the best teacher of good is doing, testing by practice and tasting what is good.

43. As an innocent little child is delighted when it sees a wonder worker, and follows the doer of marvels out of guilelessness; so too our soul, being simple and good—for it was made so by its good Master—is delighted by the fantastic suggestions of the devil and being deceived it runs to that wily one as though he were good, as the dove runs to one who sets nets for her children; and so it mingles its own thoughts with the fantasy of the devil's suggestion. If there should chance the face of a beautiful woman, or something else that is plainly forbidden by the commandments of Christ, it wishes as it were to contrive something to bring into reality the lovely thing which it has seen; and then having identified with the thought, it goes on and brings into effect by means of the body, to its own condemnation, the unlawful thing that it has seen in thought.

44. This is the art of the evil one, and with these arrows he poisons every victim. And for this reason it is not safe, until the mind has had long experience of the warfare, to allow thoughts to enter into the heart; especially in the beginning, when our

soul is still in sympathy with the suggestions of the demons, takes pleasure in them and follows them eagerly; but it is necessary, as soon as we are aware of the thoughts, immediately to cut them off, at the very moment of their impact and our finding them. But when after a long time the mind is practised in this wonderful work, and knows all there is to know about it, and comes to be skilled in waging this war, so as to discriminate between thoughts correctly—and as the prophet says, is able easily to take 'the little foxes' (Song of Solomon ii. 15)—then it may cunningly let them enter, and fight against them with the help of Christ, expose them and throw them out.

45. As it is impossible for fire and water to pass together through one channel, so it is impossible for sin to enter into the heart, unless it first knocks at the door of the heart through the fantasy of an evil suggestion.

46. First comes suggestion; secondly coupling, when our thoughts and the thoughts of the wicked demons are mingled together; thirdly, merging, when thoughts of both kinds take counsel together, resolve on evil and plan what must be done; and fourthly, comes the visible action, that is, the sin. If then the mind is steadfast in sobriety, pays attention to itself, and by resistance and calling on the Lord Jesus drives away the suggestion on its impact, that which would usually follow does not happen. For the evil one, being mind without body, cannot lead souls astray except by means of imagination and thoughts. From among these actions David says of suggestion: 'I will early destroy all the wicked of the land' (Ps. ci. 8). And the great Moses says about merging: 'Thou shalt make no covenant with them' (Exod. xxiii. 32).

47. Mind is invisibly engaged in battle with mind—the demon's mind with our mind. And for this reason it is needful for us to cry out of the depths at each moment to Christ, that He will drive away from us the demon's mind and give us the prize of victory, as He loves men.

48. Let a man holding a mirror and gazing attentively into it be an example to you of silence of the heart. And then (if you imitate him) you will see mentally inscribed in your heart both wicked things and good.

49. Watch always that there be no thought in your heart, neither seemly nor unseemly, that so you may easily recognise the aliens, that is, the first-born sons of the Egyptians (meaning suggestions).

50. How good and delightful, most sweet and bright, beautiful, fair of face and lovely a virtue is sobriety, which is led on its way by Thee, O Christ, Who art God, and which journeys watchfully in great humility of the human heart! For it stretches forth its branches to the sea and to the great deep of contemplation, and its offshoots to the rivers of sweet and Divine mysteries, and it waters the mind which has for long been withered up by impiety, by the brine of wicked thoughts, and by the frenzied wilfulness of the flesh, in which is death.

51. Sobriety is like the ladder of Jacob, above which God stood and by which the angels ascended. It takes all evil from us; it cuts off talkativeness, railing, slandering, and the whole catalogue of sensory passions; for it cannot bear on their account to be deprived even for a little while of its own sweetness.

52. Let us, brethren, follow after this zealously; but while we soar in purity of heart with Christ Jesus, and in contemplation of Him, let us keep in view also our sins and our former life; that being made contrite and humbled by the memory of our sins, we may possess and not be parted from the help of Jesus Christ our Lord in the invisible warfare. For as soon as we are deprived of the help of Jesus through pride, or love of self, or vainglory, we are deprived too of purity of heart, through which God lets Himself be known to man. For the former is the cause as it is the promise of the latter (purity of heart—seeing God) (Matt. v. 8).

53. Along with the other good things which it will find from its constant exercise of watchfulness, the mind, that does not neglect its own hidden work, will also find that the five senses of the body no longer cooperate with the sinful temptations that come from without. For in attending wholly to its own virtue —sobriety—and wishing always to rejoice in good thoughts, it does not let itself be robbed by the five senses, by which material and vain thoughts enter it; but knowing the danger of their seductiveness it curbs them from within by a strong effort of will.

54. Be steadfast in attention of the mind, and you shall not be overburdened by temptations. Retreat from this, and suffer what befalls.

55. As those who have lost their appetite and taste for food are helped by bitter wormwood, so for those who have bad habits suffering is useful.

56. If you wish not to suffer evil, then wish not to do evil, for one follows inevitably on the other. For that which a man sows that shall he also reap. When then we sow willingly that which is bad and reap it against our will, we ought to be filled with wonder at the justice of God.

57. The mind is blinded by these three passions: love of money, vainglory and love of pleasure.

58. Knowledge and faith, which are ours by nature, are blunted by nothing other than these three.

59. It is through these that wrath and anger, murders and the whole catalogue of passions are greatly strengthened among men.

60. He who does not know the truth cannot have true faith; for in the nature of things knowledge goes before faith. What was spoken in the Scriptures was spoken, not only that we may know it, but that we may do it.

61. Let us then start doing. For if we press forward in this way, we shall find that not only hope in God, but also firm faith, and inner knowledge, redemption from temptations, the gifts of grace, heartfelt confession, and copious tears, are given to the faithful through prayer; and not only these, but also endurance of the troubles that come upon us, and sincere forgiveness of our neighbours, understanding of spiritual law, finding the righteousness of God, the visitation of the Holy Spirit, and the gift of spiritual treasures, and all the things that God has promised to give to believers now and in the world to come. In one word—it is impossible for the soul to appear in the image of God, except through God's grace and man's faith—when a man remains in his heart in deep humility and unwavering prayer.

62. It is in truth a great good, as we have found from experience, that he who wishes to cleanse his heart should call constantly on the Lord Jesus against our mental enemies. See how the word which I have spoken from experience agrees with the

testimony of the Scriptures: 'Prepare to meet thy God, O Israel'45 (Amos iv. 12). And the Apostle says: 'Pray without ceasing' (1 Thess. v. 17). And our Lord says: 'He that abideth in me, and I in him, the same bringeth forth much fruit: for without me ye can do nothing. If a man abide not in me, he is cast forth as a branch, and is withered' (John xv. 5, 6). Prayer is a great good, and a good which contains all blessings, for it purifies the heart in which those who have faith see God.

63. The treasure of humility, since it is elevating and loved of God, and destructive of all those things in us which are evil and hated by God, is therefore hard to win. You may perhaps easily find in a man the partial working of many other virtues, but if you search for the odour of humility in him you will hardly find it. Hence there is need of great zeal and efforts in order to obtain this treasure. And the Scriptures speak of the devil as unclean, since from the beginning he rejected this good treasure of humility, and loved pride; wherefore he is called an unclean spirit in all the Scriptures. For what bodily uncleanness could be wrought by a being who is immaterial and has neither body, flesh nor limbs that for that reason he should be called unclean? It is plain that he was called unclean because of pride; and from being a pure and bright angel he came to be named evil. 'Every one that is proud in heart is an abomination to the Lord' (Prov. xvi. 5). For it is said that pride is the beginning of sin (Ecclus. x. 15). 'I know not the Lord,' said Pharaoh, 'neither will I let Israel go' (Exod. v. 2). Thus spoke a proud man.

64. There are many activities of the mind which can procure for us the good gift of humility, if we are not unmindful of our salvation. There is the remembrance of our sins in word, deed or thought, and the remembrance of many other things greatly contributes to humility when they are revised in the mind. And true humility is created also by this—by a man's revolving every day in his own mind the virtues of his neighbours, and extolling their other natural qualities, comparing their qualities to his own. And so when the mind sees its own worthlessness, and how far it falls short of the perfection of others, a man naturally starts counting himself as dust and ashes, and not a man but a dog, as

45 The Slavonic text reads: 'Prepare to call on thy God.' (Translators' note.)

though in all respects he comes behind all rational beings on earth, is more poor and empty.

65. It is said by the pillar of the Church, our great Father Basil, the mouth of Christ: 'It is a great help towards not sinning and not falling into the same sins on the following day, if at the end of the day we judge ourselves in our conscience, as far as we can, what we have done wrong and what we have done right. This also Job did on behalf of himself and his children.' For this daily examination throws light on what happens every hour (teaches us to examine ourselves hourly, in order to see every hour how to act rightly).

66. And another[46] of those who are wise in Divine things has said: 'The beginning of fruit bearing is the flower, and the beginning of active life is abstinence.' Let us then practise abstinence and this by measure and weight as the fathers teach. And let us pass the whole day of twelve hours in guarding the mind; for if with God's help we do this with a certain forcing of ourselves, we shall be able to quench and diminish wickedness in us; since the virtuous life, through which the kingdom of heaven is given us, must be won by forcing ourselves.

67. The way to knowledge is through passionlessness and humility, and without these no one shall see the Lord.

68. He who unceasingly occupies his time with that which is within is chaste. And not only this, but he knows contemplation, the word of God, and prayer. And it is of this that the Apostle speaks when he says: 'Walk in the Spirit, and ye shall not fulfil the lust of the flesh' (Gal. v. 16).

69. He who does not know how to journey on the spiritual road pays no attention to his passionate thoughts (that is, he does not drive them away), but all his time is concerned with the flesh; either he is a glutton and lives riotously; or he is distressed and angry, and bears grudges, and thence his thoughts are darkened; or he may practise immoderate asceticism, and so harm his heart.

70. He who renounces worldly things such as women and wealth and so on, makes the outer man a monk, but not yet the inner man. But he who renounces the passionate thought of these things, makes a monk of the inner man as well, that is, the mind.

46 Nilus of Sinai. (Footnote in 'Dobrotolubiye'.)

Such a man is a true monk. One can easily make the outer man a monk if one wishes, but it is no small struggle to make a monk of the inner man.

71. Who is there in this generation who is wholly free from passionate thoughts, who has acquired the pure immaterial ceaseless prayer, which is the distinguishing feature of the inward man?

72. Many passions are hidden in our souls, but they are discovered only when that (object, cause) which arouses them appears.

73. Let not all your attention be upon the body, but, allotting to it work compatible with its strength, turn your whole mind upon the things that are within. For it is said: 'Bodily exercise profiteth little: but godliness is profitable unto all things' (1 Tim. iv. 8).

74. If passions are inactive merely because their causes (objects) are removed, or the demons are in deceptive retreat—pride follows.

75. Humility and hardship (bodily privations) free man from all sin: the first by cutting away the passions of the soul, and the second by cutting away those of the body. And for this cause the Lord saith: 'Blessed are the pure in heart: for they shall see God' (Matt. v. 8). That is, they shall see Him, and the treasures that are in Him, when through love and abstinence they purify themselves; and so much the more as their purification is increased.

76. The watch-tower (look-out) over words, to acquire all the virtues, means guarding of the mind, as David's watchman of old signified circumcision of the heart (2 Samuel xviii. 24).

77. When we look at something harmful on the level of the senses we are hurt, so too it is on the level of the mind.

78. He who wounds the heart of a plant causes the whole plant to wither. So let us think of the heart of man. We must be on our guard at every moment, for the thieves never sleep.

79. The Lord, wishing to show that every commandment is obligatory, and that sonship of God is a gift won for men by His very blood, says: 'When ye shall have done all those things which are commanded you, say, We are unprofitable servants: we have done that which was our duty to do' (Luke xvii. 10). For the kingdom of heaven is not the reward of our work, but it is a gift

of grace from our Lord, prepared for His faithful servants. The servant does not ask for his freedom as a reward; but if he receives it he gives thanks for it like a debtor, and if not, he awaits it as a mercy.

80. According to the Scriptures Christ died for our sins. So He gives freedom to those who serve Him well. For He says: 'Well done, good and faithful servant; thou hast been faithful over a few things, I will make thee ruler over many things: enter thou into the joy of thy Lord' (Matt. xxv. 23). He who trusts himself to bare knowledge (of the duties of a slave) is not yet a faithful servant, but he who shows his faithfulness by obeying the commandment given by Christ.

81. He who honours his master does that which he is bidden; and if he errs or overlooks something, endures what happens to him as his due. Be you then both a lover of learning and a lover of labour (of course, in fulfilling the commandments). For bare knowledge puffs a man up.

82. The temptations which come to us unexpectedly serve to teach us to become lovers of labour.

83. Peculiar to a star is the light that surrounds it. And peculiar to those who worship and fear God are poverty and humility. For there is nothing so distinctive, nor is there so plain a sign, of the disciples of Christ, as a humble spirit and an unpretentious appearance. All four Gospels speak of this. And he who does not live thus humbly loses his portion in Him Who humbled Himself willingly, even unto the cross, and unto death; Who was also Himself the lawgiver of Divine commandments in the holy Gospels, and has shown (by His deeds and His life as described in the Gospels) the commandments obligatory for us.

84. It is said: 'Ho, everyone that thirsteth, come ye to the waters' (Is. lv. 1). And you who thirst for God come in purity of mind and heart. But he who flies high in this must look also to the earth of his beggarly state. For no one is higher than he who is humble. As when there is no light all things are obscure and dark, so when there is no humility all our acts are foolish, vain and barren.

85. 'Let us hear the conclusion of the whole matter: Fear God, and keep his commandments' (Eccles. xii. 13), both in

thought and outwardly. For if in thought you compel yourself to keep them, you will seldom need to struggle for that in outward things. For David says: 'I delight to do thy will, O my God: yea, thy law is within my heart' (Ps. xl. 8).

86. If a man shall not do the will of God and the law of God in his belly, that is within his heart, neither will he be able easily to do it externally. And moreover, he who is not sober but indifferent says to God, as it were: I 'desire not the knowledge of thy ways' (Job xxi. 14). Such a man is altogether wanting in Divine illumination. For he who partakes of this illumination shall not only keep the law in his heart with full conviction, but shall also have strength to live in accordance with it.

87. As material salt gives a savour to bread and to all food, and keeps meat from rotting, even for a long time; so in this same way should you think of guarding the inner savour of the mind and the wonderful doing in the heart. For it sweetens divinely both the inner and the outer man, drives away the evil smell of wicked thoughts, and preserves us continually in what is good.

88. From suggestions come many thoughts, and from these comes the actual evil deed. But he who with Jesus straightway quenches the former, has escaped that which comes after. And he will become rich in the sweet Divine knowledge through which he will see God, present everywhere. And placing before God the mirror of his mind, he will be illumined by Him, like pure crystal that mirrors the visible sun. And then at length the mind, having reached the furthest point of its desire, will find in itself repose from all other contemplation.

89. Since every thought enters the heart through imagining something sensory (and the sensory hinders the mental), so the light of the Deity begins to illumine the mind only when it is freed of everything and is totally empty of form (without representation of shape or form). For this illumination is manifested in a mind already pure, on condition that it is free of all thoughts.

90. In so far as you have perfect attention in your mind, by so much will you pray to Jesus with warm desire. And again, in so far as you watch over your mind carelessly, by so much will you become distant from Jesus. And as perfect attention entirely fills

the air of the mind with light, so too, to be without sobriety and without the sweet invocation of Jesus makes it wholly dark. And the matter is naturally such as we have said it to be and not otherwise. This you will find by experience, if you will test it in practice; since virtue and especially this light-giving and sweet work is naturally learned only by experience.

91. To call on Jesus perpetually with warm desire, full of sweetness and joy, fills the air of the heart with joyous stillness; and this comes from extreme attention. But He Who perfectly purifies the heart is Jesus Christ alone, the Son of God and God, the Cause and Maker of all good things. For He says, 'I make peace . . . I the Lord' (Is. xlv. 7).

92. The soul that is benefited and sweetened by Jesus repays its benefactor, acknowledging Him with exultation and love. And it renders thanks, and with sweetness of heart calls upon Him Who gives peace, for it sees Him, within itself, disperse the fantasies of evil spirits.

93. And David says: 'Mine' (mental) 'eye also shall see my desire on mine' (inner) 'enemies, and mine ears shall hear my desire of the wicked that rise up against me' (Ps. xcii. 11). And I saw 'the reward of the wicked' being accomplished in me from God (Ps. xci. 8). If there are no fantasies in the heart, the mind stands in its natural state, and is ready to be moved to every contemplation that is sweet, spiritual and loving.

94. So then, as I said, it is in the nature of these two things, sobriety and prayer to Jesus, to be in union one with the other. For sobriety is complete attention and constant prayer; and prayer in turn means the utmost sobriety and attention of mind.

95. A good teacher both of the body and the soul is perfect remembrance of death, when a man, looking beyond everything that is between (that is, between the present moment and the hour of death), is always seeing forward to that bed upon which we shall one day lie, breathing out our life; and at that which comes after.

96. It is not possible, brethren, for him who wishes to remain unwounded through everything, to let himself sleep. One of two things must happen: either he must fall and perish, stripped of his virtues, or he must stand on guard through everything, with

his mind armed. For the enemy too stands always arrayed for battle (watching).

97. There comes to be a Divine state in our mind from perpetual remembrance and calling on our Lord Jesus Christ, if we do not neglect constant prayer to Him, and continual sobriety, and the work of overseer or door-keeper (that is, letting in friends and turning away enemies). And indeed, let it always be in this way that we practise calling upon Jesus Christ our Lord, crying out with a burning heart, so that we may have a share (taste) in His Holy Name (so that we may have it embedded in our heart). For constancy (frequent repetition of the same thing) is the mother of habit both in virtue and in vice; and habit is then as binding as nature. When the mind attains such a state it seeks its enemies of its own accord as a hound seeks a hare in a thicket. But the hound seeks its prey to devour it, and the mind —to strike it down and drive it away.

98. And so every time it happens that wicked thoughts multiply in us, let us throw among them the invocation of our Lord Jesus Christ; and we shall at once see them dispersed like smoke in the air, as experience teaches. And then, when the mind is left free (without confusing thoughts), let us start again with constant attention and invocation. So let us act every time we suffer such temptation.

99. As it is not possible to go into battle naked, or to swim over a great sea fully clothed, or to live without breathing, so without humility and constant supplication to Christ, it is not possible to learn the secret war of the mind; nor are we able skilfully to put to flight and strike down the enemies.

100. The great David, experienced in deeds, says to the Lord: 'Because of his strength will I wait upon thee' (Ps. lix. 9) (that is, I turn to Thee for help). Even so it is the help of the Lord that preserves in us the power for silence of heart and mind—that silence out of which all the virtues arise. For the Lord gives us commands and He drives away from us accursed sloth. And if we constantly call on Him He defends us against unseemly forgetfulness, which is above all destructive of our peace of heart, as water is of fire. Therefore, brother, do not from negligence sleep unto death, but scourge thy enemies with the name of Jesus; and

as some wise man 47 has said: 'Let His most sweet name be joined to thy breath; and then shalt thou know the profit of silence.'

101. Whenever we unworthy ones are thought worthy to be admitted, with fear and dread, to the Divine and undefiled mysteries of Christ, our God and King, then let us all the more show forth sobriety, watchfulness of mind and strict attention, so that our sins and our small and great uncleannesses may be destroyed by the Divine fire, that is, by the Body of our Lord Jesus Christ. For when it enters into us it straightway drives from our heart the spirits of wickedness, and it does away with our sins of the past, and the mind is left empty of the restless importunities of evil thoughts. If after this we guard the mind strictly, and stand in the gate of our heart, each time we are again counted worthy, the holy Secret Divine Body will more and more brighten the mind, and make it shine like a star.

102. Forgetfulness naturally extinguishes the guarding of the mind, as water extinguishes fire. But constant prayer to Jesus with unflagging sobriety finally evaporates forgetfulness from the heart. Prayer needs sobriety, just as a small lantern needs a candle (perhaps as a lantern needs windless calm to burn like a candle).48

103. Great care should be taken to preserve that which is precious. But for us only one thing is truly precious—that which preserves us from all evil, both sensory and mental. And this is guarding the mind with invocation of Jesus Christ, that is, always looking into the depths of our heart and keeping our thought constantly silent. I will say even more:—we should strive to be empty even of thoughts which appear to come from the right, and in general of all thoughts, lest thieves are concealed behind them. But however painful the labour of patiently remaining in the heart, relief is nearby.

104. A heart constantly guarded and not allowed to accept the forms, images and fantasies of dark and wicked spirits naturally gives birth to thoughts full of light. As coal engenders flame, still more will the Lord Who dwells in our heart since our holy baptism, set alight our mental power of contemplation, and make

47 St. Gregory the Theologian. (Footnote in 'Dobrotolubiye'.)
48 The meaning of this passage is not clear. (Translators' note.)

it burn like a wax candle, if He finds the air of our heart pure of the winds of evil and guarded by our mind.

105. We should always be turning the Name of Jesus Christ round the spaces of our heart, as lightning circles round the skies before rain. This is well known by those who have spiritual experience in inner warfare. Let us conduct this mental war in the following order. The first thing is attention; then, when we notice a wicked thought draw near, let us wrathfully hurl a heart-felt curse at it. The third thing is to turn the heart to the invocation of Jesus Christ and pray Him to disperse forthwith this phantom of the demons, lest the mind runs after this fantasy like a child attracted by a skilful juggler.

106. Let us compel ourselves to call: 'Lord Jesus Christ!' Let our throat be exhausted (lose its voice), but may our inner eyes never cease to look on high, waiting like David in hope for our Lord God (Ps. lxix. 3).

107. If we always remember the parable of the unjust judge which our Lord gave for our instruction, showing that we must always pray and not give way to despair (and act accordingly), we shall reap benefit and be avenged.

108. It is impossible for a man to look at the sun, and the pupils of his eyes not glitter with the light. So too a man, who constantly penetrates into the air of the heart, cannot but shine with light.

109. It is impossible to live our present life without food and drink. So, too, it is impossible for the soul to attain anything spiritual and pleasing to God, or to be free of inner sin, without guarding of the mind and purity of heart, in other words, without sobriety, no matter how much a man strives to refrain from committing sins in deed through fear of future torment.

110. Still, those who force themselves to refrain from committing sin in deed are also blessed before the Lord, the angels and men, since 'the violent take' the kingdom of heaven 'by force' (Matt. xi. 12).

111. The most wonderful fruit of silence of the mind is this, that sins which start merely as thoughts knocking at the door of the mind and would, if accepted by the mind, become coarse visible sins, are all cut off mentally in our inner man by the

virtue of sobriety, which prevents them from coming in and becoming transformed into evil deeds, by a movement of the hand and the intercession of our Lord Jesus Christ.

112. The Old Testament is the image of external achievements of body and senses; but the holy Gospels, which are the New Testament, are the image of attention or purity of heart. The Old Testament did not lead to perfection, did not satisfy the inner man in his work of pleasing God, nor did it give him a guarantee; as the Apostle says: 'The law made nothing perfect' (Heb. vii. 19), it only barred gross sins. (To cut off wicked thoughts and desires from the heart for the sake of preserving its purity, which is a commandment of the Gospels, is higher, for example, than being forbidden to tear out your neighbour's eye or tooth.) You should understand the same about bodily righteousness and bodily labours, about fasting, I mean, and abstinence, about sleeping on bare earth, standing, vigils and other works usually undertaken to subdue the body and to quieten the sinful movements of the passionate parts of the body. Naturally, all this is also good, as is said of the Old Testament (that the law is good), because it serves to educate our outer man and to protect him from passionate deeds. But these labours do not guard us against mental sins or prevent them; in other words, they are powerless to free us from envy, anger and the like.

113. But when purity of heart, that is, watching and guarding the mind, the image of which is the New Testament, is observed by us as it should be, it cuts off from the heart all passions and all evil. It uproots evil and brings in its place joy, good hope, contrition, mourning, tears, knowledge of ourselves and of our sins, memory of death, true humility, immeasurable love for God and men and Divine zeal of the heart.

114. Just as a man cannot walk on the earth without cleaving the air; so a human heart cannot avoid constant attacks by the demons or being subject to their hidden influence, however strictly he may struggle with the flesh.

115. If you wish not only to appear to be a monk in the Lord —good, meek and always united with God—but to be so in actual deed, strive with all your efforts to cultivate the virtue of attention, which consists in watching and guarding the mind and

in establishing a sweet silence of the heart and a blessed state of the soul, free of fantasies—an achievement not to be found in many.

116. This virtue of attention is called mental love of wisdom. Practise it with great sobriety and zealous warmth, with prayer to Jesus, with humility and constancy, with silence of your physical and mental lips, with abstinence in food and drink, withdrawing from all sin. Practise it by following the mental path skilfully with good judgement, and with God's help it will reveal to you things you never expected, will give you knowledge, will enlighten you, make you wise and will teach you things which formerly your mind could not even receive, when you were walking in the obscurity of passions and dark deeds, plunged in the abyss of forgetfulness and confusion of thoughts.

117. As valleys produce rich harvests of wheat, so this virtue will produce in your heart a rich harvest of all good things—or, rather, our Lord Jesus Christ will Himself give you this, since without Him we can do nothing. In the beginning you will find it a ladder, then a book which you will read and, finally, progressing further and further, will find it a city, the heavenly Jerusalem. And you will actually see with your mental vision the Christ of Israel, the Lord of hosts, together with His Consubstantial Father and the Holy Spirit Who is worshipped with Them.

118. The demons lead us into sin always by means of deceptive fantasies. Thus they moved the impious Judas to betray our Lord, God of all, by dreams of riches and love of gain. By false dreams of physical well-being, worthless in itself, of honour, wealth, glory, they drove him to kill God and later to kill himself by hanging, and thus they prepared eternal death for him—the exact opposite of all they pictured to him in their dreams or suggestions, the deceitful ones.

119. So look and learn how the enemies of our salvation cast us into perdition by deceptive dreams and empty promises. Satan himself fell like lightning from the heights of heaven in just the same way, when he dreamt himself equal to God. Later by the same means he cut Adam off from God, suggesting to him the dream of godly rank (omniscience). In this way this false and deceitful enemy habitually seduces all sinners.

120. Our heart is filled with the bitter poison of evil thoughts when, growing negligent through forgetfulness, we stay away for a long while from attention and the Prayer of Jesus. But when, moved by our love for Divine things, we begin zealously to work at attention and prayer in the mental workshop of our heart, with firm determination, it becomes once more filled with the sweet sensation of delight and Divine joy. Then it is that we come to a steadfast resolve always to remain in silence of the heart, for no other reason than for the sake of the blessed sweetness and delight it brings to the soul.

121. The science of sciences and the art of arts is the capacity to master harmful thoughts. The best method and remedy against them is to watch with God's help for the appearance of their suggestion and always to keep the thought pure, just as we protect our physical eye, watching sharply for anything which might injure it and not letting even a speck of dust come near it.

122. Snow does not produce fire; water does not produce flame; nor the thorn figs. In the same way the heart of man will never become free of thoughts, words and deeds coming from the demons, if his inner man is not purified and he does not combine sobriety with prayer to Jesus, does not acquire humility and inner silence, and does not press forward with all zeal. A soul which does not watch itself is inevitably barren of good and perfect thoughts, like a barren mule, for it has no understanding of spiritual wisdom. Invocation of the Name of Jesus and freedom from passionate thoughts is indeed a blessed practice, for it brings peace to the soul.

123. When the soul enters into a wicked agreement with the body, the two together build the city of conceit and the pillar of pride and beget unclean thoughts to live there. But by fear of hell the Lord breaks up their agreement and separates them, compelling the mistress—the soul, to think and say things which are alien and opposed to the body—the slave. This fear creates a rift between them, as is said: 'Because the carnal mind is enmity against God: for it is not subject to the law of God' (Rom. viii. 7).

124. Our daily deeds should be weighed hourly by paying attention to them, and in the evening we should lighten their burden by repentance, as far as lies in our power, if we wish to

conquer evil in ourselves with Christ's help. We should also watch to see whether we perform all our outer and visible deeds according to God, under the eye of God and for the sake of God alone, lest through our foolishness we are robbed by some wrong feelings.

125. If with God's help we gain something daily through our sobriety, we should take care not to enter into communication with other people without discrimination, lest we suffer loss through our converse with them and are led into temptation. Even more should we disdain all vanities for the sake of the beauty and beneficence of this most sweet and lovable virtue (sobriety).

126. We should give to the three powers of our soul the right direction, conforming to their nature and the intentions of their Creator—God. Namely: we must move the excitable power against our outer man and against the serpent—Satan. 'Stand in awe,49 and sin not' it is said (Ps. iv. 4). This means be wroth with sin, that is, with yourselves and with the devil, so as not to sin against God. The desiring power should be directed towards God and virtue, and the thinking power must be placed over the other two as their mistress, to keep them in order with wisdom and good judgement, teach them, chastise them and rule over them as a king rules over his subjects. Then the reason we have in us will govern us according to God (that is to say, when it rules over them instead of submitting to them). Even if passions rise up against reason, we shall not lose command, so that reason rules over them. For the Lord's brother says: 'If any man offend not in word,50 the same is a perfect man, and able also to bridle the whole body' (James iii. 2). To tell the truth every sin and wickedness is the work of these three powers, and every virtue and every deed of righteousness is the work of the same three powers.

127. If a monk talks with someone about worldly things, or has an inner conversation about them, or when his mind and body are vainly lent to something sensory, or when he gives himself up to worldly vanities (or bustling about), his mind becomes

---

49 The Slavonic text reads: 'Be wroth . . .'. (Translators' note.)

50 'Ἐν λόγῳ means in word and reason. Hesychius understands the Apostle to mean the latter: who offends not in reason. (Footnote in 'Dobrotolubiye'.)

darkened and barren. For straightway after this he immediately loses warmth, contrition, daring towards God and knowledge (he forgets God and the ways of God). Therefore inasmuch as we keep our mind attentive we are enlightened, and inasmuch as we are inattentive we are darkened.

128. He who strives daily towards peace and silence of the mind, and who seeks it with diligence, will easily scorn all sensory things, lest he labour in vain. But if he deceives his conscience by some false arguments (that there is no harm in being occupied in something sensory), he will fall asleep in the bitter death of forgetfulness. To be saved from such sleep, the divine David prays, saying: 'Lighten mine eyes, lest I sleep the sleep of death' (Ps. xiii. 3). And the Apostle says: 'Therefore to him that knoweth to do good, and doeth it not, to him it is sin' (James iv. 17).

129. The mind returns from negligence to its natural state and to sobriety, if, as soon as we feel it cooling, we again intensify our zeal and once more with warmth and diligence set it to its habitual work (sobriety and prayer).

130. The miller's donkey cannot go straight ahead, but must move with the grindstone to which it is tied (it goes round and round on the same spot until the grindstone is stopped). Similarly the mind can make no progress in the virtue that creates perfection (that is, progress in sobriety which leads to perfection) if it does not put the inner man in order (by stopping thoughts turning round and round). For such a man's inner eye is always blind and he has no possibility to see virtue and the radiance of Jesus.

131. A good strong horse gallops joyfully when the rider mounts it. In the same way the mind rejoices in the light of the Lord when it enters His house in the morning, free of all thoughts (Ps. v. 3). Spurring himself on, he will pass 'from strength' of active mental love of wisdom to miraculous 'strength' of contemplation and of ineffable mysteries, and of virtues. And when at last he receives and absorbs in his heart the measureless depth of high Divine thoughts, then the 'Lord God of hosts' (Ps. lxxxiv. 8) will appear to him as far as his heart can contain Him. Then filled with wonder, the mind sings praises to God, Who sees and

is seen, and Who saves the man the eyes of whose mind are turned towards Him.

132. Silence of the heart, practised with wisdom, will see a lofty depth; and the ear of the silent mind will hear untold wonders.

133. Setting out on a long, difficult and trackless journey and fearing to lose his way home, a wayfarer sets up signs to mark the route and so help him to find his way back. A man journeying on the path of sobriety and likewise afraid, must use the words of the fathers as marks showing him the way (lest he go astray or turn back).

134. But for the wayfarer, return to his starting place is a source of joy; while for a man who practises sobriety, return does harm to his intelligent soul and is a sign of turning away from deeds, words and thoughts pleasing to God. Then, in the death-bearing sleep of his soul, he will have thoughts which will prick him like spikes and wake him up, reminding him of the depths of darkness and debility to which he has sunk through his negligence.

135. If we are cast down into trouble, despair and hopelessness (into helpless extremities from which there is no hope of extricating ourselves), we should do as David—pour out our heart and our supplication before God, and show our trouble before the Lord, such as it is (Ps. cxlii. 2). For we confess to God as to One Who can wisely dispose all that concerns us, and, if need be, make our distress light (easy to bear and easy to cast off), and free us from the harmful and destructive trouble.

136. Unnatural anger against men and ungodly trouble and despondency are all equally destructive of good and intelligent thoughts. But if we confess them to the Lord, He disperses them and brings back joy.

137. Prayer to Jesus, practised with sobriety from the deepest thoughts of the heart, destroys the thoughts which have insinuated themselves into our heart against our will and are dwelling therein.

138. We shall receive much relief and joy in the distress we suffer from the multitude of useless thoughts, if we reproach

ourselves sincerely and impartially, or if we confess all to God as to a man (a close friend). By these two means we shall find rest from all (that disturbs us).

139. The holy fathers regard Moses the lawgiver as the image of the mind. He sees God in a flaming bush, his face shines and he is sent to the Pharaoh as a god by the God of all gods; then he strikes Egypt with plagues, leads Israel forth and gives the law. All this, taken allegorically in a spiritual sense, depicts the functions and prerogatives of the mind.

140. And Aaron, the brother of the lawgiver, serves as the image of the external man. Thus, wrathfully hurling accusations at him (the external man) let us speak to him as Moses spoke to Aaron who had sinned: What did Israel (the mind which sees God) unto thee, that thou hast brought so great a sin upon them, making them abandon the Almighty Living God our Lord? (that thou hast enticed them by thoughts away from the contemplation of God in sobriety?) (Exod. xxxii. 21).

141. Among many other good examples, our Lord, when preparing to raise Lazarus from the dead, showed (by the fact that He forbade the Spirit) that we must, by strict forbidding, curb our soul when, like a woman, it gives way to a weakening excess of emotion, and generally strive to establish a stern attitude to ourselves. This attitude, I mean self-reproach, can free the soul from pandering to itself, from vanity and pride.

142. As it is impossible to cross the expanse of the sea without a large ship, so without calling on Jesus Christ it is impossible to banish from the soul the suggestion of a wicked thought.

143. Opposition usually bars the further progress of thoughts, and invocation of the name of Jesus Christ banishes them from the heart. As soon as suggestion is formed in the soul by an image of some physical object, such as a man who has wronged us, or a beautiful woman, or silver and gold, or when thoughts of all these things come to us in turn, it immediately becomes clear that these fantasies were brought to our heart by the spirits of ill-will, lust and avarice. If our mind is experienced, trained and accustomed to protect itself from suggestions and to see clearly, as by the light of day, the seductive fantasies and beguilements of the demons, then, by resistance, contradiction and prayer to Jesus

Christ, it immediately and easily repels the red-hot arrows of the devil. It does not allow passionate fantasies to entice away our thoughts and forbids our thoughts to attach themselves to the suggested image or to fraternise and allow it to multiply or to identify with it, for evil deeds follow upon all this as inevitably as night follows day.

144. If our mind is inexperienced in the practice of watchful sobriety, it immediately attaches itself with predilection to the suggestion which presents itself, whatever it may be, and begins to converse with it, accepting unseemly questions and giving similar answers. Then our thoughts become mingled with the demon's fantasies, which thereby multiply in order to appear even more attractive, beautiful and pleasing to the mind they set out to seduce. Thereupon our mind finds itself in the position of innocent lambs, grazing in some valley, among whom a dog suddenly appears. As soon as they see it, the lambs run to it as to their mother, but this is useless and they only get defiled by its uncleanness and evil smell. In the same way, through inexperience, our thoughts run to all the fantasies of the demons which appear in our mind and, as I have said, mingle with them, as though holding a consultation about the best means for the body to bring into effect what has appeared to them so attractive and delightful, under the influence of the demon's suggestion. This is how downfalls of the soul are organised within, after which, what has matured in the depths of the heart is, of necessity, brought out to the surface.

145. Our mind is something mobile and guileless, easily captivated by fantasies and irresistibly susceptible to evil thoughts, unless it has within it a thought which, as ruler over passions, constantly deters and curbs it.

146. Contemplation and knowledge promote and guide a man in strictness of living, for they lift up the heart on high and thus make it despise earthly pleasures and all worldly delights as something utterly worthless.

147. And conversely, an attentive life, led in Jesus Christ and married to humility, is the father of contemplation and knowledge and the origin of Divine ascents and wise thoughts, as the divine prophet Isaiah says: 'They that wait upon the Lord shall

renew their strength; they shall mount up with wings as eagles' (Is. xl. 31).

148. To keep one's soul silent of all thought seems to men too strict and hard a practice. And indeed it is most difficult and painful. For to confine the incorporeal in a corporeal home, and keep it there, is most difficult and painfully hard, not only for those who are not initiated into the mysteries of spiritual warfare, but also for those who are experienced in this inner unsubstantial war. But a man who constantly keeps Jesus Christ our Lord in his breast by ceaseless prayer, who, according to the prophet, has 'not hastened from being a pastor to follow thee: neither' has 'desired the woeful day' (Jer. xvii. 16) for the sake of the beauty and sweetness of Jesus and pleasure in Him; he is not ashamed of his enemies—unclean demons walking round him, but speaks 'with the enemies in the gate' (Ps. cxxvii. 5) and drives them away by the Name of Jesus.

149. When after death the soul soars into the air to the gates of heaven, it will not be shamed by its enemies even there, if it has Christ with it and for it; but then, as now, it will boldly 'speak with the enemies in the gate'. So long as it does not grow weary of calling to our Lord Jesus Christ, Son of God, day and night till death itself, He will avenge it speedily, according to His true promise, given in the parable of the unjust judge: 'I tell you that he will avenge them speedily' (Luke xviii. 8)—both in this life and after leaving the body.

150. While crossing the mental sea, be bold in Jesus. For He is within you, in your heart, secretly calling to you: 'Fear not, thou worm Jacob, and ye men of Israel', 'the Lord thy God will hold thy right hand' (Is. xli. 14, 13). 'If God be for us, who can be against us?' (Rom. viii. 31). God is for us, He Who has given rest to the pure in heart and has ordained that the most sweet Jesus, the Sole pure One, should fill pure hearts with His divinity and dwell in them. Let us then never cease to exercise our mind unto godliness, according to divine Paul (1 Tim. iv. 7).

151. He who does not accept the countenance of man, but condemns the iniquity in his own heart, will delight himself in the abundance of peace (Ps. xxxvii. 11). In other words, he who does not accept the images of evil spirits and does not, through

these images, devise sinful deeds, but judges severely and passes a strict verdict on the soil of his heart, renders sin its due. In some of their writings the great and wise fathers call demons men, owing to their intelligence. And the Lord says in the Gospels: 'An enemy hath done this' (Matt. xiii. 28), that is, sowed tares among wheat (meaning the devil, since He says later: 'The enemy that sowed them is the devil' [Matt. xiii. 39]). If we do not immediately oppose these evil-doers we become overwhelmed by thoughts.

152. Having begun to live in attention of the mind, if we combine humility with sobriety and prayer with resistance, we shall progress on our mental journey with the holy and adored name of Jesus Christ, which will light our way like a lamp. Thus we will sweep the house of our heart clean of sin and will set it in order and adorn it. But if we put our trust solely in our own attention and sobriety, we shall be speedily attacked and overcome by the enemy. Then these wicked evil-doers will begin to overpower us in everything, and we shall become more and more enmeshed in evil desires as in a net. Or we shall be completely put to death by them, since we shall not have with us the victorious sword—the name of Jesus Christ. For only this sacred sword, if it is constantly wielded in a heart swept clean of all images, can turn them to flight, slay and scorch them and devour them as fire devours straw.

153. The task of constant sobriety, so fruitful and profitable to the soul, is instantly to observe the fantasies forming in the mind. The task of resistance is to denounce and put to shame a thought which attempts to enter the air of our mind by means of an image of some physical object. But invocation of the Lord is that which at once stifles and disperses every evil design of the enemy, every word, every fantasy, every idol and every pillar of malice. And we ourselves see in our mind the mighty defeat they suffer at the power of Jesus, our great God, and the vengeance He wreaks upon them for the sake of our humble, beggarly and good-for-nothing selves.

154. Many people do not know that our thoughts are nothing but dream images of physical and worldly things. But when we persevere for a long time in prayer and sobriety, prayer frees our mind of every material image of deceitful thoughts and teaches

it to understand the words of the wicked ones (possibly the meaning of thoughts in general, what they are; or the plans and intentions of the enemies in sowing thoughts), and to experience the benefit of prayer and sobriety. 'Only with thine eyes shalt thou behold and see the reward of the wicked' (Ps. xci. 8), that is, you shall yourself see and understand mentally the reward of the mental evil-doers, as the blessed David says.

155. If possible, let us constantly remember death, for from this remembrance is born the exclusion of all cares and vanities, the guarding of the mind and constant prayer, non-attachment to the body and hatred of sin. To tell the truth, practically every living and active virtue arises from it. Therefore, if possible, let this remembrance be as continuous as our breathing.

156. If the heart is completely freed of fantasies, it begins to give birth to Divine and mysterious thoughts, which play within it as fishes play and dolphins leap in a calm sea. The sea is fanned by a light breeze, but the depths of the heart—by the Holy Spirit. And the Apostle says: 'And because ye are sons, God hath sent forth the Spirit of his Son into your hearts, crying, Abba, Father!' (Gal. iv. 6).

157. Every monk will be doubtful and hesitant to undertake spiritual doing before acquiring sobriety of mind, either because he has not as yet experienced its beauty or because, having experienced this, he lacks the zeal to give him strength for the undertaking. But this hesitation will undoubtedly cease as soon as he begins the work of guarding the mind, which is and is called mental love of wisdom or active love of wisdom of the mind. For then he will find the way of Him Who said: 'I am the way, the truth, and the life' (John xiv. 6).

158. Again he will hesitate at the sight of the abyss of thoughts and the crowd of the children of Babylon. But Christ will again disperse this hesitation if we place the foundation stone of our mind on Him, firmly and constantly, and destroy the children of Babylon, by dashing them against this foundation stone (Ps. cxxxvii. 9), thus fulfilling, as is said, our desire on them (our hatred of them). For the Wise One says: 'Whoso keepeth the commandment shall feel no evil thing' (Eccles. viii. 5). And the Lord says: 'Without me ye can do nothing' (John xv. 5).

159. He is a true monk who keeps sobriety, and he is truly sober who is a monk in heart (in whose heart there is only himself and God).

160. A man's life goes forward in a procession of years, months, weeks, days and nights, hours and minutes. Along with them we too should go forward (towards perfection) till our very end, with our virtuous deeds, I mean, sobriety, prayer, sweetness of heart and a never abating silence.

161. One day the hour of death will come upon us. Come it will, for no one can avoid it. Oh, may the prince of the power of the air of this world come then and find our trespasses small and insignificant, and may He be unable to accuse us with justice! Or else our tears will come, but will then avail nothing. For the Lord says: 'And that servant, which knew his lord's will, and prepared not himself, neither did according to his will, shall be beaten with many stripes' (Luke xii. 47).

162. Woe to those who have ruined their hearts! What shall they do when the Lord shall visit them? (Ecclus. ii. 14). Let us strive harder, brethren, in the work of the heart.

163. Simple and passionless thoughts are followed by passionate ones, as we have ascertained by long experience and observation. And the first serve as a door to the second—the passionless to the passionate.

164. Indeed a man must cleave himself in two by his will, must rend himself by wise thought, must truly become the most implacable enemy to himself. If we wish to fulfil the first and greatest commandment, that is, blessed humility, which is life in Christ, Divine existence incarnate, we must have the same, or even a worse, attitude towards ourselves as we have towards a man who has mortally offended and insulted us. Therefore the Apostle says: 'Who shall deliver me from the body of this death?' (Rom. vii. 24). 'For it is not subject to the law of God' (Rom. viii. 7). Showing that to make the body subject to the will of God is one of the tasks laid upon us, he said: 'For if we would judge ourselves, we should not be judged. But when we are judged, we are chastened of the Lord' (1 Cor. xi. 31, 32).

165. The beginning of the fruit-bearing is the flower; but the beginning of sobriety of mind is abstinence in food and drink,

renunciation and cutting off of all thoughts and silence of the heart.

166. When, empowered by Jesus Christ, we begin to press forward in firmly established sobriety; then, first, there appears in our mind a lamp, as it were, which the hand of our mind holds aloft to guide our mental steps; thereafter comes a full moon, circling in the sky of the heart, and, at last, like the sun, comes Jesus, radiant with truth like the sun, that is, both revealing Himself and illumining contemplation with His all-brilliant rays.

167. These things He mysteriously reveals to a mind keeping with constant zeal His commandment which says: 'Circumcise therefore the foreskin of your heart' (Deut. x. 16). Yea, marvellous are the truths which diligent sobriety teaches a man. God is no respecter of persons. Therefore the Lord says: 'For whosoever hath, to him shall be given, and he shall have more abundance: but whosoever hath not, from him shall be taken away even that he hath' (Matt. xiii. 12, 13). And: 'We know that all things work together for good to them that love God' (Rom. viii. 28). How much more so do these virtues (sobriety and prayer) work together in this?

168. A ship will not move forward without water; a man will in no way succeed in guarding his mind without sobriety, humility and prayer to Jesus Christ.

169. The foundations of a house are stones; the foundation of this virtue (guarding the mind) and its roof is the holy and worshipful name of our Lord Jesus Christ. A foolish navigator who dismisses his sailors, throws the sails and oars overboard and lies down to sleep, will soon suffer shipwreck in a storm. Still more easily will a soul suffer shipwreck from the demons if, when suggestions assail it, it neglects sobriety and invocation of the name of Jesus Christ.

170. What we know we pass on by writings, and what we have seen on our journey we testify to those who wish to accept our words. The Lord Himself speaks of this, saying: 'He that abideth in me, and I in him, the same bringeth forth much fruit: for without me ye can do nothing. If a man abide not in me, he is cast forth as a branch, and is withered; and men gather them, and cast them into the fire, and they are burned' (John xv. 5, 6). As

it is impossible for the sun to shine without light, so it is impossible for the heart to be cleansed of the filth of wicked thoughts without prayer in the Name of Jesus. If this is true, as I have seen (by experience), let us utter this Name as often as we breathe. For it is light, and those others (wicked thoughts) are darkness. And He (the Jesus we invoke) is God and Almighty Lord, whereas the others are servants of the demons.

171. The guarding of the mind is rightly and worthily called light-giving, producer of lightning, source of light and bearer of fire. For it truly exceeds all the greatest bodily virtues, no matter how many a man may have. Therefore it behoves us to call this virtue by the most exalted names, for the radiant lights born of it. Its lovers are transformed by the power of Jesus Christ from wicked sinners, evil men, ignorant, foolish, unrighteous into righteous, good, pure, saintly and wise men. And not only that: they begin also to contemplate mysteries and to speak in knowledge of God. Becoming contemplatives they make their abode in this pure and infinite Light, they touch It in an ineffable manner, live and act by It, since they have tasted the goodness of the Lord. Thus the word of the divine David becomes fulfilled in those angelic beings: 'Surely the righteous shall give thanks unto thy name: the upright shall dwell in thy presence' (Ps. cxl. 13). And indeed they alone truly invoke the Lord, and confess to Him, and always love to commune with Him, since they love Him.

172. Woe to the inner from the outer; for the inner man suffers much from the outer senses. But when he suffers something he must use a whip against these outer senses. He who does what is needful according to the letter has already understood what is needful according to theory.

173. Our fathers say that if our inner man keeps sobriety he has the strength to preserve his outer man as well. They also say that we and the wicked demons commit sins jointly: the demons merely present to the mind pictures of the sins they wish us to commit, painting them in thoughts or fantasies; but we commit sins both inwardly in thoughts and outwardly in deeds. Since the demons have no carnal bodies, they prepare torment, for us and for themselves, solely by means of thoughts, wiles and seductions. But if these wicked ones had carnal bodies, they would sin un-

ceasingly in deeds also, since their will is always evil and ready to commit wickedness.

174. But prayer of the heart to the Lord routs them, and turns their temptations to dust. For Jesus, God and Son of God, if constantly and diligently invoked by us, does not allow them even to begin introducing sin into us (what is called suggestion). He does not let them present any kind of image in the mirror of our mind, nor to say a single word to the heart. If no kind of image finds its way into the heart, then, as we have said, it will also be empty of all thought. For it is through thoughts that the demons habitually hold secret converse with the soul and incite it to evil.

175. Thus ceaseless prayer keeps our mental air free from the dark clouds and winds of the spirits of evil. And when the air of the heart is pure, there is nothing to prevent the Divine light of Jesus shining in it, as long as we are not puffed up by pride, vanity, conceit and a boastful showing off, and we do not strive towards the unattainable and are not therefore deprived of Christ's help. For Christ, being the image of humility, hates all those things.

176. So let us practise prayer and humility, those two weapons with which, together with sobriety, spiritual warriors arm themselves against the demons as with a flaming sword. If we live thus we shall be able to hold in our heart a secret feast of rejoicing every day and every hour.

177. There are eight principal sinful thoughts which embrace the whole field of such thoughts and give birth to them all. They all approach the doors of our heart and, finding it unguarded by the mind, enter it one after the other, each in its own time. Whenever one of these eight thoughts, rising to the heart, enters it, it brings with it a whole swarm of unclean thoughts and thus darkens the mind and heart, excites the body and leads it to commit shameful deeds.

178. But he who watches the head of the serpent (the suggestion) and smites the face of the enemy as with a clenched fist with wrathful words of opposition, thereby puts an end to the battle. For, having destroyed the head, he has avoided wicked thoughts and the still more wicked deeds that follow. Thereupon

his thought remains undisturbed, for God accepts his watchfulness over thoughts, and as a reward grants him knowledge of how to overcome the enemy, and how to purify the heart from thoughts which defile the inner man, and of which our Lord says: 'Out of the heart proceed evil thoughts, murders, adulteries. . . . These are the things which defile a man' (Matt. xv. 19, 20).

179. In this way the soul is able, with the Lord's help, to regain its seemliness, beauty and righteousness, and to be as beautiful and righteous as God made it in the beginning. The great servant of God, St. Antony, says: 'When the mind in the soul is such as it should be according to its nature, the whole of the soul is one virtue.' He says also: 'For the soul to be righteous is the same as to have the mind in its natural state as it was created.' And a little further he says: 'Let us purify our mind, for I believe that if it is thoroughly cleansed and returns to its original state, it can become far-seeing and see better and further than the demons, having in itself our Lord Who gives revelations.' St. Athanasius the Great, in his life of St. Antony, has recorded these words of the blessed saint.

180. Every thought reproduces in the mind the image of some sensory object; for the Assyrian (the enemy), being a mental power, can seduce us only by using something sensory to which we are accustomed.

181. Just as it is impossible for us, as men, to chase birds in the air or to fly as they do, since it is contrary to our nature; so it is impossible for us to be free of the incorporeal thoughts of the demons, and freely and attentively to direct our mental eye to God, without sober and constant prayer. If you have not got this, you are on earth and are chasing things of the earth.

182. If you truly wish to cover thoughts with shame, to keep silence as you should and to be sober in your heart without effort, let the Jesus Prayer cleave to your breath—and in a few days you will see it in practice.

183. As letters cannot be written in the air but should be engraved on some solid body to preserve them for a long time; so we must combine the Prayer of Jesus with the most laborious sobriety, in order that the beautiful virtue of sobriety should

abide with Him in us, remaining for ever whole and so, through Him, become an inalienable part of us.

184. It is said, 'Commit thy works unto the Lord' (Prov. xvi. 3) and you will receive grace. Let us do this, lest the words of the prophet: 'Thou art near in their mouth, and far from their reins' (Jer. xii. 2) apply to you and me. No one can give your heart an abiding peace from passions except Jesus Christ, Who has combined in Himself that which is far apart (that is, the natures of God and man).

185. Mental conversations with thoughts carried on within and outward conversations and idle talk equally darken the soul. Thus those who are striving to banish all harmful things from the mind must pitilessly chase away those lovers of idle talk—both thoughts and men. They must do so for a most pertinent reason, namely, to prevent the mind from being darkened and thus weakening in sobriety. For, being darkened by forgetfulness (from conversations), we lose our mind (we become as though we had no mind at all).

186. He who steadfastly keeps the heart pure, will have as his teacher Christ Himself, the lawgiver of purity, Who will secretly impart to him His will. 'I will hear what God the Lord will speak' (Ps. lxxxv. 8) says David of this. Describing inner discussions, which the mind carries on with itself about mental warfare, and about the help and protection of God in it, he said 'So that a man shall say, Verily there is a reward for the righteous' (Ps. lviii. 11). And further, speaking of the verdict arrived at after a thorough examination of the question, he says: 'Verily he is a God that judgeth' (evil demons) 'in the earth' of our heart (ibid.). And in another place he says: 'They search out iniquities; they accomplish a diligent search: both the inward thought of every one of them, and the heart, is deep. But God shall shoot at them with an arrow; suddenly shall they be wounded' (Ps. lxiv. 6, 7).

187. Let us then always so conduct ourselves as to 'apply our hearts unto wisdom' (Ps. xc. 12), ceaselessly breathing Jesus Christ, the power of God the Father and God's Wisdom. If, through some mishap, we sink low and neglect this mental doing, the next morning let us again gird the loins of our mind

and resume our work with renewed vigour, realising that, since we know how to do good, we have no right to neglect it.

188. Soon after taking harmful food painful disorders occur in the body; if after eating it a man hastens to vomit it as soon as he feels its harmful effect, he remains safe. In the same way if the mind, having swallowed wicked thoughts, feels their harmful bitterness, it escapes all harm if it hastens to vomit them and cast them far away by prayer to Jesus, uttered from the depths of the heart. The teachings of others and personal experiences have shown that this is how, by God's mercy, those who practise sobriety should understand the matter.

189. Combine sobriety and the Name of Jesus with your breath, or the thought of death and humility; for one and another alike bring great profit.

190. The Lord said: 'Learn of me; for I am meek and lowly in heart' (Matt. xi. 29).

191. He said also: 'Whosoever therefore shall humble him-self as this little child, the same is greatest in the kingdom of heaven' (Matt. xviii. 4). And: 'Everyone that exalteth himself shall be abased' (Luke xviii. 14). 'Learn of me', He says. Do you see what we must learn? Humility. His commandment is eternal life—and this commandment is humility. Therefore whoever is not humble has abjured life and so will naturally find himself there where is its opposite.

192. If every virtue is performed by soul and body, and if, as I have said, this soul and body by which every virtue is performed are God's creation, are we not extremely foolish if we take pride and exalt ourselves in adornments of soul and body which are alien to them? Leaning on pride as on a stick, do we not thus provoke God Whose greatness is boundless? By this extreme iniquity and foolishness do we not attract upon our heads His most terrible displeasure, since 'God resisteth the proud'? (James iv. 6). Instead of imitating the Lord in His humility, by our vain and proud reasonings we fraternise with the implacable enemy of the Lord, the proud devil. Therefore the Apostle says: 'What hast thou that thou didst not receive?' (1 Cor iv. 7). Have you created yourself? If you have received from God both body and soul from which, in which and by which every virtue is

performed, 'why dost thou glory, as if thou hadst not received it?' (ibid.). For the Lord gave you all this.

193. Purification of the heart, through which we acquire humility, like every blessing which comes from above, is no other than never to allow incoming thoughts to enter the soul.

194. Guarding of the mind, practised with God's help and for the sake of the One God, if it takes firm root in the soul, endows the mind with wisdom in spiritual work in God. It also enables a man with faultless judgement to order his external actions and words according to God.

195. The distinctive ornament of the high priest in the Old Testament (a plate of pure gold on the chest, with the inscription: 'HOLINESS TO THE LORD' [Exod. xxviii. 36]) was the image of purity of heart which incites us to pay attention to the plate of our heart, lest it be blackened by sin, so that (if we find it so blackened) we should hasten to cleanse it by tears, repentance and prayer. Our mind is something light (mobile), restrained with difficulty from sinful memories. One can say, however, that it follows with equal ease both good and bad mental fantasies.

196. Truly blessed is he who cleaves with his thought to the Prayer of Jesus, constantly calling to Him in his heart, just as air cleaves to our bodies or the flame to the candle. The sun, passing over the earth, produces daylight; the holy and worshipful Name of Lord Jesus, constantly shining in the mind, produces a measureless number of sun-like thoughts.

197. When the clouds disperse, the air appears pure. When passionate fantasies are dispersed by the Sun of Truth, Jesus Christ, radiant and starlike thoughts are naturally born in the heart, for Jesus illumines the air of the heart with His light. The wise Solomon says: 'They that put their trust in him shall understand the truth; and such as be faithful in love shall abide with him' (Wisdom of Solomon iii. 9).

198. One of the saints said: 'If you wish to bear malice, bear malice against the demons, and if you wish to be hostile, be always hostile to the body. The flesh is a deceitful friend, and when pampered rises against you all the more.' And: 'Bear enmity to the body and wage war against the belly.'

199. In the preceding texts, which constitute the first and the second hundred, we have described the work of the sacred silence of the mind. They are not the result of personal experience alone but also of the teachings of wise fathers concerning purity of mind. Now, having added a few words to show the profit of guarding the mind, we shall end our writing.

200. So come, follow me to the attainment of the blessed guarding of the mind, whoever you may be, if in spirit you be one who 'desireth life, and loveth many days, that he may see good' (Ps. xxxiv. 12). And with God's help I shall teach you the visible doing and the life of incorporeal powers. Angels never tire singing praises to the Creator; nor does a mind, emulating them in purity, ever tire in the same. As insubstantial angels in heaven care not about food, so those who are substantially insubstantial (men who practise sobriety on earth) have no care of it when they enter into the heaven of silence of mind.

201. As higher powers care not about riches and possessions, so those who have purified the eye of their soul and acquired the habit of virtue (sobriety) care not about the malice of evil spirits. And as the former are distinguished by the wealth of their achievement in perfection in God, so the latter are distinguished by their desire and love of God and their striving and ascent towards the Divine. Filled with ecstasy at the taste of Divine love, they press upwards with insatiable desire (mounting the steps of spiritual perfection) and do not halt until they become akin to Cherubims. Nor do they rest from sobriety of mind but ascend full of keen desire until they become angels in Christ Jesus our Lord.

202. No poison is more deadly than the venom of viper and basilisk; and no evil worse than the evil of self-love. The offspring of self-love, those flying snakes, are these: self-praise in the heart, self-pandering, excesses of the belly, lust, vanity, envy and the height of all evil—pride, which casts down from heaven not only men but also angels and instead of light covers them with darkness.

203. This is written to you, Theodulus, by him who is silent in name (that is Hesychius), though not silent in deed. Maybe I have not said everything relating to our subject, but I have put

down all that was given me by God the Father, the Son and the Holy Ghost, praised and glorified by all creatures with reason: by angels and men and by every creature created by the ineffable Trinity, the Indivisible God. May we be granted His radiant kingdom by the prayers of the Holy Mother of God and of our blessed fathers. To Him, God exceeding all comprehension, eternal glory. Amen.

# PHILOTHEUS OF SINAI
## Short Biographical Note

Our holy father Philotheus is called 'of Sinai' because he was the Abbot of the human flock on Mount Sinai. No one knows when he lived and died. The present writing, divided into forty texts, is beautifully composed and is indescribably full of spiritual wisdom and the power of salvation; and so it seemed wrong to exclude it from the number of other writings of the fathers on sobriety. To read it requires even greater attention, for it would not be sinning against the truth to call it an exact interpretation and true rule of sobriety, guarding the mind and purity of heart.

# PHILOTHEUS OF SINAI
## Forty Texts on Sobriety

1. We have in us a mental warfare more arduous than physical warfare. The aim of the doer of righteousness, which he should pursue with his mind and towards which he should strive, is to have the memory of God treasured in his heart like a priceless pearl or some other precious stone. He should abandon everything, even the body, and disregard his present life itself, in order to have only God in his heart. For St. John Chrysostom says that mental contemplation of God is by itself sufficient to destroy the spirits of evil.

2. According to the directions of the Holy Scriptures, those who practise mental warfare must choose for themselves spiritual works, and with all zeal apply them to their mind like healing poultices. Thus someone says that from early morning one must stand courageously and steadfastly on guard at the door of the heart, with unwavering memory of God and constant prayer to Jesus Christ in the soul. Through this mental vigilance we should slay all the sinners of the earth. In other words, for the sake of the Lord we must cut off the heads of the strong, and the first sign of strife-provoking thoughts by the true, intense memory of God, which raises us on high. For we know that in the inner work of spiritual struggle too there is a certain Divine order and sequence of procedure. It is in accordance with this that a man forcing himself (for the sake of the kingdom) should conduct himself until the time appointed for taking food. After this, having rendered thanks to the Lord Who, solely through His loving-kindness, provides us with both physical and spiritual food, we must toil at the memory and meditation of death. The next day we must again command ourselves to resume our morning work. For even if we do this every day, barely, barely shall we

escape with the Lord's help from the snares of our mental enemy. But when this practice becomes established in us, it gives birth to the following three virtues: Faith, Hope and Love; of which Faith predisposes us to a true fear of God; and Hope, overcoming abject fear, leads a man to love of God. If Hope does not shame us, it naturally gives birth to the twin loves upon which hang the law and the prophets; then Love also does not abandon us, either in this life, since it causes us to obey Divine laws, or in the next.

3. Men with a silent mind are very rarely found. This is the attribute only of those who use all means to attract to themselves Divine grace and to be filled with the spiritual comfort flowing from it. Thus if, like them, we wish to practise mental doing, this philosophy of Christ, in guarding our mind and in sobriety, let us begin by abstaining from too much food and resolve to eat and drink as little as possible. Sobriety is rightly called a way, for it leads to the Kingdom—both the Kingdom within us and that of the future. It is also called the workshop of the mind, for it fashions and polishes our mental character and transforms the passionate into the passionless. Sobriety is also like a small window through which God enters and appears to the mind.

4. Where there is humility, remembrance of God with sobriety and attention, and frequent prayer directed against enemies, there is the place of God, or the heaven of the heart where the hosts of demons fear to enter, since it is the dwelling-place of God.

5. Nothing is more ruinous than talkativeness and more harmful than an uncontrolled tongue; and nothing is more destructive and disorganising to the treasure of the soul. For whatever we succeed in building in ourselves every day is destroyed by much talking, and what we collect together with great labour our soul dissipates again through this disease of the tongue. What can be worse than this (uncontrolled tongue)? It is an irresistible evil. It is imperative to put a limit to it, to curb and restrain it and, I should say, to force it to serve only what is needful. Who can express all the harm to the soul which arises from an (uncontrolled) tongue?

6. The first door leading to the mental Jerusalem—attention of the mind—is a wise silence of the lips, although the mind is not

yet silent. The second is a precisely measured abstinence in food and drink. The third is a constant memory and meditation of death, which purifies both mind and body. Once I had seen the loveliness of this latter not by eye but in spirit, I became pierced with delight in it and with a longing to have it as my companion for my whole life, for I conceived a love for its splendour and beauty. How humble it is, how sorrowfully glad, how pensive, how afraid of the just torment of the future, and of the prolongation of (the accidental happenings of) life! Its physical eyes are wont to shed a healing living water, and its mental eyes are a rich spring of wise thoughts which gladdens the mind with its swift, leaping flow. As I said, this daughter of Adam, that is, memory of death, I have longed always to keep as my companion, to sleep with it, to converse with it and to question it as to my destiny after I leave this body. But pernicious forgetfulness, that dark daughter of the devil, has often prevented me from so doing.

7. There is a warfare where evil spirits secretly battle with the soul by means of thoughts. Since the soul is invisible, these malicious powers attack and fight it invisibly, in accordance with its nature. And it is possible to see on both sides weapons and plans (disposition of armies and military strategy), deceptive artifices and intimidating attacks (impetuous charges aiming at intimidation), and hand-to-hand battles; and victories and defeats on both sides. The only thing lacking in this mental warfare we describe, as compared with physical warfare, is a definite moment of declaration of war. In physical warfare it is customary to establish a time and to conform to certain rules. But mental warfare starts suddenly, without any declaration, with an onslaught directed at the very depths of the heart. Thereupon, having won the cast of votes (in other words, having turned the scale through the heart consenting to the suggestion), it slays the soul by means of sin. Why and wherefore are those attacks and onslaughts directed against us? To prevent us from fulfilling God's will of which we pray: 'Thy will be done' (Luke xi. 2), that is, God's commandments. Anyone who sets his mind firmly in perfect sobriety in the Lord, free from wandering, and carefully observes these invasions (of the heart) by invisible enemies and the mêlées (skirmishes with the sober mind) which take

place in the dreams of fantasy, will learn all this in practice. This is why evil demons are the target at which the Lord aims. Being God and thus foreseeing their plots, He established His commandments to oppose their aim, with threats against those who transgress them.

8. When we have acquired a certain skill in abstinence and withdrawal from visible evils produced by the five senses, we shall be able also to guard our heart with Jesus, to have it illumined by Him and with a warm disposition to savour His blessings in our mind. For the only reason why we were given the law of purifying the heart is to have the clouds of evil thoughts driven away from the atmosphere of the heart, and dispersed by constant attention, so that we can see clearly, as on a bright fine day, the Sun of truth—Jesus, and can be in some measure illumined in our mind by the words of His glory. For as a rule they are revealed not to all, but only to those who cleanse their understanding.

9. Every day we should keep ourselves as though we were to appear before God. For the prophet Hosea says: 'Keep mercy and judgment, and wait on thy God continually' (Hosea xii. 6). Again, the prophet Malachi says from the Lord: 'A son honoureth his father, and a servant his master: if then I be a father, where is mine honour? and if I be a master, where is my fear? saith the Lord of hosts unto you' (Malachi i. 6). And the Apostle writes the same: 'Let us cleanse ourselves from all filthiness of the flesh and spirit' (2 Cor. vii. 1). And wisdom teaches: 'Keep thy heart with all diligence; for out of it are the issues of life' (Prov. iv. 23). And the Lord Himself commands: 'Cleanse first that which is within the cup and platter, that the outside of them may be clean also' (Matt. xxiii. 26).

10. The fruit of misplaced empty talk is at times hatred of us by those who listen, and at times reproaches and ridicule if they realise the foolishness of our speech; at other times our conscience becomes defiled, and sometimes we incur condemnation from God and cause sorrow to the Holy Spirit, which is the most terrible of all.

11. If a man purifies his heart and uproots from it all sin against the Lord; if he labours diligently to acquire Divine knowledge

and succeeds in seeing with his mind that which is invisible to many, he must not through this exalt himself over others. Who among creatures is purer than an incorporeal being and who has more knowledge than an Angel? Yet, having exalted himself he was cast down from heaven like lightning. His pride was regarded by God as impurity. You know what men do when they dig gold out of the earth; (that is, just as they go beneath the earth, you must go below all men to obtain the gold of knowledge).

12. The Apostle says: 'Every man that striveth for the mastery is temperate in all things' (1 Cor. ix. 25). For it is impossible with a full belly to go to battle with principalities, with hostile powers, if a man is tied to the flesh, which is heavy and always lusting against the spirit. 'For the kingdom of God is not meat and drink' (Rom. xiv. 17). 'Because the carnal mind is enmity against God: for it is not subject to the law of God, neither indeed can be' (Rom. viii. 7). It is obvious that it cannot be, because it is earthy, composed of juices, blood and humours, has always a predilection for earthly things and takes pleasure in the pernicious delights of the present life. 'For to be carnally minded is death' (Rom. viii. 6). 'So then they that are in the flesh cannot please God' (Rom. viii. 8).

13. If we sincerely wish to guard our mind in the Lord, we have need of great humility, first in relation to God and, second, in relation to men. We should always strive to make our heart contrite, seeking for and putting into practice every means for humbling it. It is well known that what renders the heart humble and contrite is memory of our former life in the world, if it is recollected by us as it should be. Another thing is memory of all our sins from youth onwards; if the mind examines them in detail, this recollection habitually makes us humble, brings tears and moves us to a whole-hearted gratitude to God; so too does a constant and active (deeply felt) memory of death which gives birth to sweetness, glad mourning and sobriety of mind. The thing which pre-eminently humbles our mind and disposes us to keep our eyes downcast to the ground is memory of the passion of our Lord Jesus Christ, if a man goes over it in his memory and remembers it in detail. This also engenders tears. In addition our soul is made truly humble by the great mercies of God towards us

personally, if we examine and enumerate them in detail; for our fight is with proud demons (who are ungrateful to God).

14. Let not your self-love turn you aside from these salutary remedies of the soul, if you are in need of them. For otherwise you are no longer a disciple of Christ nor an imitator of Paul who says of himself: 'I am . . . not meet to be called an apostle' (1 Cor. xv. 9). In another place he confesses to having been before 'a blasphemer, and a persecutor, and injurious' (1 Tim. i. 13). Do you see, proud man, how even a saint did not forget his former life? All saints, from the beginning of creation to our times, have always clothed themselves in this last holy garment of God (that is in humility). Our Lord Jesus Christ Himself was clothed in humility throughout His life in the flesh, despite being God the incomprehensible, the unknowable and the ineffable. So that holy humility should rightly be called a Divine virtue, the Lord's commandment and garment. Likewise the angels and all the Divine powers of light practise and keep this virtue, knowing of the terrible downfall of the proud Satan who, because of his pride, has shown himself before God as the most wicked of all creatures, and who now lies in the abyss as an example of how all angels and men should fear to be cast down (for this sin). We know too how Adam fell through pride. Keeping these examples before our eyes, let us strive to attain this high virtue and let us humble ourselves by all the means in our power, using the remedies we mentioned above. Let us be humble in soul and body, in mind, in desire, in speech, in thought, in outward appearance; humble without and within. We must have special concern that Jesus Christ, Son of God and God, Who is for us, should not become against us. For the Lord 'surely . . . scorneth the scorners: but he giveth grace unto the lowly' (Prov. iii. 34). 'Everyone that is proud in heart is an abomination to the Lord' (Prov. xvi. 5). 'Everyone that exalteth himself shall be abased' (Luke xviii. 14). 'Learn of me; for I am meek and lowly in heart' (Matt. xi. 29), says the Saviour. So take heed.

15. 'Take heed to yourselves', says the Lord, 'lest at any time your hearts be overcharged with surfeiting, and drunkenness, and cares of this life' (Luke xxi. 34). 'Every man that striveth for the mastery is temperate in all things' (1 Cor. ix. 25).

Knowing all such sayings addressed to us in the Holy Scriptures, let us spend our life in abstinence. First of all, renouncing variety of food, let us accustom our body to a virtuous order and mode of life, giving it food according to measure. For in this way the leapings of lust and, to tell the full truth with all conviction, the movements of anger too are easily curbed and subjected to reason. All-round abstinence makes it easier also to refrain from all other sins, for in the opinion of those, who practise virtues in actual deed and have learned from experience, this virtue helps one to withdraw from all evil. Thus, after God, the giver and source of all blessings, the means of purity is a constant and daily abstinence in food, determined by measure.

16. As Satan, desiring to prevent God's will, that is, the commandments from being done, opposes God and through us fights against Him by trying to hinder their fulfilment; so too God, desiring that we should fulfil His holy will, that is, as I have said, the Divine life-giving commandments, through us defeats by a movement of His hand the pernicious intent of the evil one. The insane desire of the enemy to oppose God by instigating transgression of His commandments God himself defeats in the medium of human weakness. And look, is it not so? All Divine commandments lay down laws for the tripartite soul and give it health through their ordinances. He who follows them strictly has the three parts truly sane and sound. At the same time the devil, day and night, wages an unending war against the same three parts of the soul. If Satan wages war against these three parts, it is clear that thereby he fights against Christ's commandments, for through these commandments Christ imposes laws on the tripartite soul, that is, the excitable, the desiring and the thinking powers of the soul. Look now: the threat that 'whosoever is angry with his brother without a cause shall be in danger of the judgment' (Matt. v. 22), and the commandments that follow are remedies for the excitable part. This and other commandments, given together with it, the enemy tries to overthrow within by means of thoughts of arguing, spite and envy. This adversary (ours and God's) knows that the ruler of the excitable part is the thinking power. Consequently he directs his first arrows against it by means of thoughts, as I have said, of

suspicion, envy, argumentativeness, quarrelsomeness, deceit, vanity and presses the mental power to abandon its natural authority and relinquish the reins of government to excitation itself, thus leaving it with no government. Then excitation, overthrowing its master, unrestrainedly pours out through the lips everything that the enemy had previously implanted in the heart, and concealed there by means of thoughts allowed by negligence of mind. Then the heart shows itself as filled not with the Spirit of God and Divine thoughts, but with unbridled malice, for, as the Lord says, 'of the abundance of the heart his mouth speaketh' (Luke vi. 45). When in this way the evil one brings a man to the state when he pours out in words what was previously secretly devised within, then this captive (of the enemy) will not only say to his brother *Raca* or *Fool*, but will utter the most offensive things and may later even go as far as murder. These are the wiles used by the evil one in relation to the commandment given us by the Lord of not being angry without cause. And yet it is possible not to come to offensive words and what follows if, immediately upon the appearance of the excitable suggestion, the thoughts, which inflame the heart, are driven away by prayer and by attention to what takes place within. Thus this destroyer of souls attains his evil ends only when he finds a man ready to transgress the Divine commandments under the influence of thoughts introduced into his heart.

17. And what is ordained by the Divine commandment for the desiring part? 'Whosoever looketh on a woman to lust after her hath committed adultery with her already in his heart' (Matt. v. 28). And what is the snare woven by the wicked one in the mind against this commandment? Since the objects which can excite lust are removed, he steals in and once there excites a lustful revolt against the said commandment. This he does by painting and imprinting in the soul lustful images; at times even words are heard which excite passion, and many other things happen which are known to those practised in mental warfare.

18. And what commandment establishes guiding rules for the thinking part? 'But I say unto you, Swear not at all. . . . But let your communication be, Yes, yea; Nay, nay' (Matt. v. 34, 37). And: 'Whosoever he be of you that forsaketh not all that he

hath, he cannot be my disciple' (Luke xiv. 33), and: 'Enter ye in at the strait gate' (Matt. vii. 13). These are commandments for the thinking part. Wishing to make this thinking part, like some brave general, serve his own ends, our adversary first deprives it of good sense by means of thoughts of gluttony and negligence. Having thus deprived it of the proper authority it has over the other powers and putting it to ridicule as a drunken leader, he forces it to obey his own suggestions and wishes, using as his helpers excitability and lust. Like obedient slaves these powers, that is the lusting and the excitable, being abandoned by the thinking power, begin to turn all our five senses into weapons for visible sins. What trespasses and downfalls follow upon this! When the mind does not curb and fetter the senses from within, then the eyes dart curious glances everywhere, the ears enjoy listening to vain things, the sense of smell becomes fastidious, the lips unrestrained and the hands stretch out to touch what they should not. Thereupon, there follows instead of righteousness—unrighteousness, instead of wisdom—foolishness, instead of chastity—adultery, instead of courage—cowardice. These four chief virtues, that is, righteousness, wisdom, chastity and courage, are such that when they are sound and in force in the soul, they govern its three parts rightly; and properly governed, the three parts restrain the senses from everything unseemly. Then the mind remains in stillness and, when the other powers are obedient and well governed in God, it easily gains victory in mental warfare. But when, through lack of attention, it allows the other powers to fall into confusion, then, being overcome by evil suggestions, it transgresses Divine commandments. Transgression of commandments is followed either by corresponding repentance or by torment in the life to come. Thus it is very beneficial for the mind always to be sober, for, firmly set in the position it should naturally occupy, it becomes a true guardian of Divine commandments.

19. A (sin-loving) soul, being fenced off and surrounded by evil spirits as by a wall, is bound by the fetters of darkness, and because of this enveloping darkness cannot pray as it should: for it is bound by darkness in secret (in its own secret depths and all unwittingly) and its inner eyes are blinded. But when (coming to

itself) it starts running to God in prayer, and while praying strives to practise sobriety as well as it can, then, through the power of the prayer it begins, little by little, to be freed from this darkness; otherwise it has no possibility whatever of becoming free. Then it learns that there exists in the heart another, an inner, warfare, another battle, another struggle in thoughts, instigated by the spirits of evil, as the Holy Scriptures testify, saying: 'If the spirit of the ruler rise up against thee, leave not thy place' (Eccles. x. 4). The place of the mind is its firm standing in virtue and sobriety. A man can take a stand in virtuous life or a stand in sinful life. For the Scriptures say: 'Blessed is the man that walketh not in the counsel of the ungodly, nor standeth in the way of sinners' (Ps. i. 1). And the Apostle teaches: 'Stand therefore, having your loins girt about with truth' (Eph. vi. 14).

20. Let us hold on to Christ as firmly as we can, for many are those who try in every way to remove Him from the soul. Nor must we ourselves allow such a state of affairs that Jesus should convey 'himself away, a multitude' (of thoughts) 'being in that place' (of the soul) (John v. 13). But to keep Him is impossible without painful labour of the soul. Let us try to trace the footsteps of His life in the flesh, in order to spend our own life in humility. Let us receive His passion into our feeling, in order to imitate Him in patiently enduring all suffering. Let us taste of His ineffable loving kindness to us, in order that, having tasted it in our soul, we should understand how good is the Lord. And over it all, or before it all, let us have firm faith in everything He says, and every day let us hope to have His care directed upon us. Whatever befalls, whatever we may meet with, let us accept it with thankfulness, love and joyous content, in order that we should learn to look on the One God, Who rules over all according to the Divine laws of His wisdom. When we have done all this, we shall not be far from God. (We should also know that) devotion to God is perfection which has no end, as said one of the saints, perfect in spirit.

21. A man who successfully redeems the time of his life, and is constantly occupied with thoughts and memory of death and, through this, wisely removes his mind from passions, usually

sees the hourly appearance of evil suggestions more sharply than a man who spends his life without memory of death, and who hopes to purify his heart solely by the action of reason, instead of by keeping always to this sad and tear-provoking thought. Relying on the quickness of his mind to keep in hand all the bad passions, and not realising how much he is tied by one of them, the worst of all, he falls into conceit (as one who expects to succeed in anything) without God. Such a man must practise very strict sobriety, lest he lose his reason through his arrogance. For the Apostle Paul says (1 Cor. viii. 1) that people who collect knowledge here and there are usually puffed up over those who, in their opinion, know less than they. And I think that the reason for this is that they lack the spark of love that edifieth. A man who keeps a constant remembrance of death has sharper eyes than a man who lacks it. He notices the suggestions of the demons, and easily trampling them underfoot he drives them away.

22. Sweet memory of God, that is, of Jesus, coupled with heart-felt wrath and beneficent contrition, can always annihilate all the fascination of thoughts, the variety of suggestions, words, dreams, gloomy imaginings and, in brief, everything with which the all-destructive enemy arms himself to sally forth, daringly seeking to devour our souls. Jesus when invoked easily burns up all this. For in no other place can we find salvation except in Jesus Christ. The Saviour Himself confirmed this saying: 'Without me ye can do nothing' (John xv. 5).

23. And so every hour and every moment let us zealously guard our heart from thoughts obscuring the mirror of the soul, which should contain, drawn and imprinted on it, only the radiant image of Jesus Christ, Who is the wisdom and the power of God the Father. Let us constantly seek the kingdom of heaven in the heart, and we are sure mysteriously to find within ourselves the seed, the pearl, the drink and all else, if we cleanse the eye of our mind. This is why our Lord Jesus Christ said: 'The kingdom of God is within you' (Luke xvii. 21), meaning by this the Deity dwelling in the heart.

24. Sobriety cleanses conscience till it shines brightly. Being thus cleansed, conscience drives away all darkness from within,

as a light which suddenly shines forth, when a veil which covered it is removed. If true and constant sobriety is continued after darkness is driven away, conscience again shows what has been forgotten or what has remained hidden without being realised. At the same time, again by means of sobriety, it teaches invisible struggle with the enemies, waged by the mind, and the warfare of thoughts. It teaches how to throw spears in this single combat, how skilfully to shoot the darts of good thoughts (against the enemy) and how to prevent the enemy arrows from wounding the mind, by making it speed like an arrow to seek protection in Christ, and thus gain the refuge of the light of our desire, in place of the darkness of destruction. He who has tasted this light understands of what I am speaking. Once tasted, this light tortures the soul all the more with hunger for it, for the soul feeds on it but is never satiated, and the more it tastes it, the more it hungers. This light, which draws the mind as the sun draws the eyes, this light, inexplicable in itself, which however becomes explicable, only not in words but by the experience of him who receives its influence, or rather who is wounded by it—this light, commands me to be silent, although the mind would still have enjoyed conversing on this subject.

25. 'Follow peace with all men, and holiness, without which no man shall see the Lord' (Heb. xii. 14) for the sake of acquiring love and purity: for they are peace and holiness. Anger should be roused only against the demons with whom we wage mental war and who are incensed against us. But hear how this war, waged hourly in us, should be carried on, and do thus: with sobriety combine prayer, and sobriety will strengthen prayer and prayer sobriety. Constantly watching everything within, sobriety notices the enemy trying to gain entrance and, barring the way with its whole strength, at the same time invokes the help of our Lord Jesus Christ to drive away these evil combatants. In this, attention bars the way by opposition, and Jesus, when invoked, drives away the demons with their fantasies.

26. Guard your mind with extreme intensity of attention. As soon as you notice a (hostile) thought, immediately resist it and at the same time hasten to call on Christ our Lord to wreak vengeance. While you are still calling to Him, sweet Jesus will

say: I am with you to protect you. But when by your prayer the enemies are subdued, you must again diligently pay attention to your mind. Here come waves (of thoughts), more numerous than ever, again rushing against you, one after another, so that the soul is almost engulfed in them and is about to perish. But Jesus, being God, when the disciple appeals, again forbids the evil winds (of thoughts, and they become subdued). But you, having found an hour or a moment of respite from attacks of the enemy, glorify Him Who has saved you, and plunge deep into meditation upon death.

27. Let us pursue our way with the strictest attention of the heart on the sensations of the soul. Attention, when daily combined with prayer, produces something like the fiery chariot of Elias, lifting a man up to heaven. What am I saying? In a man firmly grounded in sobriety, or striving to be grounded in it, his pure heart becomes an inward heaven with its own sun, moon and stars and confines God, the Unconfinable, through mysterious vision and ascent (mental ecstasy). Let him who loves Divine virtue strive at every moment to utter the name of the Lord and with all zeal to translate words into practice. A man who uses a certain violence against his five senses to curb them, lest they harm the soul, makes the work of the heart and inner warfare much easier for the mind. So learn to be skilful in repulsing everything external (suggestions and impressions harmful to the soul) and struggle against thoughts born of them by the means given us by God, the guidance of spiritual art, namely: by the labour of vigils curb impulses to carnal pleasures, be abstinent in food and drink, and reduce your body sufficiently to render the war of the heart easy for yourself in advance; and it is you yourself who will profit from all this. Torture your soul with thought of death, and by memory of Jesus Christ collect your dispersed mind; especially do so at night when the mind is habitually more pure and full of light and able to contemplate God and Divine things more clearly.

28. Neither should we disregard physical labours, for as wheat grows out of the earth, so spiritual joy and experience in good grow out of them. Let us not repulse the demands of conscience by false arguments, for its suggestions are practical and

lead to salvation; it always tells us what is our duty and what we should do, especially when it is purified by a living, active and subtle sobriety of the mind. In this case, owing to its purity, it generally has a clear judgment (of everything that happens, a judgment that is just and decisive) and excludes all doubt. Therefore we should not be led astray by false theories, for conscience teaches us inwardly how to lead a life pleasing to God, and severely accuses the soul when it has defiled our understanding by sin. It also shows us how to rectify our trespasses, suggesting to the fallen heart that it must repent and showing it the remedy with sweet convincingness.

29. The smoke of wood fire is painful to the eyes; but later when light appears it brings delight in place of discomfort. In the same way attention, constantly straining the eyes of the mind, is painful and tiring to the head. But Jesus, being invoked in prayer, when He comes brings light to the heart. Remembrance of Him together with illumination (of our inner man) brings us the highest blessing of all (that is, the Lord Himself).

30. Having acquired the habit of disturbing our mind, the enemy wishes to incline us towards eating earth, together with him, so that, though created in the image of God, we should crawl on the belly. But God has said: 'And I will put enmity between thee and' the other (Gen. iii. 15). Therefore it behoves us always to call to God with sighs, so as to spend every day impervious to the red-hot arrows of the devil. The Lord says in the Psalms of David: 'I will set him on high, because he hath known my name' (Ps. xci. 14). And: 'Surely his salvation is nigh them that fear him' (Ps. lxxxv. 9).

31. The blessed Apostle, this chosen vessel who spoke in Christ and who had a long experience in the invisible mental warfare which takes place in us, said in the Epistle to the Ephesians: 'For we wrestle not against flesh and blood, but against principalities, against powers, against the rulers of the darkness of this world, against spiritual wickedness in high places' (Eph. vi. 12). And the Apostle Peter also says: 'Be sober, be vigilant; because your adversary the devil, as a roaring lion, walketh about, seeking whom he may devour: whom resist steadfast in the faith' (1 Peter v. 8, 9). Our Lord Jesus Christ

Himself, speaking of the different dispositions with which the word of the Gospel is heard, said: 'Then cometh the devil, and taketh away the word out of their hearts', which robbery he commits by bringing evil forgetfulness, 'lest they should believe and be saved' (Luke viii. 12). And the Apostle Paul again says: 'For I delight in the law of God after the inward man: But I see another law in my members, warring against the law of my mind, and bringing me into captivity to the law of sin which is in my members' (Rom. vii. 22, 23). They said all this in order to teach us and reveal what is hidden from us.

32. When reason loses self-reproach and humility, it habitually exalts itself deeming itself to be above many others. If we wish to gain a realisation of our infirmity, let us argue like him who said: 'Brethren, I count not myself to have apprehended: but this one thing I do, forgetting those things which are behind, and reaching forth unto those things which are before, I press toward the mark for the prize of the high calling of God in Christ Jesus' (Phil. iii. 13, 14). Again: 'I therefore so run, not as uncertainly; so fight I, not as one that beateth the air: But I keep under my body, and bring it into subjection: lest that by any means, when I have preached to others, I myself should be a castaway' (1 Cor. ix. 26, 27). See what humility and at the same time what striving towards virtue! See also how great is the humility of St. Paul, in spite of what he is. (But listen to what he says further.) 'Christ Jesus came into the world to save sinners; of whom I am chief' (1 Tim. i. 15). And how can we avoid being humble when our nature is so bad? For what is worse than earth? We should remember God, because that is the purpose for which we are created; and we should accustom ourselves to works of abstinence, so as to follow more easily in the steps of our Lord.

33. If a man gives way to evil thoughts, it is impossible for his outward man to be pure of sin. Those who do not uproot evil thoughts from the heart cannot fail to manifest them in corresponding evil deeds. The reason why a man looks with lustful eyes is that before this his inner eye has committed adultery and has become darkened. In the same way the cause of desire to listen to shameful things lies in our willingness to listen with the ears of our soul to all that the evil demons whisper within to our ruin.

We must cleanse ourselves in the Lord, both within and without. Each of us must guard his senses and daily cleanse himself from sins and the actions on us of passions. In the past, in the days of our foolishness, when we lived and moved in the world, our mind in confusion, we served sinful prelest with all our mind and senses. But now, having adopted a life in God, it behoves us to serve the living and true God, God's righteousness and God's will with all our mind and senses.

34. First comes *impact* (προσβολή—contact, action, when a thing thrown hits the thing at which it is thrown); then comes *coupling* (συνδυασμος—joining together; attention is fettered to the object so that there exist only the soul and the object which has impinged upon it and occupied it); next comes *merging together* (the object, which has impinged upon the soul and occupied the attention, has provoked desire—and the soul has consented to it—has merged with it); then comes *captivity* (the object has captivated the soul which desired it and is leading it to action like a fettered slave); finally comes passion (πάθος— sickness of the soul) inculcated in the soul by frequent repetition (repeated gratification of the same desire) and by habit (of actions, by which it is gratified) which has thus become a quality of the soul (a feature of character). This is the field for gaining victory in the warfare which takes place within us! Thus also it is defined by the holy fathers.

35. And they say that *impact* is a bare thought, or the image of some thing, just born in the heart and presenting itself to the mind. *Coupling* is conversing, whether passionately or passionlessly, with (the object or image) which has presented itself. *Merging together* is the inclination of the soul with enjoyment towards the object seen by the eye of the mind. *Captivity* is the forcible and involuntary leading of the heart away (into captivity), its retention there and its merging as it were into one life (συνουσία) with the object which has enslaved it; this merging results in the disappearance of our good state (loss of peace). They say that *passion* generally inculcates itself into the soul through long passionate attachment (to some object). Of all these (actions or states) the *first* is sinless, the *second*—not altogether; the *third*—according to the state of him who is

striving (maybe according to the degree of his efforts and resistance); and *warfare* is the cause either of crowns (if a man stands firm) or torment (if he falls).

36. *Captivity* is different when at prayer and when not at prayer. *Passion* is undoubtedly subject either to an equivalent (counterbalancing) repentance, or to future torment. He who resists the first, that is, impact, or remains passionless towards it, at once cuts off everything shameful. Such is the war waged by evil demons against both monks and non-monks, in which, as we have said, there are victories and defeats. Crowns await the victors and torment those who fall without repenting. So let us struggle against them mentally, in order to refrain from putting into practice their evil counsels by visible sinful deeds. Let us strive to attain the kingdom of heaven within us by cutting off all sin from the heart. By this excellent doing we shall preserve purity of heart and constant contrition before God.

37. Many monks are unaware of the prelest which the mind suffers from the demons. They strive for rectitude in their deeds, but take no heed of the mind and spend their life in guileless simplicity. In my opinion they are totally unaware of the darkness of inner passions, since they have no taste of purity of heart. Those who do not know the warfare of which St. Paul speaks have possibly no experience of good either; they regard as downfalls only sins committed in deed, and fail to take into account mental victories and defeats, invisible to the physical eye, since these are hidden and known only to God, Who inspires our strivings, and to the conscience of the man who strives. The following saying of the Scriptures seems to refer to such people: 'Saying, Peace; and there was no peace' (Ezek. xiii. 10). We should pray for those brethren who are in such a state through simpleness, and teach them, as far as is possible, to refrain not only from visible wrong actions, but also from the evil which acts in the heart. But for those who are filled with Divine desire to cleanse the eye of the soul (the vision of the soul) there is another doing in Christ, and another mystery.

38. Many indeed are the virtues contained in a deep remembrance of death. It gives birth to mourning, gives guidance in all-round abstinence, it reminds a man of hell, it is the mother of

prayer and tears, the guardian of the heart, the means of going deep into oneself and of good judgment; their offspring are a great fear of God and purification of the heart from passionate thoughts, offspring which embrace many of the chief commandments. In such a heart there is then seen struggle and endeavour borne with extreme effort. And many of Christ's warriors have this as their whole care.

39. Some accidental happening or adversity habitually destroys inner attention and, tearing the mind away from its good and salutary state, extinguishes its desire of the best and entices it towards sinful argument and discord. The cause of such woeful calamity is the fact that we have no vigilance for temptations (which are ready at every moment to assail us from any side).

40. None of the sorrows which are ready at every hour to confront us will sadden or disturb us as long as we realise that all this is inevitable and constantly keep this realisation in our thoughts. Thus the divine Apostle Paul says: 'Therefore I take pleasure in infirmities, in reproaches, in necessities, in persecutions, in distresses for Christ's sake' (2 Cor. xii. 10). And: 'Yea, and all that will live godly in Christ Jesus shall suffer persecution' (2 Tim. iii. 12). To Him be glory for ever and ever. Amen.

# HOLY FATHERS
## BARSANUPHIUS AND JOHN
### Short Biographical Note[51]

St. Barsanuphius was an Egyptian by birth. From early age he burned with desire to lead a life of spiritual endeavour. Once, passing by a racecourse, he went in and seeing them all competing with one another, said to himself: 'See how hard they compete for crowns that perish.—Should not we—heirs to the kingdom of heaven—try even harder?' And he left the racecourse, burning with still greater zeal for effort.

It is not known whether he entered any monastery in Egypt. The records show him already a monk in Palestine. Coming to Jerusalem on pilgrimage to the holy places, he remained there and lived first under the tutelage of the Staretz Marcellus, and later in the community of Abba Serid near Gaza. Aspiring to the highest feats, he built himself a small cell outside and lived there a hermit's life, enjoying the sweetest silence.

At the beginning of this life of silence they brought him from the community only three small loaves a week. But since he devoted himself to mourning and received much sweetness from tears, the sensation of this ineffable sweetness often made him content with only one small loaf, and frequently he forgot to eat even that. Thus at times he ate only twice a week, at times only once; for he was often ravished to spiritual food, the sweetness of which made him forget physical food.

Thus washing himself in ceaseless tears, in the course of time this saint so cleansed his heart of the passions of soul and body, that he became immune to the arrows of the enemy, acquired peace of thoughts, in which gifts of the Holy Spirit are received,

[51] Taken from their lives composed by Nicodemus of the Holy Mountain. (Footnote in 'Dobrotolubiye'.)

and attained a state when all the stirrings and wiles of passions fell asleep, or rather died in him, so that he called his seclusion—a tomb.

When he had cleansed his heart of passions and had become a temple and dwelling-place of the Holy Spirit, through this purity he became enriched by an elevating, true and perfect humility which made him consider himself dust and ashes, not only in words but in actual fact. He was always saying to himself: Who am I? And who considers me somebody?

Through this humility he was granted the greatest of all virtues—right judgment, which God gives a monk to rule him.

From right judgment the great Barsanuphius became endowed with vision by which, according to the interpretation of St. Peter of Damascus, are comprehended the immaterial hidden essences of sensory and immaterial creatures.

Through vision he was granted the gift of clairvoyance and prophecy—he could see distant happenings as though they were close, and the future as though it were the present. Through grace he also saw the hearts of men and answered their questions not according to their words but according to the trend of their mind and thoughts.

In accordance with the words of the divine David, ceaselessly striving to ascend to God in his heart, and adding humility to humility, silence to silence and love to love, he was finally granted the greatest gift of all—being ravished to God, when he would rise to the seventh heaven, not on the wings of imagination, but through the ineffable power of the Spirit. There he received blessings and saw indescribable glories and the mysteries of the kingdom of God, and whether he was in the body or out of the body, like the great Paul, he could not tell (2 Cor. xii. 3).

Thereupon he was given a gift of performing many miracles, so that by the Name of the Lord Jesus Christ he could raise the dead, cast out demons, cure incurable diseases and do many other miracles and, like Elias, open and close heaven.

These are the great gifts and the high perfection in virtues attained by St. Barsanuphius, great among the fathers. At the same time, these great gifts were accompanied by temptations such that few men would comprehend if they heard of them, let alone endure them in practice. He was also subjected to grievous diseases, but suffered them with such courage that, when he was ill, he not only refrained from lying down to rest, but never gave up working with his hands.

This saint lived in the sixth century in the reign of the Emperor Justinian, and for fifty years or more no man saw him. Only once did he appear to some brethren and washed their feet to banish all doubt of his existence. And once, towards the end of his life, he parted from his beloved silence for the good of the Church, when Justinian began to oppress those who did not accept the doctrine of Aphthartodocetism which he favoured. In this difficulty, the Patriarch of Jerusalem persuaded the great Abba to go to the Emperor with a petition for mercy. The mission was successful. Convinced by the force of the Abba's argument, the Emperor abandoned the intention to persecute those who, as he thought, were rebelling against him personally, and restored the Church of Jerusalem to his favour, even sending it gifts by St. Barsanuphius.

The great Abba died in A.D. 563. Some accounts place his death before the year 600, without being more precise.

The other staretz, St. John, practised the same life of silence as St. Barsanuphius and was granted the same gifts of the Spirit, in particular the gift of clairvoyance and prophecy, for which reason he was called the Prophet.

No one knows where he was born and from whence he came to that community. He lived in the great Barsanuphius's first cell, after the latter had built himself another close to the same community, and spent eighteen years there in silence, until he died. No one ever saw him smile, or be agitated, or take communion of the Divine Mysteries without tears, as the Abbot has testified.

Through his gift of foreknowledge, St. John predicted many things which came to pass later exactly as he had foretold. He also foretold his own death, saying: 'A week after Abba Serid's death I shall die. Had Abba Serid lived longer, I would have lived another five years. But since God concealed this from me and has taken him, I shall not live longer.'

But since Abba Helian was still young at the time he took the vows and was made Abbot of the monastery and did not know the monastic statutes or how to govern the brotherhood, he implored the blessed John: 'Give me at least two weeks so that I can ask you questions about the monastery and how to govern it.' The staretz took pity on him and the Holy Spirit dwelling in him made him say: 'Very well, I shall stay with you another two weeks.'

And so Abba Helian questioned him about everything concerning the governing of the community. At the end of two weeks the saint called together all the brotherhood of the monastery, greeted every one of them individually and dismissed them to their cells. Then in peace he gave up the ghost into the Lord's hand.

After the death of St. John, St. Barsanuphius ceased to speak altogether and gave no answers to any questions asked of him, as Abba Dorotheus says in the beginning of his second chapter; for, after St. Barsanuphius closed his lips, Dorotheus left the monastery and formed his own religious community.

These blessed fathers loved their neighbours with their whole heart; not only did they load them with benefits during their life but continued to do so after death, having left us the soul-saving book of their wise counsels, as an inheritance from fathers to their children; so that, reading it with diligence, we should gain great profit for our soul.

This book contains 850 answers to various questions asked by different people: bishops, priests, monks, laymen, old, young, sound and infirm. Some of these answers were written by St. John, the second staretz as he was called; but most were given by the great Staretz Barsanuphius himself. St. Barsanuphius did not himself write these answers, but they were taken down by Abba Serid.

The following incident stirs our wonder. When the great Barsanuphius began to give his answers, he called Abba Serid, told him his answer and ordered him to write it down (the answer was to John, a monk of the monastery of Beersheba). Not expecting to retain in his memory all the words said to him by the saint, Abba Serid was in a quandary as to how to write down so many words and expected the saint to tell him to bring paper and ink, in order to take the answer down word for word as he listened. By his gift of clairvoyance, St. Barsanuphius read the secret thought of Serid; his face became radiant like a flame and he said to Serid:

'Go, write it down and fear not. Even if I say innumerable words for you to write down, know that the Holy Spirit will not let you write one single word more or less than what I have said, even though you wish it, but will guide your hand in writing down everything correctly and in right order.'

Such is this book! Rich in marvellous judgment it solves the most intractable questions. It teaches patience, roots out complaints, acts as a sword cutting off self-will, as an axe to slay pandering to man; it is a guide to true and perfect humility, teaching us to regard ourselves as nothing; a messenger of repentance, the parent of mourning and intercessor for the salvation of our souls, and for perfection in Christ Jesus.

# HOLY FATHERS
## BARSANUPHIUS AND JOHN
### Directions in Spiritual Work

(All the selected texts refer to spiritual work and to struggle with passions, and are in the order in which they occur.)

1. Dispose yourself to give thanks to God for everything, hearkening to the word of the Apostle: 'In every thing give thanks' (1 Thess. v. 18). Whether you are assailed by tribulation, or suffer want or persecution, or have to bear physical hardships and infirmities, give thanks to God for all that befalls for 'we must through much tribulation enter into the kingdom of God' (Acts. xiv. 22). So let not your soul be assailed by doubt, nor your heart weaken; but remember the word of the Apostle: 'Though our outward man perish, yet the inward man is renewed day by day' (2 Cor. iv. 16). If you do not endure sufferings, you will not be able to mount the cross and share its fruit which brings salvation.

2. While the ship is at sea, it is a prey to dangers and winds. When it reaches a calm and peaceful harbour, it no longer fears dangers, calamities or winds, but remains safe. In the same way, while you are among men you must expect tribulation, dangers and mental buffetings. But when you reach the harbour of silence prepared for you, then you will have no fear.

3. Do not lose heart in sufferings and in labours of the flesh, which you bear for the sake of the community, for this too means 'to lay down our lives for the brethren' (1 John iii. 16), and I hope the reward for this labour will be great. As the Lord placed Joseph in Egypt in the position to feed his brethren in time of famine (Ps. xxxiii. 19), so He placed you in the position to serve the community. And I repeat to you the word of the

Apostle: 'Thou therefore, my son, be strong in the grace that is in Christ Jesus' (2 Tim. ii. 1).

4. One man reaches peace in the Lord by his godly labour; another attains the same by humility. But you should strive to obtain peace in return for both the one and the other, when anger has died in your heart through the taming of irritation. Then the word of the Scriptures will be fulfilled for you: 'Look upon mine affliction and my pain;[52] and forgive all my sins' (Ps. xxv. 18). May the Lord preserve your soul, your body and your spirit from all evil, from all adversity inflicted by the devil and from all fantasies, inciting rebellion of thoughts.

5. Above all beware of the spirit of despondency, from which all evil and a variety of temptations are born. Why does your heart weaken and despair because of sufferings caused you by Christ's flock? Listen attentively to my words: longsuffering is the mother of all blessings. Look at Moses, who chose 'rather to suffer affliction with the people of God, than to enjoy the pleasures of sin for a season' (Heb. xi. 25).

6. Beware, lest you be robbed by evil serpents and become poisoned by their venom (ill temper). It is deadly. No one will ever do good by means of evil, because he himself is overcome by evil. Good, on the contrary, overcomes evil (Rom. xii. 21). You stand in the arena; perforce you have to fight with beasts like the Apostle who conquered the beasts at Ephesus (1 Cor. xv. 32). You are thrown into the stormy sea; so you are bound to suffer many dangers and fight against the onslaught of the waves. Having conquered them with God's help, you will enter a quiet harbour in Christ Jesus, our Lord.

7. You have no peace from thoughts, which impel you to trouble others, and in turn to be troubled by others. But know, my brother, that if we offend by word or deed, we are thereby ourselves offended a hundredfold. Be longsuffering in all things and refrain from letting your own will enter into anything. Carefully examine your thoughts lest they infect your heart with deadly poison (ill temper) and make you take a gnat for a camel, a pebble for a cliff, and lest you become like a man who has a beam in his own eye but beholds the mote in the eye of another.

[52] The Slavonic text reads: 'my humility and my labour'. (Translators' note.)

8. You call yourself a sinner, but in effect you show that you do not feel yourself to be one. A man, who admits himself to be a sinner and the cause of many evils, disagrees with no one, quarrels with no one, is not wroth with anyone, but considers every man better and wiser than himself. If you are a sinner, why do you reproach your neighbour and accuse him of bringing afflictions upon you? It seems that you and I are as yet far from regarding ourselves as sinners. Look brother, how base we are: we speak with our lips only; our actions show something different. Why, when we oppose thoughts, do we not receive the strength to repulse them? Because, previously, we have surrendered to criticising our neighbour and this has weakened our spiritual strength. So we accuse our brother, being ourselves guilty. Put all your thoughts in the Lord, saying: God knows what is best, and you will be at peace and, little by little, will be given the strength to endure.

9. If a man cannot bear being reviled, he will not see glory. If he is not cleansed of gall, he will not savour sweetness. You have come among brethren, and their various occasions, to be tempered and tried: and gold can be tried only by fire. Never set your tasks yourself, for otherwise you will subject yourself to cares and struggles; but with the fear of God, test what suits a particular time, and do nothing on impulse. Flee anger as much as you can, judge no one and love especially those who tempt you. If you think deeply, you will find that it is they who lead us to achievement.

10. Be longsuffering in tribulation, as one who has attained to the Lord's testament: 'In the world ye shall have tribulation: but be of good cheer; I have overcome the world' (John xvi. 33); and may you thus gain that unconquerable love which leads its possessors into the king's palace and makes them brothers of Christ.

11. Churn the milk and you will bring forth butter; but if you wring the nose, you will bring forth blood (Prov. xxx. 33). If a man wants to bend a bough or a vine into a hoop, he bends it gradually, lest it break, for if he suddenly bends it too much, it snaps. (This refers to strict measures of abbots and excessive asceticism of monks.)

12. Why be overcome by tribulation like a man of the flesh? Have you not heard that tribulation awaits you? Do you not know that 'Many are the afflictions of the righteous' (Ps. xxxiv. 19), and that men are tried by them like gold in a furnace? Therefore, if we are righteous, let us subject ourselves with good cheer to the test of afflictions; but if we are sinners, let us suffer them as our due. Let us bring to mind all the saints from the beginning of the world, and let us remember how much they endured in doing good, speaking good and steadfastly remaining in truth. They were hated and persecuted by men to the very end, but, according to the words of the Saviour, prayed for them which despitefully used them, and persecuted them (Matt. v. 44). Were you sold like the chaste Joseph? Have you, like Moses, suffered enmity from childhood to old age? Were you persecuted like David at the hands of Saul? Or like Jonah were you cast into the sea? Why then does your thought weaken? So do not fear and grow timid like one devoid of courage, lest God's promises be lost to you. Do not be stricken with terror like an unbeliever, but put courage into your unbelieving thoughts. Love afflictions in all things, so that you may become a skilled son of the saints.

13. No man who wishes to reach a city lies down on the ground; no man who wishes to work gives himself up to laziness when he sees the sun rise; no one who wishes to manure his field leaves it neglected. But a man who wishes to enter the city hastens to reach it before dusk falls; a man (who wishes to complete his work) takes it up briskly on seeing the sun rise, lest something detain him; and a man who wishes to manure his field exerts himself to do so before it has become derelict. 'He that hath ears to hear, let him hear' (Matt. xi. 15).

14. Do you wish to be free of afflictions and not to be burdened by them? Expect greater ones, and you will find peace. Remember Job and other saints, and the afflictions they suffered. Acquire their patience, and comfort will come to your spirit. Be of good courage, stand firm and pray.

15. Mourn, weep, do not seek to be regarded as somebody, do not compare yourself to others in anything. Leave the world, mount the cross, discard all earthly things, shake the dust from off your feet, 'despising the shame' (Heb. xii. 2); do not light

the furnace with the Chaldeans, lest the wrath of God burns you with them. Regard every man as better than yourself—weep over your dead—take out your beam—rebuild your ruined house, cry: 'Son of David, have mercy on me . . . that I may receive my sight' (Luke xviii. 38, 41).

16. While we have time, let us have attention in ourselves and learn to be silent. If you wish to be untroubled by anything, be dead in relation to every man, and you will find peace. I speak here touching thoughts, touching all kinds of activities, relationships with men and cares.

17. You wrote asking me to pray for your sins. And I will say the same: pray for my sins. For it is said: 'As ye would that men should do to you, do ye also to them likewise' (Luke vi. 31). Although I am accursed and lower than all men, I continue to do so as much as I can, according to the commandment: 'Pray one for another, that ye may be healed' (James v. 16).

18. If you cannot discourse about faith, do not try to. If a man is firm in faith he will never be confused in discussions and disputes with heretics or unbelievers, because he has in him Jesus, the Lord of peace and quiet. After a peaceful discussion, such a man can lovingly bring many heretics and unbelievers to the knowledge of Jesus Christ our Saviour. As for you, since discoursing on some subjects is beyond you, keep to the royal road, that is to the faith of the 318 holy fathers (and for us now, to the faith established by the seven oecumenical councils), into which you were baptised. It contains everything stated exactly for perfect understanding. But most of all have attention in yourself, meditating on your sins and on how you will be received by God.

19. When you hear someone praising you, remember the words of the Scriptures: 'O my people, they which lead[53] thee cause thee to err, and destroy the way of thy paths' (Is. iii. 12). Such praise prevents us from seeing the abomination of our actions; it probably does harm even to those who have attained a measure (of spiritual achievement) and separates man from faith in God, Who says: 'How can ye believe, which receive honour one of another?' (John v. 44). He who accepts the

---

53 The Slavonic text reads: '. . . they which praise thee, flatter thee . . .'. (Translators' note.)

humility of the Apostle will rather choose to be 'a fool, that he may be wise' later (1 Cor. iii. 18). But if a man shows himself clever rather than spiritual, it would surprise me if he escaped the judgment reserved for boastfulness.

20. (In reply to a question about fears at night.)

Citizens fear enemy invasions so long as they have no help from the king. When the news comes that a military commander has entered their town, they cease to worry in the knowledge that the authorities will take care of them. Even if they hear that the enemy approaches, they are not afraid since they have a protector. In the same way, if we believe in God, we do not fear the demons, for God sends us His help.

21. The hours and psalmody are customs of the Church and are wisely established to conciliate all men (in prayer), as well as to unite the many in communities. Those who live in sketes do not read the hours or psalmodise, but occupy themselves in solitude by working with their hands, reading and meditation and from time to time stand up to pray. When you stand at prayer you should pray to be delivered from the old Adam, or say the Lord's Prayer, or both together, and then again sit at your handiwork. As to how long you should stand at prayer I would say: if you 'pray without ceasing' (1 Thess. v. 17) as the Apostle says, the length of time is not important.

22. As regards sleep at night, pray for two hours in the evening counting from sunset, and when you have finished the doxology, sleep for six hours. Then get up for your vigil and stay awake for the remaining four hours. In summer time do the same, but reduce doxology and read fewer psalms in accordance with the shortness of the night.

23. The Lord has taught us how to acquire wise humility, saying: 'Learn of me; for I am meek and lowly in heart: and ye shall find rest unto your souls' (Matt. xi. 29). If you too want to find perfect rest, understand what the Lord has endured and suffer the same; and cut off your will in all things. The Lord Himself says: 'For I came down from heaven, not to do mine own will, but the will of him that sent me' (John vi. 38). And perfect humility consists in enduring blame and abuse and other things which our Teacher, Christ Jesus, has suffered. The same is also

a sign that a man has touched perfect prayer—namely the fact that he is no longer troubled even if the whole world were to abuse him.

24. The approach to perfect prayer is when a man is freed from dispersion of thoughts and sees his mind, enlightened in the Lord, filled with joy. A man has attained perfection in prayer if he makes himself dead to the world with its ease. But when a man does his work diligently for the sake of God, it is not a distraction but a thoroughness, which pleases God.

25. About the measure of abstinence in food and drink, the fathers say that one should partake of the one and the other in a measure somewhat less than one's actual need, that is, not to fill the stomach completely. Everyone should establish a measure for himself, whether in cooked food or in wine. Moreover the measure of abstinence is not limited to food and drink but embraces also conversations, sleep, garments and all the senses. Each of these should have its own measure of abstinence.

26. How to establish a measure of food and drink, at less than one needs. Take away about one ounce from the total quantity of bread and other foods. As regards water and wine taken together, take away less than half a cup. If you have attention in yourself and it is not hard for you to drink only once a day, it would be well to do so; if you cannot, drink twice a day, but each time less than you need. At times when thoughts are troubled and at war, even the customary quantity of food and drink should be reduced, that is, food by another ounce and all drink by a cup, so that in all food is reduced by two ounces and drink by one cup.

27. How to establish the needful measure or to find out how much a man should eat and drink? By observing himself over several days in relation to the total amount of food, that is, bread, other foods and vegetables, a man can learn by experience how much food and drink his body requires (to be satisfied without overloading it). This measure he should reduce by one ounce of food and half a cup of drink. And at times of struggle he should reduce it by another ounce and another half cup.

28. What does it mean to abstain according to one's strength? —To abstain according to one's strength means precisely to use food and drink as I said, namely: to take slightly less than one

needs. The same applies to sleep. But if owing to hardship and exhaustion a man somewhat increases the measure, this will not mean an infringement of the rule: 'according to one's strength'. You will ask: What should be the measure of sleep? The fathers set it as half the night. As regards food—stop eating when you would like to have a little more, and in this way always take it in moderation.

29. What does it mean to take food to satisfy a whim, and what to satisfy natural requirements? To satisfy a whim means to want to take food not because the body needs it but to pander to the belly (and the palate). But if you notice that your body takes some foods more willingly than others, not for pleasure, but because it is lighter, then to take it would not be a whim. If the nature of some demands sweet food, the nature of others—salt food and the nature of yet others—acid food, that is not a whim. But to be particularly fond of some kind of food and to lust for it is a whim—serving gluttony. If you wish to find out whether you are addicted to the passion of gluttony, you can find it out in the following manner. If food captures your thought (so that you cannot resist it)—you are a glutton. If you are not possessed by it and partake freely of all kinds of food to the extent your body requires it, you are not a glutton.

Another sign of gluttony is to have a craving for food before the appointed time. This should never be allowed, unless there is some valid reason for it.

30. If the passion (of gluttony) does not trouble me beforehand but appears when I am taking food, what should I do—leave off eating or not?—If you are having a meal with someone else, do not leave off but, calling on the name of God for help, banish lust and eat a little, bearing in mind that the food will soon be transformed into stench. But when you are alone and hungry, eat bread and some other food towards which you are not drawn.

31. Should one question one's staretz about all the things born in the heart?—One should not question about all thoughts born in the heart but only about those which linger in a man and fight against him. It is the same as when a man sets at nought all unpleasantness and remains untroubled no matter how many people vex him. But if someone rises to attack him, he denounces him to the ruler.

32. Should one contradict the thought which attacks one?—
Do not contradict; because the enemies desire it and (seeing
the contradiction) will not stop attacking. But pray to the
Lord for help against them, casting your weakness at His feet;
He has the power not only to banish them, but to destroy them
altogether.

33. Night dreams and defilements occur either from vainglory, or from surfeit, or from the envy of the devil. About the
latter one should remember that when vainglory or surfeit on our
part do not help the enemy, he cannot repeat these things often.
As a man labours in vain at building a house if he cannot find the
necessary material, so it is with the devil.

34. I want to curb my belly and reduce the amount of food—
and cannot. Even if sometimes I reduce it, I very soon return
again to the old measure. It is the same with drink. Why is this
so?—No one is freed from this except a man who has attained to
the measure of him who said: 'I forget to eat my bread. By
reason of the voice of my groaning my bones cleave to my skin'
(Ps. cii. 4, 5). Such a man quickly succeeds in reducing his food
and drink; for tears serve him as bread—and he finally reaches a
state when he is fed by the Holy Spirit. Believe me, brother—I
know a man of such stature; once or twice in the course of a
week, and sometimes more often he is transported towards
spiritual food, and its sweetness makes him forget physical food.
When he is about to eat bread, he is like one fully satiated and has
no desire for it; and, when he does eat it, reproaches himself saying: Why am I not always in that state? And so wishes to attain
to still greater achievement.

35. How to reach such a state? When all man's thoughts form
one whole in God, then the flesh too follows the thought of God
and the joy of the Spirit comes to the heart, feeding the soul and
strengthening the body, and so fortifies both. Such a man no
longer weakens or grows despondent, for from then onwards
Jesus becomes his Intercessor and sets him at the door of that
place where 'sorrow and mourning shall flee away' (Is. li. 11).
And so the word of the Scriptures becomes fulfilled in him:
'Where your treasure is, there will your heart be also' (Matt.
vi. 21). And what brings a man to such a state is humility.

36. How to distinguish a natural infirmity of the flesh (brought about by abstinence) from one simulated by the demons, and how much food should one eat?—About infirmity I should say: if receiving daily food (with the habitual measure of abstinence) the body grows weak—it is from the demons. In the opposite case (if the measure of abstinence is increased)—the infirmity is natural. The usual measure of abstinence is to get up from the meal slightly hungry, as the fathers laid down for beginners. Later when a man becomes firmly established in this and in a still greater measure of abstinence, experience will have taught him to know clearly how much he should eat.

37. 'Pray for me; I am sorely tried.'—Those who completely die to the world come to the measure of stature through patience and trials, O beloved brother! The Lord has suffered on the cross. Should you not rejoice in sufferings, the endurance of which leads you to the kingdom of heaven? That you suffer is a good sign. Do you not know that sufferings and temptations become multiplied when the Lord prepares His mercy? And, generally, do not seek bodily ease if the Lord does not grant it to you, for bodily ease is abomination in His eyes. And the Lord has said: 'In the world ye shall have tribulation' (John xvi. 33).

38. How to allot oneself daily food? If you allot yourself daily food in the cell, it will lead you to cares and struggles. Be content with what God provides. 'He that walketh uprightly walketh surely' (Prov. x. 9).

39. When I read psalms, should I say the Lord's prayer after every psalm?—To say the Lord's prayer once is sufficient.

40. Walk the path which we have trodden, following in the footsteps of our fathers. I do not remember an instance when, having found perfect rest, we have taken advantage of it, for we have always tried to add to it some small straitness and suffering, fearing Him Who said: 'Thou in thy lifetime receivedst thy good things' (Luke xvi. 25); and remembering that: 'we must through much tribulation enter into the kingdom of God' (Acts xiv. 22). We behaved thus also when many possessions came into our hands, and God knows in what poverty we lived for the sake of Him Who beggared Himself for us. It is not good to give oneself

ease in everything. He who seeks this lives for himself and not for God, for such a man cannot cut off his will.

41. The Lord wishes you to regard every man as superior to yourself. Show obedience to your staretz in all things and do all that he tells you, whether it refers to food or drink or some other matter. If they slander you, rejoice—it is most useful. If they insult you, endure it, for 'he that endureth to the end shall be saved' (Matt. x. 22). Give thanks to God for all things, because thanksgiving is intercession before God for our weakness. Judge yourself always and in everything as a sinner and as one seduced— and so God will not judge you; be humble in everything and you will receive grace.

42. Let us have recourse to humility on all occasions; for the humble lie prone on the ground, and how can a man fall if he lies on the ground? But a man who stands on a height can easily fall. If we have been converted and have mended our ways, it did not come from ourselves but was a gift of God, for 'The Lord openeth the eyes of the blind: the Lord raiseth them that are bowed down' (Ps. cxlvi. 8).

43. Sickness is a lesson from God and serves to help us in our progress if we give thanks to God. Was not Job a true friend of God? And yet what did he not suffer, blessing and glorifying God? And finally patience brought him unexampled glory. So do you also endure a little (in sickness), and you will 'see the glory of God' (John xi. 40). And do not grieve that, owing to sickness, you cannot keep fasts. God never demands labours beyond a man's strength. And after all what is fast except chastisement of the body, to curb a healthy body and render it weak, for the sake of its passions, according to the word of the Apostle: 'When I am weak, then am I strong' (2 Cor. xii. 10). But sickness is more than this chastisement and so replaces fasting and is even considered of greater value. If a man bears it with patience and gives thanks to God, then as a reward for his patience he receives the fruit of salvation. A sick body is weakened by infirmity and so there is no need to reduce its strength by fasting. So thank God that you are freed from the labour of fasting. Do not worry even if you eat ten times a day: you will not be judged for this, since you do not do it for the sake of pandering to yourself.

44. Moved by envy (of the fruits of faith) the demons bring us unbelief; and if we accept it we become their servants and accomplices.

45. (Daily exercises.) You should spend some of your time in psalmody, some of your time in reciting prayers (by heart), and you must allow some time to examine and guard your thoughts. Do not set limits to yourself as regards psalmody and oral prayer, but do as much as the Lord gives you strength for; do not neglect reading and inner prayer. Do some of one, some of another, and so you will spend your day in a manner pleasing to God. Our fathers, who were perfect, had no cut and dried rule, but spent the whole day in following their own rule: some psalmody, some recital of prayers aloud, some examination of thoughts, and some, though little, care of food. They did all this in fear of God, for it is said: 'Whatsoever ye do, do all to the glory of God' (1 Cor. x. 31).

46. Let not the enemy confuse you in your affliction. Can temptation or affliction ever assail anyone without God's leave? No. God allows this for the profit of our soul, but the devil shows us things in a different light, as he did of old when he banished our ancestors from the garden of Eden. But we are not mindful of this and forget that God sends us trials to cleanse us of all filth—and so we become troubled and despondent. If you wish to be saved, do not trust your thought; for the demons sow an evil seed in you and represent one thing in place of another. Never accuse anyone of anything, but strive always to please your neighbour. And never think evil of anyone, for through this you become evil yourself, since an evil man thinks evil, and a good man thinks good. When the thought comes to you: 'They say about me . . .' know that it is the enemy who whispers it in your ear. Never have such suspicions. Endure everything with joy and gladness, for great is the reward of endurance. As to demons —do not trust them, for reality is not as they represent it. All they care about is to confuse you in every possible way.

47. ('Again an insult'.) I marvel at your simplicity, brother. Do you imagine that the devil ever stops tempting anyone?— Moreover, is it possible to accuse the possessed who fall down on the ground and foam at the mouth? In the same way it is

impossible to accuse those who are moved by the devil to oppose
and insult us. It is not them we should blame but the passion and
its instigator. You are being tempted by the enemy—and you do
not look at your own sins, but see clearly the sins of your
brother. You rehearse your brother's trespasses, and forget about
your own. And who are you, to look at other people's sins?
Remember Lazarus, how long he endured, giving thanks to God.

48. 'I fall into (unseemly) fantasies (in sleep).'—God lets 'is
fall into fantasies and other passions to make us see our infirmity,
and force us to lay our trust and hope not in ourselves but in God
alone. Yet do not think that we fall into fantasies or other passions at God's will. God allows this to happen because of our
negligence, and in His loving kindness and for our salvation, leads
us to humility by means of the evil (which manifests itself in us).
So learn what you are like and humble yourself, not only before
God but also before men, and put all your cares in Him Who can
do infinitely more than we ask for or can think of.

49. 'I am worn out by temptations.'—Do not get worn out,
brother; God has not forsaken you and will not forsake you.
Know that the verdict brought by the Lord against our common
ancestor Adam: 'In the sweat of thy face shalt thou eat bread'
(Gen. iii. 19)—is immutable. As gold heated in the furnace
becomes pure and suitable for the royal crown, so a man, from
the fire of suffering, becomes the son of the Kingdom, if he
endures with thankfulness. So believe that all that happens to
you is for your own good, to endow you with daring before God.

50. (To a sick man who has lost heart.) Kiss the sufferings of
our Saviour—as though, together with Him, you were suffering
abuses, wounds, degradations, the insult of being spat upon, the
disgrace of the scarlet robe, the shame of the crown of thorns,
the vinegar with gall, the pain of the nails, the piercing with the
lance, the flow of water and blood—and from this receive solace
in your sickness. The Lord will not let your efforts go unre-
warded. He lets you suffer a little sickness in order that you should
not be a stranger to the saints when you behold them at that hour,
endowed with the fruit of their endurance of affliction and made
glorious, but so that you should be companion to them and to
Jesus, and with the saints have daring before Him. So do not

grieve; God has not forgotten you, but cares for you as for a sincere son of His who is not an 'adulterer'.

51. May our great Brother grant His help to us all; I mean our Lord Jesus Christ, Who has deigned to make us His brethren (Heb. ii. 11). And we have already become His brethren, and the angels praise us. Oh, Whom we have for Brother! He is Mighty to give us strength, Firm to divide the gains, a Warrior to strike down the enemy's attack in the time of battle; the Healer, to heal our inner man, together with the outer, subjugating the latter to the former; the Provider, to give us spiritual food; the Living One, to give us life; the Merciful, to grant us mercy; the Bountiful, to bestow bounty upon us; the King, to make us kings; God, to make us gods. Thus, knowing that all is contained in Him, pray to Him, and He will grant you your heart's request, unless you yourself hinder Him.

52. May the Lord Jesus, Who said: 'Ask, and ye shall receive' (John xvi. 24), grant all your requests. Only prepare your house, and sweep it thoroughly to receive the Divine gifts. They remain secure only in a house swept clean, and exude their sweet scent only where there is no impurity. He who tastes of them becomes a stranger to the old Adam; he becomes crucified to the world as the world is to him, and lives always in the Lord. No matter how much the waves of the enemy beat against him, they do not break his ship. And from then onwards he begins to inspire fear in his enemies, for they see on him the sacred seal; and the more he becomes their foe, the more he becomes a sincere and welcome friend of the Great King.

53. Let not the worries caused by the passions and fantasies of the demons weaken you. Believe that, although the demons disturb and tempt us, they will achieve nothing, but will only increase our virtue, if we do but keep attention in ourselves with diligence and have a little patience. Thus do not let us diminish our efforts, lest we lose what is promised us by the loving and merciful God. It is for Him to give, but for us to keep. And do not be surprised if, after the sacred promises and the unstinted gifts of God, the demons again instigate shameful passions to rise against you, hoping to steal the measureless treasure; but remember how shameless they were after God Himself had given His

testimony of Job, by what temptations and wiles they attacked him to break down this pillar of longsuffering. Yet they did not overcome him and were unable to steal the treasure of his radiant faith and thankfulness. The gold was made more pure by fire, that is, the righteous man by many temptations. God gave permission and leave for His servant to be tempted even after His special testimony about this righteous man, for the greater glory and honour of the Lord and the confusion of the enemies. So do not lose heart. The seals of the covenants are intact; but 'wait on the Lord' (Ps. xxvii. 14). 'He that shall endure unto the end, the same shall be saved' (Matt. xxiv. 13) in Christ Jesus our Lord.

54. (Answers.) Confusion of thoughts happens with you because your heart is inconstant.—There is no need to give up wine (from grapes) altogether, but use it sparingly.—To sleep in a sitting posture leads later to humility.—In all things give up the whole of yourself to God, in the fear of the Lord.

55. Keep attention in yourself; the demons seek to entice you towards things that are of little value, such as: sleeping in a sitting posture, or doing without a pillow, which is the same as 'mint and anise and cummin,' and incite you to omit 'the weightier matters of the law' (Matt. xxiii. 23), that is, extinguishing anger, withering irritability and acquiring obedience in all things. They sow this in you in order to exhaust your body, from which you fall into sickness and involuntarily require a soft bed and variety of food. It is better for you to be content with a pillow and to rest on it with fear of God. Put into your pot such immaterial condiments as: humility, obedience, faith, hope, love, for he who possesses them spreads a banquet before Christ the Heavenly King.

56. 'I was attracted by a blasphemous thought.'—For a long time has the demon of blasphemy been waging war against you— a demon who slays the souls of those who accept him. He has caught you by your neck-chain (passions) to put you to death. Oh, may my God not let him take you captive at his will! (2 Tim. ii. 26).—But do not despair. Behold, God stands before you, accepting your penitence. Awake from the beguilement of captivity—but first extinguish anger and irritability, knowing

that they lead a man to soul-destroying blasphemy against God. Acquire humility, which scorches the demons, obedience, which opens the door for the Son of God to enter a man, faith which saves a man, hope which makes him unashamed; and love which lets not a man fall away from God. You took no care of these virtues, but have chosen the opposite—anger, irritability and what is total ruin—blasphemy. Strive to mend your ways, looking at the goodness of God and meditating how good the Lord is. —The past is forgiven you, but from now on mend your ways.— For forty days offer penitence to God, making three bows daily and saying: 'Forgive me, who blasphemed against Thee, my God!' And profess your faith in Him three times a day, with those lips that blasphemed, saying: 'Glory be to Thee, my God, and blessed art Thou for ever, Amen.' Do not fall again into this sin, lest something worse befall you. From insensibility of your heart you fell into anger, and from anger passed to withdrawing from the Holy Communion; then, being wholly captured, you fell into the moat of blasphemy.—Had not the hand of the merciful God and the prayers of the saints prevented it, your soul would have fallen into the destruction of despair. Behold, God says to you through me, the least of all: you have sinned—sin no more. Pray also for your past sins. God is merciful and if we wish (to mend our ways) He forgives our sins.

57. (The Abba grieves me, for he gives preference to others.) —Brother! It is you who are tempting yourself. Do you not know that 'every man is tempted, when he is drawn away of his own lust, and enticed' (James i. 14)? Heed no one but yourself nor be curious about others, for all this is in no way profitable for you. Look, with what a worthless matter Satan has disturbed your heart! Arise then, supported by the hand of God, and do not trust your thoughts, through which the demons represent things to you as they wish.

58. (When one is offered some attention, signifying respect.) —Preserve yourself from this lest you enjoy being considered somebody, but show obedience which banishes argument, so hateful to God and to those who love Him. Hold on to obedience which leads to heaven and fashions those who acquire it in the likeness of the Son of God.

59. (How to begin repentance?)—If you wish to begin to repent, see what the sinful woman did: she 'began to wash his feet with tears' (Luke vii. 38). Mourning cleanses every man from sins. But a man attains mourning through labour, through long instruction in the Scriptures, through patience, meditation on the last judgment and eternal shame, and through self-denial, as the Lord says: 'If any man will come after me, let him deny himself, and take up his cross, and follow me' (Matt. xvi. 24). To deny oneself and to take up one's cross means to cut off one's will in all things and to regard oneself as nothing.

60. (Owing to physical infirmity I cannot work like the fathers did.)—If you are infirm and cannot endure much, do as much as your strength allows and take bread and drink in a quantity somewhat less than you need. For God accepted the two mites of the widow and was more pleased with them than with all else. Teach yourself not to be uncontrolled in your behaviour towards others—and you will be saved.

61. (Thoughts arise in me and say: go to a foreign land and there you will find salvation.)—This comes from the enemy who offers it to you, disguised as what is right, to mock you, make you an object of temptation to many, that you may be condemned for them. Moreover you are subjected to this for your negligence and vanity. And to this negligence and vanity the demons add their own wiles to ruin your soul. Keep attention in yourself diligently and struggle against thoughts, banishing all negligence and vanity. Do nothing of your own will and do not accept the thoughts and the self-justification which arise in you —otherwise you will suffer a grievous fall. Acquire steadfastness, and it will set aside your freedom of behaviour with your neighbours, which is the cause of all evil in man. Renounce all cares—and you will be free to serve God. Become dead to every man—and you will be at large. Regard yourself as nothing—and your thought will not be troubled. Do not think that you have done something good—and your reward will be kept whole for you. In addition, remember that you will not remain long in the body, so strive to make it possible for yourself to say daringly on that day: 'I made haste and delayed not' (Ps. cxix. 60). Brother! No one can live without labour and no one is crowned without

effort. Compel yourself to work for your salvation, and God will help you, for He 'will have all men to be saved, and to come unto the knowledge of the truth' (1 Tim. ii. 4).

62. Not all who live in monasteries are monks; but he is a monk who does the work of a monk. The Lord says: 'Not everyone that saith unto me, Lord, Lord, shall enter into the kingdom of heaven; but he that doeth the will of my Father which is in heaven' (Matt. vii. 21).

Brother! Why do you allow the enemy to mock you and subject you to the dangers of downfall? You ask for advice—but you do not try to do what you are told. Again you ask, and vaingloriously you repeat it to others, to gain favour with men—and thus you yourself hinder the speed of your progress.

Time is given to us in order that, having learned our passions, we should work at curing them, with groans and mourning.

If, when you are in your cell, your thoughts are dispersed, blame yourself and cast your infirmity before God.

63. He who wants to be a monk must in no way have any will of his own. Christ our Lord taught us this when He said: 'I came down from heaven, not to do mine own will' (John vi. 38). But if you obey in one thing and refuse to obey in another, you will show by this that you are wiser than him who directs you, and this is the same as being mocked by the demons. So you must obey in everything, even if it should seem to you that what is ordained is not without sin. The Abba who ordains you to do it will bear your sin and will have to answer for you. If something is extremely difficult and dangerous for you, or above your strength, explain this to the Abba, and do what he decides.

64. (When I am drawn into a conversation I am carried away and forget myself; and later I feel sad and ashamed.)—In order that a weak man should not fall into this danger, and into vainglory, he must at all costs avoid much talk and break off conversation, excusing himself under some pretext and withdrawing from the discussion.—When conversation is useful and does not interfere with more necessary work, stand by while it is going on. But if it is not useful, say: forgive me, I feel weak—and withdraw.

65. How to behave on meeting others? When you meet someone, limit yourself to a bare greeting; then say: pray for me, I am busy—and withdraw. And if you are asked about something and you know it, say what you know, and pass on; if you do not know, say: I do not know, and go your way.

66. I want to stop meeting people: should I do it at once or little by little?—If you stop meetings at once, you will be at peace; otherwise you will cause much trouble both to yourself and to others.

67. (The infirmary-attendant asks whether he should read medical books.) Read them, but in reading them or in asking someone about medicines, do not forget that no one can be cured without God. He who gives himself up to the art of healing must surrender himself to the name of God, and God will send him help. The art of healing is not an obstacle to piety; but you must practise it as you would practise manual work, for the sake of the community. Do what you have to do with the fear of God and the saints will protect you with their prayers.

68. 'I am busy the whole day long—and this prevents me from remembering God.'—It happens sometimes that a man has heard much about a certain city, but when he comes thither he does not realise that it is the same city about which he had heard so much. It is the same with you, brother: all day long you remember God without being aware of it. The meaning of obedience and remembrance of God is precisely to have a commandment and to try to keep it, as coming from God.

69. We are daily in need of food, but we must not savour it with delight. If we take it, giving thanks to God Who has provided it and condemning ourselves as unworthy, God makes the food we eat sanctify us and it becomes a blessing.

In the same way, if you are in need of something and it is granted to you, give thanks to God Who has helped you and condemn yourself as unworthy; and God will banish passionate attachment from you.

70. Each man loves his neighbour according to his own measure. The measure of perfect love is to love one's neighbour as oneself, for the sake of the love one has for God. The young suffer downfalls from foolish love of one another and from coming

together for private conversations. The measure of their love for one another should be as follows: not to slander one another, not to hate one another, not to humiliate others, not to seek only one's own gain, not to love one another for the sake of physical beauty, or for the sake of some physical occupation, not to keep one another company without extreme need, lest one falls into the temerity which destroys all the fruit of a monk's labours and makes him like a withered tree.

71. 'I want to be saved, but I do not know the way to salvation.' Brother! Through the Holy Scriptures and through our fathers God has shown us the way to salvation, saying: 'Ask thy father, and he will show thee; thy elders, and they will tell thee' (Deut. xxxii. 7). So if you wish not to go astray on the path of salvation, do nothing without asking the spiritual fathers, and you will not err, thanks to the grace of God 'Who will have all men to be saved, and to come unto the knowledge of the truth' (1 Tim. ii. 4).

72. 'My thought tells me that if I go somewhere and live alone, I shall attain perfect silence.'—Before He was crucified, our Lord Jesus Christ suffered much vexation and reviling, and only later mounted the cross. In the same way no one can reach perfect and fruitful silence and perfect and holy peace if he has not previously suffered with Christ (living among brethren) and has not undergone all His sufferings, remembering the words of the Apostle: 'If so be that we suffer with him, that we may be also glorified together' (Rom. viii. 17). Do not be deceived: there is no way but this to salvation.

73. (To a sick man.) You are stricken by this sickness lest you depart barren to God. If you endure and give thanks to God, this sickness will be accounted to you as work, since you have not been a monk for long.

74. One should not go anywhere without being ordered to do so, for nothing we do in obedience to our own thoughts is pleasing to God. But when you go somewhere by command, then this obedience to him who sent you is in itself both prayer and a pleasing of God, Who says: 'For I came down from heaven, not to do mine own will, but the will of him that sent me' (John vi. 38).

75. (I am overworked in my obedience. Should I ask for an assistant?) Brother! He who wants to come to Jesus and to walk on the path of salvation should expect temptations and afflictions every hour. The Scriptures say: 'My son, if thou come to serve the Lord, prepare thy soul for temptation' (Ecclus. ii. 1). And the Lord said: 'If any man will come after me, let him deny himself, and take up his' (daily) 'cross, and follow me' (Matt. xvi. 24). So a man who wants to be His disciple must keep obedience till death itself. To remain alone and be somewhat overworked is better for you than to ask for someone else. Uncontrolled behaviour is not increased so much when a brother merely helps you as it is when he is constantly with you.

76. (Whom to ask about thoughts, and is it needful, having asked one, to ask another the same question?)—It is necessary to ask someone in whom you have faith, and to know that he can carry your thoughts, and whom you believe as you would God. But to ask another about the same thought is unbelief and curiosity. If you believe that God speaks through His saint, why verify and where is the need to tempt God by asking another about the same thing?

77. 'How many times should one pray to be advised in thought about some action?'—If you cannot ask your staretz, pray three times about every action, and thereupon watch whither the heart inclines, be it by a mere hair's breadth—and then act thus. For the heart is aware of the advice and clearly understands it.

78. 'How to pray three times—at different times or all at once? Sometimes it is impossible to delay.'—If you have time, pray three times in the course of three days; but if the need is urgent, such as during the betrayal of the Saviour, follow His example when He withdrew three times to pray and prayed three times, saying the same words (Matt. xxvi. 44).

79. (About guidance.) When the ship is buffeted by waves, if it has a captain, he saves the ship by the wisdom given him by God; and he who sails in it rejoices at its security. In the same way, a sick man greatly rejoices when he remembers the physician and even more so his skill; and a wayfarer in danger of attack by brigands is heartened by the voices of watchmen, and still more by their presence. If this is really so, how much more should

everyone who hears rejoice at the answer of the father, especially if it is connected with a diligent prayer to God Who said: 'Pray one for another, that ye may be healed' (James v. 16).

80. He who declares his trespasses is acquitted of them, according to the words of the Scriptures: 'Declare thou, that thou mayest be justified' (Is. xliii. 26). And: 'I acknowledged my sin unto thee, and mine iniquity have I not hid. I said, I will confess my transgressions unto the Lord; and thou forgavest the iniquity of my sin' (Ps. xxxii. 5). Let us guard ourselves henceforth; as to our past iniquities—God has forgiven them.

81. If anyone, while keeping fast, adds something to it by his own will, or if he fasts seeking men's praise or some gain from it, such a fast is abomination in the eyes of God. And so it is in all things. Every good action, which is done not merely from love of God, but is mingled with one's own will, is unclean and unpleasing to God. The same can also be seen from the Divine law which says: 'Thou shalt not sow thy field with mingled seed: neither shall a garment mingled of linen and woollen come upon thee' (Lev. xix. 19; Deut. xxii. 9–11).

82. While learning psalms by heart, do not have exalted ideas, lest it proves that you are filling the air with useless words serving to condemn you. The word of God is the seed of good; if it remains in you without fruit, you will be condemned together with him who buried the silver, which he was given to increase.

83. How can our lips give thanks to Him Who first created us, then granted us help against the enemy and, most important of all, gave room for our repentance, and surrendered His own Body and Blood to redeem our sins and make firm our heart? Never will our thanks to Him be worthy; yet let us give all our strength to thanking Him with our lips and in our heart, and especially by enduring all for His sake till our very death; and in His loving kindness He will compare it with the widow's mites.

84. If the chance of some godly action appears, but an opposing thought resists it, this very fact shows that the action is truly godly. But apply yourself to prayer and watch: if during prayer your heart is confirmed in the good and this good grows instead of diminishing, then, whether the opposing thought which troubles you remains or not, know that the action is godly. For

all good necessarily suffers painful opposition caused by the envy of the devil; but the good overpowers it through prayer. But if the apparent good is suggested by the devil, and the opposition also comes from him, then through prayer the apparent good diminishes together with the apparent opposition. In this case it is clear that the enemy opposes a thought which he himself has suggested for the sole purpose of making us mistake this thought for good.

85. When thought praises you, and you cannot avoid this evil, try to invoke the name of God and say to your thought: 'The Scriptures say: "O my people, they which lead thee cause thee to err, and destroy the way of thy paths" (Is. iii. 12).' Do the same when others praise you, remembering also that those who accept the praise of men receive no profit, as the Lord Himself says: 'How can ye believe, which receive honour one of another?' (John v. 44).—Altogether one should keep in mind and heart the remembrance that 'he that glorieth, let him glory in the Lord' (2 Cor. x. 17), for everything we have of God we have only with God's help. Therefore the Apostle, in spite of having attained a high measure, did not glory in himself, but cried saying: 'But by the grace of God I am what I am' (1 Cor. xv. 10).

86. When during psalmody or prayer or reading, a bad thought comes to you, heed it not but pay closer attention to psalmody, prayer or reading, to gain strength from the words you utter. If the thought persists, exert yourself in invoking the Lord's name and the Lord will help you and will suppress the wiles of the enemies.

87. 'How to have tender feeling in prayer, reading and psalmody?'—To have tender feeling in prayer comes from remembering one's sins. The man who prays should bring to his memory his actions, the verdict which awaits those who are guilty of such actions, and the terrible voice exclaiming: 'Depart from me, ye cursed, into everlasting fire' (Matt. xxv. 41). And during reading and psalmody, tender feeling comes if a man makes his mind attentive to the words he utters and receives into his soul the force contained in them. If notwithstanding this you still remain insensitive, do not weaken but urge yourself to

patient efforts. For merciful, bountiful and longsuffering is the Lord, and He accepts our diligence. Remember always the words of David: 'I waited patiently for the Lord; and he inclined unto me, and heard my cry' (Ps. xl. 1). So persevere in the hope that God's mercy will soon visit you.

88. If during psalmody, or when you find yourself among people, you have occasion to invoke God, do not think you cannot invoke Him without spoken words, but remember that He knows the hearts of men and looks into their hearts—and so invoke Him in your heart. This is what is meant in the Scriptures: 'Enter into thy closet, and when thou hast shut thy door, pray to thy Father which is in secret' (Matt. vi. 6). Even if you do not utter the Name of God in your heart, but simply remember about God, it is still quicker than invocation, and sufficient to bring you help.

89. True mourning, joined with tenderness of feeling, erases former transgressions and washes off the filth; with constant calling on God's Name, it protects a man who has acquired it, banishes laughter and distraction, and maintains ceaseless contrition. It is the shield which repulses all the fiery darts of the wicked (Eph. vi. 16); he who possesses this shield is immune from all dangers if he is among men, and even if he find himself among whores.

90. Imperfect mourning comes and goes as the thought of (zeal for) salvation alternately flares up and dies down. But when warmth becomes permanent, a man has great and constant tenderness of feeling, and in its turn this leads to true mourning. It is this mourning which one should exert oneself to obtain.

91. Humility consists in cutting off one's own will in all things and to have no cares in anything. To cut off the root of passions (lust, gluttony, love of money) means to cut off one's will, to mortify oneself as much as possible and to compel the organs of sense to keep their place, instead of misusing them. This cuts off the root not only of these but also of other passions.

92. Surrendering everything to God's will protects a man from confusion by perturbation,54 no matter what happens. But

54 The Russian word смущеніе often implies disturbance by *temptation*. (Translators' note.)

perturbation may still come and prevent a man from accepting what happens with thankfulness and joy. In this case it is necessary to struggle against this disturbance, reviving one's submission to God's will, by reaffirming one's conviction that all things come from God and that all that comes from God is for our good.—No good can be achieved solely by our own efforts, but by God's will and power. At the same time, God demands efforts on our part, but these efforts must correspond to His will and not be based on some craftiness or lies, which come from the evil one.

93. Silence of the lips is better and more wonderful than any edifying conversation. Our fathers embraced it with reverence and were glorified through it. But since, in our weakness, we cannot yet follow the path of the perfect, let us talk of what edifies, and speak of such things with reference to the words of the fathers, without undertaking to interpret the Scriptures; for this latter is fraught with dangers for the ignorant. The Scriptures are written in the language of the spirit, and men of the flesh cannot understand spiritual things. It is best to use the words of the fathers in our conversations, then we shall find the profit they contain. But let us be moderate even in the use of these words, remembering him who said: 'In the multitude of words there wanteth not sin' (Prov. x. 19). And lest we fall into high and boastful thoughts, let us keep in mind that unless we practise what we say, we speak to our own condemnation.

94. If silence of the lips is considered more useful than good conversation, it is even more useful than talk about indifferent things (cities, villages, trade, war and peace and suchlike). If we cannot refrain from speech but are drawn into talk on such subjects, let us at least not prolong the conversation, lest through much talk we fall into some snare of the devil.

95. If you find yourself among men talking about worldly or spiritual things, permit yourself also to say something containing no harm, but do this with good judgment, solely to avoid being praised by the others for your silence. But when you act thus, that is, when you say little, beware of judging others who say much.

96. When you intend to do something and see that your thought is perturbed, and if after invoking God's Name it remains

perturbed even by a hair's breadth, know from this that the action you mean to commit is from the evil one and refrain from committing it. For nothing done with perturbation is pleasing to God. But if a man resists perturbation (if he has a thought in him which resists perturbation), then he should not at once consider the proposed action as harmful, but should examine it to see whether it is good or not, and if it is bad he should leave it, but if it is good—do it, disregarding what perturbs him.

97. If, having begun a conversation, you suddenly see that it is sinful, stop it, saying: 'No, let us not talk about this', or, after a short silence, say: 'I have forgotten what I was speaking about', and pass to another and harmless subject.

98. What is self-justification?—Self-justification is when a man denies his sin, as we see in the case of Adam, Eve, Cain and others who have sinned but, wishing to justify themselves, denied their sin.

99. As is said, every thought and every action should be examined to see whether it is good or not; thereupon one should do what is good and repulse what is bad. Yet to avoid the good being accompanied by perturbation, one should examine the thought governing the proposal and see for what purpose it undertakes to do something. When you question it with fear of God, God will not let you fall into error. In any case never forget to invoke God's Name.

100. (To a man who received a blow from a brother and wanted to part from him.) Do not give way to indignation, lest you do something precipitate, especially in relation to a man thrown into confusion by thoughts suggested by the envious devil. Some men are sick and, when their reason is obscured by grievous fever, they unwittingly vex the healthy who look after them, because their illness possesses them completely. In the same way, a man who is tempted destroys his soul but is not aware of it, for the enemy makes him drunk with the passion of his disease and always distorts everything in his eyes, in order to cast him into the moat of destruction. He is worthy of pity and compassion rather than anger and revenge. Through such people God allows us too to be tempted, but does so deliberately, to test our skill before Him. So let us be tolerant to our neighbour in time of his

physical and mental distress; for it is said: 'Bear ye one another's burdens, and so fulfil the law of Christ' (Gal. vi. 2). Do not attempt to leave your place and part with your brother, for this would not be doing God's will but the will of the devil; and if you do decide on this, the enemy will not rest but will redouble his attacks. Better pray for your brother with your whole soul and love him in Christ Jesus, our Lord.

101. (To a brother troubled with fears.) Brother! You should glorify God for justifying in you the words of the Scriptures, which say: 'God is faithful, who will not suffer you to be tempted above that ye are able' (1 Cor. x. 13). He lets you acquire skill in spiritual warfare according to your strength; but great men He tries with great temptations in accordance with their strength, and they rejoice in it; for temptation leads a man to achievement. Wherever good is to be attained, struggle is necessary. So do not fear temptations, but rejoice in them, for they lead to achievement. Disregard this temptation. God helps and protects you.

102. Strive to acquire humility and submissiveness. Never insist that anything should be according to your will, for this gives birth to anger. Do not judge or humiliate anyone, for this exhausts the heart and blinds the mind, and thereon leads to negligence and makes the heart unfeeling. Watch constantly, learning to understand God's law, for this warms the heart with heavenly fire, as is said: 'While I was musing the fire burned' (Ps. xxxix. 3). Guard your lips from an idle word, or empty talk, lest the heart gets used to evil words. Cast yourself before God, saying: 'God be merciful to me a sinner' (Luke xviii. 13), and He will have mercy upon you and will keep and protect you from all evil, to lead you from darkness to true light, from prelest to truth, from death to life in Christ Jesus, our Lord.

103. Give the body as much (food) as it needs, and you will not suffer harm even if you eat three times a day. Even if a man eats only once a day but ill-judgedly, what good is that to him? Overeating is followed by an uprising of lusts and thereupon the enemy makes the body heavy with sleep to defile it.

104. Do not be surprised that at times you feel great weakness in performing your rule and in working with your hands. Such is this way: at times a man feels himself so, at other times other-

wise; just as a wayfarer at times follows a smooth path and at others strikes ravines and mountains, and then once more comes out on a level road. Pay no attention to weakness, but do everything and do your work.

105. (To a sick man forced to take food not in accordance with the statutes.) If a man eats not for pleasure but from bodily infirmity, God does not judge him. Food is forbidden to us in order to protect us from surfeit and stimulations of the body. But infirmity abolishes their activity, for where there is infirmity, there too is invocation of God.

106. (To a sick man asking for prayers in his prostration.) My repining and despondent brother! Why do you fret? Why do you cry? Why do you send afar for help when Jesus stands near you and desires you to call for His help! Call to Him: 'Teacher!' and He will answer you. Touch the edge of His garment, and He will cure you not only of this affliction but of all your passions. If your mind were where it should be, the stings of poisonous snakes and scorpions could not drive you thence to the sensation of bodily sickness. 'I forget', says David, 'to eat my bread. By reason of the voice of my groaning' (Ps. cii. 4, 5). Do not fret: God's mercy is near you.

107. Despise your body, which will be eaten by worms; it will be no help to you when it is given up to corruption. The Apostle says: 'Make not provision for the flesh, to fulfil the lusts thereof' (Rom. xiii. 14).

108. (A sick man: should one indulge the flesh by reason of infirmity?)—God gave us reason to guide us on the right path through Divine Scriptures. The Apostle says: 'Prove all things; hold fast that which is good' (1 Thess. v. 21). A man must only observe lest he uses something or does something from passion. But what he does from infirmity or need is not counted as sin or indulgence. In a healthy state, to seek bodily ease incites lusts But when we support our body out of need it will help us to do our works. If we care for the animals who serve our needs, how much more must we care for the body as a tool of the soul. When the tool is blunted, it hinders the artist, even if he is quick and skilful. Bearing in mind the infirmities of St. Timothy and the weakness of his stomach, the Apostle ordered him to drink wine

(1 Tim. v. 23) although he told him to 'endure afflictions' in doing 'the work of an evangelist' (2 Tim. iv. 5). A man should keep to right judgment in all things and he will not easily stumble.

109. 'Warfare against me increases more and more.'— Brother! Time of warfare is the time of doing: do not weaken, but do. Fight; and when the battle increases in strength, increase you too your strength by calling: 'Lord Jesus Christ! You see my weakness and my affliction; help me and deliver me from my persecutors (Ps. cxlii. 6) for I flee unto Thee to hide me!' (Ps. cxliii. 9); and pray to be given strength to serve God with a pure heart.

110. Two gifts God gave to men, by which they may be saved and delivered from all the passions of the old man: humility and obedience. But we do not strive after them, do not desire to abide in them, nor be guided by them. Leave off all evasions, bend your neck to humility and obedience, and you will receive mercy. If you practise with humility and obedience what you hear from the fathers, God will grant you His blessed help not only in the work you are doing, but will make all your works successful, for He protects the path of those who fear Him and watches over their progress. Why are you indignant? Why do you argue? God's mercy will help you if you constantly remain in Godly patience. Cease being ill-tempered, irritable and envious. Die to every man. Say to your thought: Who am I?— 'Dust and ashes' (Gen. xviii. 27), and a dog (Matt. xv. 27). Do not discuss others, belittling and ridiculing them. Compel yourself not to say: 'What is this? Wherefore is that?' (Ecclus. xxxix. 21). Why have I not the same as this or that man has? But work diligently at your small manual tasks with fear of God, and you will receive no small reward.

111. When despondency brings sleepiness, which interferes with the work you have to do, get up to pray and do not stop praying—and through prayer the Lord will banish sleepiness.

112. (To a man who wanted to be last, if only he were accepted into the community.)—It is not your business to seek to be last. That depends on your Abbot. Your business is to prepare yourself for obedience.

113. If a man does not make efforts to the fullness of his strength and does not add his own endeavours to the prayers of the saints, he will receive no profit whatever if the saints pray for him. If they fast and pray for him while he himself panders to his lusts and leads a disorderly life, what good can praying for him bring? For here the word of the Scriptures is fulfilled: 'When one buildeth, and another pulleth down, what profit have they then but labour?' (Ecclus. xxxiv. 23). And the Apostle says: 'The effectual fervent prayer of a righteous man availeth much' (James v. 16), that is, when a holy and righteous man prays for a sinner, the sinner must assist the prayer of the righteous by repentance according to his strength.

1.14. If a man is asked for something he has not got, he will not be judged for not giving what is asked of him. The Apostle Peter himself, when a lame man asked him for alms said: 'Silver and gold have I none' (Acts. iii. 6); and did not borrow to give him alms. In the same way, if a man has only enough of something for his own immediate needs, he must not give it away in alms, lest it happens that later, in time of want, he suffers affliction, being unable to bear privations. If the other persists and importunes him, and he replies: 'Forgive me, I have nothing to give you,' it will not be a lie, for if he has only enough for his own essential needs, he has indeed nothing to give another. Let him say to one who begs: 'Forgive me, I have only enough for my own needs.' Remember the five virgins who answered, when the others asked for oil for their lamps: 'Not so; lest there be not enough for us and you' (Matt. xxv. 9). And the Apostle Paul writes to the Corinthians: 'Now at this time your abundance may be a supply for their want' (2 Cor. viii. 14) but: 'I mean not that other men be eased, and ye burdened' (2 Cor. viii. 13).

115. When you wish to give alms but your thought brings doubt as to whether it is best not to give, test your thought and if you find that the doubt comes from avarice, give a little more than you intended.

116. How can he, who has nothing to give, come to have a share in blessedness? Blessedness is promised not only to those who give alms. 'Blessed are the poor in spirit,' 'blessed are they that mourn,' and so forth (Matt. v. 3, etc.). So if you cannot give

alms, be poor in spirit, that you may inherit the kingdom of heaven together with the saints. Mourn over your sins in this world, to be comforted with those that mourn. Acquire meekness, that you may inherit the earth. Be pure in heart, that you may see God in His glory. For the sake of the Lord, suffer reviling, persecution and all manner of evil said against you falsely, to rejoice and be exceeding glad at the great reward you will receive in heaven.

117. If the law of the Lord commands one thing and the laws the world establishes the opposite, what must one do?—The law of God is more important, for it speaks of the salvation of the soul. The law of the world, being of the flesh, speaks to the flesh.

118. Your love asks me about the fact that at times you look with passion on a man and your soul is carried away. This obviously refers to attacks by the devil. At those moments you should imagine how we will change in our coffins, the corruption and stench of our bodies after death. Keep also before your eyes the future last judgment of God, and imagine the lot of those who behave thus: how will you bear the great shame when our actions are revealed before the angels and archangels, before all men and before the just Judge? And imagine how the lips of those who performed such actions will then be closed. Let us fear him who said: 'Be not deceived: neither fornicators, nor idolaters, nor adulterers, nor effeminate, nor abusers of themselves with mankind . . . shall inherit the kingdom of God' (1 Cor. vi. 9). And 'Whosoever looketh on a woman to lust after her hath committed adultery with her already in his heart' (Matt. v. 28). You must remember this and not pay frequent visits to those who cause this struggle in you. But do not reveal to them why you withdraw from them, lest you give rise in them to all kinds of thoughts. And if you have to converse with them, call to your help the holy Name of God, saying: 'Lord Jesus! Protect me and help my weakness.' And do not fear; He will break the enemy bow, for His Name renders evil ineffective. Instead of saying much, say little; do not give freedom to your ears and thoughts, but conduct yourself with propriety and without confusion lest anyone notices what is happening. If through this you are given strength, do not be bold in relation to your enemies, for they are shameless

and return to the attack even after a thousand defeats. But God the Victorious helps a man in his humility, since He desired of His own free will to assume a human body for the sake of man.

119. 'How is mind enticed to a lustful thought?'—The enticing or abduction (and captivity) of mind occurs not only in relation to the passion of lust, but also on other occasions. The mind is subjected to it through being dispersed, and when this happens, a man must recall himself, saying: 'Lord, forgive me for the sake of Thy holy Name; I fell a prey to this through negligence. Free me from dispersal and from every net of the enemy.' And the sign by which you can recognise such abduction is the following: if a man converses with another while his mind darts hither and thither, it happens that while he speaks of one thing his mind passes to something else. This is what abduction means. In exactly the same way we are abducted by a lustful thought. A man happens to converse with another and if the enemy succeeds in distracting his mind from righteous sobriety, then through this distraction a lustful desire may appear in the mind. This too is abduction, because it occurs not as a result of thinking or remembering, but as a result of forgetting. On coming to himself, such a man should recall himself as was said above, and appeal to God for His mercy. The Lord is kind and will receive him as an erring son. But when this warfare arises without distraction of thoughts, one should practise sobriety and not delight in such thoughts, nor let them linger, but run quickly to our Lord God.

120. It is best of all to avoid all conversation with women. If necessity forces us to communicate with them, let us try to do it through someone else. If this is impossible, then, when we meet them, let us behave like a man approaching fire. Such a man takes every precaution not to be scorched; so we must do the same, and if we thus deal with women as though they were fire, we shall become firmly established in the fear of God. Let us not look at women, whatever happens. Let us not give rein to our eyes, nor linger in conversation with them, for this gives birth to the fire of desire; but let us try to withdraw as soon as we can, praying God to save us in this difficult hour from the nets of the devil spread before us; and let us constantly remember God—

and His great power will protect our weakness in Christ Jesus our Lord.

121. 'Is it good for me to leave my wife in order to enter a monastery?'—You must not leave her of your own accord, for you will thus break the commandment of the Apostle who says: 'Art thou bound unto a wife? seek not to be loosed' (1 Cor. vii. 27). If (after you leave her) she sins and begins to lead a bad life, the sin will be on you; unless you have left her by mutual consent, agreeing that it will be profitable. But leave this matter to God; in His loving kindness He will do what pleases Him.

122. On no account must you grieve about anything of this world, but only about sin. Also, 'to rejoice with those who rejoice' means to share in the joy of those who progress in godly virtue and who rejoice in the hope of future blessings. And 'to mourn with those who mourn' means to share in the sufferings of repenting sinners.

123. (About 'Blessed are the peacemakers'.)—It is best to make peace in your own heart. This is proper for everyone, and blessed are those who do it. But to make peace between those who have quarrelled is not proper for everyone, but only for those who can undertake it without harm to themselves. A weak man must rejoice when there is peace among all men; but he must not make himself an intermediary for the reconciliation of all men, but only of those whom he loves in God, and even this only if there is no risk of harming his own soul.

124. 'I suffer wrong from a certain man: what should I do?'— Do good to him.

125. 'When one father or another comes to visit me, I possess none of the necessary things to offer him—and I grieve.' Such thought is from the devil. It is sufficient to offer them what you have, according to the words: 'Be content with such things as ye have' (Heb. xiii. 5)—and God will inform them of your zeal. And when you yourself happen to go somewhere, do not expect to find comfort there—and you will not be disturbed. But when you expect but fail to find it, and begin to criticise the man who has received you, this criticism is death to the soul. Give thanks for everything; for in this consists the spiritual food and rest which profit the soul.

126. He who questions the fathers imitates Christ, Who 'humbled himself . . . and took upon him the form of a servant' (Phil. ii. 8, 7). A man who lives without counsel is his own enemy, for the Scriptures say: 'Be not confident in a plain way' (Ecclus. xxxii. 21). It is more profitable to question with humility, than to follow one's own will. For the Lord Himself puts the right words in the mouth of the answerer in return for righteousness and humility in the heart of the questioner.

127. Never dispute about faith. God does not demand this of you, but only that you should believe rightly in what you received from the holy Church at baptism, and that you should keep His commandments. Keep to this—and you will be saved. If you are asked, say 'Forgive me holy fathers, this is beyond me.'

128. Speculate on nothing that God does not demand of you but, as I said above, be content to profess the right faith, and do not be curious about anything beyond this.

129. If you happen to be among laymen, and they start to talk idly, withdraw if there is no special need to remain. But if you must stay, turn your mind to prayer, without judging them, but recognising your own weakness.—However, if they are well disposed towards you and you know that they listen readily to the word of God, try to turn from empty to useful talk, telling them something from the lives of the saints.

130. If someone you know inclines towards heretical theories, exhort him to become acquainted with the right faith, but do not argue with him; do not seek to hear his theories, lest you become infected with his poison. If he expresses a desire to hear about true faith, bring him to the holy fathers, who can be of service to him in Christ. In this way you will help him in God without harm to yourself. But if, after the first and second admonition, he does not acknowledge his error, then in the words of the Apostle, such a man should be 'rejected' (Titus iii. 10).

131. 'My thought tells me that I should not leave my house often, but it happens sometimes that there is a Church service several times in the course of a week. Should I go there or is it better to stay at home and be occupied (with prayer)?'—If you know that when you go out and meet people it does you harm, then it is better for you not to leave your home often, even to go

to Church, except from time to time. For silence frees us from many evils.

132. 'If it is necessary for me to go out, either for my own needs or for the needs of the fathers, would it not be putting a burden on my conscience if (in that case) I do not go to Church?' —If it is necessary for you to go out of your house for some essential need, or in obedience to the command of the fathers, try to do what you have to do with fear of God, and do not trouble about not attending a Church service, but return home and occupy yourself there with recollection of your sins. But if you leave your house out of laziness and inattention, then it is better to go to Church and keep attention in yourself without distraction.

133. 'Is it good to go to Church for night vigil, or is it better to keep vigil according to one's strength at home?'—It is better to keep vigil at home, for in Church conversations occur.

134. 'My thought shows me the insufficiency of my means, suggesting that my household and I cannot subsist on them—and I find myself overburdened.' This is a human burden. If we had trust in God He would rule over us according to His will. So 'Cast thy burden upon the Lord, and he shall sustain thee' (Ps. lv. 22). He has the power to provide everything needful to you and your household without burden or anxiety. Say to Him: 'Thy will be done' and He will not abandon you in your anxiety and burden.

135. 'If I do something unjust and then mend my ways, my thought becomes puffed up, suggesting that I have done something good. What should I say to my thought on such occasions?' —Say to it: 'Without God we can do nothing good,' as He Himself said: 'Without me ye can do nothing' (John xv. 5). And the Apostle says: 'What hast thou that thou didst not receive? now if thou didst receive it, why dost thou glory, as if thou hadst not received it?' (1 Cor. iv. 7). So, if we cannot glory in the good we do, how much less can we glory in withdrawing from evil. It is a great folly to sing our own praises for not sinning.

136. 'Every kind of food contains a natural sweetness: does it harm the man who partakes of it?'—Almighty God has imparted sweetness to every kind of food, and a man who receives it with

thankfulness suffers no harm. But passionate attachment should always be avoided, for it does harm to the soul.

137. 'Is it proper to strive to do a clean piece of work, for example, in building a house or doing something else?'—To see that the thing you make is clean and beautiful is not improper if it is done for the sake of the use it serves, without passionate attachment. For the Lord rejoices in all kinds of clean workmanship. But if you observe in yourself a passionate attachment to anything, remember the end which awaits it, since it is subject to rot and corruption, and you will find peace. For not a single thing remains constantly in the same state, but all are subject to change and corruption.

# THEOLEPTUS, METROPOLITAN OF PHILADELPHIA
## Short Biographical Note

Theoleptus, a truly great luminary of Philadelphia, lived in the reign of Andronicus, the second Palaeologus, about 1325. At first he led a life of spiritual endeavour on the Holy Mountain, but later was called away and given charge in Philadelphia. Among the pupils who received his spiritual guidance was St. Gregory[55] of Thessalonica, to whom he gave most excellent instruction in holy sobriety and revealed the mysteries of mental prayer, even while the latter was still occupied with worldly affairs, as is related in Gregory's life written by the Patriarch Philotheus.

The present writing, composed by him with loving care, is an exact description and a true rule of the secret doing in Christ. This and the additional texts, in which Divine thoughts are beautifully combined with purity of expression, are offered here side by side with other writings of the fathers, for they are more instructive than many, and precious to those who wish to have a brief survey of the wise teaching of spiritual philosophy in its entirety.

[55] i.e. St. Gregory Palamas. (Translators' note.)

# THEOLEPTUS, METROPOLITAN OF PHILADELPHIA

## A Word which expounds the secret doing in Christ and shows briefly in what the main work of monks consists

1. Monkhood is a tall and fruitful tree, the root of which is renunciation of everything worldly; its branches—absence of passionate attachments in the soul and of sympathy with things once renounced; its fruit—the wealth of virtues and love inspired by God, and the joy which is inseparable from them. 'The fruit of the Spirit is love, joy, peace' and so forth, says the Apostle (Gal. v. 22).

2. Withdrawal from the world provides refuge in Christ. By world I mean love for things of the senses and for the flesh. He who alienates himself from all this, because he has understood the truth, becomes absorbed by Christ for the sake of love for Him; when, through this love, a man has become estranged from all worldly things, he has bought this one precious pearl—Christ.

3. You were clothed in Christ by the Baptism which gives salvation. In this Divine bath all the filth of sin was washed away; it gave you the light of spiritual grace and restored to you your original nobility. But what happened later? Or rather what has man suffered later through his foolishness? By love for the world he altered the Divine features, by compassion for the flesh he distorted the image; and the darkness of passionate thoughts has blackened the mirror of his soul, which should have reflected Christ the inner sun.

4. Now you have again nailed your soul to the fear of God; you have realised the darkness of worldly confusion; you have understood the dispersion of thoughts, introduced into the mind

by worldly cares; you have seen the vanity of the vortex into which man is inevitably plunged by the turbulence of life; you have been wounded by the arrow of love of silence; you have sought peace from thoughts, hearkening to the word of the prophet: 'Seek peace, and pursue it' (Ps. xxxiv. 14); you have desired the ensuing rest of the soul, according to the words of the same prophet: 'Return unto thy rest, O my soul' (Ps. cxvi. 7). Because of all this the thought has come to you once again to incline your will towards the good, and so restore in yourself the nobility you received by grace at baptism, and later rejected through inclining your will towards evil, when you slaved for passions in the world. You have taken action to make this restoration by coming to this holy school, by clothing yourself in the honourable garment of repentance and by a whole-hearted vow to remain a monk until death.

5. This is already your second covenant with God. The first (was made) when you entered this life on earth, and the second —when you conceived the desire to end this life (worthily). Then, you were united with Christ by faith; now, you have adhered to Him through repentance. Then you received grace, now you have undertaken obligations. Then, in your childhood, you were unaware of the high rank bestowed upon you, although later, coming to manhood, you became conscious of the greatness of the gift and realised the curb you carry in your mouth. Now, having gained full understanding, you see clearly the force of this vow. Take care (keep your word), lest you again break your promise and are cast like a shattered vessel into outer darkness, where there is weeping and gnashing of teeth. For there is no way to salvation except through repentance.

6. Hear what David says to you: 'Thou hast made the Lord, . . . even the most High, thy habitation' (Ps. xci. 9). Full of suffering is the life you have chosen in the spirit of Christ; so let no evil approach you, for it clings to us if we move among things of the world. You have undertaken the burden of repentance; so let not love of possessions, comforts, honours, adornments and unbridled senses follow upon your footsteps; let the foolish 'not stand in thy sight' (Ps. v. 5):—wandering thoughts, captivity of mind, dissoluteness of ever-changing fancies and every other

arbitrary deviation from the right path, and confusion. Let not love of parents, brothers, friends and comrades stand in your way, for already it has become untimely and unprofitable to meet and converse with them.

7. If you conceive such a love for renouncing the world, both in soul and body, the scourge of suffering will not come near your soul, and the arrow of grief will not wound your heart or cloud your face. The sting of sorrow is blunted for those who have forsaken the love of pleasure, and have cast away passionate attachment to all we have described. For Christ comes to the striving soul and gives ineffable joy to the heart—and neither pleasures of this world nor its bitter griefs can ever rob you of this spiritual joy. Blessed meditations, soul-saving memories, Divine contemplations and words of wisdom serve and protect a true monk on all his paths of activity which are pleasing to God. This is why he tramples under foot all foolish lust and arrogant rage as a viper or a basilisk, and slays the lion of anger, and the snake-like love of pleasures. The reason why he has relinquished all hope of men and of what we have described and is cleaving to God, enriched by knowledge of Him and always mentally invoking His help, is the following promise: 'Because he hath set his love upon me,' says the Lord, 'therefore will I deliver him: I will set him on high, because he hath known my name. He shall call upon me, and I will answer him: I will be with him in trouble; I will deliver him, and' (also) 'honour him' (Ps. xci. 14, 15).

8. Do you now see the struggles of those who work in the Lord, and what are their rewards? Then strive to put this calling into practice, withdrawing from thoughts about things, as you have withdrawn in the body. You have changed your garment, then make yourself also (in the feelings of the heart) an exile; cast away even the words (habitual in the world), as well as your natural kin. For if you do not stop the wanderings of thought without, you will not be able to rise against those which ambush you within. If you do not conquer those who fight against you by visible things, you will not put invisible slanderers to flight. When, having put an end to external distractions, you also master inner thoughts, the mind will begin to rise to spiritual

words and actions (or to be awake in them). Then instead of rules observed in dealings with your relatives and friends, you will carefully observe the rules of right doing, and instead of vain words multiplied by worldly talk (which darken the soul), the examination and elucidation of Divine words moving in the memory will enlighten you and teach wisdom to your soul.

9. The unloosing of the senses lays fetters on the soul; fetters on the senses give freedom to the soul. When the sun sets, night comes; when Christ leaves the soul, the darkness of passions envelops it and mental beasts of prey rend it. When the physical sun rises, beasts hide in their holes; when Christ rises in the firmament of the praying heart, all feeling for the world stops, pity for the flesh vanishes and the mind sallies forth to do its work—to think of God—till evening, not limiting its doing of the spiritual law to a certain time, nor keeping to a definite measure; but it works on till this life comes to an end and the soul is forced to leave the body. The prophet speaks of this, saying: 'O how love I thy law! it is my meditation all the day' (Ps. cxix. 97); by day meaning the whole course of every man's life. Thus put an end to outer talking with the outer world until you find the place of pure prayer and the home in which dwells Christ, Who enlightens and gladdens you by His knowledge and visitation, and makes you count as joy all sufferings for His sake, and repulse worldly pleasures like wormwood.

10. Winds raise waves in the sea, nor till the winds cease will they be lulled, neither the sea be stilled. Likewise, in the soul of the negligent, evil spirits raise memories of his parents, brothers, relatives and friends, as well as of banquets, festivals, theatres and other pleasure-serving inventions; and they incite him to meet the former and take part in the latter with eyes, tongue and body; so that he uselessly wastes the present as well as the time after, when he sits alone in his cell, in empty recollections of what he has seen and heard. Thus monks waste their life fruitlessly, if they allow memories of worldly affairs to become imprinted in their mind, just as a man walking on snow leaves tracks of his footsteps. If we go on giving food to the beasts, when shall we starve them to death? If in deed and thought we continue to be occupied with foolish friendships and customs, when shall we

put to death the whims of the flesh? And how shall we be able
to live a life in Christ as we have vowed? Footsteps on the snow
vanish, either melting in the rays of the sun or washed away by
rains; and memories of deeds and objects of sensual pleasures are
annihilated either by Christ, Who shines forth in the heart
through prayer, or when the rain of tears (of sincere contrition)
comes with deepest tenderness and feeling.

11. When shall a monk who acts foolishly efface the old impressions previously imprinted in his mind? The practice of
virtues is as yet only that of the body, when you abandon the
customs of this world. Blessed memories are imprinted and
Divine words come to dwell in the soul and remain there, only
when you have effaced from your mind memories of your past
actions by frequent prayer, coupled with warm tenderness of
feeling. The light, which comes from remembering God with
faith, together with contrition of heart, cuts off bad memories
like a razor. Imitate the wisdom of the bees. When they see a
multitude of wasps swarming round, they remain inside their
hive and thus escape the harm those evil-doers may cause.
Understand by wasps, communion with the world and with men
of the world. Avoid them with all care, remain in the secret
chamber of your holy dwelling-place and strive from there to
enter the innermost watch-tower of the soul where Christ
abides, bringing you peace, joy and untroubled stillness. These
are the gifts of Christ, the inner Sun which He sends forth like
rays and bestows as a reward upon a soul, which welcomes Him
with faith and love of good.

12. Thus, sitting in your cell, remember God; and, moreover,
withdrawing your mind from everything, prostrate it speech-
lessly before God. Pouring out your heart to Him, cleave to Him
with love. Remembrance of God is contemplation of God, Who
attracts to Himself the vision and striving of the mind and illumines it with His light. Having cut off all images of existing
things and turning to God, the mind sees Him without form or
image, and thus has its vision cleared despite its imperfect comprehension of the Object of its contemplation, Whose glory
is utterly inaccessible. Although it cannot comprehend the
Object of its contemplation, since He is incomprehensible, the

mind then truly knows that it is He Alone Who is, and Alone has transubstantial being. Feeding its love for Him and satisfying its striving by the wealth of goodness pouring out of God, it is granted eternal and blessed rest in Him.

13. Such are the qualities of true remembrance of God. But prayer is mental speaking to the Lord, in which words of prayer are uttered, with the eye of the mind turned towards God alone. When thought frequently invokes the Name of the Lord, and the mind gives intense heed to this invocation of the Divine Name, then the light of recognising God, as his God, envelops man's whole soul like a radiant cloud.

14. True and diligent remembrance of God is followed by love and joy. 'I remembered God, and was troubled,'[56] says the prophet David (Ps. lxxvii. 3). And pure prayer is followed by knowledge of God and tenderness of feeling. 'When I cry unto thee,' says the same prophet, 'this I know; for God is for me'[57] (Ps. lvi. 9). And again: 'The sacrifices of God are a broken spirit' (Ps. li. 17). When mind and thought stand before God through intense concentration of the eye upon Him and warmth of prayer, the heart is moved to tenderness. When mind, word and spirit (heart) press close to God, the first by attention, the second by invocation, the third by tenderness of feeling, then the whole of the inner man serves God, as the Lord ordains: 'Thou shalt love the Lord thy God with all thy heart . . .' and so forth (Luke x. 27).

15. I wish you to know the following, lest, thinking that you are praying, you remain far from prayer and so labour uselessly and 'run, in vain' (Gal. ii. 2). Just as during oral prayer it sometimes happens that psalmody is performed while the mind wanders somewhere outside among passionate thoughts of worldly objects, and so all the meaning of the utterances is lost, so it happens in mental prayer. Often thought repeats the words of prayer, but the mind (attention) is not there; it does not direct its eye to God, to Whom the words of the prayer refer, but insensibly wanders off to other thoughts. And, although thought

---

56 The Slavonic text reads: '. . . and rejoiced.' (Translators' note.)
57 The Slavonic text reads: 'this I know, that Thou art my God.' (Translators' note.)

utters the words by habit, the mind slips away from knowledge of God (remembrance of Him and standing before Him with understanding). Then the soul becomes disorganised, and as if unconscious; for the mind wanders about in various fantasies, or turns round and round either in things which enticed it un-wittingly away and robbed it, or in things towards which it has drifted deliberately. When there is no harmony in the soul for prayer, when the man who prays is not even conscious before Whom he prays, and about what he prays, how can his prayer be a joy to him? How can the heart rejoice in prayer if a man only appears to be praying, instead of having true prayer working within? 'Let the heart of them rejoice that seek the Lord' (Ps. cv. 3). But a man is seeking the Lord if he clings to Him with his whole thought and with warm disposition, rejecting every worldly thought for the sake of gaining knowledge and love of God, engendered by pure and frequent prayer.

16. In order to explain what contemplation should be present in the mind while remembering God, and what supplication in the thought during pure prayer, I shall borrow an illustration from the physical eye and tongue. What the pupil is to the eye and the uttering of a word to the tongue, so is memory (of God) to the mind and prayer to thought. Just as the eye, receiving through the sense of sight a visual impression of an object, utters no sound but obtains knowledge of what it sees by the very act of seeing, so the mind, directing its loving attention (consciousness) towards God and cleaving to Him with ardent feeling, in the silence of most single contemplation, is illumined by Divine radiance and receives therein a token of the light to come. And again: as the tongue, when uttering words, reveals to the hearer the hidden wishes of the heart, so thought, uttering the brief words of the prayer frequently and warmly, reveals to the all-seeing God the supplications of the soul; and by persistent con-stancy in prayer and unceasing contrition of heart it opens the bowels of compassion of the merciful God, and so receives the riches of salvation. For the prophet says: 'A broken and a con-trite heart, O God, thou wilt not despise' (Ps. li. 17).

17. Another illustration which may guide you in understand-ing what pure prayer should be, is the customary behaviour of

those who stand in the presence of an earthly king. If you chance to gain admittance to the king, you make your body stand before him (as is seemly), and you beseech him with your tongue, and you fasten your eyes on him (with supplication)—and in such manner you win his benevolence. Do likewise in prayer, whether you are with others in church or pray alone in your cell. When you come to church to take part with your brethren in a common prayer to the Lord, as your body stands before Him and your tongue utters psalmody, so keep also the attention of your mind on the words and on God, clearly conscious of Him with Whom you converse and to Whom you address yourself. Remember that if thought is zealously and purely occupied with prayer, the heart is endowed with ineffable peace and joy that cannot be taken away. When you are alone in the cell, keep mental prayer with sobriety of mind and contrition of heart—and in return for sobriety you will be given vision, in return for prayer knowledge will come to dwell in you, and in return for your tenderness of feeling wisdom will descend upon you, banishing all foolish love of pleasures and replacing it by Divine love.

18. Believe me, I tell you the truth: if every work you do is inseparably connected with prayer—the mother of all good—prayer will not rest until it has shown you the bridal chamber and has led you within, filling you with ineffable bliss and joy. Removing all obstacles, it smooths the path of virtue and renders it easy for those who seek (salvation).

19. Look now on the picture of mental prayer! Converse (inner utterances in this prayer) destroys the stirrings of passions; directing the mind to God banishes worldly thoughts, tenderness of feeling cuts off love of the flesh. It is evident that prayer, which consists of an unceasing invocation of the Divine Name, is the harmony and union of mind, word and soul (heart). 'For where two or three are gathered together in my name, there am I in the midst of them' (Matt. xviii. 20) says the Lord. Thus, in recalling the powers of the soul from their dispersion among objects of passion, and in uniting them with one another and with the tripartite soul itself, prayer mirrors the One God in three hypostases. When, by means of the various virtues, it has first erased the shame of sin from the soul, and then has depicted

therein the beauty of the Divine features by means of its own holy knowledge, prayer finally presents the soul to God. The soul straightway recognises God as its Creator, for it is said: 'When I cry unto thee, then . . . this I know; for God is for me' (Ps. lvi. 9). And in its turn it becomes known to God, for it is said: 'The Lord knoweth them that are his' (2 Tim. ii. 19). The soul knows God because its image is pure, for every image is attracted to its prototype. And it is known by Him because of its likeness in virtue, through which it both knows God and is known by Him.

20. He who wishes to gain the king's benevolence, uses a threefold means to this end; he either implores the king in (suitable) words, or stands silent before him (as a supplicant), or casts himself at his feet, since the king alone can help him. In the same way pure prayer, having united in itself mind, (inner) word and spirit (heart), invokes the name of God in words, looks up at God, Whom it is invoking, with a mind free from wandering, and shows contrition, humility and love in spirit (in heart). Thus it inclines towards itself the eternal Trinity, the Father, the Son and the Holy Spirit—the One God.

21. As variety in foods provokes the desire to taste them, so different kinds of virtue (spiritual perfections) provoke zeal in the mind (towards acquiring them). Therefore, in your progress on the mental way, repeat the words of the prayer and speak to the Lord, calling to Him constantly and never losing heart. Pray steadfastly, imitating the importunate widow who inclined the implacable judge to mercy. Then (it will mean that) you walk in the spirit, that you do not listen to the lusts of the flesh and do not interrupt the ceaseless flow of prayer by worldly thoughts, but are a temple of God in which He is praised without distraction. If you practise mental prayer in this way, in the end you will attain to constant remembrance of God, will gain access to the inaccessible hidden treasure of the mind and in secret contemplations will see Him Who is Unseen, serving the One God in oneness and solitude, in outpourings of love understood by yourself alone.

22. When you notice that you begin to weaken in prayer, take up a book and, paying attention to what you read, try to understand its meaning. Do not read the words cursorily, but examine

them with deliberation (searching out their meaning) and store what you have understood in the treasure-house of your mind. Then begin to reflect on what you have read, so as to gladden your heart with understanding and make what you have read unforgettable. Meditations on Divine things will kindle warmth in you, as David says: 'While I was musing the fire burned' (Ps. xxxix. 3). As food gives pleasure to the taste when properly chewed, so Divine words feed the mind and gladden the heart when turned over in the soul by reflection. 'How sweet are thy words unto my taste!' says the same prophet (Ps. cxix. 103). Learn also by heart the words of the Gospels and the sayings of the holy fathers, and study their lives in order to have all this as subjects for meditation during the nights.

23. If after reading and meditation on Divine words you are still in need of reviving your thought, since it is too weak to pray, and of making it once more alive and active in prayer, practise oral psalmody, but in a low voice and with attention of mind, not allowing yourself to leave uncomprehended anything of what is uttered by the tongue. If in the course of this practice something eludes the attention of the mind, again return to the same verse, no matter how many times this happens, until finally the mind is made to follow what the tongue utters with unfailing attention. The mind has enough strength to psalmodise with the lips and at the same time to remember God. Learn this from experience. If a man converses with someone, he talks to him and at the same time looks at him with his eyes. In the same way you can practise psalmody with your lips and look at God with the eye of the mind.

24. Do not neglect kneeling. Kneeling represents falling into sin, implying also confession of sin. Rising up from the knees represents repentance, suggesting a vow of virtuous life. Each time you kneel make a mental invocation of Christ, casting yourself body and soul at the feet of the Lord, to incline the God of souls and bodies favourably towards you.

25. If while practising mental prayer, you take up some undistracting work with your hands, this also will be a help to you in this most difficult task of prayer. All the works indicated, when connected (as weapons) with prayer, sharpen attention, banish

despondency, give youthful vigour to the soul and render the mind more acute in vision and warmly zealous in the exercise of mental doing.

26. As soon as the gong has sounded leave the cell, your physical eyes downcast and your thought plunged deeply into remembrance of God. When you have gone into church and joined the number of the worshippers, do not let your tongue indulge in idle chatter with the neighbouring monk, nor let your mind wander in vanities. Occupy your tongue solely in psalmody, and keep your mind firmly at prayer. At the end of the service go back to your cell and take up the work ordained by your cell rule.

27. On entering the refectory do not peer at the helpings of your brethren and do not injure your soul by improper spying around. Look only at what is put before you and touch nothing else; give food to your body, the hearing of what is read to your ear and prayer to your soul, so that, being fed in body and spirit, you may be able to give full praise to Him Who has so mercifully satisfied your desire. Then get up, enter your cell modestly and in silence and, like an industrious bee, readily resume your proper occupations. If you do some work with your brethren, let the hands work, while the lips are silent and the mind remembers God. If someone starts vain talk, to stop such unseemly behaviour, get up and make a bow.

28. Repulse thoughts and do not allow them to run through the heart and settle there. Passionate thoughts settling in the heart revive passions and kill the mind. Therefore, as soon as they come near, from the first moment of their appearance in the mind, hasten to strike them down by the arrow of prayer. If they persist, pushing at the door of attention and troubling thought, know that they are reinforced by a hidden desire for them which has preceded this attack. So they trouble and importune the soul, as though by right because your will has wavered. In this case it is necessary to pillory them by confession, for evil thoughts immediately turn to flight as soon as they are exposed. As darkness vanishes with the coming of light, so passionate thoughts disappear in the light of confession, for they themselves are darkness. For example, if vanity and the passion of lust have gained place in your thoughts, they are immediately banished by the shame of

confessing them, and by the suffering caused by the penance imposed. After this, thoughts of all kinds find the mind free of passions and occupied with ceaseless contrite prayer and so hasten away, covered with shame.

29. If a man strives to cut off (by prayer) the thoughts that trouble him and manages for a time to drive them away and to stop their frequent appearance, but cannot get completely free from them, and so remains in the state of one now vanquishing, now vanquished, this happens because he has a fondness for the causes of those troubling thoughts—bodily comfort and worldly ambitions, because of which he does not hasten to confess his thoughts. And so he has no peace, since he keeps in himself what gives the enemies the right to attack him. If a man steals things that do not belong to him, how can he avoid being tortured for this by those to whom they do belong? And how can a man hope to be set free by his adversaries if, being tortured, he does not restore what he has wickedly appropriated? But when by effort a monk has become strengthened by memory of God and so welcomes the degradation and vexation of the flesh and confesses his thoughts without fear of shame, the enemies immediately retreat and thought, becoming free, keeps constant prayer and uninterrupted contemplation of Divine things.

30. Cut off drastically any suspicion that may arise in the heart against other people, for it destroys peace and love. But accept any calamity which may come from without with courage, for it gives an opportunity for profitable patience—a patience which will be rewarded in heaven by peace and joy.

31. Spending thus your days, you will pass the present life in a manner good for your soul, inspired by blessed hope; and when death comes you will leave this life unafraid, and will enter the abode of rest prepared for you by the Lord, to share in His kingdom as a reward for your present labours. To Him be glory, honour and worship, with His eternal Father, and His all-holy, righteous and life-giving Spirit, now and for ever, and through the ages of the ages. Amen.

# Nine texts on the same subject

1. The mind that withdraws from the external and is collected within, returns to itself and thus becomes united with the mental word natural to it. By this word, essentially inherent in it, it takes up prayer. By prayer it ascends to consciousness of God with the whole force of love and disposition of the heart. Then lusts of the flesh depart; all pleasure-loving sensations cease, and all the beauties of this earth delight it no longer. For then the soul, having left behind all that is in the body and around the body, is drawn in the wake of the beauty of Christ and pursues it by worthy activities and purity of thought. Then it sings: 'She' (the king's daughter) 'shall be brought unto the king' (Ps. xlv. 14); it sees Christ and sets Him before it, as in the words of the prophet: 'I have set the Lord always before me: because he is at my right hand' (Ps. xvi. 8). It cleaves to Christ with love and calls: 'Lord, all my desire is before thee' (Ps. xxxviii. 9); its eyes ever turned towards Christ, it cries: 'Mine eyes are ever toward the Lord' (Ps. xxv. 15); by pure prayer it converses with Christ, thus joyously delighting Him and saying: 'My meditation of him shall be sweet: I will be glad in the Lord' (Ps. civ. 34). For God, being loved, and named, and asked for help, accepts the converse of prayer and gives ineffable joy to the praying soul; and the soul, remembering God in prayerful converse, rejoices in the Lord and says with the prophet: 'I remembered God, and was troubled'[58] (Ps. lxxvii. 3).

2. Guard the senses, and you will abolish delight in sensory things. Flee also mental fantasies of sensory pleasures, and you will abolish pleasure-loving thoughts. When the mind is free of fantasies, and neither receives impressions nor suffers changes from objects of pleasure or lustful thoughts, it abides in pure simplicity; being above all sensory and mental things, it rises in

[58] The Slavonic text reads: '. . . and rejoiced.' (Translators' note.)

thought towards God, and, constantly remembering Him, has but one cry in the depth of the heart—the Name of the Lord—calling to Him as a child calls to his father. As Adam was fashioned by God's hand out of clay and then God breathed into him a living soul; so the mind, re-created by virtues, through frequent invocation of the Lord with pure thought and warm feeling, undergoes a Divine change, gaining new life and creation by knowledge and love of God.

3. When ceaseless prayer of the heart has led you out of lusting after things of the earth and when your thought falls asleep to everything that is lower than God and you are firmly grounded in memory of God alone: then love of God will arise like a helpmeet within you. For the cry of the heart born of prayer brings forth Divine love, and Divine love prepares the mind for understanding what is hidden. Then the mind, in harmony with love, becomes fruitful in wisdom, and, under the influence of wisdom, announces wondrous things. For God the Word, invoked by Name in the praying heart, takes out discursive reason like a rib, and gives knowledge. Putting right order in its place, He bestows virtue, creates light-giving love and brings it to the mind withdrawn into ecstasy, asleep and at rest from every earthly lust. This love becomes a helpmeet to the mind at rest from foolish attachment to sensory things, because it incites the mind to words of wisdom. Then, beholding it with delight, the mind makes known to others unstintingly the hidden dispositions of virtue and the invisible actions of intellect.

4. Step out of everything sensory and abandon the law of the flesh—and spiritual law shall be inscribed in your heart. For as those who walk in the Spirit do not fulfil the lust of the flesh (Gal. v. 16), so a man who steps out of the senses and sensory things, that is the flesh and the world, attains a state where he walks in the spirit and thinks on spiritual things. You can understand this from what God did for Adam before his transgression.

5. A man who endeavours to keep the commandments, who abides in the paradise of prayer and stands before God in ceaseless remembrance, is lifted by God out of the lustful influences of the flesh, all stirrings of the senses and all fantasies of sensory things in thought. Making him dead to passions and sin, God

grants him participation in Divine life. As a sleeping man though living is like one dead—dead in body, but alive in the activity of his soul; so a man, who is dead to the flesh and the world, is alive in the workings of the spirit.

6. If you understand what you chant, you receive knowledge: knowledge leads to consciousness or conscience (in relation to what you know); from conscience springs putting what you know into practice; from this putting into practice grows the fruit of knowledge from experience; knowledge from experience leads to true contemplation; and true contemplation makes the light of wisdom shine forth, filling the immaterial air with the radiant words of grace and interpreting hidden things to those who are without.

7. First the mind seeks and finds, then it unites with what is found. Its search is with the reason, and its union is through love. It seeks with the reason for the sake of truth, and achieves union through love for the sake of good.

8. He, who stands above the flowing nature of the things of this life, and who is alien to lusting after the transitory, looks not at the valley below and yearns not for earthly beauties. His eyes are open to the peaks above, he sees the blessings on high and aims to share in pure bliss. For the heavens are closed to a man who heeds only the material blessings of the earth and is inclined towards indulging the flesh, since his mental eyes are darkened. But a man who despises what lies below and turns away from it, has his mind transported to the heights, sees the glory of eternal blessings and comprehends the radiance of light promised to the saints. Such a man receives the love of God descending on him from above, and he becomes a temple of the Holy Spirit. He yearns for the fulfilment of God's wishes, is guided by the Holy Spirit, is granted sonship and attains God's benevolence and pleasure. 'For as many as are led by the Spirit of God, they are the sons of God' (Rom. viii. 14).

9. Do not abandon prayer under the pretext of infirmity even for one day, so long as you have breath, and listen to the words of the Apostle: 'When I am weak, then am I strong' (2 Cor. xii. 10). Acting thus you will gain much profit, and prayer will soon restore you by the action of grace. For where there is comfort of the Spirit, there is no room for weakness and despondency.

# PART THREE

# THE HOLY FATHER
# ST. PHILEMON THE ABBA
## Short Biographical Note

Historical records of the fathers tell us nothing about when our Father Philemon lived—the most saintly, the most sober and the most contrite father of them all. But that he was a man of the greatest devotion and experience, that he loved silence better than any of the other startzi, being the strictest imitator of the great Arsenius, will be seen from this narrative. For he spent his days and nights patiently in a small cave in the wilderness, in prayer and supplication, washing himself in the ever-flowing springs of the sweetest tears and, in his ardent love of God, rising above all sensory and mental things. Like one deaf and dumb he stood always in the presence of God and was miraculously illumined by Divine grace. Enlightened thereby as by the rays of the sun, this revered saint, in his extreme silence and stillness, was enriched not only by the highest gifts of discrimination and wisdom, but also by vision and foresight. The narrative offered here bears true testimony of this, since it gives his most wise teaching on holy sobriety, from both the practical and the contemplative point of view, based on long personal experience. Thus whoever wishes to divest himself of the filthy and abominable garment of passions, or, which is the same thing, to cast off the old man, and to become clothed in the radiant garment of passionlessness and grace, or the new man in Christ Jesus, will gain his desire unhindered if he studies diligently the teaching of this staretz and puts into practice what he has understood, as far as lies in his power.

# THE MOST PROFITABLE
# NARRATIVE OF ABBA PHILEMON

1. It is said of Abba Philemon, the Hermit, that he shut himself up in a cave a short distance from a Lavra called Romaios and gave himself up to works of spiritual effort, mentally repeating, we are told, the words the great Arsenius used to say to himself: 'Philemon, why have you come here?' He spent a long time in this cave. His occupation was to make ropes and baskets which he gave to the steward and received in return small loaves which were his only food. He ate nothing but bread and salt, and even that not every day. He seemed not to care at all for his body, but practising contemplation, was illumined by Divine light, and being secretly guided thereby remained in a state of spiritual joy. On his way to church on Saturdays and Sundays, he always walked alone, deeply collected within himself, allowing no one to come near him, lest his mind be diverted from its inner doing. While in church, he chose a place in a corner and, with his face to the ground, wept floods of tears, filled always with contrition and revolving in his mind the memory of death and images of the holy fathers, especially that of Arsenius the Great, in whose footsteps he endeavoured to follow.

2. When a heresy appeared in Alexandria and the surrounding countryside, he left there and went to the Lavra of Nikanor. The God-loving Paulinus welcomed him, gave up his own secluded place to him, and arranged for him a life of complete silence. For a whole year he allowed no one to see him, and himself refrained from troubling him, except for bringing him the bread he required. Easter came and when, on their meeting, the conversation touched upon hermit life, Philemon realised that the most devout brother Paulinus was also filled with the excellent desire of becoming a solitary. Thereupon he sowed him richly with words of spiritual endeavour, from the Scriptures and the fathers, to

prove that it is impossible to please God without utter seclusion, as Moses, the father enlightened of God, had said of old; silence gives birth to endeavour, endeavour gives birth to mourning, mourning to fear, fear to humility, humility to opening of the eyes, opening of the eyes to love, and love makes the soul sound and passionless, and then a man realises that he is not far from God.

3. He (Philemon) said to him: 'By means of silence you must thoroughly cleanse your mind and give it constant spiritual occupation. As the eye turned on sensory objects looks closely at what it sees, so a pure mind, turned towards immaterial things, is uplifted by the object of its spiritual contemplation so that it cannot be torn away. And in the measure that silence strips it of passions and purifies it, so is it given knowledge (of these spiritual things). The mind becomes perfect when it enters into the sphere of essential knowledge and is united with God. Having thus attained kingly rank, the mind no longer feels poor and is not carried away by false desires, even if all the kingdoms of the world were offered it. Thus, if you wish to reach such blessings, hasten to run from the world and follow diligently upon the footsteps of the saints; abandon all care of your appearance; wear poor garments and humble attire. Keep your disposition simple, your speech without guile, your walk without arrogance, your voice sincere. Love to live in scarcity and to be disregarded by all men. Above all, strive to guard your mind and to practise sobriety, be patient in strait circumstances and try at all costs to preserve unharmed and unchanged the spiritual blessings you have already acquired. Keep attention in yourself diligently, and do not accept any of the lusts which secretly try to steal in. For, although silence tames the passions of the soul, they are wont to rage all the more if they are allowed to flare up and become acute, and with redoubled force they lead those, who let this happen, into sin. They are like bodily sores, which, being rubbed and worried, become incurable. Even a single word can deflect the mind from memory of God, when the demons are pushing and the senses concur. To guard the soul is a great work and a great fear. Thus you should renounce the world completely and, tearing your soul away from all compassion to the flesh, become

cityless, homeless, devoid of possessions, money, acquisitions, worries, companions; ignorant of all human affairs, humble, compassionate, good, meek, even-tempered, ready to receive the teachings which Divine knowledge imprints in your heart. For, as Basil the Great teaches, you cannot write on a wax tablet unless you erase the letters previously engraved on it. Such were the saints who, having entirely renounced all worldly habits, and preserving heavenly thoughts undisturbed within, became enlightened by Divine laws and shone with righteous deeds and words, having mortified their "members which are upon the earth" (Col. iii. 5) by abstinence, fear of God and love. For constant prayer and study of the Divine Scriptures open the inner eyes of the heart to see the Lord of hosts. Then great joy reigns and an irresistible Divine desire is set aflame in the soul, whereupon, by the action of the Spirit, even the flesh is ravished on high and the whole of man becomes spiritual. These are the gifts in store for those who practise blessed silence and the strictest life of struggle, and who, having withdrawn from every human consolation, constantly converse in solitude with our Lord in heaven alone.'

4. On hearing this the devout brother's soul was pierced by Divine love; (he left his place) and went with (Philemon) to the skete where the greatest among the fathers had completed their path of righteousness. They settled in the Lavra of St. John Kolobos, entrusting the steward of the Lavra with all care for them, since they wished to remain in silence. And so, by the grace of God, they remained there in complete silence, coming out on Saturdays and Sundays to take part in divine services with the community; but on all other days they stayed in their own place. Moreover, each of them prayed and performed his rule independently of the other.

5. The holy staretz (Philemon) kept to the following rule: during the night he recited all the psalms and the nine canticles (included in the Psalter), without haste or restlessness; then he read the beginning of one Gospel, and thereupon sat down and repeated within: 'Lord have mercy!' with his whole attention and for a considerable time, until he could no longer continue the invocation. Finally he allowed himself to sleep. At dawn he

again chanted the first 'hour' and sitting down on his stool, his face turned to the East, alternately chanted (psalms) and read what he chose from the Apostle or the Gospels. In this way he spent the whole day, in constant psalmody and prayer, and the joy of contemplating heavenly things. Often his mind was so enravished in contemplation that he no longer knew whether he was on earth or not.

6. Seeing him practise his rule of prayer with such diligence and observing how at times his whole aspect changed through Divine thoughts, his brother said to him: 'Is it difficult for you, father, to mortify yourself so in your old age and to subjugate your flesh?' He replied: 'Believe me, God has put into my soul such zeal and such love for prayer that I lack strength wholly to satisfy this longing. As to physical infirmity, it is conquered by love of God and hope of future blessings.' Thus his whole desire was mentally soaring on wings to heaven, and this at all times, even while eating.

7. The brother who lived with him asked him once: 'What are the mysteries of contemplation?' Seeing his persistence and realising that he sincerely sought instruction, he said to him: 'I tell you, my son, that to him whose mind is completely purified God reveals visions of the very powers and hierarchies (of angels) which serve Him.'

8. The same brother asked him also: 'Why is it, Father, that of all Divine Scriptures you take the greatest joy in the Psalter and why, when reciting psalms in a low voice, do you seem to be talking with someone?' To this he replied: 'God has engraved the force of the psalms in my soul as deeply as in the Prophet David himself, and I cannot tear myself away from delighting in the various contemplations contained in them; for they embrace everything in all the Divine Scriptures.' This he confessed to the questioner with the greatest humility, for the latter's profit and after long and persistent questioning.

9. A certain brother named John, came to this great father Philemon from the seashore and, embracing his feet, said to him: 'What should I do, Father, to be saved? For my mind wanders hither and thither, where it should not be.' After a brief silence he replied: 'This sickness (of the soul) is the attribute of those

who are external, and it abides in them. It is in you too, for you have not yet reached a perfect love of God; the warmth of loving and knowing Him has not yet come to you.' The brother said to him: 'What should I do, Father?' Philemon said to him: 'Go, acquire secret instruction in your heart, and it will cleanse your mind of this.' The brother, not being initiated in the meaning of what he was told, said to the staretz: 'What is this secret instruction, Father?' And he replied: 'Go, practise sobriety in your heart, and in your thought repeat soberly, with fear and trembling: "Lord, Jesus Christ, have mercy upon me!" This is what blessed Diadochus recommends for beginners.'

10. The brother went back and, with the help of God, and assisted by the prayers of the staretz, found rest and enjoyed this instruction for a while. But later the joy left him and he could no longer keep sobriety and do the work of prayer. Therefore he went again to the staretz and told him what had happened. The staretz said to him: 'Now you have had some experience of the path of silence and mental doing, and you have tasted the sweetness which comes of it. Keep it always in your heart; whether you eat, or drink, or converse with someone, whether you travel or sit in your cell, with sobriety of thought and a mind free from wandering never cease to keep this prayer, and continue to practise psalmody and gain instruction from prayers and psalms. Even when satisfying your most urgent needs, do not allow your mind to be idle, but compel it to continue secretly to learn and to pray. In this way, you will be able to understand the depths of the Divine Scriptures and the power concealed in them, and will give your mind a constant occupation in obedience to the word of the Apostle: "Pray without ceasing" (1 Thess. v. 17). Keep attention diligently in yourself and guard your heart from accepting bad thoughts, or thoughts that are idle and unprofitable. But always, whether you sleep or rise, eat or drink, or converse with someone, make your heart mentally and in secret either seek instruction in psalms, or pray: "Lord, Jesus Christ, Son of God, have mercy upon me!" In the same way, when you utter psalms with your tongue, pay attention lest your lips say one thing and your thought be diverted towards something else.'

11. The brother said to him: 'I have many idle fantasies when I sleep.' The staretz replied: 'Do not be lazy or faint-hearted; but before falling asleep say many prayers in your heart, and resist thoughts and the attempts of the devil to lead you where he wills. May God encompass you. Take as much care as you can to go to sleep with psalms on your lips and instruction in your mind; and do not let your mind accept alien thoughts through negligence. Whatever thoughts you had during prayer, draw instruction from them: and when you lie down on your bed make them remain in you while you sleep and converse with them when you awake. Recite also the holy Symbol of the Orthodox faith before you drop asleep, for to profess true faith in God is the source and preservation of all blessings.'

12. Yet again the brother asked him: 'Of your charity, Father, tell me what is the doing which occupies your mind? Teach me, so that I too may be saved.' He said: 'Why are you curious to know?' The other got up, embraced the feet of the saint and, kissing them, implored him to tell him. After a considerable time the staretz said: 'You cannot as yet do it. To give suitable work to each one of the senses is proper to a man accustomed to move among the blessings of truth. But it is impossible to be granted this gift, unless a man is completely cleansed of the vain thoughts of the world. Therefore, if you truly desire it, keep the secret instruction in a pure heart. For if prayer and learning from the Scriptures are constantly in you, the eyes of your soul will be opened, and it will be filled with great joy and a certain ineffable burning sensation, so that even the flesh is warmed by the Spirit, and the whole man becomes spiritual. Thus, if God grants you undistracted prayer with purity of mind, whether it be by day or at night, leave your ordinary rule and strive with your whole strength to cleave with your mind and heart to God. And He will enlighten your heart in the spiritual doing which you have undertaken.'

Then he added: 'Once a staretz came to me, and when I asked him about the state of his mind, he told me: "For two years I have remained in prayer before God, imploring Him with my whole heart and zeal to let the prayer He gave to His disciples be constantly and undistractedly imprinted in my heart. And, seeing my labour and patience, the merciful Lord granted me what I asked.'''

He told him also: 'Thoughts about vain things which are found in the soul are a disease of an idle and negligent soul. Therefore the Scriptures teach us to guard our mind with all diligence, to psalmodise with understanding and without distraction, and to pray with a pure mind. So, brother, God wants us to show our zeal for Him first by our works (of endeavour and right actions), then by love and constant prayer—and He will show us the way to salvation. And it is clear that there is no other way leading to heaven except complete withdrawal from all evil, acquisition of all good, perfect love for God and union with Him, in righteousness and in His likeness. If a man has all this he will speedily ascend to heaven. Moreover, every man wishing to ascend on high must not delay in mortifying his members which are upon the earth. But when our soul delights in the contemplation of true bliss, it no longer returns to any of the passions incited by sinful lusts, but turning away from every bodily pleasure, welcomes the coming of God with pure and undefiled thought. Thus it is necessary to guard ourselves in every possible manner, to suffer much physical labour, and to purify our soul that God may dwell in our hearts. Then, through the grace of the Spirit instilled into us, He will help us to fulfil His commandments without sin, and will Himself teach us to keep steadfastly His laws, radiating His influences upon us like rays of the sun. By labours and trials we must purify the image in which we were created as intelligent beings, capable of all understanding and of likeness to God; if we keep our senses cleansed of all filth, by reforging them in the furnace of trials, we become transmuted to the rank of king. When God created human nature He made it able to participate in every bliss, to contemplate inwardly the exultation of the angels of glory, of principalities, of powers, of might, of dominion, to see inaccessible light and radiant glory. But when you have acquired some virtue, take care lest your thought exalts itself over your brother for having practised it, while he was negligent; for this is the beginning of pride. When you struggle with some passion, take care not to be dejected or faint-hearted if it resists your efforts, but arise and cast yourself down before

God, saying from the bottom of your heart, with the prophet: "Fight", O Lord, "against them that fight against me" (Ps. xxxv. 1), for I am powerless against them! Then, seeing your humility, He will speedily send you His help. If you travel with a companion, do not accept idle talk, but give your mind its usual spiritual occupation, to keep this good habit in it and, making it forget worldly delights, force it to stay in the harbour of passionlessness.'

These and many other words did the staretz say to the brother, and then let him go.

13. But after a short time the brother again came to him and asked: 'What should I do, Father? During the practice of my night rule I become heavy with sleep, which prevents me from praying with sobriety and keeping a longer vigil. So I would like to take on some work with my hands while I do psalmody.' The staretz replied: 'When you can pray with sobriety, do not touch any work with your hands. But if sleep tends to overcome you, after struggling for a while with your thoughts and resisting them, take up manual work.' The brother asked: 'And you yourself, Father, do you not get heavy with sleep during your vigil?' The staretz replied: 'Not so easily. Yet, when at times I become assailed with sleepiness, I am affected a little. But I begin to read the Gospel of St. John from the beginning, raising the eyes of my mind to God, and sleepiness immediately disappears. I do the same in respect of thoughts, namely, if one of them comes upon me, I quench it like a flame with tears and it vanishes. You cannot as yet struggle with them in this manner; but hold fast to your secret instruction and perform with all zeal the daily prayers established by the holy fathers, such as the third, sixth and ninth hours, vespers and the night services. And strive with all your strength to do nothing simply to please men, nor to have any enmity towards any of the brethren, lest you separate yourself from your God. Try also to hold your mind undistracted and to keep its attention carefully on your inner thoughts. When you are in church, preparing yourself for the communion of the holy Mysteries of Christ, do not leave until you have acquired perfect peace. Standing in one place, do not move from there till dismissal. Think inwardly that you are in

heaven, standing before God with His holy angels and preparing to receive Him into your heart. Prepare yourself for this with fear and trembling, lest you are unworthy to have communion of the holy powers.'

Having thus strengthened the brother and entrusting him to the Lord and to His Spirit of grace, the staretz let him go.

14. A brother who lived with him related the following. Once sitting near him, he asked whether he had been tempted by the demons while living in the desert. He said: 'Forgive me, brother—if God let you suffer the same temptations from the devil as I underwent, I do not think you could endure their bitterness. I am in my seventieth year and more, I have suffered numerous temptations living in many wild places in complete silence. But it is not useful to relate to those, who have not yet been tried by silence, the bitterness I have experienced and suffered from those demons. During such temptations I always followed the same rule; I put my trust in God, to Whom I made vows of renunciation, and He speedily freed me of every want. So now, brother, I no longer think of providing for my needs, but knowing that He takes care of me, bear with ease any trial that befalls. Only one thing I do to bring Him on my side— constant prayer. It is no small help in this to trust that the greater the tribulations and afflictions, the greater the crowns prepared for the sufferer: for the righteous Judge makes them balance one another. Knowing this, brother, do not give way to faintness of heart. You have undertaken the struggle in order to fight; so fight, inspired by the thought that those who fight on our side against the enemy of God are very many, and outnumber the enemy hosts. How could we dare to resist this terrible foe of our race if the mighty hand of God the Word did not hold, protect and cover us? How could human nature resist his suggestions? For, as Job says: "Who can open the doors of his face? his teeth are terrible round about. . . . Out of his mouth go burning lamps, and sparks of fire leap out. Out of his nostrils goeth smoke, as out of a seething pot or cauldron. His breath kindleth coals, and a flame goeth out of his mouth. In his neck remaineth strength, and sorrow is turned into joy before him. . . .59 His

59 The Slavonic text reads: '. . . perdition flows before him. . . .'

heart is as firm as a stone; yea, as hard as a piece of the nether millstone. . . . He maketh the deep to boil like a pot: he maketh the sea like a pot of ointment. He maketh a path to shine after him; one would think the deep to be hoary. . . . He beholdeth all high things: he is a king over all the children of pride" (Job. xli. 14–34). This is whom we have to fight, brother! This is how words describe this tyrant! Yet victory over him is easy for those who live a solitary life as they should, for they have nothing that belongs to him, since they have renounced the world, since they practise high virtues and since we have Him, Who fights for us. For tell me, what man has not had his nature transformed if he came to the Lord and kept the fear of Him in his mind? What man who has enlightened himself by Divine laws and deeds has not made his soul radiant and able to shine with Divine thoughts and understandings? Such a man never allows his soul to be idle, since he has in him God, Who incites the mind to strive insatiably after light. And the spirit does not allow a soul constantly affected by such influences to get unruly through passions, but like a king, breathing terrible wrath and interdictions, cuts them off without mercy. Such a man never turns back, but by practice (of virtues), by raising his hands to heaven and by inner prayer gains victory in battle.'

15. The same brother related: 'Among other virtues, Abba Philemon had also the following: he could not bear to hear an idle word; if someone, forgetting himself, began to tell of something not concerned with profit to the soul, he never showed any response. Also, if I had to go away on some business, he never asked: "Why do you go?" And when I returned, he never asked: "Where have you been?" or "What have you done and how?" Thus I once took a ship to Alexandria on urgent business and from there went to Constantinople on some affairs of the Church, without letting him know. Then, after spending a considerable time there and visiting the local devout brethren, I finally returned to his skete. On seeing me the staretz was filled with joy, but after the usual greeting, said a prayer and sat down; he asked me no questions but remained occupied with his customary inner doing.

16. 'Once, wishing to try him, I refrained from giving him bread for several days. He never asked me for bread or said

anything. Then, bowing low to him I asked: "Of your kindness, Father, tell me, were you offended that I have not brought you to eat, as usual?" He replied: "Forgive me, brother! Even if you omit to give me bread for twenty days I will not ask for it, for so long as my soul endures my body endures also." To such an extent was he occupied with the contemplation of true blessings.

17. 'He used to say: "From the time I came to the skete I would not let my thought go beyond the walls of my cell, but accepted no thought into my mind other than fear of God and future judgement, keeping in memory the verdict which threatens sinners, eternal fire and outer darkness, remembering also how the souls of the righteous and the sinners live and what blessings are prepared for the just, and the fact that each receives his reward according to his efforts: one for spiritual endeavour, another for bestowing mercy and for sincere love; a third for uncovetousness and complete renunciation of the world; yet another for wise humility and complete silence; another for extreme obedience, another for estrangement from the world. Keeping all this in my mind, I do not allow other thoughts to act in me and can no longer be with people or occupy my mind with them, lest I be withdrawn from Divine thoughts."

18. 'He added to this a narrative about a certain solitary, saying that he had already achieved passionlessness, and received food from the hands of an angel, but through laziness (weakening of attention) was deprived of this honour. For when the soul relaxes the scrutiny and intense attention of the mind, night sweeps over it. Where God does not shine all is blurred, as in darkness. And then the soul can no longer look only towards God and tremble at His words. "Am I a God at hand, saith the Lord, and not a God afar off? Can any hide himself in secret places that I shall not see him? saith the Lord. Do not I fill heaven and earth?" (Jer. xxiii. 23, 24). He also remembered many others who have suffered a similar fate. He cited too the downfall of Solomon who, as he said, had received such wisdom and was so glorified by all men that, like the sun rising in the morning, he illumined all by the radiance of his wisdom—and yet he lost this glory for a petty lust. Thus it is dangerous to pander to laziness; but one should pray without ceasing, lest

some incoming thought should part us from God, and something other than Him present itself to our mind. Only a pure heart, becoming the abode of the Holy Spirit, sees in itself clearly, as in a mirror, the true God of all that is.

19. 'Hearing this,' says the brother who lived with Father Philemon, 'and seeing his works, I understood that passions of the flesh had completely ceased to work in him and that he loved perfection with such zeal, that he always appeared transfigured by the Divine Spirit (from glory to glory), sighing inexpressible sighs, communing with himself within himself, weighing himself (holding himself evenly-balanced, as on scales) and striving in every possible way to prevent anything from disturbing the purity of his mind, or from letting some filth secretly cling to him.

'Seeing this,' he says, 'and fired by an ardent desire to imitate his mode of life, I begged him earnestly, saying: "How can I acquire a purity of mind like yours?" He replied: "Go—work; for this requires work and heart-felt suffering. Spiritual blessings, worthy of zealous search and labour, cannot be attained if we lie on our beds and sleep. Even earthly blessings are not acquired without labour. He who wants to succeed must first of all abandon all desires of his own, and acquire constant mourning and uncovetousness. Pay attention not to the transgressions of others, but only to your own, and mourn over them day and night; and form vain friendships with no man. For a soul, sorrowing over its perilous state and wounded by memories of past sins, is dead to the world, just as the world is dead to it; that is, passions of the flesh then become inactive and man becomes inactive in relation to them. Moreover a man who has renounced the world and has united with Christ, a man who abides in silence, loves God, preserves His image and is enriched by His likeness; for God sends him from above the gift of the Spirit, and he becomes the house of God, instead of the abode of the demons, and offers righteous deeds to God. Thus the soul that is pure in its life, free from defilements of the flesh, and that harbours no filth or vice, becomes finally crowned with truth and shines with the beauty of the virtues.

' "But he in whom in the beginning of renunciation there is no mourning, no spiritual tears, no memory of torment without end, no true silence, no ceaseless prayer, no psalmody and instruction in Divine Scriptures, a man in whom all this has not become a habit so that, through constant practice, he no longer has any need to be compelled by his mind to do it against his will; a man in whose soul fear of God does not hold sway: such a man still rests in his friendship with the world and cannot keep his mind pure in prayer. For only righteousness and fear of God purify the soul from passions, and, liberating the mind, lead it into the contemplation natural to it, and allow it to approach knowledge of God, which it receives in the form of bliss ('Blessed are the pure in heart, for they shall see God'), which to those who acquire it even in this life serves as a token (of the future) and preserves (their spiritual state) unshakeably.

'"So let us strive with all our strength after practical doing (of virtues and spiritual efforts), which lead us to piety, that is, mental (spiritual) purity, the fruit of which is contemplation of God, natural (to the mind). For doing is ascent towards contemplation, as the most farseeing and divinely enlightened mind (of Gregory the Theologian) says. Therefore if we neglect this doing, we shall be strangers to all love of wisdom. For even if a man reaches the very summit of virtue, he will still be in need of spiritual efforts and endeavours, to curb the unruly tendencies of the body, and in need of strict guarding of thoughts. Even by this means we are barely able to have Christ dwell in us. For the more our righteousness grows, the more we achieve spiritual maturity, until finally the mind reaches perfection and cleaves entirely to God, illumined by Divine light—and then ineffable mysteries become revealed to it. Then it truly knows where is wisdom, where power, where the faculty for knowing all, where life and long life, where light of the eyes, and peace. For so long as a man is occupied with struggle against passions he has no means of enjoying this, since both virtues and vices blind the mind: the latter prevent it from seeing virtues, the former from seeing vices.

'"But when a man has achieved rest from warfare and is granted spiritual gifts, he is constantly acted upon by grace, and so becomes permeated with light and can no longer be turned from the contemplation of spiritual things. Such a man is attached to nothing in this world; for he has passed from death into life. A man who has undertaken to imitate excellence in his life, and who yearns to come near God, should have a chaste heart and pure lips, so that with clean words from clean lips he can glorify God worthily, since his soul cleaves to Him and ceaselessly converses with Him. So, brethren, let us aim at achieving this height of virtue, and let us cease crawling on the ground, attached to passions. A man who strives and who is close to God, who shares in His holy light and is wounded by love of Him, delights in an ineffable spiritual delight in the Lord, as the Divine psalm says: 'Delight thyself also in the Lord; and he shall give thee the desires of thine heart. . . . And he shall bring forth thy righteousness as the light, and thy judgment as the noonday' (Ps. xxxvii. 4, 6). And what love can be so strong and so irresistible as the love which God pours into the soul cleansed of all evil? Such a soul speaks from the true disposition of the heart and says: 'I am sick of love' (Song of Songs ii. 5). Beyond speech and beyond description is the dazzling of Divine beauty! Word cannot utter, nor ear comprehend it. Compare it with the radiance of day, with the brightness of the moon or the light of the sun, all these are as nought to that glory; before true light they are poorer than the blackest night or the deepest darkness before the clear midday. Thus was it described too by Basil, great among teachers, who comprehended and learned it from experience." '

20. This and much else did the brother who lived with the Abba narrate. But who will not be filled with wonder also at the following proof of his great humility? Although he had been ordained into priesthood long ago, and though his life and mind were so long permeated with heavenly things, he always avoided officiating, as being a burden, so that through many years of his spiritual struggle he very seldom consented to officiate at the Holy Communion. In spite of this life of extreme watchfulness, he refrained from receiving the communion of the Divine Mysteries if he happened to meet people and talk with them, even though during such conversations he never said anything earthly, but only things profitable to the souls of those who sought to speak with him. And preparing to receive the holy sacrament of

the Divine Mysteries, he importuned God for a long time, imploring His mercy by prayers, psalmody and confessions. He trembled at the voice of the priest when he calls out before communion: 'Holiness to the holy.' For, he used to say, at this moment the church is filled with holy angels and the Lord of hosts officiates Himself mysteriously transforming bread and wine into His body and blood and, thereupon, through the Holy Communion, entering our hearts. Therefore, he used to add, we should dare to receive the Holy Communion of the immaculate Mysteries of Christ only in a state of purity and chastity, being as it were outside the flesh, without doubt or hesitation, in order to share in its enlightenment. Many of the holy fathers saw angels who warned them (of everything unseemly); therefore they kept complete silence, refraining from all talk.

21. The brother related yet another thing: when the staretz was forced to sell his handiwork himself, then to avoid any lies or swearing, or idle words, or some other sin which may occur during conversations and bargaining, he stood mute, pretending to be witless. Thus anyone who wanted to buy his handiwork took it from him and gave for it whatever he chose. He made small baskets, and received thankfully what people gave for them, saying nothing.

# INDEX OF PROPER NAMES

417

# INDEX OF PROPER NAMES

# INDEX OF PROPER NAMES

419

# INDEX OF PROPER NAMES